Culture and
Human Development

Culture and Human Development

The importance of cross-cultural research for the social sciences

Edited by
Wolfgang Friedlmeier,
Pradeep Chakkarath
and Beate Schwarz

Ψ Psychology Press
Taylor & Francis Group

HOVE AND NEW YORK

First published 2005 by Psychology Press
27 Church Road, Hove, East Sussex, BN3 2FA

Simultaneously published in the USA and Canada
by Psychology Press
270 Madison Avenue, New York, NY 10016

Psychology Press is a part of the Taylor & Francis Group

Printed and bound in Great Britain by
TJ International Ltd, Padstow, Cornwall
Cover design by Jim Wilkie

British Library Cataloguing in Publication Data
A catalogue record for this book is available from the British Library

Library of Congress Cataloging-in-Publication Data
Culture and human development: the importance of cross-cultural
research for the social sciences / [compiled by] Wolfgang Friedlmeier,
Pradeep Chakkarath, and Beate Schwarz.
        p. cm.
    Includes bibliographical references and index.
    ISBN 1-84169-568-8
    1. Developmental psychology – Cross-cultural studies – Congresses.
2. Ethnopsychology – Congresses. I. Friedlmeier, Wolfgang, 1960–
II. Chakkarath, P. (Pradeep), 1960 – III. Schwarz, Beate. IV. Title.
    BF712.5.C86 2005
    155.8–dc22
2004022494

ISBN 1-84169-568-8

Contents

Biographical Notes   *ix*

Preface   *xvii*

Introduction   **1**

Part I: Theory and Methods in
Cross-Cultural Research   **7**

The Psychological Study of Culture: Issues and
Questions of Enduring Importance   *9*
   Walter J. Lonner

What can Western Psychology Learn From Indigenous
Psychologies? – Lessons From Hindu Psychology   *31*
   Pradeep Chakkarath

Using Cross-Cultural Psychology to Design Afterschool
Educational Activities in Different Cultural Settings   *53*
   Michael Cole

Part II: On the Development of
Developmental Theories   **73**

Universal and Culture-Specific Aspects of Human Behavior:
The Case of Attachment   *75*
   Klaus E. Grossmann, Karin Grossmann, and
   Anika Keppler

Attachment and Culture: Bridging Relativism and
Universalism   *99*
   Fred Rothbaum and Gilda Morelli

Emotional Development and Culture: Reciprocal
Contributions of Cross-Cultural Research and
Developmental Psychology   *125*
   Wolfgang Friedlmeier

Spatial Language and Cognitive Development in India:
An Urban/Rural Comparison   *153*
   Ramesh C. Mishra and Pierre R. Dasen

Part III: Intergenerational Relationships   **181**

Changing Value of Children: An Action Theory of Fertility
Behavior and Intergenerational Relationships in
Cross-Cultural Comparison   *183*
   Bernhard Nauck

Relations between Value Orientation, Child-Rearing Goals,
and Parenting: A Comparison of German and
South Korean Mothers   *203*
   Beate Schwarz, Esther Schäfermeier and
   Gisela Trommsdorff

Adolescent Future Orientation: Intergenerational
Transmission and Intertwining Tactics in Cultural and
Family Settings   *231*
   Rachel Seginer

Part IV: Social Change   **253**

Modernization Does Not Mean Westernization: Emergence
of a Different Pattern   *255*
   Çigdem Kagitçibasi

Modernization and Value Change   *273*
   Helmut Klages

Part V: Acculturation   **289**

Acculturation   *291*
   John W. Berry

Long-Term Effects of International Student Exchange
Programs   *303*
   Alexander Thomas

Collective Self-Esteem and Acculturation: A Case Study of European and Japanese Internship Students   *321*
  Makoto Kobayashi

Author Index   *341*

Subject Index   *349*

Biographical Notes

John Berry is Professor Emeritus of Psychology at Queen's University, Kingston, Canada. He received his B.A. from Sir George Williams University, Montreal, Canada (1963) and his Ph.D. from the University of Edinburgh, UK (1966). He was Lecturer at the University of Sydney, Australia, for three years, Fellow at the Netherlands Institute for Advanced Study and Visiting Professor at a number of universities in Estonia, Finland, France, India, Japan, Norway, Switzerland, and the UK. He is Past Secretary-General, Past President, and Honorary Fellow of the International Association for Cross-Cultural Psychology. In 2001, he received honorary doctorates from the universities of Geneva, Switzerland, and Athens, Greece. He is the Senior Editor of the *Handbook of Cross-Cultural Psychology* (rev. ed., 1997), co-author of two textbooks in the field, and author or editor of thirty books in the areas of cross-cultural, social, and cognitive psychology. He is particularly interested in the application of cross-cultural psychology to public policy and programs in the areas of acculturation, multiculturalism, immigration, health and education.
Address: Department of Psychology, Queen's University, Kingston, ON, K7L 3N6, Canada

Pradeep Chakkarath is Lecturer at the Department for Cultural Sciences of the University of St. Gallen, Switzerland, and co-organizer of the university's East Asian Studies Program. He is also a free research associate at the Department for Developmental and Cross-Cultural Psychology at the University of Konstanz, Germany, where he has served as a research assistant and lecturer (1996-2003). He teaches courses in Developmental and Cultural Psychology, Asian studies, and Intercultural Training. He received his M.A. in Philosophy and History (1986) and his Ph.D. in Psychology (2000) at the University of Konstanz. His main interests are the philosophy of science with a focus on psychological theory and methodology, cultural psychology, and the role worldviews play in societal and individual development.
Address: University of Konstanz, Department of Psychology, Box D 14, 78457 Konstanz, Germany

Michael Cole is Professor of Communication, Psychology, and Human Development at the University of California, San Diego, USA. He received his Ph.D. in Psychology at Indiana University, USA (1962). He is Director of the Laboratory of Comparative Human Cognition at the University of California, San Diego. M. Cole received honorary doctorates from Copenhagen University, Sweden (1996) and from the University of Helsinki, Finland (2000). He is a member of the American Academy of Arts and Sciences, the National Academy of Education (USA) and the Russian Academy of Education. His major research interest is the role of culture in

human development, currently with an emphasis on the study of culturally mediated learning and development in children, and mediational theories of mind.
Address: Laboratory of Comparative Human Cognition, 0092, University of California, San Diego, La Jolla, California 92093, USA

Pierre R. Dasen is Professor of Anthropology of Education and Cross-Cultural Psychology in the Department of Psychology and Education at the University of Geneva, Switzerland. He studied Developmental Psychology in Geneva, was assistant to J. Piaget, and received his Ph.D. (1971) from the Australian National University. He studied the cognitive development of Aboriginal children in Australia, Inuit in Canada, Baoulé in Côte d'Ivoire, and Kikuyu in Kenya. He has also contributed to research in cognitive anthropology in Bali and among the Yupno of Papua-New Guinea. His research topics have included visual perception, the development of sensorimotor intelligence, the causes and effects of malnutrition, the development of concrete operations as a function of eco-cultural variables and daily activities, definitions of intelligence, number systems, and spatial orientation. His current interests are in everyday cognition, informal education, and parental ethnotheories. He heads a research team working on intercultural education, concerned with the access of migrant adolescents to professional training. P. Dasen is co-author and co-editor of several volumes and textbooks on cross-cultural psychology and intercultural education.
Address: FPSE, Université de Genève, 9 rte de Drize, CH-1227 Carouge, Switzerland

Wolfgang Friedlmeier received his master's degree in Psychology from the University of Bamberg, Germany (1988), and his doctorate in Psychology from the University of Konstanz, Germany (1993). He obtained a grant for a research stay at the University of North Carolina at Chapel Hill, USA (1993) before he became Assistant Professor at the University of Konstanz (1993-1999). There he was appointed University Lecturer ("Habilitation") in 2001. He was Visiting Chair at the University of Osnabrueck, Germany (2002-2003) and a Visiting Professor at Nagoya City University, Japan (2003-2004). He obtained several grants for research stays in Brazil and Japan. W. Friedlmeier is currently Assistant Professor for Cross-Cultural Psychology at the Grand Valley State University in Grand Rapids, Michigan, USA. His main research areas are emotional and social development, socialization, and cross-cultural psychology.
Address: Grand Valley State University, Department of Psychology, 140 Lake Michigan Hall, Allendale, MI 49401, USA

Karin Grossmann, studied Mathematics and English at the University of Arkansas, USA (B.A. 1965), Psychology in Freiburg and Muenster (M.A. 1977) and in Regensburg, Germany (Ph.D. 1984). She is a "free" senior researcher at the Department of Psychology, University of Regensburg, and a Lecturer at the Department of

Psychology, University of Salzburg, Austria. She has done extensive research in longitudinal and cross-cultural studies on attachment (together with Klaus E. Grossmann) and several research stays at the National Institute of Child Health and Human Development in Bethesda, at the University of Colorado in Denver, USA, and at Hokkaido University in Sapporo, Japan. Her publications focus on the application of attachment theory on family matters.
Address: University of Regensburg, Department of Psychology IV, Universitätsstr. 31, 93040 Regensburg, Germany

Klaus E. Grossmann studied Psychology in Hamburg, Germany (M.A. 1961), obtained a Fulbright grant for New Mexico State University (1961-1962), and received his Ph.D. from the University of Arkansas, USA (1965). He continued in comparative ethology towards his "Habilitation" in psychology and behavioral biology in Freiburg, Germany. He was full professor in Bielefeld (1970-1977) and in Regensburg, Germany (from 1977 - 2003). Research stays in Minneapolis, Bethesda, San Diego (all USA) and in Sapporo, Japan. His research emphasis is on Developmental Psychology, Comparative and Cross-Cultural Psychology and on attachment development in humans under a life-span perspective (together with Karin Grossmann).
Address: University of Regensburg, Department of Psychology IV, Universitätsstr. 31, 93040 Regensburg, Germany

Gustav Jahoda is Professor Emeritus of Psychology at the University of Strathclyde, Glasgow, Scotland. He studied at the University of London and received his PhD at the London School of Economics (1951). After a spell as a lecturer at the University of Manchester he went to the then University College of the Gold Coast (now Ghana). There, in the 1950s, he conducted fieldwork in cross-cultural psychology before that term existed. His subsequent research was mainly in Africa, but also India and Hong Kong. His varied interests included the psychological effects of social change, space perception and illusions, and socio-cognitive development. Past president of IACCP, he was Visiting Professor at the universities of Cape Town, Geneva, Harare (Zimbabwe), Legon (Ghana), New York, Osaka, Paris and Tilburg. After retiring he retreated to the library and is writing on theoretical and historical themes. He has published several books, many chapters and numerous research papers.
Address: University of Strathclyde, Department of Psychology, Graham Hills Building, 40 George Street, Glasgow G1 1QE, Scotland, United Kingdom

Çigdem Kagitçibasi is Professor of Psychology at Koc University in Istanbul, Turkey. She received her Ph.D. from the University of California, Berkeley, USA. She has served as Vice President of the IUPsyS and President and Honorary Fellow of the IACCP. She is a member of the Turkish Academy of Sciences and received the American Psychological Association and the International Association of Applied

Psychology Awards for Distinguished Contributions to the International Advancement of Psychology. Her extensive publications include *Family and human development across cultures* (1996) and (co-editor) *Handbook of cross-cultural psychology*, Vol. 3 (1997).
Address: Koc University, College of Arts and Sciences, Istinye, 80860 Istanbul, Turkey

Anika Keppler is a research and teaching assistant at the Department of Psychology, University of Regensburg, Germany, where she received her master's degree (2000). Currently a Ph.D. candidate, she is doing longitudinal and cross-cultural research together with Klaus E. and Karin Grossmann with a special interest in attachment theory.
Address: University of Regensburg, Department of Psychology IV, Universitätsstr. 31, 93040 Regensburg, Germany

Makoto Kobayashi received his master's degree in Educational Psychology at Keio University in Tokyo, Japan (1989) and his doctorate at the University of Konstanz, Germany (1994) under the supervision of Gisela Trommsdorff and with the support of a DAAD scholarship. He obtained a grant for a research stay at the University of Konstanz (1995-1997) and was Lecturer at Keio University (1997-2001). He was appointed Associate Professor for developmental psychology at Kyoto Koka Women's University (2001). Currently, he is an Associate Professor for Developmental Psychology at Tamagawa University, Japan and a research advisor for the educational program "Culture of Peace" by the National Federation of UNESCO Associations in Japan (NFUAJ). His main research areas are self and moral development in cross-cultural comparison, self-esteem, and psychological research for intercultural tolerance.
Address: Tamagawa University, College of Education, Tamagawa-Gakuen 6-1-1, Machida, Tokyo 194-8610, Japan

Helmut Klages received his master's in Macroeconomics at the University of Erlangen, Germany (1953) and his doctorate in Economics at the University of Hamburg, Germany (1955). He was appointed University Lecturer ("Habilitation") in sociology at the University of Erlangen-Nuernberg (1960) and University of Muenster (1961). He became a Full Professor at the Technical University of Berlin in 1964 and declined several calls from other universities before he accepted to take the Chair of Sociology at the German University of Administrative Sciences in Speyer (1975). He is now Professor Emeritus. He was frequently invited for guest professorships and research stays in USA, Japan, and the Republic of Korea. His main research areas are social change, value change, modernization, organizational dynamics, institutional reform, strategies of innovation, strategies and techniques of empowerment, and actualization of human potentialities.

Address: Deutsche Hochschule für Verwaltungswissenschaften Speyer, Postfach 1409, 67324 Speyer, Germany

Walter J. Lonner is Professor Emeritus in the Department of Psychology, Western Washington University, Bellingham, Washington. He is also Director of Western's Center for Cross-Cultural Research. W. Lonner has been involved in cross-cultural psychology for over 35 years. A charter member of the International Association for Cross-Cultural Psychology, he has served as the Association's President (1986-88) and in 1994 was made an Honorary Fellow. He is Founding Editor and currently Senior Editor of the *Journal of Cross-Cultural Psychology* and has been involved with many books in the area of cross-cultural psychology. Among the books, which he has either authored or edited, are *Cross-Cultural Research Methods* (1973), the six-volume *Handbook of Cross-Cultural Psychology* (1980), and *Counseling across Cultures*, which now appears in its 5th Edition. For more than 25 years he was co-editor of the Sage Publications book series, *Cross-Cultural Research and Methodology* (later changed to Cross-Cultural Psychology). W. Lonner was a Fulbright Scholar in Germany (1984-85) and has collaborated in research and scholarship with colleagues in numerous countries.
Address: Center for Cross-Cultural Research, Department of Psychology, Western Washington University, Miller Hall 328A, Bellingham, WA 98225-9089, USA

Ramesh C. Mishra is Professor of Psychology at Banaras Hindu University, India. A D. Phil. from Allahabad University, India, he has been Post-doctoral Research Fellow, Shastri Research Fellow and Visiting Professor at Queen's University, Canada. He has also been Visiting Professor at the University of Geneva and Jean Piaget Archives, Switzerland. His principal interest is in cultural influence on human development, and he has contributed numerous articles to professional journals, both in India and abroad, in the fields of cognition, acculturation, schooling, and cross-cultural studies. He has extensively contributed chapters to books, including the *Handbook of Cross-Cultural Psychology* and *Handbook of Culture and Psychology*. He is the co-author of *Ecology, Acculturation and Psychological Adaptation: A Study of Adivasis in Bihar*, and co-editor of *Psychology in Human and Social Development: Lessons from Diverse Cultures*.
Address: Department of Psychology, Banaras Hindu University, Varanasi 221005, India

Gilda A. Morelli received her Ph.D. from the University of Massachusetts-Amherst in 1986 and was a NIMH Postdoctoral Fellow, University of Utah (1986-1989). She is an Associate Professor in Psychology (1989-present) and Acting Associate Dean (2002-present) at Boston College, SRCD Policy Fellow and consultant to Department Health and Human Services on welfare reform and children's learning and development (1996-present). She has written numerous articles on culture and young children's social and emotional development, especially of children of hunting gath-

ering and horticultural societies in the Democratic Republic of Congo. She is also a Co-director of the "Ituri Forest People's Fund."
Address: Department of Psychology, Boston College, Chestnut Hill, MA 02467, USA

Bernhard Nauck received his master's degree in Educational Sciences (1972) and his doctor's degree in Sociology (1977) from the University of Cologne, Germany. He was an Assistant Professor at the universities of Cologne, Bonn, and Oldenburg, Germany (1972-1984) and was appointed University Lecturer ("Habilitation") at the Universities of Bonn (1983) and Augsburg, Germany (1987). Professorships followed for Sociology at the Universities of Wuppertal (1985/86) and Cologne (1988/1989), and at the Pädagogische Hochschule Weingarten (1990/92). Nauck was the founding Head of the Department of Family Research at the Bavarian State Institute for Early Education and Family Research (1986/88). Since 1992 he has been Founding Professor of the Department of Sociology at the University of Technology in Chemnitz, Germany. His main research areas are family, population, life course, migration, minorities, social structure and social reporting, cross-national and cross-cultural comparisons.
Address: Chemnitz University of Technology, Department of Sociology, Reichenhainer Str. 41, D-09107 Chemnitz, Germany

Fred Rothbaum received his Ph.D. from Yale University, USA, in 1976. He was an Assistant Professor at Bryn Mawr College (1976-1979) and at Tufts University, USA (1979-1982) where he became Associate Professor later on (1982-1992) and has been a Professor of Psychology since 1992. He has written many articles on parental caregiving and child functioning. He is Principal Investigator of a study on "Web based information about children and families" from the William T. Grant Foundation, 2001-2004. His main research areas are parenting and child functioning; culture and parent-child closeness, Web-based dissemination of child development information.
Address: Tufts University, Eliot-Pearson Dept. of Child Development, 105 College Ave., Medford, MA 02155, USA

Esther Schäfermeier received her master's degree (1999) and her doctorate in Psychology (2003) from the University of Konstanz, Germany. She was an exchange student at the Université René Descartes in Paris (1994 and 1998) and was a research intern at Princeton University, USA (1997). As a research assistant at the Department of Developmental and Cross-Cultural Psychology at the University of Konstanz (1999-2003), she obtained a grant for a research stay at the Federal University Fluminense, Brazil (2001). Currently she is undergoing child psychotherapist training. Her main research areas are cross-cultural psychology, socialization and social development, stereotypes and prejudices.

Address: University of Konstanz, Department of Psychology, Box D 14, 78457
Konstanz, Germany

Beate Schwarz received her master's degree (1989) at the Technical University of
Berlin, Germany, and her doctorate in Psychology (1996) at the University of Giessen, Germany. She worked as a research assistant in the Berlin Youth Study and in
longitudinal studies on adolescent development in East and West Germany after
unification at the University of Giessen and on family development after separation
and divorce at the University of Munich, Germany. Since 2000 she has been Assistant Professor at the University of Konstanz. Her main research interests focus on
social relationships and problem behavior in adolescence, children and adolescents
in divorced and stepfamilies, parent-child-relationship in adulthood, and cross-
cultural psychology.
Address: University of Konstanz, Dept. of Psychology, Box D 14, 78457 Konstanz,
Germany

Rachel Seginer received her B.A. in Psychology and Sociology from Hebrew University in Jerusalem, Israel, her M.Sc. in Child Development from Cornell University, USA, and her Ph.D. in Psychology from the Hebrew University in Jerusalem.
Her research interests focus on socio-cultural and familial contexts of adolescent
development, mainly applying to future orientation and school functioning. She
teaches developmental psychology at the Faculty of Education, University of Haifa,
Israel. Her teaching, as her research, focuses on adolescent development in the family and the school with special emphasis on the relevance of socio-cultural settings
to these issues.
Address: University of Haifa, Faculty of Education, Mount Carmel, Haifa 31905,
Israel

Alexander Thomas received his master's degree (1968) and his doctorate (1973) in
Psychology at the University of Muenster, Germany. He was a professor of Sport
Psychology at the Free University of West-Berlin (1973-1979) and has been Profes-
sor of Psychology (Social Psychology and Applied Psychology) at the University of
Regensburg, Germany (since 1979). A. Thomas has conducted cross-cultural re-
search in many European and non-European countries, e.g., in China, India, Japan,
and the USA. His main research areas are action psychology, cross-cultural psychol-
ogy, psychology of intercultural action, and organizational psychology.
Address: University of Regensburg, Institute of Experimental Psychology, 93040
Regensburg, Germany

Gisela Trommsdorff studied Sociology and Psychology at the University of Göt-
tingen, Germany, the University of North Carolina at Chapel Hill, USA, and at
Mannheim University, Germany, where she received her doctorate (1970) and her
"Habilitation" (1976). In 1978 she became a Professor in Educational Psychology at

the Technical University (RWTH) in Aachen, Germany, and holds the Chair for Developmental and Cross-Cultural Psychology at the University of Konstanz, Germany (since 1987). G. Trommsdorff was a Visiting Professor at Keio University and Kansai University, Japan, and was invited for several research stays at foreign universities, e.g., in India, Indonesia, Japan, and the Republic of Korea. Her research interests cover cross-cultural psychology, future orientation, lifespan development, intergenerational relationships, social change, subjective developmental theories, motivation and intentionality.

Address: University of Konstanz, Department of Psychology, Box D 14, 78457 Konstanz, Germany

Preface

The famous work of Rivers during the Cambridge Expedition to the Torres Strait is usually regarded as the origin of cross-cultural psychology. Less well known are some of the German antecedents of ideas in this field. Already Herbart warned against undue concentration on the unrepresentative "cultured person," and speculated about the psychological consequences of educating a Maori in Europe. Waitz, who put forward the notion of "psychic unity" at a time when biological racism was in the ascendant, noted that there are many reports on the mental life of "uncivilized" peoples, but they are far from conveying a complete picture. He commented that one has looked on their religion and customs as mere curiosities, without trying to understand them.

Early in the 20th century Thurnwald, working in the Solomon Islands, undertook empirical research on higher cognitive functions which Rivers, influenced by Wundt, had at that time regarded as beyond the capability of "natives." There followed an interregnum of almost half a century when very little was done, until a fresh start was made in the 1950s and '60s.

As far as I know there was at that time little interest in Germany in issues of psychology and culture, the sole exception being Ernest Boesch at Saarbrücken who established an Institute. Injecting a personal note, I might mention that one of my former Ghanaian students spent some time there and found the experience greatly enriching.

Things began to move in Germany during the 1970s and '80s, and one of the earliest and most active people in the field was Gisela Trommsdorff who is being honored by the present volume. Like several now prominent cross-cultural researchers, she began as a social psychologist, soon moving from "social" to "cultural." Her contributions are impressive in terms of quality, quantity, and range of topics covered, from general theory to specific comparative studies, the *Schwerpunkt* being in the developmental sphere. It is therefore appropriate that it should be the major theme of this volume.

The book itself is a felicitous mélange. On the one hand it offers an excellent and very welcome, though of course by no means comprehensive sample of what is going on in culturally oriented developmental psychology in Germany today. On the other hand it is adorned by contributions from a sample of the most outstanding exponents from the rest of the world, who are thereby paying homage. Generally, this book reflects the variety and liveliness of current cultural/developmental psychology and thereby constitutes a valuable source for both scholars and students.

Gustav Jahoda

Introduction

In March 2002, several social scientists from various corners of the world gathered together in Konstanz, Germany, on the picturesque shore of Lake Constance, to celebrate Gisela Trommsdorff's 60th birthday and honor her academic work by participating in a conference on the relationship between "Culture and Human Development." Focusing on central themes in their colleague's work, the participants discussed important contributions that cross-cultural research has made to the social sciences as well as its relevance for future research in the field. The group itself also reflected these two aspects, as some of the participants number among the most renowned scholars in the field of psychological and sociological cross-cultural research and others were Gisela Trommsdorff's former pupils.

In order to pay tribute to Gisela Trommsdorff's achievements as a researcher and a teacher as well as highlight some of the major topics in current cross-cultural investigation, the meeting focused on four main goals:

The first goal was to provide a forum for discussion aimed at resolving seemingly irresolvable *theoretical and methodological disputes* in the field of cross-cultural research, thus improving our insight into the relationship between culture and human development. The symposium's second goal was to examine different theoretical and methodological approaches to the *analysis of psychological and sociological mechanisms and processes* involved in the relationship between culture and human development. The combined use of psychological and sociological theories and methods should help us to better understand the nature of the intergenerational transmission of culture as well as socialization and internalization processes. The third goal was to discuss the meaning of such an analysis for a *better understanding of social change and modernization* and to consider how to take transformation processes into account when describing and explaining the relationship between societal and individual development. The fourth goal was to reflect on how the rapid societal change of today's world affects the ecological niches in which individuals develop, thus emphasizing *potential practical uses of cross-cultural research*, e.g., with regard to the increasing frequency and perhaps importance of intercultural encounters.

This volume aims to capture some of the ideas and results presented at the conference in order to show how intriguing and challenging cross-cultural research has been and will continue to be for the further investigation of human development. Of course, the following chapters cannot cover the entire range of research topics currently being discussed in the scientific community, but these chapters will point to very different areas and at the same time illustrate how they are interrelated with regard to theoretical, methodological and interdisciplinary aspects. To this end the volume has been divided into five parts. In accordance with the symposium's main goals, each part is interconnected with the preceding as well as the following part.

The first section deals with theoretical and conceptual problems that cross-cultural research has to face and to which it must also offer solutions. It begins with Walter J. Lonner's synopsis of key issues and questions that have guided scientists who study human thought and behavior and who often differ with regard to their theoretical positions that he calls the three "isms": absolutism, relativism, and universalism. While summarizing historical factors as well as contemporary perspectives, he shows how enduring the importance of the ongoing debates are when considering (1) the assumptions one makes when conducting research in other cultures, (2) the questions one asks (or doesn't ask) in such research, (3) how researchers interpret data and other information that have been gathered, and (4) what is viewed as important as opposed to trivial in culture-oriented psychological inquiries. In the second chapter, Pradeep Chakkarath deals with the increase in attention to so-called "indigenous psychologies," i.e., psychologically relevant concepts that were not developed in mainstream Western psychology, but in the cultures being studied, thus also reflecting the particular way of thinking inherent in these cultures. Using Hindu psychology as an example, the focus is on the question concerning what impact different worldviews, images of man, self-concepts, and values as well as their relevance to action orientations on an individual level may have for theories and assumptions developed in Western psychology. In the last chapter of this section, Michael Cole summarizes the basic principles of an approach to cultural psychology which understands the mediation of human action through artefacts as the defining characteristic of homo sapiens. He presents results from a decade-long experiment in designing afterschool activities that has been run in different institutions in a number of different countries with children from different home cultures. These results serve as an example of the need for new methodological approaches that help to gain more insight into the processes and dynamics involved in children's development and the role of the cultural contexts they live in. At the same time, this chapter gives an example of how culture-sensitive aspects of research and application can gain from each other.

The second section presents examples for more recent insights and refinements within some of the classical developmental theories. First, Klaus E. Grossmann, Karin Grossmann, and Anika Keppler take on the case of attachment in order to show how universal as well as culture-specific phenomena influence human behavior. Based on empirical evidence from different cultures, including the authors' own studies on infant attachment behaviors in Japan and on the Trobriand Islands, it is claimed that the four core concepts of attachment theory, i.e. the concept of universality, of security being the norm, of parental sensitivity leading to secure infant attachment, and of security leading to higher competence, are universally valid. In a second chapter on attachment theory, Fred Rothbaum and Gilda Morelli review cross-cultural evidence that supports but in some cases also questions the relevance of some of the theory's central hypotheses in non-western cultures. The authors propose ways in which the hypotheses might be revised to accommodate extant evidence and discuss the kinds of research needed to definitely test the revised hypotheses adequately. In his chapter on the development of emotions Wolfgang Friedlmeier also points to more recent attempts to identify culture-specific emotional reactions based on different cultural norms and values. At the same time, the developmental perspective sharpens the attention for the relation between individual and culture, because it includes the question of transfer and mediation. Thus, there are reciprocal effects between cross-cultural research and developmental psychology that can provide a more fruitful perspective on the development of human emotions. The section is concluded by a chapter on cross-cultural and related ecological differences on the development of language and spatial concepts. Pierre Dasen and Ramesh Mishra present new empirical findings from urban and rural regions of India and Nepal that serve as the starting point for a critical review of classical, e.g., Piagetian and neo-Piagetian theories on cognitive development. The authors try to show how culture-sensitive research can help to detect some general methodological shortcomings in psychological research and help to more adequately explain internal processes that most have considered universal by definition.

The third section takes up different psychological and sociological aspects of intergenerational relations, a topic that has gained some attention lately, especially against the background of social change within a growing number of rapidly changing countries. In his chapter on the value that children have for their parents, Bernhard Nauck tries to provide a more thorough sociological explanation of fertility behavior than proposed by demographic and micro-economic approaches. Here, children are seen as strategic intermediate goods that fulfill basic needs of their (potential) parents and that are oriented towards (1) work and income needs, (2) insurance needs, (3) status needs, and (4) emotional needs. The author unfolds his theory's explanatory potential for six essential dimensions of the culturally varying family system (size, durability, context opportunities and restrictions, resources, intergenerational relationships, and gender). In their cross-cultural comparison of German and South Korean samples Beate Schwarz, Esther Schäfermeier, and Gisela Trommsdorff investigate the interplay between value orientation, child-rearing goals, and parenting as well as the role that cultural factors may have on related psychological processes. Discussing their empirical findings within the concept of the developmental niche, they also elaborate on the role of subjective child-rearing theories for human socialization, including intergenerational and intercultural differences. The role of intergenerational relationships for adolescent future orientation is at the centre of the study conducted by Rachel Seginer. Her main proposition is that the development of future orientation requires both the freedom to make choices and the support of knowledgeable others and that these are differentially provided by cultural blueprints and by the family. The analyses of the relationships between these two developmental milieus and future orientation are based on comparisons between Jewish and Arab adolescents in Israel and complemented by a discussion of the implications the findings may have for intergenerational transmission.

While the topic of social change already surfaced in some of the preceding chapters, it is at the core of the fourth section, especially since it is the classical concept of modernization that once promoted cross-cultural scientific research and at the same time provided some of its most aggravating pitfalls. In this section a psychologist and a sociologist take a critical look at modernization theory and research and propose a more adequate view with regard to concepts and research methods. In the first chapter, Çigdem Kagitçibasi portraits the modernization paradigm as a social evolutionist worldview that considers whatever is different from the Western pattern as deficient and bound to change (e.g., towards Western individualism) with socioeconomic development. With regard to social groups, she shows that what really emerges in "modernizing" societies is a more complex pattern in family/human relationships which can be seen as "cultures of relatedness." The author discusses the implications of this revised model for a better understanding, e.g., of the processes of social change and the resultant development of the self. From a sociological point of view, Helmut Klages deals with two major questions concerning value change in modernizing societies: first, the question concerning causality in the relationship between modernization and value change; second, the question concerning the qualitative character and the consequences of a possibly mutual causal interaction between modernization and value change. Moreover, the author shows that analyses and interpretation of the available cross-cultural data can be interpreted in a perspective quite different from classical and influential interpretations offered by Inglehart, Hofstede and others.

The last section of this volume takes the investigation of acculturation processes as an example to show in more detail the application-related potential of cross-cultural research. Starting with an overview of the unidimensional and unidirectional conceptualizations of acculturation, John Berry uses new empirical findings in order to identify the more complex and variable processes and the factors on which they depend. One factor is what collectives and individuals are attempting to do during their acculturation. These acculturation strategies (assimilation, integration, separation, marginalization) are defined, and evidence for their role in acculturation is reviewed. In addition, the author shows how these concepts and empirical findings can be applied to politics and social work. Alexander Thomas presents results of a study conducted in order to investigate the long-term effects of international exchange programs on Australian and German children and teenagers. Following Epstein's theory of personality and based on his own empirical findings, the author outlines a theory concerning how such exchange programs can affect the development of self-efficacy as well as self-decentralization. Besides the effects on personality development and individual variations in the chronology of influential effects will be discussed. Makoto Kobayashi explores the role of collective self-esteem for acculturation processes during international internships. His study was conducted among European students who were on a 2-month internship in Japan. The comparison of the data with their as well as their host company's evaluation of the internship revealed certain discrepancies between the two evaluations. On account of the results, the author proposes a process model according to which a stable collective identity fosters a positive image of the host country, which in turn intermediates positive communicational grounds for acculturation.

Taking these sections and the individual chapters together, the volume aims to show the interrelationship of interdisciplinary theoretical and empirical approaches, exemplifying it through a broad range of topics in different areas of current cross-cultural and developmental research, including perspectives from various cultures and cultural groups. Thus, it not only represents the academic interests and work of Gisela Trommsdorff, but also reflects the state of the art and the future tasks of social scientific cross-cultural research.

We would like to thank a number of people who helped us to organize the symposium and put this volume together. We especially wish to thank Hans-Joachim Kornadt for his support and advice during our preparation of the symposium. We are grateful that he and Doris Bischof-Köhler participated in the meeting and enriched it by serving as discussants. For offering their various skills and thus contributing to the symposium's success we thank Esther Schäfermeier, Rozalia Horvath, Bert Neidich, Marian Jimenez, Christine Stellfeld, Tamara Herz, and Dong-Seon Chang. The stimulating atmosphere in which the discussions took place was due in part to the wonderful venue, Schloss Akademie Seeheim, and we thank Ariane Zettier for her hospitality and for her patiently fulfilling our every wish.

As for the volume itself, our thanks go first and foremost to all the participants who presented the papers that laid the groundwork for this volume. In addition, we thank John Berry and Alexander Thomas for adding to the selection although they were not able to attend the meeting, and we express our great appreciation to Gustav Jahoda for writing the foreword. We are also indebted to Walt Lonner for his helpful advice and encouragement concerning this volume. We could not have completed this book without the help of Gabriella von Lieres, who participated in revising and editing most of the manuscripts. We would also like to thank Rozalia Horvath and Agnes Günther, who assisted in preparing figures and tables and the final copies of the manuscripts, as well as Tamara Herz, who helped us put the finishing touches to the volume. Hale Ruben and Lizzie Catford from Psychology Press deserve special acknowledgement for patiently accompanying the editors at every step.

We hope that this book will find many interested readers among scholars as well as students from all fields of the social sciences. Moreover, we hope that they will benefit from reading it.

Wolfgang Friedlmeier, Pradeep Chakkarath, Beate Schwarz

Part I

Theory and Methods in

Cross-Cultural Research

1

The Psychological Study of Culture: Issues and Questions of Enduring Importance

Walter J. Lonner

Introduction

This chapter gives a brief overview of the nature and purpose of cross-cultural psychology. The celebratory nature of the gathering for which this chapter was prepared permits comments that are both historical and somewhat autobiographical. It also permits brief commentary on contemporary perspectives in topical areas of interest to cross-cultural psychologists as well as an overview of several methodological issues and problems that are of enduring importance. The gathering converged precisely to the month with the publication in March 1970 of the inaugural issue of the *Journal of Cross-Cultural Psychology* (JCCP) and almost exactly with the 30th anniversary of the founding of the International Association for Cross-Cultural Psychology (IACCP), formed in 1972. As founding editor of JCCP as well as a charter member of IACCP, I have witnessed for over 35 years the growth of what has often been called the "modern movement" in cross-cultural psychology. All participants in this symposium have had discussions with various proponents who identify either with cross-cultural psychology, cultural psychology, indigenous psychology, ethnic psychology, or psychological anthropology and, occasionally, other perspectives such as semiotics, evolutionary psychology, ethnopsychiatry, and multicultural psychology. The latter is primarily identified with gender, ethnicity and other "diversity" issues within the United States (Bronstein & Quina, 2003). Division 45 (Society for the Study of Ethnic Minority Issues) of the American Psychological Association is active in the great diversity within a single country. All the others are more concerned with the "big picture" in global, pancultural scale. All psychologists affiliated with these "culture-oriented" perspectives generally agree that any psychology or neighboring discipline that fails to take culture into account, regardless of geographic scope, is bound to give an incomplete and inconclusive picture of human behavior in its many and complex forms.

By dint of historical developments, most of my involvement in cross-cultural psychology has been through activities associated with JCCP. I continue to measure the progression of cross-cultural psychology in terms of JCCP's growth and continued success. For instance, it is now published six times a year, its trim size and overall appearance have received several facelifts, and there has been about a four-fold increase in publication space. These changes can mainly be attributed to the growing interest in cross-cultural psychology, but also to the formation of IACCP. Commencing with the 1973 issue (Volume 4), JCCP has been published by Sage Publications. With the exception of yours truly, who is now Senior Editor, none of the members of original interdisciplinary Editorial Advisory Board is currently associated with it. Several have died, but a few are still quite active in the field. Moreover, while manuscripts with an interdisciplinary focus are still welcome, the current Editorial Advisory Board consists mainly of psychologists. The EAB consists of an Editor, Founding and Senior Editor, five Associate Editors, about 46 Consulting Editors, and a Book Review Editor. Approximately 20 countries are currently represented on the EAB.

Despite these changes at the operational level, a strong thread of continuity governs the Journal's policy. The key parts of the original publication policy include the following: That it will publish exclusively cross-cultural (transcultural, cross-national) research; that studies focusing on psychological phenomena (motivation, learning, attitudes, perception, etc.) as they are influenced by culture, as well as other social and behavioral research which focuses on the individual as a member of the cultural group, rather than the macroscopic groups. Studies that were not replicable were discouraged, and the criterion of relevance of the research for cross-cultural comparisons of psychological variables must be clear. The printed policy also stated that while JCCP is "broadly a psychological journal, the closely related disciplines of anthropology, sociology, criminology, psychiatry . . . are expected to contribute heavily to the cross-cultural understanding of human behavior," and papers from these disciplines were invited. Casting a broad interdisciplinary net, our early promotional flyers contained the phrase " . . . to consult all that is human."

A Historical Perspective on Cross-Cultural Psychology

Cross-cultural psychology prior to JCCP and IACCP

Historical details about cross-cultural efforts in psychology have been the subject of reviews by Jahoda (1980, 1990); Klineberg (1980), Hogan and Tartaglini (1994), Jahoda and Krewer (1997), and Adamopoulos and Lonner (2001). However, sandwiched between these earlier efforts and the "modern era" of cross-cultural psychology, interest in culture's influence on behavior was generally diffuse and disorganized, and characterized by sabbatical opportunism and "jet-age" forays into different and often exotic cultures. More often than not, researchers (usually from the United States) would design a study where culture or cultures were essentially treated as (quasi-) independent variables and dependent variables were various "instruments" such as so-called intelligence tests, personality or values inventories and attitude scales, visual illusions, and devices designed to measure stages of human development, factors associated with learning and thinking, and so on. Typically, researchers would make a brief trip to some other place requiring a valid passport and then return to their comfortable offices to analyze the data and publish the results in mainstream journals whose editors and readers warmly welcomed manuscripts featuring reports of cultural differences (a strong interest in the nature and origin of similarities has emerged in recent years). It was largely because of this prototypical research and the way it has been imitated and reified over the years (in contrast to the more sophisticated nature of contemporary cross-cultural research) that cross-cultural psychology has often been described and even criticized as being "nothing more than" or "nothing but" an extension of the logical positivistic ways in which psychologists trained in the EuroAmerican tradition have conducted psychological research (e.g., Gergen, Gulerce, Lock, & Misra, 1996; Tyler, 1999, 2001).

Nevertheless, and despite the many methodological and conceptual errors that in retrospect most psychologists made when studying behavior in other cultures, these earlier efforts clearly demonstrated that some psychologists, regardless of when and where they were conducting research, have always been interested in how culture influences behavior. Research forays and other inquisitive ventures, in some instances, go back hundreds of years (Jahoda, 1980). The problem is that their efforts were neither guided by solid research guidelines nor supported by a network of like-minded and sympathetic colleagues.

The modern movement in cross-cultural psychology
Several independent events or factors converged to create what is now regarded as organized, institutionalized cross-cultural psychology. The first seems to have been a small conference of approximately 100 social psychologists from numerous countries who met at the University of Nigeria during the Christmas/New Year holiday period of 1965-66. A major product of that meeting was the inauguration of the mimeographed Cross-Cultural Social Psychology Newsletter. Harry Triandis, one of the key figures at that meeting, briefly edited it. It is the predecessor of the much more sophisticated *Cross-Cultural Psychology Bulletin*, thanks to the creative editorship of William K. Gabrenya, Jr. Another factor was the publication of the first of a continuing series of directories of psychologists who were identified as serious scholars of culture and behavior. The first Directory, assembled by John Berry, listed the names and addresses of approximately 110 psychologists from numerous countries. It appeared as a small appendix in a 1968 issue of the UNESCO-sponsored *International Journal of Psychology*, which began publication in 1966. Over the years a series of IACCP-sponsored and -oriented membership directories

have been published, the most recent of which was in 1998. Another influencing factor was a meeting in Istanbul, Turkey that featured the cultural adaptation of "mental tests" (Cronbach & Drenth, 1972). And in 1966 a meeting held at the East-West Center in Hawaii was attended by psychologists representing the Western world and the Eastern world. No publications resulted directly from that meeting, but it did stimulate collaboration. I only recently learned that a small conference sponsored by UNESCO, held in Bangkok, Thailand in 1958 might have predated all post-World War II conferences that were explicitly concerned with various problems and methodological issues in cross-cultural (Boesch, 1958). It would not surprise me to learn that solid and sophisticated conferences took place even earlier than this.

An important component in the development of modern, organized cross-cultural psychology was JCCP (see above). The picture was completed when IACCP was formed. At the initiative of the late John L. M. B. Dawson, the inaugural IACCP meeting took place in August 1972 at the University of Hong Kong, where Dawson was Head of the Department of Psychology. Although records are conflicting, apparently approximately 110 people attended that meeting. The conference proceedings contain all the papers that were delivered (Dawson & Lonner, 1974). As an example of continuity and dedication, the same person – Gustav Jahoda, an acknowledged pioneer in the area who has been a significant presence and somewhat of a super-ego for many cross-cultural psychologists for nearly half a century – wrote a foreword for that book just as he has written one for the present volume. At that meeting it was also agreed that, with the permission of the copyright holder, Western Washington State College (now Western Washington University), IACCP could call JCCP one of its official publications (see Lonner, 2004, for an historical overview of JCCP).

These converging factors ushered in an impressive outpouring of books, monographs, meetings, and other efforts. Why these independent events took place in the mid- to late-1960s – or earlier (see Boesch, 1958) – has been the subject of much discussion. Was it because two relatively recent, horrible world wars and then the Viet Nam conflict triggered many further questions about humanity and the state of the world? Did an increasing number of scholars recognize more than ever before that nations of the world had better recognize that an interdependent and mutually understanding world gives all nations a better chance of survival? Were better communication and the ubiquity of international air travel making collaboration more possible than ever before? Was psychology maturing as a science, finally ready and able to address psychological questions of universal concern? Whatever the cause, psychologists, like never before, were focusing on the construct of "culture" as an important factor in shaping human behavior. While the number of truly dedicated cross-cultural psychologists still tends to be small, a growing number of psychologists are giving the phenomenon increased respect and attention.

Central Issues in Cross-Cultural Psychology

What is cross-cultural psychology?

Despite nearly 30 years as an organized, institutional entity, there is no crisp and clear definition of cross-cultural psychology with which everyone agrees. However, a popular recent definition, included in a chapter reviewing culture and human development (Gardiner, 2001), states that it is "the systematic study of relationships between the cultural context of human development and the behaviors that become established in the repertoire of individuals growing up in a particular culture" (Berry, Poortinga, & Pandey, 1997, p. x).

Other definitions abound, but primarily cross-cultural psychology is an enterprise involving research and scholarship whose goal it is to help psychology develop into a more mature and broad-banded science. Its purpose is to help contribute to the development of a more global understanding of human thought and behavior. This means that all topics or domains with psychology and their dynamic interactions within and between individuals from any culture are candidates for inclusion in an extensive and increasing network of research projects involving a variety of methods. Table 1 shows what would be involved in this effort.[*]

Column A in Table 1 lists many of the domains and topics within Psychology (the topical areas of psychology without which the discipline would hardly have anything to study and which almost certainly transcend culture). All of these domains and their constituent parts are, as in "mainstream" psychology, candidates for an unlimited number of within-culture and cross-cultural explorations.

Column B includes some examples of rationale for making meaningful comparisons. Aberle, Cohen, Davis, Levy, & Sutton (1950) argued that there nine "functional prerequisites of society" – that is, for a society to exist (and therefore qualify for comparison with other functioning societies) it must have all of these elements. Examples of numerous additional common denominators or guidelines include Piaget's hypothesized stages of cognitive growth, Super and Harkness's (1986) "developmental niche," various models such as those developed by Bronfenbrenner (1979,

---

[*] Components of Table 1 were influenced by numerous discussions of "emics and etics" that for many years have been part of the "insider" versus "outsider" debate regarding approaches that one may take in the study of culture by behavioral and social scientists (Berry, 1989; Headland, Pike and Harris, 1990). However, Table 1 was primarily influenced by the methodological insights of D. T. Campbell and D. W. Fiske (1959) who recommended the use of convergent and discriminant validation by the multitrait-multimethod matrix. Campbell and Fiske outline what should be taken into account when "traits" (concepts, ideas, hypotheses, etc.) and "methods" (e.g. questionnaires, rating scales, systematic observations, interviewing, experiments, etc.) interact with researchers who differ with regard to the paradigms, theories, or assumptions they bring into an inquiry or research project. One would be on relatively safe ground if findings from multiple "traits" using multiple "methods" as employed by multiple researchers converged to validate some aspects of human behavior in question. Among other things, such considerations would help guard against "own-culture bias" in culture-comparative research.

Table 1 An Idealized Theoretical Framework for a Potentially Complete Understanding of the Relationships Between Culture and Appropriate and Relevant Psychological Topics

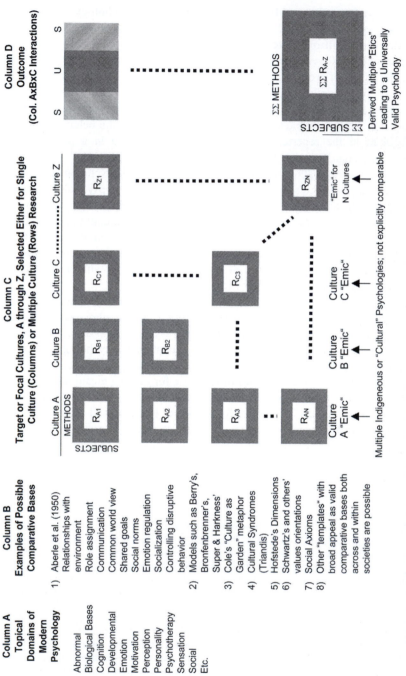

Column A
Topical Domains of Modern Psychology

Abnormal
Biological Bases
Cognition
Developmental
Emotion
Motivation
Perception
Personality
Psychotherapy
Sensation
Social
Etc.

Column B
Examples of Possible Comparative Bases

1) Aberle et al. (1950) Relationships with environment
Role assignment
Communication
Common world view
Shared goals
Social norms
Emotion regulation
Socialization
Controlling disruptive behavior

2) Models such as Berry's, Bronfenbrenner's, Super & Harkness'

3) Cole's "Culture as Garden" metaphor

4) Cultural Syndromes (Triandis)

5) Hofstede's Dimensions

6) Schwartz's and others' values orientations

7) Social Axioms

8) Other "templates" with broad appeal as valid comparative bases both across and within societies are possible

Column C
Target or Focal Cultures, A through Z, Selected Either for Single Culture (Columns) or Multiple Culture (Rows) Research

Culture A   Culture B   Culture C ············· Culture Z

METHODS

R_{A1} R_{B1} R_{C1} R_{Z1}

R_{A2} R_{B2}

R_{A3} R_{C3}

R_{AN} R_{ZN}

SUBJECTS

Culture A "Emic"   Culture B "Emic"   Culture C "Emic"   "Emic" for N Cultures

Multiple Indigeneous or "Cultural" Psychologies; not explicitly comparable

Column D
Outcome (Col. AxBxC Interactions)

S   U   S

ΣΣ METHODS

$\Sigma\Sigma\ R_{A-Z}$

ΣΣ SUBJECTS

Derived Multiple "Etics" Leading to a Universally Valid Psychology

Notes: For example, R_{A1} would be Research Report No. 1 for Culture A, which would use a specific sample and a specific method or theory. R_{A2} would be Research Report No. 2 for Culture A using its specific (and different) sample and specific (different) method or theory. S = Specific, U = Universal.

1993) McClelland (1961), and Berry (1995), Hofstede's (2001) or Schwartz's (1994) perspectives on human values, and Cole's (1996) "garden metaphor." These and many other views on the nature of human nature as it interacts with culture ostensibly guarantee meaningful comparisons across cultures (provided methodological care is taken to produce valid results). Column C could potentially include conducting exhaustive research in a large number of (theoretically all) cultures, making sure in each that multi-methods are used, that representative and equivalent samples of persons are selected in each, and that researchers representing different philosophical perspectives (e.g., cognitive, psychodynamic, behavioral, etc., to guard against method bias) are used, not only for each society (here labeled A, B, C . . Z) but across them all. In this way one could have multiple indigenous psychologies (i.e., looking down each column separately) with no aspirations to be comparative. While these must be understood on a column-by-column basis, one should also be able to find the common denominators by going across the columns. This is where the frameworks in Column B may be instructive as guidelines. Column D would then be involved in trying to determine what is shared or common (U, tentatively universal) across all cultures as well as what is unique or specific (S) in each society. Summing all the elements across the rows and down the columns (the lower right-hand corner), we potentially would have a truly universal psychology.

Obviously it would be impossible to complete what the overall structure in Table 1 implicitly demands: encouraging a huge number of replications of many studies and experiments across a large number of societies. It would, in fact, be a logistical nightmare to take just one topic – infant development for instance – and deal with it exhaustively both within and across cultures. Two reminders: First, when we talk about culturally unique and non-comparative psychological characteristics of a specific culture we are only "reading" down a specific column. Second, when we talk about "universals" we are generalizing across the collection of cultures. These strategies may represent, respectively, cultural psychology (and/or indigenous psychology) and cross-cultural psychology.

Three "isms" in the psychological study of culture

Probably the most familiar and debatable conceptual issue in conducting research across cultures is the "emic-etic," or insider versus outsider, debate (Headland, Pike, & Harris, 1990). While many dislike this simple dichotomy, it does pose an important question: Can anyone outside any specific human group (culture) understand completely the workings of the group (culture) to the same degree an insider does? Is the internal structure of any specific group so intricately learned and dynamically subtle that only an insider can truly understand the complexities of the interactions? Even worse, is it an imposition and possibly a major blunder for an outsider to be so pretentious as to think that he or she knows exactly what to study inside a group about which he or she may know so little that he or she cannot respectable research on it? Many psychologists have disavowed and/or avoided research in other cultures for these reasons, preferring to let anthropologists deal with culture – ironically a concept that many anthropologists say doesn't exist in the first place.

This debate is one of the more pervasive issues in the psychological study of other societies. Regardless of one's allegiance in the cultural sciences, it is often a central part of methodological and conceptual issues. Discussions often feature the three "isms" mentioned earlier -- absolutism, relativism, and universalism. Table 2 depicts the basic details of this simple yet highly debatable situation.

Unabashed absolutists rigorously follow the stringent demands of hardheaded experimentation and no-nonsense empiricism (e.g., Skinner's radical behaviorism). Absolutists believe that cultures are essentially vaguely defined superficial and colorful groups of people that are remarkable only because they have such things as quaint languages, different music and interesting clothing. It has often been said that absolutists are culture-bound and culture-blind, and many of them seem content to stay that way. Absolutists may also argue that there is no such thing as tangible and static "culture" to which someone can be bound or toward which someone can be blind (e.g., Hermans & Kempen, 1998). The "orange peel" analogy is often used in this context: the extremely thin and colorful skin of an orange merely masks a wealth of commonalities among all humans throughout the world. This allegation of relatively superficial aspects of culture implies that it really doesn't matter in psychology. John Berry (personal communication) has often reported a pertinent story: An absolutistic psychologist once said to him that culture is nothing more than "noise" that has to be tuned out in "real" psychological research. Berry's response: "Culture may be noise to you, but to me it is music." Culture-oriented psychologists would quickly agree. At the other extreme are the radical relativists. Relativists tend to reject comparativism or reductionism and believe that culture and mind are co-constructed. All cultures are totally unique (the S in Column 4 of Table 1), constructed from within and must be understood on their own terms and preferably by

Table 2
The Three "Isms" in the Psychological Study of Culture

		Is the phenomenon of one's culture an important factor in influencing one's thought and behavior?	
		No	Yes
Is it reasonable to assume that there are commonalities, continuities, and patterns in thought and behavior across cultures?	No	N/A	Relativism
	Yes	Absolutism	Universalism

individuals who are either members of the group being studied or completely familiar with the group's history, language, and so forth, This leaves universalism, a position that is somewhat of a compromise and a position with which most cross-cultural
psychologists strongly identify or, at minimum, understand and endorse. At the risk
of being over-inclusive, I would say that all cross-cultural psychologists believe that
humans and their interactions with their cultures are much more similar than they are
different, but that culture exerts such a strong force on the behavior and thought of
all sentient individuals that to disregard it runs the risk of having a narrow and incomplete psychology. This idea of universalism corresponds to the U in Column 4
of Table 1.

Cross-cultural psychological research: The standard approach

When cross-cultural psychologists design and conduct research, a relatively standard
method of inquiry is usually followed. As indicated above, they tend to more comparative and universalistic in their thinking than most other psychologists. However,
because the assumption of universality without strong evidence would be incautious
and presumptuous, a major goal of the cross-cultural psychologist has been to cast a
broad net by using a more or less standard "transfer and test" approach (Berry et al.,
2002). In this strategy psychologists essentially take (transfer) previously culture-
bound hypotheses and findings to other cultures in an effort to test their generalizability. However, there is also a "discovery" or "exploration" aspect in the standard
design. Because it is quite possible – indeed, more or less expected and welcomed –
that new and unusual (to the outsider) phenomena will be observed in other societies, it is the obligation of cross-cultural psychologists to try and understand what
dynamic processes have been encountered or uncovered. In the final process, the
goal of the cross-cultural psychologist is to "fold back" into mainstream psychology
the findings of research projects elsewhere. If nothing else happens, the results of
cross-cultural research will help enrich psychology by indeed "studying all that is
human."

The standard model of research is, however, not the only one used by cross-
cultural psychologists. Van de Vijver and Leung (1997) described a taxonomy of
cross-cultural studies. As shown in Table 3, this taxonomy includes four common
types of comparative approaches.

Hypothesis-driven studies aim to contribute to (or refute) the generalizability of
some psychological finding or principle. They are among the most common procedures used in cross-cultural research (e.g., do social psychology "laws" generalize
across cultures?) Primarily because psychological theory and principles of behavior
as studied for over a century in the "highly psychologized" western world were used
to develop research strategies, these approaches may also have received the most
criticism as being "nothing more" than an extension of the western model of logical
positivism by treating cultures as "quasi-independent variables." This is especially
true of theory-driven studies that paid little attention to the cultural context or to the
implications of such to the inhabitants of the cultures in question.

Table 3
Four Common Types of Cross-Cultural Studies

Should contextual factors be considered?	Orientation more on	
	Hypothesis Testing	Exploration
Yes	Generalizability	Psychological Differences
No	Theory-Driven	External Validation

Source: van de Vijver and Leung, 1997, p. 20.

In studies that are oriented more toward exploration, those that assess psychological differences are the most frequently cited in the cross-cultural literature. Because they are "instrument-driven," this approach typically involves selecting some personality, attitude, or values scale and collecting responses from individuals in two or more cultures. Means, standard deviations, response sets, factor structures and other aspects of measurement are then examined. Usually not propelled by some overarching theory, post hoc explanations may then be invoked to help interpret the differences as well as the similarities.

The Ongoing Maturation of Cross-Cultural Psychology

Prior to the mid-1960s, psychologists who designed and conducted research in other cultures had little guidance from the psychological literature. There were no books on cross-cultural research methods and there were few journal articles to serve as solid methodological models. Research done in other cultures was published in scattered journals throughout the world. In the U.S. , only the *Journal of Social Psychology*, which in the mid-1960s began publishing a short section, entitled "Cross-Cultural Notes," offered occasional insights. A few journals scattered among British Commonwealth countries published occasional reports, especially those based on research conducted in Asia and the Pacific or in Africa. When the "modern movement" of cross-cultural psychology started about 35 years ago, a groundswell of published resources began. Influential books such as Segall, Campbell, and Herskovits (1966), Naroll and Cohen (1970), Przeworski and Teune (1970), Triandis (1972), Cole, Gay, Glick, and Sharp (1971), Brislin, Lonner, and Thorndike (1973), Berry and Dasen (1974), Cole and Scribner (1974), among others, became increasingly numerous. JCCP was inaugurated, joining the *International Journal of Psychology* as a publication with a truly international focus. These efforts begat even more publication activity, such as the *Handbook of Cross-Cultural Psychology* (Triandis et al., 1980) the inauguration of the Sage Publications series, *Cross-Cultural*

Research and Methodology, and, of course, the biennial publication of the proceedings of the IACCP, the most recent of which is Lonner, Dinnel, Forgays, and Hayes (1999) and Boski, Van de Vivjer, and Chodynicka (2002) and the pending volume containing selected papers from the IACCP conference held in Yogyakarta, Indonesia in July, 2002 (Setiadi, Supratiknya, Lonner, & Poortinga, 2004). More recent publications include the second edition of the *Handbook of Cross-Cultural Psychology* (Berry et al., 1997), the *Handbook of Culture and Psychology* (Matsumoto, 2001), and many other authored and edited books. Various overviews have appeared (e.g., Segall, Lonner, & Berry, 1998). In addition, a number of texts aimed for undergraduates have been written (e.g., Brislin, 2000; Matsumoto, 2000; Segall, Dasen, Berry, & Poortinga, 2000). A free and easily accessible web-based project entitled "Online Readings in Psychology and Culture" was recently inaugurated (Lonner, Dinnel, Hayes, & Sattler, 2001). Several journals are now part of the established literature, such as the *International Journal of Intercultural Relations*, the *Interamerican Journal of Psychology*, *Cross-Cultural Research*, *Culture and Psychology*, the *International Journal of Testing*, and of course the *Journal of Cross-Cultural Psychology*. Different associations have emerged, including the Association pour la Recherche Interculturelle (ARIC) and the International Academy of Intercultural Research (IAIR). In 1965 one could have discussed relevant published literature over a quick cup of espresso. Today it would take a seven-course meal just to list all the available resources and their relative merits.

This extensive literature has been most helpful in clarifying the various ways that culture influences thought and behavior. It has also contributed immeasurably to a maturing science of psychology and culture and, one hopes, to breaking down of walls between the various factions of psychologists whose careers revolve around the study of culture. Ernest Boesch, who identifies himself as a cultural psychologist, wrote of his "conversion" from cross-cultural psychology (read: the extension of western experimental psychology to other cultures) to cultural psychology. Boesch (1996) discussed the seven "flaws" of cross-cultural psychology. However, his "flaws" are another person's "methodological challenges." Regardless of interpretation, Boesch said that the choice is not one of either-or – either subscribe to cross-cultural psychology or to cultural psychology. Rather, it is basically a statement in support of the proposition that a good cross-cultural research project should be preceded by insights and astute culture-sensitive observations of the researchers themselves, by cultural psychologists, and by any other informed source. In short, the cultural sciences need each other. Campbell (1961) wrote an influential chapter entitled "The mutual methodological relevance of anthropology and psychology." The various psychological approaches to culture share much methodological as well as conceptual relevance. It is only through a continued spirit of cooperation and mutual respect that unyielding critics of any single approach will finally be silenced.

Contemporary Trends in Cross-Cultural Psychology

When the modern movement in cross-cultural psychology was still a toddler, it was noted that several domains of research were prominent when carried into other cultures (Brislin, Lonner, & Thorndike, 1973). They included 1) measures of modernism, 2) Piagetian research, 3) Witkin's theory of psychological differentiation, 4) Dawson's bio-social psychology, 5) achievement motivation, 6) measuring subjective culture, and, of course, and 7) measuring intelligence and abilities across cultures. Other topics were studied, of course, especially in the area of social psychology (prejudice, stereotypes, social distance, and so forth). The research landscape has changed substantially during the past thirty years. Currently, there are many perspectives that tend to receive much of the attention. For instance, research on the psychology of acculturation (e.g., Ward, 2001), the definition and function of families across cultures (e.g. Georgas, Berry, van de Vijver, Kagitcibasi, & Poortinga, in press; Georgas et al., 2001; Kagitcibasi, 1996), the study of culture and personality (Church, 2001; Church & Lonner, 1998), and the value of children (e.g., Trommsdorff, 2001; Trommsdorff & Kornadt, 2003) are among many topical areas receiving considerable attention. Focusing on one of the currently popular topics, however, will help us understand various ongoing issues, concerns, and questions that persist in numerous psychological approaches to understand behavior and thought in and across other cultures. Thus, we turn briefly to an example of studying the venerated psychological tradition of studying individual differences in personality across the globe.

The study of culture and personality has been popular for many decades. Indeed, the study and understanding of individual differences ("personality" variations) is one of the great traditions in psychology. Once primarily the province of cultural anthropology, attempts to understand the influence of culture on individual differences in characteristic modes of interacting with others are led by psychologists who tend to identify with either cross-cultural psychology or cultural psychology. The latter are heavily context-oriented and tend to use qualitative methods with little interest in examining individual differences. They may be more likely to have an interest in, for example, how a specific culture and the perception of self within that culture are mutually constituted (e.g., Markus & Kitayama, 1991). The former are more likely to use quantitative methods, such as scales and inventories, in attempts to find basic factors of human personality that can be used for intraindividual comparisons both within and across cultures. Special issues concerning personality and its measurement across cultures have recently appeared in both the Journal of Cross-Cultural Psychology (1998) and the Journal of Personality (2001). Much attention has been given to how many "pure" factors of personality there are and why, if there really are a finite number of pure factors, they exist in the first place.

Research involving the NEO-PI-R has been especially active. This is a paper-and-pencil personality inventory that, like so many other devices, is designed to measure an individual's traits or characteristic modes of behaving. Using the NEO-

PI-R, Jeff McCrae, Paul Costa and their international network of colleagues have developed a convincing case for the universality of the so-called "Big Five" factors of personality – Openness (O), Conscientiousness (C), Extraversion (E), Agreeableness (A), and Neuroticism (N). There is insufficient space here to go into many of the details of this research. However, an interesting problem of interpretation (or lack thereof) is, according to McCrae (personal communication), perhaps the central current issue in culture and personality research. One would assume, McCrae says, that the personality structure of a particular culture is highly related to "national character" and therefore easy to see in the aggregate profiles of different cultures. After all, as McCrae (2001) noted, the "moody and melancholic temperament of Spaniards matches their high N scores." Similarly, high O scores are consistent with Germany, the land of Dichter und Denker. But the industrious and team-oriented Japanese score low in C and Hispanics, known for concepts such as sympatia and familia, scored low in A, scores that surprised McCrae.

These inconsistencies motivated McCrae to conduct a study aimed at determining to what extent aggregate scores for 26 cultures are consistent with perceptions of national character. To assess this, he enlisted the assistance of a panel of experts. McCrae explained his methodology as follows:

On five separate sheets of paper presented in random order, I listed the seven lowest and seven highest scoring cultures for each factor. I asked the experts to identify the personality factor that had been used to rank the cultures on each page. Which personality factor, for example, is lowest among Hong Kong Chinese and South Koreans, but highest among Norwegians and Americans? Judges were instructed not to consult the literature, but simply to rely on their own impressions (p. 838).

In his instructions he guessed that the task would take 10-20 minutes. However, nearly all the experts agreed that this was an extremely difficult task. Several gave up immediately, finding it impossible to complete. Of the 25 judgments made, only 4 were correct – about chance expectations. These results were puzzling. The internal consistency and external correlates of the factors should, in theory, make this a relatively easy task. What does it mean for real-world applications if the "experts" can't exceed chance expectations on something that is seemingly so simple?

McCrae (2001) noted several possible explanations for these poor performances. For instance, "it is possible that the scores, and thus the rankings, are seriously distorted by response biases, different standards of self-presentation, or quirks of sampling" (p. 838). Among other possibilities are that the judges were insufficiently familiar with all cultures listed and thus couldn't make truly informed judgments or that expert judges "are relatively insensitive to differences in average levels of personality traits in large groups and that mean trait differences are not reflected in obvious ways in social institutions and customs" (p. 839). McCrae suggested that an implication of the last interpretation is that "intercultural analyses may uncover many new and hitherto unsuspected findings because, like microscopes, they operate at a level of analysis inaccessible to the 'naked eye'" (p. 839). This interpretation is consistent with the last part of the "transfer-test-discovery" rationale in standard cross-cultural research methodology, mentioned earlier in this chapter that characterizes much psychological research involving other cultures. Another explanation is that the notions of national stereotypes, national character, and modal personality, terms that have been soundly criticized and vilified for being too superficial are probably too gross or general to be useful in such situations.

Using other data sets from many cultures, tasks like McCrae's can be replicated. Indeed, Schwartz is currently doing it by using aggregate scores on his culture-level value dimensions from many societies. Thus far it appears that his task is somewhat easier than McCrae's. This may be because the seven value dimensions he used on a matching task have clearer margins and are more face valid (in the good sense of that term) than the more subtle or muted configurations presented in McCrae's NEO-PI-R task. It may also be that observers of a society can sense cultural differences more easily than personality profiles. Culture is manifest in the functioning of institutions and the widespread practices in societies. Observers are likely to experience these consistent overt expressions of culture when visiting or studying a society. They are less likely to be exposed to a representative set of individual members of that society who exhibit a shared personality profile. Similar tasks can be developed for Hofstede's (2001) five dimensions, for Gannon's (2001) "metaphorical journeys across nations," and so on. Incidentally, Hofstede warned against committing the "ecological fallacy" – the fallacy of assuming that characteristics found at the group level are also true at the level of the individual. Smith (2002) noted that this "level of analysis" problem occurs in many areas of investigation and not just in cross-cultural psychology. As Smith succinctly stated, "there is no logical reason why the relationship between two variables at one level of analysis should be the same at another level of analysis" (p. 5). Part of the problem is that the basic unit of analysis in psychology has historically been the individual. When psychologists take that level of analysis up one or more notches, especially to the macroscopic level of entire cultures, complex problems of analysis can easily emerge (see the special section, "Levels of Analysis in Cross-Cultural Psychology: Promises and Challenges" in the January 2004 issue of the *Journal of Cross-Cultural Psychology*.)

The practical implications for research of this kind are significant. Questioning what is happening here is a sign of a maturing science of psychology and culture. Puzzlements such as these were not a major concern when psychologists started using personality and values scales and questionnaires in other societies. In the early days of cross-cultural explorations the primary motive was to look for and explain differences. Most readers would - and did - accept these explanations as perfectly valid because of the (absolutistic) belief that devices used to measure personality were fairly accurate and, more importantly, stable and equally useful across cultures. Currently there is as much interest in explaining similarities as there are in focusing on differences. How different factors or dimensions, which may be valid in a global sense, manifest themselves in different societies is of interest to many. This leads to the topic of psychological universals.

The Search for Psychological Universals Revisited

My chapter, "The Search for Psychological Universals," appeared in Volume 1 of the *Handbook of cross-cultural psychology* (Lonner, 1980). The reason I was invited to write a chapter on this topic was because I had expressed an opinion, early and often, that there are far more similarities in human behavior than there are differences and that it therefore may be more profitable for cross-cultural psychologists to search for the basic, underlying reasons for these similarities instead of dwelling on a cascade of differences and post hoc musings for them. Moreover, because one of the goals of cross-cultural psychology is to contribute to a more inclusive, perhaps even universally valid, psychology, it was natural to include such a chapter. It was useful then, and it still is, to quote Kluckhohn and Murray (1948): "Every man [sic] is in certain respects a) like all other men, b) like some other men, and c) like no other man" (p. 35).

As explained in more detail elsewhere (Lonner, 2000), I began to search for a structure that would present a solid case for ideas and concepts that may qualify as psychological universals. Hoping to cover a wide range of topics, I used a structure that included seven levels or types of universals. These levels were labeled (1) Simple universals (e.g., the absolute facticity of human aggression), (2) Variform universals (e.g., aggression can be seen in various forms in different cultures, but it always occurs, even if muted and implicit rather than blatant and explicit), (3) Functional universals (societal variations that have the same social consequences, but equilibrated for local relevance – for instance, the punishment of children or the marriage of a daughter), (4) Diachronic universals (universals of behavior that are temporally invariant, but interpreted differently in historical context – for instance, yesterday's blacksmith is today's rocket engineer); (5) Ethologically-oriented universals (those with phylogenetic, Darwinian links, such as the facial display of emotions); (6) Systematic behavioral universals (various subcategories with psychology, and there are many of them,) and (7) Cocktail party universals (those things that all people feel and share with others but can only be discussed as phenomena that defy measurement, as in "I know exactly how you felt when you saw the Acropolis"). This structure worked pretty well in that context more than 20 years ago. It was broad enough and flexible enough to permit the incorporation of a good number of perspectives that were viable at the time. Indeed, the structure could still be used effectively because it was designed to be sufficiently broad to accommodate changes and new ideas.

While strategies and reasons to look for them may vary, the search for universals is still one of the more fundamental reasons why culturally oriented psychologists are attracted to studying thought and behavior in other places. One might even say that the search for psychological universals is itself a universal! Most cross-cultural psychologists still, I believe, would define a good part of what they do as a search for universals, for common denominators, for some sort of template that may help us understand individual differences throughout the world – both within and across cultures. The hunger for finding pancultural regularities is still real, viable and palpable. What has changed, primarily, is that the items worthy of studying are currently more numerous and varied. Moreover, efforts to pursue them have become more energetic, sophisticated, and perhaps even more contentious and methodologically problematic. If I were to begin a chapter on universals today, I would undoubtedly start where I did about 25 years ago: searching the relevant and much larger literature and try to catalog what people have been doing in this area. There would be plenty from which to choose. With several journals now featuring culture, ethnicity, and related terms suggestive of some form of "group-belongingness" and many more books than were available earlier, one would have no trouble finding strong evidence that psychologists interested in other cultures are using assumedly universal templates in guiding their research. Many of these perspectives have been mentioned in this paper. All of them would be candidates for Column 2 in Table 1 – the idea of common denominators that make it more defensible to conduct culture-comparative research.

In addition, a current overview of psychological universals would have to consider the friendly discussions between cultural psychologists and cross-cultural psychologists. In the late 1970s these somewhat contrasting viewpoints were yet to flourish as viable alternative ways to view human thought and behavior. There were radical relativists in anthropology and linguistics (e.g. the Whorf-Sapir hypothesis), but with only a few exceptions among psychologists the strident challenge of universality and/or culture-comparative inquiry had not yet emerged. I continue to believe what I recently wrote:

I hope this is not an oversimplification, but cross-cultural psychologists seem to be looking for the simplest way to explain the enormous complexities of thought and behavior, at the same time embracing the way that such patterns can be interpreted in culturally-specific ways. Cultural psychologists seem to be searching for reasons why it is inappropriate to reduce thought and behavior to some kind of simple structure, eschewing comparativism. The debate involving absolutism, relativism, and universalism continues, and I suspect that it will not be resolved soon. I believe that the one-size-fits-all mentality encompassed in absolutism is completely unacceptable. I also believe that radical relativism and a total and uncompromising reliance on non-comparative contextualism is too extreme. That leaves universalism, and I still argue that searching for the common denominators in human thought and behavior is both tenable, justifiable, and rather interesting. Science, even social science, is, after all, essentially a search for patterns, regularities, causal factors, and threads of continuity in antecedent conditions. It is also an open, honest, and unbiased system that must accommodate those things that are temporarily inexplicable.
Regardless of the approach that cultural scientists prefer, the search for psychological universals will continue. Why shouldn't it? Abandoning the search would amount to neglecting one of the main canons of science. (Lonner, 2000, p. 37)

Concluding Remarks

I shall end this chapter by turning once again to one of the major elements of the modern movement in cross-cultural psychology, and the element I know best: the *Journal of Cross-Cultural Psychology*. When the Journal was founded I had both the privilege and the obligation to do what I consider best. With no recipe for success to guide me, I tried to "get it right" and capture the essence of what seemed to be the best way to proceed. Had I known then what I know now, I would have done several things differently. The main thing I would have done is to capture the essence of what is currently the most important part of our current publication policy:

[the Journal] publishes papers that focus on the interrelationships between culture and psychological processes [that] report results from either cross-cultural comparative research or results from other types of research concerning the ways in which culture (and related concepts such as ethnicity) affect the thinking and behavior of individuals as well as how individual thought and behavior define and reflect aspects of culture.

I believe that the above captures the essence of what cross-cultural psychology has been trying to do for many years. We may be close to "getting it right" – but who knows what "right" is? Part of any answer to this very large question is provided by the others who were present at the event that led to this book. Fortunately, some of their important views on the matter are included in this volume. A reading of this entire book will provide a respectable overview of the various ways that culturally oriented psychologists ask questions, conduct research, and attempt to make sense of the important connections between psychology and culture.

References

Aberle, D. F., Cohen, A. K., Davis, A., Levy, M., & Sutton, F. X. (1950). Functional prerequisites of society. *Ethics, 60*, 100-111.

Adamopoulos, J., & Lonner, W. J. (2001). Culture and psychology at a Crossroad: Historical perspective and theoretical analysis. In D. Matsumoto (Ed.), *Handbook of culture and psychology* (pp. 11-34). New York: Oxford University Press.

Berry, J. W. (1989). Imposed etics-emics-derived etics: The operationalization of a compelling idea. *International Journal of Psychology, 24*, 721-735.

Berry, J. W. (1995). The descendents of a model. *Culture and Psychology, 1*, 373-380.

Berry, J. W., & Dasen, P. R. (Eds.). (1974). *Culture and cognition*. London: Methuen.

Berry, J. W., Poortinga, Y. H., & Pandey, J. (Eds.). (1997). *Theory and method: Handbook of cross-cultural psychology: Vol. 1*. Boston: Allyn and Bacon.

Berry, J. W., Poortinga, Y. H., Segall, M. H., & Dasen, P. R. (2002). *Cross-cultural psychology: Research and applications* (2nd ed.). Cambridge: Cambridge University Press.

Boesch, E. E. (1958). *Expert meeting on cross-cultural research in child psychology: Problems and methods in cross-cultural research. Bangkok, Thailand: United Nations Educational, Scientific, and Cultural Organization.* Unpublished manuscript.

Boesch, E. E. (1996). The seven flaws of cross-cultural psychology: The story of a conversion. *Mind, Culture, and Activity, 1*, 2-10.

Boski, P., van de Vijver, F. J. R., & Chodynicka, A. M. (Eds.). (2002). *New directions in cross-cultural psychology: Selected papers from the Fifteeenth International Congress of the International Association for Cross-Cultural Psychology.* Warsaw, Poland: Polish Psychological Association.

Brislin, R. W. (2000). *Understanding culture's influence on behavior.* Fort Worth, TX: Harcourt.

Brislin, R. W., Lonner, W. J., & Thorndike, R. M. (1973). *Cross-cultural research methods.* New York: John Wiley.

Bronfenbrenner, U. (1979). *The ecology of human development.* Cambridge, MA: Harvard University Press.

Bronfenbrenner, U. (1993). The ecology of human development: Research models and fugitive findings. In R. Wozniak & K. W. Fischer (Eds.), *Development in context* (pp. 3-44). Hillsdale, NJ: Lawrence Erlbaum Associates.

Bronstein, P., & Quina, K. (Eds.). (2003). *Transforming the teaching of psychology: Resources for gender and multicultural awareness.* Washington D.C.: American Psychological Association.

Campbell, D. T. (1961). The mutual methodological relevance of anthropology and psychology. In F. Hsu (Ed.), *Psychological anthropology* (pp. 333-352). Homewood, IL: Dorsey Press.

Campbell, D. T. & Fiske, D. W. (1959). Convergent and discriminant validation by the multitrait-multimethod matrix. *Psychological Bulletin, 56*, 81-105.

Church, A. T. (Ed.). (2001). Culture and personality [Special Issue]. *Journal of Personality, 69* (6).

Church, A. T., & Lonner, W. J. (Eds.). (1998). Personality and its measurement across cultures [Special Issue]. *Journal of Cross-Cultural Psychology, 29* (1).

Cole, M. (1996). *Cultural psychology: A once and future discipline.* Cambridge, MA: Belknap/Harvard.

Cole, M., & Scribner, S. (1974). *Culture and thought: A psychological introduction.* New York: Wiley.

Cole, M., Gay, J., Glick, J., & Sharp, D. (1971). *The cultural context of learning and thinking.* New York: Basic Books.

Cronbach, L. J. C., & Drenth; P. J. D. (Eds.). (1972). *Mental tests and cultural adaptation.* The Hague, The Netherlands: Mouton.

Dawson, J. L. M. B., & Lonner, W. J. (Eds.). (1974). *Readings in cross-cultural psychology*. Hong Kong: International Association for Cross-Cultural Psychology (Libra Press Ltd.).

Gannon, M. (2001). *Understanding global cultures: Metaphorical journeys though 23 nations* (2nd ed.). Thousand Oaks, CA: Sage Publications.

Gardiner, H. (2001). Culture, context, and development. In D. Matsumoto (Ed.), *Handbook of culture and psychology* (pp. 101-117). New York: Oxford University Press.

Georgas, J., Berry, J. W., van de Vijver, F. J. R., Kagitcibasi, C., & Poortinga, Y. H. (Eds.). (in press). *Cultures, family and psychological functioning*. Cambridge: Cambridge University Press.

Georgas, J., Mylonas, K., Bafiti, T., Christakopoulou, S., Poortinga, Y. H., Kagitcibasi, C., Orung, S., Sunar, D., Kwak, K., Ataca, B., Berry, J. W., Charalambous, N., Goodwin, R., Wang, W.-Z., Angleitner, A., Stepanikova, I., Pick, S., Givaudan, M., Zhuravliova-Gionis, I., Konantambigi, R., Gelfand, M. J., Velislava, M., McBride-Chang, M., & Kodic, Y. (2001). Functional relationships in the nuclear and extended family: A 16-culture study. *International Journal of Psychology, 36*, 289-300.

Gergen, K. J., Gulerce, A., Lock, A., & Misra, G. (1996). Psychological science in cultural context. *American Psychologist, 51*, 496-503

Headland, T. N., Pike, K. L., & Harris, M. (1990). *Emics and etics: The insider/outsider debate*. Newbury Park, CA: Sage Publications.

Hermans, H. J. M., & Kempen, H. J. G. (1998) Moving cultures: The perilous problems of cultural dichotomies in a globalizing society. *American Psychologist, 53*, 1111-1120.

Hogan, J. D., & Tartaglini, A. (1994). A brief history of cross-cultural psychology. In L. L. Adler and & U. P. Gilen (Eds.), *Cross-cultural topics in psychology* (pp. 15-23). Westport, CT: Praeger.

Hofstede, G. (2001). *Culture's consequences: Comparing values, behaviors, institutions, and organizations across nations* (2nd ed.). Thousand Oaks, CA: Sage Publications.

Jahoda, G. (1980). Theoretical and systematic approaches in cross-cultural psychology. In H. C. Triandis & J. W. Berry (Eds.), *Handbook of cross-cultural psychology: Perspectives* (Vol. 1, pp. 69-142). Boston: Allyn and Bacon.

Jahoda, G. (1990). Our forgotten ancestors: In R. A. Dienstbier & J. J. Berman (Eds.), *Nebraska Symposium on Motivation: Cultural perspectives* (Vol. 37, pp. 1-40). Lincoln, NE: University of Nebraska Press.

Jahoda, G. (1980). Theoretical and systematic approaches in cross-cultural psychology. In H. C. Triandis & J. W. Berry (Eds.), *Handbook of cross-cultural psychology: Perspectives* (Vol. 1, pp. 69-142). Boston: Allyn and Bacon.

Jahoda, G., & Krewer, B. (1997). History of cross-cultural and cultural psychology. In J. W. Berry, Y. H. Poortinga, & J. Pandey (Eds.), *Handbook of cross-cultural psychology: Theory and method,* (Vol. 1, pp 1-42). Boston: Allyn and Bacon.

Kagitcibasi, C. (1996). *Family and human development across cultures: A view from the other side.* Mahwah; NJ: Lawrence Erlbaum Associates.

Klineberg, O. (1980). Historical perspectives: Cross-cultural psychology before 1960. In H. C. Triandis & W. W. Lambert (Eds.), *Handbook of cross-cultural psychology: Perspectives* (Vol. 1, pp. 31-68). Boston: Allyn and Bacon.

Kluckhohn, C., & Murray, H. A. (1948). *Personality in nature, society, and culture.* New York: Knopf.

Lonner, W. J. (1980). The search for psychological universals. In H. C. Triandis & W. W. Lambert (Eds.), *Handbook of cross-cultural psychology: Perspectives* (Vol. 1, pp. 143-204). Boston: Allyn & Bacon.

Lonner, W. J. (2000). Revisiting the search for psychological universals. *Cross-Cultural Psychology Bulletin, 34* (1&2), 34-37.

Lonner, W. J. (2004). JCCP at 35: Commitment, continuity and creative adaptation. *Journal of Cross-Cultural Psychology, 35,* 123-136.

Lonner, W. J., Dinnel, D. L., Forgays, D. K., & Hayes, S. A. (Eds.). (1999). *Merging past, present, and future in cross-cultural psychology: Selected papers from the 14th International Congress of the International Association of Cross-Cultural Psychology.* Lisse, The Netherlands: Swets and Zeitlinger.

Lonner, W. J., Dinnel, D. L., Hayes, S. A., & Sattler, D. N. (Eds.). (2001). *Online readings in psychology and culture.* Bellingham, WA: Western Washington University, Center for Cross-Cultural Research, from http://www.ac.wwu.edu/~culture/readings.htm.

Markus, H. R., & Kitayama, S. (1991). Culture and self. *Psychological Review, 98,* 224-253.

Matsumoto, D. (2000). *Culture and psychology: People around the world.* Pacific Grove, CA: Brooks/Cole.

Matsumoto, D. (Ed.). (2001). *Handbook of culture and psychology.* New York: Oxford University Press.

McClelland, D. C. (1961). *The achieving society.* Princeton, NJ: Van Nostrand.

McCrae, R. R. (2001). Trait psychology and culture: Exploring intercultural relations. *Journal of Personality, 69,* 819-846.

Naroll, R., & Cohen, R. (Eds.). (1970). *A handbook of method in cultural anthropology.* New York: Natural History Press.

Przeworski, A., & Teune, H. (1970). *The logic of comparative social inquiry.* New York: Wiley, 1970.

Schwartz, S. H. (1994). Are there universal aspects in the structure and content of human values? *Journal of Social Issues, 50,* 19-45.

Segall, M. H., Campbell, D. T., and & Herskovits, M. (1966). *The influence of culture on visual perception.* Indianapolis, IN: Bobbs-Merrill.

Segall, M. H., Dasen, P. R., Berry, J. W., & Poortinga, Y. H. (1999). *Human behavior in global perspective: An introduction to cross-cultural psychology* (2nd ed.). Boston: Allyn and Bacon.

Segall, M. H., Lonner, W. J., & Berry, J. W. (1998). Cross-cultural psychology as a scholarly discipline: On the flowering of culture in behavioral research. *American Psychologist, 53,* 1101-1110.

Setiadi, B. N., Supratiknya, A., Lonner, W. J., & Poortinga, Y. H. (Eds.). (2004). *Ongoing themes in psychology and culture: Selected papers from the XVI. International Conference of the International Association of Cross-Cultural Psychology.* Yogyakarta, Indonesia: Kanisius.

Smith, P. B. (2002). Levels of Analysis in Cross-Cultural Psychology. In W. J. Lonner, D. L. Dinnel, S. A. Hayes, & D. N. Sattler (Eds.), *Readings in psychology and culture.* Bellingham, WA: Center for Cross-Cultural Research Web site: http://www.ac.wwu.edu/~culture/readings.htm.

Super, C. M., & Harkness, S. (1986). The development niche: A conceptualization at the interface of child and culture. *International Journal of Behavioral Development, 9,* 545-570.

Triandis, H. C. (1972). *The analysis of subjective culture.* New York: Wiley.

Triandis, H. C., Lambert, W. W., Berry, J. W., Lonner, W. J., Heron, A., Brislin, R. W., & Draguns, J. G. (Eds.). (1980). *Handbook of cross-cultural psychology* (Vols. 1-6). Boston: Allyn and Bacon.

Trommsdorff, G. (2001). Eltern-Kind-Beziehungen im interkulturellen Vergleich [Parent-child relations in cross-cultural comparison]. In S. Walper & R. Pekrun (Eds.), *Familie und Entwicklung: Perspektiven der Familienpsychologie* (pp. 23-50). Goettingen, Germany: Hogrefe.

Trommsdorff, G., & Kornadt, H.-J. (2003). Parent-child relations in cross-cultural perspective. In L. Kuczynski (Ed.), *Handbook of dynamics in parent-child relations* (pp. 271-306). Thousand Oaks, CA: Sage Publications.

Tyler, F. L. (1999). Cross-cultural psychology: Is it time to revise the model? In: W. J. Lonner, D. L. Dinnel, D. K. Forgays, & S. A. Hayes (Eds.), (1999). *Merging past, present, and future in cross-cultural psychology: Selected papers from the 14th International Congress of the International Association of Cross-Cultural Psychology* (pp. 116-134). Lisse, The Netherlands: Swets and Zeitlinger.

Tyler, F. L. (2001). *Cultures, communities, competence, and change.* New York: Kluwer/Plenum.

van de Vijver, F. J. R., & Leung, K. (1997). *Methods and data analysis for cross-cultural research.* Thousand Oaks, CA: Sage Publications.

Ward, C. (2001). The ABCs of acculturation. In D. Matsumoto (Ed.), *Handbook of culture and psychology* (pp. 411-445). New York: Oxford University Press.

Segall, M. H., Dasen, P. T., & Berry, J. W. (1998). Cross-cultural psychology as a scholarly discipline: On the flowering of culture in behavioral research. *American Psychologist*, 53, 1101–1110.

Takahashi, K. (2002). Variations in retrospective accounts of ...

Triandis, H. C. (2000). ...

2

What can Western Psychology Learn From Indigenous Psychologies? – Lessons From Hindu Psychology[*]

Pradeep Chakkarath

Introduction

In this article I will reflect on the meaning of Indigenous Psychologies by focusing on its role in structuring of the developmental niche and for subjective theories of life-span development and child rearing. These topics of psychological research have gained some interest lately, but have rarely been investigated with regard to their reciprocal relationship and its implications for empirical research. Thus, the aim of the following considerations is to show the fruitfulness of an integrative perspective on these topics and to support my argumentation using some examples of indigenous concepts that might prove to be relevant for research within the frame-

[*] This article is based on research done within the framework of the project "Subjective Developmental Theories in Cross-Cultural Comparison," which was part of the interdisciplinary Collaborative Research Center 511 "Literature and Anthropology," Project 15 "Subjective developmental theories in cross-cultural comparison," and supported by grants from the Deutsche Forschungsgemeinschaft (DFG) to Gisela Trommsdorff and Wolfgang Friedlmeier, University of Konstanz.

work of subjective theories on human development and child rearing. Of course, in view of the innumerable indigenous theories that could serve as examples for this purpose, the tradition of Hindu thinking is just one of many (for other examples, see Chakkarath, in press). My selection of this particular theory pays tribute to the fact that the so-called "Indian culture" has contributed some of the oldest, most systematized and still most influential theories on many aspects of human development. Moreover, since Indian religious and philosophical worldviews, concepts of man as well as a variety of social theories have influenced many parts of South Asia and South East Asia, their scope reaches beyond the Indian subcontinent and therefore sufficiently justifies having a closer look at some of those elements within the Indian tradition of thinking that are also of interest to mainstream psychology as developed in the West. At the same time, the topic of the article as well as the examples chosen reflect that it is a growing number of especially Asian psychologists who demand a more thorough investigation into the meaning and function of indigenous psychologies for a better understanding of culture and its influence on human development (Ho, 1998; Kim, 2001; Sinha, 1997). In accordance with these preliminary remarks, the following considerations will consist of four parts:

First, an understanding of Indigenous Psychology and its meaning for the refinement and development of psychological theory and research will be given. Our further investigation will be based on that understanding. Following this, some psychologically relevant indigenous concepts will be presented and it will be shown why considering these concepts is important for a sounder understanding of subjective theories of human development within Indian contexts. Finally, I will reflect on some of the implications that our results might have for further research on human development in cross-cultural and cultural psychology.

What is "Indigenous Psychology"?

The last decades have seen many theoretical and methodological debates between mainly two well known approaches of investigating the psychological significance of culture. On the one hand there is a so-called cross-cultural psychology with its goal to pursue the universal validity of psychological theories across a variety of cultures and which upholds the idea of an objective reality that can be separated and distinguished from the individuals under investigation; on the other hand, there is a so-called cultural psychology with its rather relativistic view, its emphasis on culture specificities, and its notion that since individuals and the culture they live in make each other up culture cannot be treated as an objective entity apart from the person.

More recent attempts to integrate some of the theoretical convictions of both approaches have made it clear that the relevance of culture-specific contexts has been increasingly acknowledged even by cross-cultural psychologists (Berry, 2002; Lonner, in this volume; Segall, Lonner, & Berry, 1998; Shweder, 2000). This can be seen, for example, in the role that some important concepts play in research carried out by cross-cultural as well as cultural psychologists: the model of the developmental niche (Super & Harkness, 1997), culture-specific conceptualizations of the self (Markus & Kitayama, 1991), the research on interculturally varying cognitive styles (Nisbett, Peng, Choi, & Norenzanan, 2001), and the efforts to take the concept of individualism-collectivism to a higher level of differentiation (Oyserman, Coon, & Kemmelmeier, 2002; Triandis, 2001), to name just a few.

It is against this background that one can understand the growing interest in so-called "indigenous psychologies," that first gained attention in cultural anthropology (Heelas & Locke, 1981) and more recently in psychology (Ho, 1998; Kim, 2001; Kim & Berry, 1993; Sinha, 1997; see also the Special Issue of the *Asian Journal of Social Psychology* on "Indigenous, cultural, and cross-cultural psychologies," 2000). The term "indigenous psychology" is generally used to mark psychologically relevant concepts that were developed in the culture of investigation and that need not necessarily be congruent with psychological concepts that were developed by western mainstream psychology. Since indigenous psychologies carry important aspects of how certain cultures "think," they allow essential insights into the self-understanding of these cultures, into their worldviews, their picture of man, including their preference for certain values and attitudes, for example, with regard to the relationship between individual and the collective.

Moreover, indigenous psychologies are of special interest to western mainstream psychology because they provide ideas, theories, and explanations concerning human development that may help to critically reflect on some of the assumptions traditionally held by western psychology. From an indigenous psychological perspective, western psychology is indigenous itself (Gergen, Gulerce, Lock, & Misra, 1996) and repeatedly has changed considerably within its own history (Chakkarath, 2003). Therefore and due to the methodological standards set by modern western psychology itself, its goal to discover universal traits and laws governing the human psyche should always be tested against competing theories, for example, indigenous psychologies provided by other cultures. At the same time this can help to generate new hypotheses in order to specify some of the commonly approved concepts or to develop new theories with a broader scope of validity.

One of the reasons why western psychology has not shown very much interest in indigenous psychological concepts may have to do with the assumption that those concepts are often integral parts of religious or other prescientific worldviews and, therefore, do not meet western scientific standards. Since indigenous psychology has been defined as a psychological understanding developed and historically rooted in a particular cultural context and designed primarily for the people of that culture (Kim, 1990), indigenous psychology appears to be "merely" part of the general knowledge of a specific culture. Though its role as an important constituent of a particular cultural context makes indigenous psychology important enough for social scientific consideration in general, definitions like this do not differentiate between folk theories about human functioning and the specific efforts of some cultures to formally and systematically, i.e., scientifically, describe and analyze psychological phenomena and their meaning for human development. Since it may be assumed that folk theories can be found in every culture, it has been a main goal of the indigenous psychological approach to take informal folk concepts that seem to be psychologically relevant and formalize them into more complex psychological theories (Greenfield, 2000). Such an attempt may be called an "indigenized" psychology (Enriquez, 1993; Sinha, 1997). In this article, however, I suggest taking a closer look at those indigenous psychological theories that were already formalized and had already integrated psychologically relevant concepts into a systematically elaborated theory before modern psychology was taken into account. In other words, I suggest focusing more attention on psychological frameworks and concepts that were indigenous right from the beginning and that provide systematic analyses and can therefore serve as a more adequate basis for comparison with concepts provided by academic western psychology. As we shall see, the mere fact that in many cases indigenous concepts are embedded in religious or other ideological worldviews should not discredit their scientific potential and their psychological relevance (Chakkarath, in press; Thomas, 1997).

In light of these considerations, the Hindu tradition of psychological thinking is a well-suited starting point for us for several reasons: For over 3000 years, Hinduism has provided a vast literature on various systems of philosophy that involves elaborate conceptual frameworks, critical thinking concerning the mind and the body, theoretical analyses of the human personality, introspective methods of observing psychological phenomena, various therapeutic techniques designed to help individuals cope with the difficulties of human life and reach higher levels of development, as well as a broad range of social institutions that reflect, facilitate, and structure the kind of personality growth that Hindu culture regards as the basis for well-being and fulfillment (Paranjpe, 1984).

There have been several attempts to show the theoretical potential of indigenous concepts for an alternative description and explanation of psychological phenomena within the cultural contexts of the Indian subcontinent (for an overview see Gergen et al., 1996). However, only a few psychologists have attempted to look more closely at the efforts of Hindu scholars to describe and analyze psychological phenomena and their meaning for human development within the framework of an original indigenous psychology (e.g., Paranjpe, 1988, 1998; Thomas, 1990).

Therefore, one of the reasons I chose Hindu psychology as an example of a non-western tradition of psychological theorizing is that we can doubtless refer to these Hindu traditions as an example of "indigenous psychology" in the sense that I suggest. It is an important constituent of Indian culture and – as confirmed empirically (e.g., Inglehart, Basanez, & Moreno, 1998; Mascolo, Misra, & Rapisardi, 2004; Saraswathi & Ganapathy, 2002) – has an influence on human values, attitudes, and judgments as well as the relationships between the groups and individuals within cultural contexts. Second, the Hindu concepts and the developmental contexts they influence may help us to identify a broader scope of psychologically relevant phenomena that could assist us in generating new hypotheses and refining some of the traditional assumptions of western psychology. Third, as I will show, from its very beginning, Hindu psychology was developed in the framework of a life-span model and could thus serve to enrich and refine some of the more recent debates among western developmental psychologists. Finally, it is of interest to psychologists to learn the extent to which very different cultures develop similar psychological concepts and what such similarity or dissimilarity tells us about universal features in psychological theorizing across cultures.

The following attempt to deal with some of the core themes of Hindu thinking can merely be exemplary. Since Hinduism has offered mankind one of the richest and most diverse traditions of philosophical and scientific thought, it is impossible to cover the whole range of ideas that are meaningful for further psychological research. Moreover, it is not possible to do justice to the elaborate systematic character of classical Hindu theories on only a few pages. It is also not possible to adequately pay tribute to the many philosophical (e.g., Buddhist, Jain, Islamic) traditions by which Hindu thinking was enriched. However, by presenting a few topics, commenting on their main features, the following may encourage the reader to consider these and other indigenous concepts more thoroughly.

The Hindu Model of Human Development

Key elements of the Hindu worldview

The term "Hinduism" refers to innumerable sects, mainly on the Indian subcontinent, that follow many different ideas, but share some central convictions which are derived from a vast corpus of sacred writings (with the *Vedas* and the *Upanishads* at the core). One of these convictions is the belief in the repetitious transmigration of the individual soul (*atman*) in a cycle of birth, death, and rebirth (*samsara*). Another central belief is that life means mainly suffering. Therefore, reaching salvation (*moksha*) from that cycle and becoming one with the world soul (*brahman*) – i.e., the absolute reality behind the visible and misleading phenomena of the world – is the ultimate goal of the Hindu practitioner.

The driving force behind the process of *samsara* is the accumulated sum total of the individual's good and bad deeds (*karma*). This quality of a person's *karma* is subject to the natural law of action and reaction, of cause and effect. Good *karma* is achieved by living according to the cosmic law of being (*dharma*). Since one of the main aspects of *dharma* is the representation of a just world in which everything has a precisely defined place and function, each Hindu must follow certain rules and norms and fulfill his or her duties. This well-defined code of conduct involves doing what is right for the individual, the family, the caste (*jati*), the society, and the universe. The rules of conduct have been laid down in various *dharma shastras*, compilations of laws that cover the realms of religious and social life in order to give Hindus orientation throughout their life course. The most famous among these is the *manava dharma shastra*, said to be written by Manu, a sage who lived in the second century B.C. These works serve to integrate the doctrines mentioned above into the social structure and thus show that, from a Hindu point of view, there is no real difference between the religious and the social spheres. Since the biological and social conditions of a Hindu's life – whether he is a mineral, a plant, an animal or a human being, a male or a female, whether he is physically attractive or unattractive, whether he belongs to a lower or a higher caste – are determined by the *karma* he accumulates, faithfully carrying out his duties as they have been laid down primarily in the caste rules is of utmost importance for reaching the goal of release from the cycle of *samsara*.

The interpretation of one's social conditions, the unequal distribution of wealth, prestige, and suffering, as well as one's membership in a particular caste, as is the result of deeds done in a former life, endows the system with divine sanction and makes it possible for each individual to perceive the social reality as being just. Thus, this interpretation has helped stabilize the elementary structures of Hindu society for thousands of years.

This short sketch of some of the basic tenets of the Hindu worldview may be sufficient to understand why Hindus themselves call it *sanatana dharma*. This approximately translates to "eternal rules" and does not mean a religion in the western sense of the word, but rather a code of conduct. Now I will try to outline how some of the central convictions mentioned above are not rooted in mere cosmological and metaphysical speculation, but in an early psychological theory of human cognition.

The human condition from a cognitive and motivational point of view

As mentioned above, one of the characteristics of Hindu thought is a general pessimism concerning the value of life – including human life – especially in light of the experiences of suffering and death. Many Hindu scholars have developed various theories to explain why the human condition is miserable and how that condition can be overcome. Interestingly enough, it is often disregarded that most of these theories are psychological in nature and begin with an analysis of human cognition. My example of this kind of analysis will focus on some of the assumptions made within the tradition of *Sankhya*, which is said to be one of the oldest orthodox schools of Indian philosophy. *Sankhya* is closely associated with the system of *Yoga*, which proposes a well-structured introspective method for verifying the core assumptions of the *Sankhya* analysis of cognitive processes. Moreover, *Yoga* also provides detailed therapeutic exercises that enable the individual to understand these processes, to cope with the problems resulting from them, and to thereby attain salvation from *samsara*.

Therefore, the Hindu philosophers do not regard the *Sankhya* theory as mere metaphysics, but as theory accompanied by empirical analysis. I will now explain some of the main features of the *Sankhya* theory.

On the first level of analysis, *Sankhya* supports the key conviction of all Indian philosophy that suffering is omnipresent and that there are countless examples of how human suffering is caused by a "three-fold misery," i.e., by internal factors

(e.g., anger, desire, greed), by other beings (e.g., relatives, enemies, friends, animals), and by supernatural factors (spirits) responsible for disasters (e.g., earth-
quakes, flooding, drought). *Sankhya* does not forbid the experience of happiness and
contentment (as it is highly celebrated in Indian art and literature), however, it
makes it clear that the everyday experience of happiness commonly ends and subsequently becomes a source of new suffering. The inevitability of death questions
both, the states of happiness as well as those of suffering, and more importantly it
questions the meaning of life as a whole and ultimately concludes that there cannot
be much value in it.

On the second level of analysis, *Sankhya* shows that the miserable human condition results from a psychological causal nexus, according to which it is assumed that
cause and effect are two identical states, with the effect always pre-existing in the
cause. To illustrate: a potter forms a pot (effect) using clay (the material cause) at a
certain point in time; however, the potential to be(come) a pot was inherent in the
clay before the pot was created.

Based on this concept of causation, *Sankhya* further assumes that the world of
human experience evolves from one single principle, which it calls *prakrti* (matter)
and in which all the diverse forms of the world's phenomena are latently inherent.
Interestingly, it is made clear that the mind, ego, and intellect evolve from *prakrti* as
a result of cognitive processes that have their beginning in the natural tendency of
the senses and the mind to discriminate between objects, to have them sorted and
named. This tendency leads the individual to fix preferences and antipathies as well
as to form intentions in order to reach certain emotional states and to avoid others.
One of the most important results of this process is the development of the ego and
the feeling of a "self" that makes the individual act self-interestedly or even egoisti-
cally. Since the satisfaction of many of these interests is often hindered by the
"three-fold misery" mentioned above, the formation of the self is one of the main
sources of human suffering.

At this point of analysis, *Sankhya* arrives at a second principle that co-constitutes
the world and which it calls *purusha* (consciousness, essential spirit). It is assumed
that there must be a subject that experiences pleasure and pain and that the ego or
the intellect cannot be that subject since they – as do the emotional states – evolve
from *prakrti*. Therefore, the experiencing and witnessing subject must be different in
nature from *purusha*: While *prakrti* is active but without consciousness, *purusha* is
passive and conscious. As illustrated in one of many analogies, *purusha* is not
touched by *prakrti*, just as the reflection of the moon does not touch the clear water
of a lake.

As we can see, *Sankhya* provides an analysis of the cognitive and motivational
mechanisms ruling the development and functions of wanting and their relation to
knowing, feeling, and behavior. Connecting these results to the tenets of Hindu
beliefs as presented before, we are now able to understand how *Sankhya* explains the
miserable condition of man: It is assumed that these mechanisms within *prakrti*
attach the human mind to the idea that *prakrti* and *purusha* are the same, thus having

no distance to emotions like pleasure, pain, and other psychological states. However, as soon as the individual is able to realize "non-attachment" (*anasakti*), he is able to discriminate between *prakrti* and *purusha* and attains spiritual salvation, the ultimate goal within the Hindu worldview. As described within the system of *Yoga*, in order to gain release from suffering, the individual has to undergo a tedious and rigorous training of moral, physical, and mental discipline, with the stages of moral and physical training being the foundation for mental governance. Moral discipline, the first prerequisite for liberation, is reached as soon as the individual is able to refrain from certain "weaknesses," e.g., thoughts and actions that could harm others, falsehood, stealing, laziness, envy, and greed. Here, within the psychological analysis of the human condition, one can easily recognize the source of some central values that will turn up again when we take a closer look at the Hindu model of human development.

The Hindu model of ideal life-span development
It would be wrong to assume that the ultimate, i.e. spiritual, goal of *moksha* necessarily collides with duties the individual has to fulfill in his social life. On the contrary, the ability to acknowledge and integrate the different needs of individuals is one of the striking features of indigenous Indian developmental theory as it is documented in the Hindu model of an ideal life-span development.

In its doctrine of the four-fold purpose of life, Hinduism acknowledges and enforces four central goals (see Table 1):

Table 1. Four Central Life Goals

dharma	Righteousness, responsibility, and moral conduct in accordance with the scriptures and including all duties – individual, social, and religious
artha	Attainment of economic success, wealth, and power in order to raise a family and maintain a household
kama	Satisfaction of the desires of the body and mind in the form of passions, emotions, and drives; moreover, satisfaction of genuine human desires such as art, music, savory food, sports, conjugal love, filial affections, clothes, jewelry, etc., as long as it does not conflict with *dharma*
moksha	Liberation from *samsara*

These four life goals reflect the essentials of a value system that allows the individuals to pursue the satisfaction of basic human needs without losing sight of the ultimate spiritual goal of salvation. Thus, Hindu ideology tries to satisfy human needs on the spiritual as well as on the social level. It does so by valuing action in the world as long as it is performed with insight and with understanding of the *dharma*. The *manava dharma shastra* mentions some essential rules for the observance of *dharma* that have to be applied for reaching each of the four goals: Patience, forgiveness, self-control, control of the senses, absence of anger, honesty, reason, knowledge (or learning), and truthfulness. These values are of the same kind as those that, according to the *Yoga* system, constitute the moral prerequisite of *moksha*.

In the *ashramadharma*, the Hindu model of ideal human development, one can see how the life cycle of an individual should be divided into four stages that allow one to reach the four consecutive essential life goals (see Table 2):

Table 2. The *ashrama dharma* (Stages of Ideal Human Development)

brahmacharya	This stage begins when a child enters school at an early age and continues until he or she has finished all schooling. The goal is to acquire knowledge, build character, and to learn to shoulder responsibilities.
grihastha	The second stage begins at marriage. In this *ashrama*, an individual pays three debts (serving God, serving the sages and the saints, and serving the ancestors), and enjoys good and noble things in life in accordance with *artha*, *kama*, and the goal of *moksha*. One of the duties one must fulfill during this stage is to have a son because there are certain religious ceremonies within the life cycle that must and should be performed by male relatives. Though marrying a daughter off and providing her with a fair dowry is also considered a duty, the scriptures do not emphasize this to the same degree.
vanaprastha	The third stage begins after the responsibilities of *grahastha ashrama* are complete (when one's children have reached adulthood). This is known as the ascetic or hermit stage of life. In this stage, one gradually withdraws from active life and begins devoting more time to the study of scriptures, contemplation, and meditation.
sannyasa	The final stage of life in which an individual mentally renounces all worldly ties, spends all of his or her time in meditation and contemplation, and ponders over the mysteries of life. In ancient times but rarely today, one would part company with one's family and become a mendicant.

A more detailed insight into the Hindu model of human life-span development can be gained by looking at some of the rituals (*samskaras*) that are traditionally performed during an individual's life. These rituals that accompany the individual through the life cycle and help structure the perception of a person's development, show that the Hindu model of development – if seen in its entirety, i.e., including the *samskaras* – does not exclude childhood from the developmental perspective, as some researchers (e.g., Thomas, 1990) assume. Actually, most *samskaras* focus on childhood (Kakar, 1981; Saraswathi & Ganapathy, 2002), though the complete range of rituals covers a whole life-cycle and thus highlights certain developmental stages within the four-stage model described above. Originally, there were about 300 rituals; today, in most parts of India, only the following are still performed, whereby the rituals performed depend on the region, the caste, and the gender of the individual. The rituals mark three different births of a child: Its biological, psychological, and social birth:

Biological birth
garbhadhara (impregnation): performed to ensure the healthy birth of a child
pumsavan: carried out during the third month of a pregnancy to foresee that the child is a male (in case of a gender preference)
simanta: the parting *of* the expectant mother's hair between the fourth and eighth month, to prepare for the event of the birth
jatakarman: various rites *associated* with the delivery; experienced mothers massage the pregnant woman; in order to stimulate the sensory and organic functions, warm and cold water are sprinkled onto the newborn's body and stones are rubbed together near its ears. Salt water is given in order to make the newborn regurgitate amniotic liquids that may have entered during the delivery.
namakarana: the ceremony of giving the child a name, takes place between the tenth and twelfth day of a newborn's life. A sacrificial fire is lit and *darbha* grass is laid to the west of it, in the north-south direction. A gold object such as a ring is placed around the child's neck. Then the child is given a name that has previously been selected by the priest or astrologer.
nish-kramana: the first outing, i.e., the process in which the child is taken outdoors for the first time. This occurs during the fourth month. A square portion of the courtyard is smeared with cow dung and clay. The child is then carried out to the victorious sound of conch shells and the chanting of various prayers and hymns. This rite is also known as the *surya-darsana* or sun showing, as the child is placed facing the sun.
anna-prasana: food eating ceremony, when the child is between five to eight months old and is fed with solid food for the first time (weaning). This marks the beginning of a gradual process of detachment from the mother.
karna-vedha: ear-piercing occurs between the ninth and the twelfth month (usually done before the child's first tooth appears) and was formerly performed on children of both sexes, but today it is mainly restricted to girls. The ear is pierced by a goldsmith who uses a gold, silver, copper, or iron needle. The hole should be large enough to allow the sun's rays to pass through. This symbolizes the interrelatedness between individual and nature.

Psychological birth
chuda-karana (tonsure): held during a male child's first and seventh year of life. This entails the shaving of the boy's head; an auspicious day is chosen and a fire is kindled. As *mantras* are chanted, the father cuts the first tuft of hair before the bar-

ber completes the job. Afterwards the parents fit their child out with a new set of clothes. While sacrificing one's hair symbolizes devotion and death, the new set of clothes indicate rebirth. Now the child is considered able to learn, fulfill obligations, and show self-control.

vidyarambha (beginning of knowledge): performed when the child commences his education. It takes *place* in the fifth year at the child's home. The gods are invoked and addressed. The child then pays homage to the teacher. The teacher writes the Sanskrit characters and recites them one by one as the child repeats them consecutively.

Social Birth

upanayana (thread ceremony): takes place during the child's eighth year. In ancient times, both girls and boys were admitted to this ceremony, but it was later restricted to boys of the traditional first three castes. The night before the ceremony is spent alone and is the first night spent without the mother. The next morning the boy eats together with his mother for the last time, and from this time on he will eat with the male members of the family. The ceremony symbolizes the boy's growing independence from his mother and his readiness for receiving sacred knowledge amidst the world of men. The boy wears a sacred thread consisting of three strands which symbolize the three *Vedas*, representing moral discipline in thought, word, and deed.

vivaha (marriage): a major ceremony and the only one permitted for the lowest caste, too. It is a binding between a man and a woman, not only in this life but for the life hereafter. The father of the bride gives his daughter along with a sufficient dowry to the bridegroom, who accepts the daughter by invoking a fire and tying a necklace around the girl's neck. The ceremony ends with *samapana* or consummation, when the bride and the groom feed each other symbolically and are also fed by the groom's mother.

antyeshti (final ceremony): performed after death and includes the *sraddha* rites that cannot be performed by *sannyasins* (individuals passing the last stage of the life cycle) or women. They are a means of paying homage to departed ancestors. Prayers are offered to gods, while the deceased ancestors are called upon to consume a large feast prepared by the grieving family. Brahmins perform the ceremony and they are paid well to represent the ancestors. It is assumed that whatever is given to them is received by the ancestors.

The early rituals of childhood indicate that, according to Hindu psychology, young children are not capable of volitional and reflected regulation of their actions. Caregivers are thus seen as playing a vital role in the early development of children and the individual's responsibility for regulating his own actions and emotions as growing considerably over the life span.

The Hindu Model of Life-Span Development as a Source of Research Questions

Human development is a lifelong process: Changes in growth, relationships, patterns of thinking, feelings, attitudes, and behavior occur throughout one's entire lifetime. The different stages of human development identified and described by the life-span perspective reflect patterns of change that result from biological, cognitive, and socio-cultural influences. Against the background of these characteristics of life-span theories in general, I will conclude my examination of Hindu developmental concepts by identifying further psychologically relevant phenomena and generating related research questions.

According to Hindu psychology, human development begins at conception and continues until one reaches salvation (*moksha*) from the cycle of birth, death, and rebirth (*samsara*). In contrast to western assumptions, Hindu theory presupposes not only one, but thousands of lives that each individual goes through. Thus, it does not acknowledge death as the end of a person's existence. This metaphysical aspect and its outflows may be the reason for most secularized western psychologists' lack of interest in Hindu contributions to psychology. However, in my opinion, it is this combination of ideological and psychological aspects that makes Hindus regard their "religion" primarily as a *code of conduct*. Moreover, it gives us reason to assume that some of the main constituents of Hindu life-span theory are of great psychological importance for the thinking, feeling, and behavior of hundreds of millions of members of the Hindu culture. Thus, in the following, I will outline some of the topics that might also be of interest to western psychologists. Since we have seen that it is the model of an ideal life cycle that facilitates and structures an individual's development and helps the person to proceed from task to task, i.e. from stage to stage, I will take that model and its implications as a starting point for my discussion.

Childhood, adolescence, and aging

In the Hindu stage model of ideal human development (*ashramadharma*), there are four stages, the first one starting in early puberty. Thus, at first glance, one might get the impression that childhood – as a stage in human development – does not exist from a Hindu point of view. However, as we can see from the rites of passage (*samskaras*), childhood does play a role and is even described as a period of life in which measures are taken that – from a western point of view – might be characterized as "dramatic" or at least stressful. For example, in early childhood, a symbolic separation of mothers and sons takes place that could be interpreted as the preparation for the subsequent severing of all social bonds that will take place at the third and fourth stage of the Hindu model, i.e., in middle and old age. Some studies have shown that Hindu mothers (e.g., in Rajasthan), pay more attention to the physical needs of their infants, assuming that in most other regards small children are all more or less the same (Hitchcock & Minturn, 1963). Hindu cognition theory assumes that intellectual growth cannot be influenced before schooling and the study of the scriptures begin and that therefore the four-stage model of an ideal life cycle does not include the period of early childhood. This may support the hypothesis that those Hindu mothers' subjective theories about child development at least partially represent a concept indigenous to their culture (Keller, 2002). Certain indigenous techniques of body stimulation (e.g., baby massage) have proven to speed up the physical development of infants (Landers, 1989). This may indicate that in cultural contexts in which children are expected to assist in chores and other tasks at an early age and in which an earlier commencement of parenthood is aimed at, an accelerated development of motor skills and mobility as well as a shorter childhood is preferred.

All things considered, it seems that the Hindu model regards childhood primarily as a stage of physical, not mental development. This is very different from more recent western theories about child development. Some researchers (e.g., Saraswathi & Ganapathy, 2002) have interpreted the indulgent attitude of Indian caretakers towards their children as an expression of the view that children are considered divine and nearly perfect during their first years. However, against the background of Hindu views as outlined above, the child can also be seen as the result of *karma*-directed processes and therefore having deficits. These deficits are characteristic of the human condition and cannot be overcome before the child is capable of understanding the concept of duty and how it is related to the important goals in life. It seems that the child is not considered a person before he/she is able to study and understand what the scriptures convey. That is why early adolescence marks the first stage in the Hindu model of human development. Since the Hindu teachings convey many of the intellectual beliefs of Hinduism as well as a system of morals upon which the society's code of conduct is founded, it is not surprising that adolescence is regarded as the key period for moral development. Also, it is the period in which the adolescent learns to set, pursue, and maintain personal goals. Since very little research has been done on this topic in India, it is unclear whether or not the goals set by adolescents correspond with the main aims in life as derived from Hindu worldview and ethics.

The main developmental tasks in the second stage (early adulthood) are to get married, have children, and support a family. Well-defined social obligations towards relatives, caste members, and the village community have to be met, following a code of conduct fixed by the caste and the scriptures. On the other hand, this is also the stage in which the individual is encouraged to pursue sensual pleasure (*kama*) and the accumulation of wealth (*artha*).

The third stage (middle age) is reached when all social obligations have been met. It entails loosening these interpersonal bonds and focusing on the goal of salvation by leading an ascetic life devoted to practical physical and mental exercises as well as to the scriptures. These efforts are expected to prove successful in the fourth stage (old age), when the individual is free to focus on nothing but achieving liberation from *samsara*. The Hindu model of development demonstrates the essentially sacramental nature of an idealized Hindu society. While people in the secular and more industrialized societies of the West look forward to a time of comfort and economic independence in their old age, in the sacramental order of the Hindu world they look forward to becoming independent of economics, indifferent to comfort and discomfort, and liberated from social obligations.

As stated above, within this model, old age is highly appreciated since it marks the stage of development in which the ultimate goal of human effort is expected to be achieved. All the other stages appear to be periods of life in which the individual is merely setting the stage for the most important performance. So, the Hindu life-span model depicts a psychological ascent, rather than a descent. Although one cannot ignore the fact that there are differences between the culture-specific conceptions of age, the Hindu model does seem to rest on ideas about lifelong developmental tasks that bear a striking similarity to assumptions made in western disengagement theory (Cumming & Henry, 1961). Even if more or less discounted in recent western psychological literature (Achenbaum & Bengtson, 1994), some of the premises of disengagement theory are similar to those in the Hindu life-span model. For example, the Hindu ideal of indifference and *anasakti* can be seen as the basis for successfully coping with the natural and inevitable withdrawal of the individual from family and society, a process that is at the core of disengagement theory. However, it is remarkable that the Hindu theory conceives of the older person as being self-directed within this process – even as being at the height of his spiritual development.

Research on social networks, life goals, and well-being as well as on questions concerning elderly – or younger – individuals' self-esteem could inform us about the psychological relevance of the idealized Hindu model and the ability (or inability) of western theories to explain these phenomena in the Indian context.

Cognition, motivation, and emotion

One of the central aims of Hindu psychology is to uncover the mechanism behind the cognitive, motivational, and emotional processes operating within an individual. This is of great importance because understanding these processes is a precondition for well-being and fulfillment on a social as well as a spiritual level. The implications of the Hindu analysis are far-reaching: Since cognitive and motivation processes cause the individual to desire certain emotional states and avoid others, they have an immense influence on a person's behavior. Hindu psychology considers this causal nexus to be the basis of man's miserable condition. It thus proposes therapeutic measures that allow individuals to develop an attitude towards the world and its objects characterized by restraint, indifference, and detachment. This kind of attitude is meant to help people to psychologically distance themselves from certain feelings and thus to develop an effective emotion regulation. Since discipline and self-regulation are central tasks within the Hindu model of an ideal life cycle and since these tasks are prerequisites for the ultimate goal of salvation, Hindu individuals may develop a pattern of emotional regulation that is different from that of western individuals with regard to the degree of regulation.

Against the background of these general features of the Hindu theory of cognition and motivation, it would be of great interest to learn more about the effect that these theoretical assumptions might have on thinking and attribution styles. Drawing on the premise of western psychology that causal explanations depend on how people perceive and describe the world – including the social world – in general, the question is, how, in their everyday life, Hindus explain why people behave the way they do and what causes their own behavior. Do they prefer to make external rather than internal attributions and how does the concept of *karma* affect their attribution style? Does the concept of causation as proposed by *Sankhya* philosophy (which is different from the western concept of causation) influence a Hindu individual's attribution style? Though some empirical research on related issues was done for the Indian and other cultural contexts (e.g., Miller, 1984; Nisbett et al., 2001), the impact of indigenous concepts of causation and reasoning as well as their interrelationship with *karma*-related explanations of behavior is still unclear.

Besides the more specific aspect of attribution, the domain of intellectual development is of general interest within the current psychological debate. According to the traditional western view of child development, intellectual development peaks in adolescence (Piaget, 1990). One of the most important contributions of life-span psychology was to show that this picture does not do justice to the lifelong process of cognitive and intellectual development and that the way it changes as well as how individuals cope with these changes is more complicated than previously assumed (Schaie & Willis, 2000; Trommsdorff & Dasen, 2001). The Hindu model of cognitive development raises some interesting questions in this area, too. It shows two different types of cognitive development: First, there is an emphasis on having children acquire cultural techniques that allow them to study the textbooks and the sacred writings in order to learn everything about the phenomenal world and to learn how to interact with objects and people within the outside world. Second, there is the method of meditative introspection that builds on the knowledge acquired and leads to the understanding of the true nature of the self. Reaching this highest level of cognition is emphasized as the main goal in middle and old age. Hindu cognition theories, e.g., *Sankhya*, make it clear that these are two different types of cognition because they differentiate between an internal process that fosters the development of intellectual abilities and a gradual process of liberation from the internal mechanisms that are achieved by the individual's rigorous efforts in the fields of moral, physical, and mental discipline as outlined in the *Yoga* system.

So, we can see that Hindu psychology makes assumptions very similar to those made by modern western life-span psychology, in so far as both would agree that there are multiple forms of intelligence and that each may reach its peak at different stages in the life course, including old age (Schaie & Willis, 2000). Interestingly, the Hindu culture attributes the higher level of intellectual development to middle and old age and – at least in this regard – values age over youth. This may be reflected in intergenerational relationships and in the individuals' self-esteem.

Attachment and interpersonal relationships

Since in India, as compared to Western and East Asian countries, only little empirical research has been carried out on western attachment theory and its meaning for relationships over the life span, it is not clear what impact the Hindu concept of *anasakti* and the ideal of indifference may have on interpersonal and intergenerational relationships. While these concepts may help an individual keep his distance from members of out-groups (e.g., members of other castes), they may at the same time complicate the relationship to his family members. Of course, these questions are of special interest with regard to the mother-child relationship, which classical attachment theory focuses on.

Hindu psychology acknowledges that there is a special bond between a mother and her son; however, it also seems to regard this bond as a hindrance for the son when he begins to reach for the higher goals as described in the Hindu value system, in which *anasakti* (i.e. indifference and "non-attachment" ") is seen as important virtue. Therefore, the *upayana* ceremony, as described above, may aim at loosening this bond between mother and son in order to prepare the child for the ideal life cycle that he will enter soon after and in which he will have to cope with indifference and "non-attachment" again.

Having mentioned the specifics of the relationship between mothers and their sons, the question arises about whether that kind of relationship and the attachment "between a mother and her son is different from a mother-daughter relationship. We could gain a great deal of insight into gender differences with regard to attachment and interpersonal relationships by doing research in cultural contexts in which an ideal life cycle and the preparation for the different stages of life seem to be restricted to boys (Chakkarath & Schwarz, 2002). However, even beyond the very special mother-child relationship, it would be interesting to learn whether or not *anasakti* influences the quality of adults' romantic relationships. It is plausible that in a cultural context in which romantic relationships outside a marriage are rare and in which most marriages are arranged by the couples' parents the attitude of indifference helps you to abstain from personal preferences and to accept the parents' choice, i.e., the partner you will have to spend many years of your life with. Nonetheless, the question remains concerning what quality romantic relationships in Hindu marriages have and in how far they are influenced by attachment "patterns formed between infants and their primary caregivers. In India, where multiple caregivers may provide multiple forms of attachment and where hierarchical relationships are typical, the developmental contexts might be of a different complexity as compared to western family contexts (Trommsdorff & Kornadt, 2003).

Self-concept

It seems that the ancient scholars were well aware of the problems that could arise from the ideal of *anasakti* for interpersonal relationships. That may also be one of the reasons why the concept of duty is so closely linked to the ultimate goal of salvation. It seems that in order to prevent people from being the ideal individualists that "non-attachment theory" would have them be, the ethics of duty and selfless service (as a means of reaching salvation) – embedded in a stage model that preserves only the last stage for uncompromising indifference – is the only way to secure certain social bonds between people which every society needs in order to function.

Moreover, the general assumption that intergenerational relationships in India are motivated more by collective than by individual goals could be just one – and maybe a too simple – way of interpreting the available data. A closer look at the role that indigenous conceptions and corresponding attitudes play in peoples' thought and behavior may, for example, help to explain why – in Hofstede's well-known study (Hofstede, 2000) – India came out as the most individualistic Asian society, although its social structure seems to be indicative of a culture with prevalent collectivistic features. The difficulty in interpreting these results may have to do with the lack of knowledge about the impact that indigenous psychological concepts have for the development of a Hindu self-concept. Since the Hindu goal and value system is still influential, as Sinha and Tripathi (1994) and Mascolo et al. (2004) have shown for the Hindu self-concept, there is a high possibility that, on a motivational level, the individuals are primarily focusing on self-fulfillment and "independence" of others as characterized by the ideal of *anasakti*. On the behavioral level, however, they may appear to be dependent and primarily oriented towards the in-group. Thus, the traditional mainstream conceptualization of individualism, defined as detachment and independence of relationships and community, may, on the motivational level, hold true for collectively behaving Hindus as well. The art of serving two kings at the same time may be a talent required for a successful life in Hindu culture which in this perspective would call its members "dividuals" rather than "individuals" (Bharati, 1985). It is obvious that the mainstream research on individualism and collectivism needs to be refined along the lines of culture specificities and to take the indigenous concepts of thinking, feeling, and behavior into consideration.

Concluding Remarks

As shown above, in the Hindu theory of human development, the foundations of which were laid over two thousand years ago, development is viewed as occurring over the entire life span. As other indigenous psychologies (e.g., in Buddhist or Confucian thought) also propose developmental theories in life span perspective, an earlier interest in these psychologies could have led western developmental theories to some of its modern concepts much earlier. The same may be true for other domains of psychological thinking.

Moreover, indigenous Hindu psychology is not content with mere observation of human behavior; it delves much deeper by studying the cognitive, motivational, and emotional phenomena that accompany behavior and by applying introspective methods. In the present chapter, our look at the Hindu life-span perspective and at motivation and self-regulation as social-cognitive mediators of personal adjustment and interpersonal relationships resulted in the generation and refinement of research questions about various domains of human development in cultural context. It is important to notice that many of Hindu psychology's hypotheses can be tested and thereby contribute to progress in empirical psychological research.

Finally, Hindu psychology is characterized by the conclusions it draws for proper personal conduct and the proper balance between individual and societal needs. To have an influence on individuals' thoughts, feelings, and behavior, i.e., to be applied by individuals, is one of Hindu psychology's main goals. Therefore, we may assume that the representation of psychological assumptions in the subjective theories of individuals is especially great in contexts in which indigenous psychologies are essential constituents of the cultural niche. This is one of the greater differences between western and Hindu psychology and between various other indigenous psychologies.

For these reasons and due to the general potential to stimulate western psychological thinking, I advocate further exploration of the role of indigenous psychologies and a focus on such questions in future developmental psychological research.

References

Achenbaum, W. A., & Bengtson, V. L. (1994). Re-engaging the disengagement theory of aging: On the history and assessment of theory development in gerontology. *The Gerontologist, 34*, 756-763.

Berry, J. W. (2002). *Cross-cultural psychology: Research and applications* (2nd ed.). Cambridge: Cambridge University Press.

Bharati, A. (1985). The self in Hindu thought and action. In A. J. Marsella, G. Devos, & F. L. K. Hsu (Eds.). *Culture and Self: Asian and western perspectives* (pp. 185-230). London: Tavistock.

Chakkarath, P. (2003). *Kultur und Psychologie: Zur wissenschaftlichen Entstehung und zur Ortsbestimmung der Kulturpsychologie* [Culture and psychology: On the scientific origin and the present state of cultural psychology]. Hamburg, Germany: Dr. Kovac.

Chakkarath, P. (in press). Religionen und Weltanschauungen [Religions and worldviews]. In G. Trommsdorff & H.-J. Kornadt (Eds.), *Kulturvergleichende Psycho-logie. Vol. 1: Theorien und Methoden in der kulturvergleichenden und kulturpsy-chologischen Forschung* (Enzyklopädie der Psychologie: Themenbereich C The-orie und Forschung, Serie VII). Göttingen, Germany: Hogrefe.

Chakkarath, P., & Schwarz, B. (2002, July). *The effects of traditional values and socioeconomic change on fertility, gender preference, and parent-child relations in India*. Paper presented at the 15th Congress of the International Association for Cross-Cultural Psychology, Yogyakarta, Indonesia.

Cumming, E., & Henry, W. (1961). *Growing old: The process of disengagement*. New York: Basic Books.

Enriquez, V. G. (1993). Developing a Filipino psychology. In U. Kim & J. W. Berry (Eds.), *Indigenous psychologies: Research and experience in cultural context*. Newbury Park, CA: Sage.

Gergen, K. J., Gulerce, A., Lock, A., & Misra, G. (1996). Psychological science in cultural context. *American Psychologist, 51*, 496-503.

Greenfield, P. (2000). Three approaches to the psychology of culture: Where do they come from? Where can they go? *Asian Journal of Social Psychology, 3*, 223-240.

Heelas, P., & Lock, A. (Eds.). (1981). *Indigenous psychologies: The anthropology of the self*. London: Academic Press.

Hitchcock, J. T., & Minturn, L. (1963). The Rajput of Khalapur, India. In B. B. Whiting (Ed.), *Six cultures: Studies of child rearing* (pp. 203-362). New York: Wiley.

Ho, D. F. Y. (1998). Indigenous psychologies: Asian perspectives. *Journal of Cross-Cultural Psychology, 29*, 88-103.

Hofstede, G. H. (2000). *Culture's consequences: International differences in work-related values* (5th ed.). Newbury Park, CA: Sage.

Inglehart, R., Basanez, M., & Moreno, A. (1998). *Human values and beliefs – A cross-cultural sourcebook: Political, religious, sexual, and economic norms in 43 societies*. Ann Arbor, MI: University of Michigan Press.

Kakar, S. (1981). *The inner world: A psycho-analytic study of childhood and society in India* (2nd edition). New Delhi: Oxford University Press.

Keller, H. (2002). Development as the interface between biology and culture: A conceptualization of early ontogenetic experiences. In H. Keller, Y. H. Poortinga, & A. Schölmerich (Eds.), *Between culture and biology: Perspectives on ontogenetic development* (pp. 215-240). Cambridge: Cambridge University Press.

Kim, U. (1990). Indigenous psychology: Science and applications. In R. W. Brislin (Ed.), Applied cross-cultural psychology. Newbury Park, CA: Sage.

Kim, U. (2001). Culture, Science, and Indigenous Psychologies: An Integrated Analysis. In D. Matsumoto (Ed.), *The handbook of culture and psychology* (pp. 51-75). Cambridge: Oxford University Press.

Kim, U., & Berry, J. W. (1993). *Indigenous psychologies: Research and experience in cultural context*. Thousand Oaks, CA: Sage Publications.

Landers, C. (1989). A psychobiological study of infant development in South India. In J. K. Nugent, B. M. Lester, & T. B. Brazelton (Eds.), *The cultural context of infancy (pp. 169-208). Norwood, NJ: Ablex*.

Markus, H. R., & Kitayama, S. (1991). Culture and the self: Implications for cognition, emotion and motivation. *Psychological Review, 98, 224-253.*

Mascolo, M. F., Misra, G., & Rapisardi, C. (2004). Individual and relational conceptions of self in India and the United States. In W. Damon (Series Ed.), M. F. Mascolo & J. Li (Vol. Eds.), *New directions in child and adolescent development, 104. Culture and developing selves: Beyond dichotomization* (pp. 9-26). San Francisco, CA: Jossey-Bass.

Miller, J. G. (1984). Culture and the development of everyday social explanations. Journal of Personality and Social Psychology, 46, 961-978.

Nisbett, R., Peng, K., Choi, I., & Norenzanan, A. (2001). Culture and system of thoughts: Holistic versus analytic cognition. *Psychological Review, 108,* 291-310.

Oyserman, D., Coon, H. M., & Kemmelmeier, M. (2002). Rethinking individualism and collectivism: Evaluation of theoretical assumptions and meta-analyses. *Psychological Bulletin, 128,* 3-72.

Paranjipe, A. (1984). *Theoretical psychology: Meeting of East and West.* New York: Plenum Press.

Paranjipe, A. (1988). A personality theory according to Vedanta. In A. Paranjipe, D. Ho, & R. Rieber (Eds.), *Asian contributions to psychology* (pp. 185-214). New York: Praeger.

Paranjpe, A. C. (1998). *Self and identity in modern psychology and Indian thought.* New York: Plenum Press.

Piaget, J. (1990). *The child's conception of the world.* New York: Littlefield Adams.

Saraswathi, T. S., & Ganapathy, H. (2002). Indian parents' ethnotheories as reflections of the Hindu scheme of child and human development. In H. Keller, Y. H. Poortinga, & A. Schölmerich (Eds.), *Between culture and biology: Perspectives on ontogenetic development (pp. 79-88).* Cambridge: Cambridge University Press.

Schaie, K. W., & Willis, S. L. (2000). A stage theory model of adult cognitive development revisited. In B. Rubinstein, M. Moss, & M. Kleban (Eds.), *The many dimensions of aging: Essays in honor of M. Powell Lawton* (pp. 175-193). New York: Springer.

Segall, M. H., Lonner, W. J., & Berry, J. W. (1998). Cross-cultural psychology as a scholarly discipline. *American Psychologist, 53,* 1101-1110.

Shweder, R. (2000). The psychology of practice and the practice of the three psychologies. Asian Journal of Social Psychology, 3, 207-222.

Sinha, D. (1997). Indigenizing psychology. In J. W. Berry, Y. H. Poortinga, & J. Pandey (Eds.), *Handbook of cross-cultural psychology, Vol. 1: Theory and method* (pp. 129-169). Boston: Allyn & Bacon.

Sinha, D., & Tripathi, R. C. (1994). Individualism in a collective culture: A case of coexistence of opposites. In U. Kim, H. C. Triandis, C. Kagitçibasi, S.-C. Choi, & G. Yoon (Eds.), *Individualism and collectivism: Theory, method, and applications* (pp. 123-136). Thousand Oaks, CA: Sage.

Super, C. M., & Harkness, S. (1997). The cultural structuring of child development. In J. W. Berry, P. R. Dasen, & T. S. Saraswathi (Eds.), *Handbook of Cross-Cultural Psychology. Vol. 2: Basic processes and human development* (pp. 1-39). Boston, MA: Allyn & Bacon.

Thomas, R. M. (1990). Hindu theory of human development. In R. M. Thomas (Ed.), *The encyclopedia of human development and education: Theory, research, and studies* (pp. 140-144). New York: Pergamon Press.

Thomas, R. M. (1997). *Moral development theories – Secular and religious: A comparative study.* Westport, CT: Greenwood Press.

Triandis, H. C. (2001). Individualism and collectivism: Past, present, and future. In D. Matsumoto (Ed.), *The handbook of culture & psychology* (pp. 35-50). London: Oxford University Press.

Trommsdorff, G., & Dasen, P. (2001). Cross-cultural study of education. In N. J. Smelser & P. B. Baltes (Eds.), *International encyclopedia of the social and behavioral sciences* (pp. 3003-3007). Oxford: Elsevier.

Trommsdorff, G., & Kornadt, H.-J. (2003). Parent-child relations in cross-cultural perspective. In L. Kuczynski (Ed.), *Handbook of dynamics in parent-child relations* (pp. 271-306). London: Sage.

3

Using Cross-Cultural Psychology to Design Afterschool Educational Activities in Different Cultural Settings

Michael Cole

Introduction

The goal of this chapter is to introduce a somewhat unorthodox cross-cultural research strategy and to show that it can be of practical use to social scientists interested in the design of environments for the development of children. The initial motivation for undertaking this work was my long term dissatisfaction with the difficulties of conducting methodologically adequate cross-cultural research involving large demographic groups or entire nations, combined with my growing interest in specifying the role of culture in development in rather precise detail. These two concerns appear to be at odds with each other, so I will begin by outlining a view of culture which I believe to be well suited to purposes of designing environments to illustrate culture's role in development. I will then go on to argue that deliberately constructed cultures offer analytic advantages to those interested in both the role of culture in development and cross-cultural comparisons, in addition to arguing for the efficacies of the particular cultures studied. While this approach does not solve problems facing those concerned with macro comparisons of culture in development, my hope is that by highlighting the issues involved, my work may inspire more effective responses to unsolved problems of cross-cultural psychology, traditionally understood.

Some Commonplace Definitions of Culture

In their often quoted book about the many definitions of culture, Alfred Kroeber and Clyde Kluckhohn (1952) offered a definition which continues to pervade cross-cultural psychological work to this day. Culture, they wrote, refers to "patterns ... of and for behavior acquired and transmitted by symbols, constituting the distinctive achievements of human groups, including their embodiments in artifacts" (p. 151). Culture also refers to traditional ideas and their attached values and constitutes both products of action and conditions for future actions.

Edwin Hutchins (1995), who, like me, has focused his recent work on cultures as they develop in small, specialized groups, refers to culture as "an adaptive process that takes place inside and outside the minds of people. It is the process in which everyday cultural practices are enacted" (p. xx).

Finally, Raymond Williams (1973) offers a definition which explicitly links the concept of culture to the process of development. By his account, since its appearance in the English language in the 16th century, culture has always been "a noun of process, the process of tending of something, basically crops or animals (e.g., horticulture, agriculture, etc.)" (p. 77).

Some Commonplace Observations Concerning the Difficulties of Applied Cross-Cultural Research

I will not rehearse here the many methodological difficulties of conducting typical cross-cultural research on large social systems. I believe that the difficulties have been well articulated and the search for methods to circumvent those difficulties have also received extensive attention (Berry, Poortinga, & Pandey, 1997; Boesch, 1997; Cole, 1996; Jahoda, 1993).

In large measure, the very reasons cross-cultural research is difficult to conduct in a methodologically satisfactory way where one's goal is to make causal attributions from culture to behavior are the very reasons one wants to conduct such research in the first place: growing up in different cultural environments presumably influences one's development, but that environment/culture exists prior to the arrival of the analyst and is a pre-existing condition that makes random assignment of people to treatment groups impossible, thereby undermining the logic of experimentation that warrants the very causal attributions one was interested in investigating the first place.

When it comes to efforts to apply knowledge learned from cross-cultural work for (presumably) beneficial purposes, the uncertain knowledge obtained from the initial research carries with it additional dangers. For both practical and usually ethical reasons as well, it is inappropriate to even contemplate changing entire cultural systems because the unintended consequences of such changes are impossible to anticipate, although there are historical circumstances that may motivate us to do so. I have in mind here the catastrophic dislocations currently occurring in parts of Africa and elsewhere as a result of AIDS epidemic. Certainly we know that relatively rapid cultural change with identifiable health benefits (for example) *can* occur (the rapid diminution of smoking among pregnant women in some parts of the world, for example), but *experimentation* in cultural change on a large-scale basis remains an unviable alternative strategy for either applied or basic research on culture and development.

These and other factors suggest that for purposes of design, we consider smaller social systems that nonetheless qualify as socio-*cultural* systems where design and experimentation are ethically acceptable. That is the course I chose to follow.

Idiocultures

Williams' emphasis on interpreting culture as the process of creating an environment to promote growth has several salutary consequences for my purposes to design experimentation on culture and development.

First, it points toward the use of environmental design, including the need to develop appropriate physical and conceptual tools to carry out our task of promoting development as a part of the design process. Hence, it links nicely to theories of the role of artifact mediation in human development (e.g., Vygotsky, 1978).

Second, it practically forces upon us a developmental/historical approach in which we study the success of our design over generations. After all, we cannot just plant the seeds and walk away. We cannot just allow the seeds to sprout, pick weeds, and walk away. We must see what natural predators appear, how to deal with them, and how to see that we have seeds enough left over from one growing season to assure the birth of a next generation.

Third, Williams' emphasis on the organization of environments rather naturally reminds us that it is necessary not only to design environments which are effective "inside the fence," but which are sustainable in the larger ecological settings within which they are embedded. So, study of culture/development over time requires a dual focus on the traditional objects of psychology, that is, people in their immediate environments, but also larger units of analysis such as the institutional context of the immediate environment as well. This latter topic is especially highlighted in the study of after school activity systems, where exclusive attention to proving that they are effective detracts attention from the fact that they often fail to be sustained in their socio-ecologies, despite their effectiveness locally.

Idiocultures: A unit of analysis to substitute for cultures characterizing large scale societies

It has been known at least since the study of culture formation in small groups during the 1950's that no sooner do two or more people get together to accomplish some task in common than they begin to develop special terminology and procedures which become routine and fade into the background of their interactions (Rose & Felton, 1955). When new people enter the group, they quickly and easily begin to use these new cultural artifacts and begin introducing new items of their own. The same is true, of course, of naturally forming groups where people congregate at work or play, giving rise to such popular expressions as "office culture," observations of which have made the American comic page character, Dilbert, famous.

In a number of his writings, particularly his ethnographic study of Little League Baseball, sociologist Gary Alan Fine (1989) has suggested the term "idioculture" to apply to such social entities. In his words,

> an *idioculture* is a cultural formation that emerges in a *small* group: system of knowledge, beliefs, behaviors, and customs shared by members of an interacting group to which members can refer and that serve as the basis of further interaction. Members recognize that they share experiences, and these experiences can be referred to with the expectation they will be understood by other members, thus being used to construct a reality for the participants. (p. 125)

This definition of an idioculture fits well the formation of cultures in the small groups ranging in size from approximately eight to 25 members present at any one time, although numbers and characteristics of participants varied from one idioculture to the next, as we shall see in the idiocultures to be described below.

Fifth Dimension: A prototype idioculture for afterschool educational activity
As will become clear, an essential feature of the idiocultures that I refer to as Fifth Dimensions is their adaptability to specific local conditions. Nonetheless, there was an "original" Fifth Dimension (LCHC, 1982) and an initial set of ideas which constituted the starting point of its development as an idioculture, which then underwent change across implementations. Consequently, it is useful to provide a description of that ideal type as a provisional benchmark for evaluating the subsequent diversity (for other descriptions, see Cole, 1996; Vasquez, 2003).

The Fifth Dimension is an educational activity system that offers school aged children a specially designed environment in which to explore a variety of off-the-shelf computer games and game-like educational activities during the afterschool hours (see Figure 1). The computer games are a part of a make-believe play world that includes non-computer games like origami, chess, and boggle and a variety of other artifacts.

College or university students enrolled in a course focused on fieldwork in a community setting play, work, and learn as the children's partners. In assisting children, the students are encouraged to follow the guideline: Help as little as possible but as much as necessary for you and the child to have fun and make progress. The presence of college or university undergraduates is a major draw for the children.

HOST INSTITUTION (Boys and Girls Club)

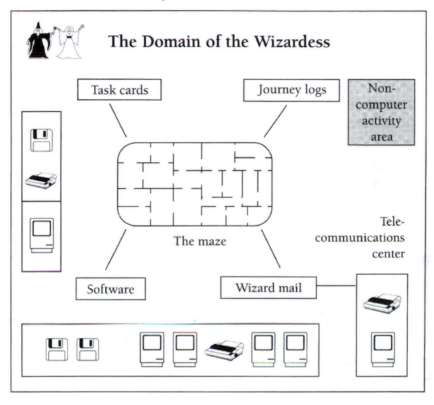

Figure 1. Layout of a Prototype Fifth Dimension

As a means of distributing the children's and undergraduates' use of the various games, the Fifth Dimension contains a table-top or wall chart maze consisting of a number of rooms, initially 20. Each room provides access to two or more games, and the children may choose which game to play as they enter each room

Games are played using task cards written by project staff members for each game. Task cards fulfill several goals. They are designed to help participants (both children and undergraduate students) orient to the game, to form goals, and to chart progress toward becoming an expert. They provide a variety of requirements in addition to the intellectual tasks written into the software or game activity itself. These additional requirements routinely include having participants externalize their thinking and learning or reflect upon and criticize the activity, sometimes by writing to someone, sometimes by looking up information in an encyclopedia, or by teaching someone else what one has learned (see Figure 1).

There is an electronic entity (a wizard/wizardess/Maga, Golem, Proteo, etc.) who is said to live in the Internet. The entity writes to (and sometimes chats with) the children and undergraduates via the Internet and they write back. In the mythology of the Fifth Dimension, the electronic entity acts as the participants' patron, provider of games, mediator of disputes, as well as the source of computer glitches and other misfortunes.

Because it is located in a community institution, the Fifth Dimension activities require the presence of a local "site coordinator" who greets the participants as they arrive and supervises the flow of activity in the room. The site coordinator is trained to recognize and support the pedagogical ideals and curricular practices that mark the Fifth Dimension as "different" – a different way for kids to use computers, a different way of playing with other children, and a different way of interacting with adults.

In short, considered in its community context, the Fifth Dimension is organized to create an institutionalized version of the form of interaction that Vygotsky (1978) referred to as a zone of proximal development for participants. Unlike the more formal interactions envisioned by Vygotsky, from time to time there is creative confusion about who the more capable peers might be, e.g., when novice under-graduates encounter children highly skilled in playing educational computer games about which they know nothing. But the general culture of collaborative learning that is created within the Fifth Dimension is designed to serve the development of all.

How does one know that one is dealing with an idioculture in the Fifth Dimension?

All I have done above is to characterize some design principles that went into con-struction of an activity where a group of children, accompanied by a few under-graduates, get together several days a week to engage in a rather peculiar mixture of play, academic work, and peer interaction. How do I know, or perhaps more impor-tantly how can I convince you, that the activity I have just described is in fact an idioculture?

For this purpose, my best alternative is to return to the classical definitions of culture provided at the beginning of this chapter, and supplement them by field notes written by undergraduate participants as part of their participation. According to the classical definitions, we should expect to encounter "patterns ... of behavior ac-quired and transmitted by symbols, constituting the distinctive achievements of human groups, including their embodiments in artifacts (...)." These patterns ought to take place in, and constitute, cultural practices and they should take place in an environment designed for the development of children. All of these definitions, including their inclusion in Fine's definition of an idioculture, are practically un-avoidable.

Here is a brief sample of field notes from newcomers at a Fifth Dimension in a Boys and Girls Club (BGC):

"It seems pretty chaotic with kids coming and going, arguments in progress, and computers blinking. Pretty soon I noticed that almost everyone seemed to know what to do. No one was bumping into or fighting with anyone else, the children seemed to enjoy themselves, and they were doing a lot of academic stuff. They are excited by invisible events, they say odd things like 'Wildcat is down!' ; 'Right 45 degrees' ; 'Katmandu' ; 'I hate the Wizard,' and so on. And it all seems to make sense to them."

"It was really odd having a young adolescent guiding us through the game. I felt sort of helpless in a way, considering that knowledge is power in this society. Here we were, elders who would soon take on the challenge of helping children develop their minds and to help them to get through the Fifth Dimension and we couldn't even finish the first round! Boy was I humiliated in a fun way!"

Over the course of any given 10 week quarter during which a group of undergraduates are present, or a year, during which three groups of undergraduates are present, the idioculture of the Fifth Dimension undergoes constant change.

The sources of change are so diverse that I have not yet been able to dimensionalize them, although a change in the hardware (the advent of the computers with large memories or the internet, for example) and the software (which began with *Pacman* and now includes highly sophisticated simulation games) certainly has played its role. But so have games which do not depend in the least upon computer hardware or software, such as the African board game mancala, which from time to time has developed its own micro-culture of devotees, invasion from Pokemon and other faddish games that appear and disappear like locusts in the deserts of Utah, or the appearance among the undergraduates of a very feminine undergraduate woman wearing long skirts who was easily the most accomplished skateboarder in the group, and so on.

Analyzing the Fifth Dimension

Participants' behavior in the Fifth Dimension can be analyzed with respect to cultural mediation of children's development both within and between different Fifth Dimension idiocultures located in different socio-cultural environments.

Cross-cultural analysis of different Fifth Dimensions
A major analytic advantage that we gain in comparing Fifth Dimension idiocultures is that we know the "original" since we created it and described it with some care at the time. Of course, the original design required a process of culture formation just as the formation of all of its subsequent varieties. And the particular formation that evolved was very much a product of the special circumstances we faced and the goals we hoped to attain. But at least we know who started it and the stated goals and outcomes of their efforts (LCHC, 1982).

Despite this presumed advantage, I was insensitive to the potential for comparative, cross-cultural research for many months after actually initiating a trio of Fifth Dimensions in a suburb north of San Diego. The three locales were a child care center, a library, and a Boys and Girls Club (BGC). I was hugely preoccupied with simply getting three systems going at one time. Each organization had its own local constraints and demands. The child care center catered to young children, roughly five to eight years old. The BGC had attendees who ranged in age from about six to 14 years of age, but with a large cluster between seven and nine years. The composition of the Library group was similar to that of the Club.

The child care center ran the Fifth Dimension in one of its classrooms. Because all the computers and other artifacts of the Fifth Dimension were absent from the classrooms, the undergraduates and researchers were required to put together the requisite materials at the beginning of each of their twice weekly visits. This research, begun in 1987, when computers were scarce, required us to carry a set of Apple 2 computers with us to each site and forced the policy of running no more than two of the three initial sites on any given day owing to both limits on the number of computers and on the number of undergraduates and researchers who could be deployed simultaneously. The Library devoted a corner cleared to allow the setup of several computers at a large table and room for other artifacts connected with the activity (to be described below). The BGC had a relatively large room where computers could be placed along the walls and two large tables for arraying the associated artifacts.

At the child care center the children all arrived simultaneously on a bus provided by the school district, and their presence was carefully documented. At the Library the children were brought by their parents, because the Library was located across the freeway from their schools and it was too dangerous for them to be left alone to walk there. At the BGC children walked from a nearby school. In all cases, children stayed for about an hour and a half, and were picked up on a haphazard schedule by their parents, according to exigencies of the day.

During the first year of research, creating, seeking to sustain, and documenting change of the children and the idiocultures that formed in each site, we discovered that just as every garden differs from every other garden, depending upon the goals of the gardeners, the conditions of the soil, the weather, the availability of nutrients, and water, etc. as well as the institutional setting of which it is a part – the garden's context, according to one ubiquitous use of that term – so too with Fifth Dimensions. As undergraduates began to experience more than one Fifth Dimension, they spontaneously commented in their field notes that no two Fifth Dimension cultures are alike. Despite a common origin, both institutionally and ideologically, and many common artifacts, the differences among different Fifth Dimension were a constant source of wonderment to the students. Yet, at the same time, each seemed to be recognizable as a Fifth Dimension. What were some of the common features, despite the variability? And how are we to describe and explain the variability?

Some similarities

Since they have been conceived of for the same purpose, have key participants who attend the same undergraduate course, and are all supervised by a single research team, it is only to be expected that different Fifth Dimensions would have similar idiocultural features and they do. All, for example, deliberately mix play and education and involve multigenerational social interactions among participants. These and other common starting points result in recognizable similarities across sites.

One of the striking similarities is what Nicolopoulou and Cole (1993) referred to as a "culture of collaborative learning." This similarity manifests itself in many ways. Primarily, perhaps, is, that activities within various instantiations of the Fifth Dimension provide little or no evidence of overt competition or hierarchy. Even though there is hierarchical potential in the existence of a site coordinator, undergraduates, and children of different ages, activities at all of the sites share what I might term a "horizontal structure." In photographs taken at different sites over a period of many years, one sees time after time that by and large (despite differences in size) the head levels of children and undergraduate participants, and even the older adults are at more or less the same level (see Figure 2).

Figure 2. Illustration of Horizontal Structure

Another striking similarity is that each site has a wide variety of activities that go well beyond the presence of different kinds of computers and different computer games. The specifics of this variety naturally differ from one idioculture to the next, but the presence of such variety bespeaks the common goal of arranging to meet the interests of a wide variety of children and to be in a position to find something interesting for children and undergraduates to engage in when computers or computer games are not working (a ubiquitous shared condition in all of the sites). Such ancillary activities range from the use of drawing materials, board games, to tasks associated with physical exercise, photography, and so on.

A third similarity is associated with the common need across sites to distribute scarce and uncertain resources to make the idioculture a place where children voluntarily come to spend their time. As mentioned in our description of a prototypical Fifth Dimension, there is a means for distributing activities among children and providing them with a variety of specific activities to choose among, instantiated in the prototype as a physical maze. Some version of such a maze is ubiquitous as a flexible means of task allocation across all Fifth Dimensions, although, again, the specifics of how this artifact is constructed vary not only across sites but within sites across time (see Figures 3 and 4).

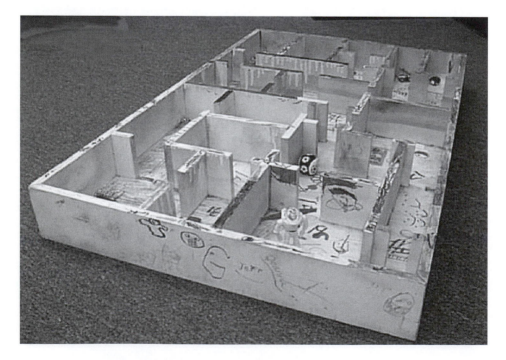

Figure 3. Example of a Fifth Dimension maze retrieved from the Fifth Dimension Clearinghouse (http://129.171.53.1/blantonw/5dClhse/clearingh1.html)

Figure 4. Further Example of a Maze

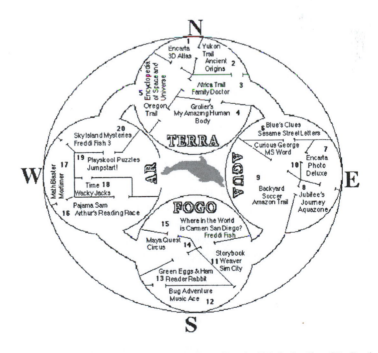

Figure 5. Map of the Fifth Dimension (Play Pen) from Escola Cidade Jardim, São Paulo, Brasil

While other similarities could be mentioned, those noted above are typical as is their source. They are common solutions to common problems. At the same time, each idioculture exists under at least slightly different institutional conditions, involves different people as participants, somewhat different specific tools (e.g., different computers, different games that have been donated or purchased) and so they differ in their specifics according to the tastes and opportunities of their users.

Differences

One of the most widely accepted ideas in cross-cultural research is that cultures represent ways of life that have evolved to meet the challenges posed by local circumstances. That is, the organization of any culture must be understood as a relationship between the "culture itself" and its environment. This principle is clearly illustrated in comparative analyses of different Fifth Dimensions.

Cultural environment

Although I have already commented that the particular way in which common features across cultures are constructed differs across instantiations of the Fifth Dimension the point is worth further examination because it is true even when we restrict our attention to Fifth Dimensions that appear to exist under very similar circumstances (e.g., they are run by a single community group, the same group of undergraduates taking the same course from the same institution, all of whom are in constant contact with each other). And, it is of course obvious when the larger cultural context of the local Fifth Dimension is taken into account: For example, a Fifth Dimension conducted in a Gypsy community in Barcelona uses a gypsy symbol of a wagon wheel as its maze, reflecting Gypsy culture, while the symbol used to represent the maze at one of the BGCs (Boys and Girls Clubs) where the Fifth Dimension currently runs is a pizza pie cut into slices because pizza parties are a locally common way to mark celebrations, such as the ascension of a child to the role of "Wizard's assistant" because she or he has completed all the games at a high level of proficiency.

But, as mentioned previously, significant differences among idiocultures arise even within a single socio-economic group, identical community organizations and in cases where the undergraduate participants come from a single course, so all have "the same idea" of what a Fifth Dimension is and how it ought to be conducted. Examination of such cases makes contact with macro-level explanations of cultural variation, and are, consequently, of special interest in understanding the process of cultural change as it relates to individual change.

Physical environment

A comparison of the idiocultures that developed in our early work with the BGC and the Library provides an especially informative case in regard to the physical environment (for more details, see Cole, 1996; Nicolopoulou & Cole, 1993).

As mentioned earlier, the Fifth Dimension in the BGC was surrounded by many other activities the children could engage in: athletics, arts and crafts, ping pong and pool, to name a few. A large swimming pool was located outside the Fifth Dimension room. Often rock music blared from a boom box in the game room outside the doors of the Fifth Dimension were always open, so children could come and go as they wished.

The situation with respect to the Library was quite different. The children were of course free to come and go from the Fifth Dimension, but their parents did not want them to leave the library. So, while they could choose to leave the Fifth Dimension at any time, their choices when they did so were restricted; they could read quietly or do homework, but they could not run around to have a good time.

As a consequence of the contrasting environments in which they were embedded, the two Fifth Dimensions bore opposite relations to each other with respect to how they related to their environments. Both mixed games, learning, and peer interaction and shared the same games, the same reading/writing tasks associated with each game, and the same set of undergraduate companions. But the BGC Fifth Dimension was, relative to its environment, a place where education was more likely to be in evidence while in the library, the Fifth Dimension play was more likely to be present than in its surroundings. If the children got excited by someone's special achievement, they were likely to make excited noises that were noticed by library patrons and librarians, and not particularly appreciated. Hence, the undergraduates and site coordinator often found themselves whispering, "Remember, this is a *library* Fifth Dimension" and in general, working to keep the atmosphere of the Fifth Dimension relatively sedate.

The consequence of these relationships is diagrammed in a crude way in Figure 6 in which the ordinate of the Figure should be interpreted as noise level. As you can see, there is good reason for undergraduates who spent time at the BGC and at the Library to see the two idiocultures as very different: one was a good deal noisier than the other. However, when considered in relationship to their local environments, it is clear that the BGC Fifth Dimension was quieter than its environment (the games room at the club) while the Library Fifth Dimension was correspondingly noisier than its environment (the reading spaces in the Library).

Other contextual factors

A large set of additional contextual factors is involved when we move beyond Fifth Dimensions that involve the same population of children to include varieties of children, neighborhoods, and other institutions. An instructive case is La Clase Mágica, an adaptation of the Fifth Dimension begun by Olga Vasquez located about the same distance from the BGC as the Library, but in a different part of town that is the largest Mexicano barrio (neighborhood) in the town. The institution which plays host to La Clase Mágica is a Catholic mission, under the control of a nearby Catholic church. The Church is predominantly Anglo and its parishioners economically well off. The parishioners of the Mission are overwhelmingly of Mexican origin –

many have lived in the town for generations, while others are recent immigrants – and economically struggling.

There are important variations in the local practices within La Clase Mágica associated with Vasquez's commitment to promoting use of the community's knowledge and resources, including knowledge of Spanish, in the design and implementation of the activity (for details, see Vasquez, 2003) as well as cultural features of the population that participates. For example, often there are many young children present because their older siblings or cousins have been put in charge of care giving and have brought them along. There are also differences which represent a combination of local necessity and ideology. So, for example, the site coordinator is a local parent who has been trained and participated in the activity when her own children were participating (the first coordinator was the catechism teacher at the Mission), which is both an externally imposed necessity – unlike the BGC, the Mission has no other ongoing afterschool program and hence no staff – and a means of engaging and empowering the local community.

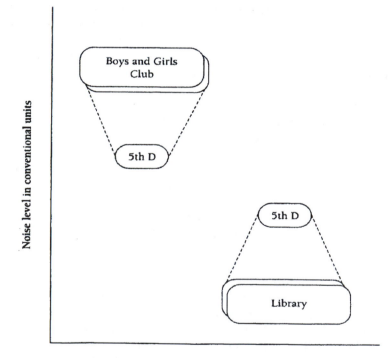

Figure 6. Comparison of Noise Levels in BGC and Library Fifth Dimensions

Such obvious cultural factors, in the usual sense of the term, are clearly important in giving La Clase Mágica its special cultural features as a member of the fam-ily of Fifth Dimension idiocultures. But just as importantly, like the Library, and unlike the BGC, the physical setting of La Clase Mágica (currently in a room that was part of a Head Start center which has expanded since the site was first opened) is not a place where children play. There is a small yard with two tables that is deserted when the Head Start program is not in operation, but the site, on the Mission grounds, is not a play yard for children, and is deserted in the afternoons. It serves exclusively as a quiet place where children who need to do homework can do so. Hence, relative to its environment, like the Library, *La Clase Mágica* is a buzzing hub of noisy activity. However, there is no effort to contain the children's enthusiasm when a child and undergraduate jointly achieve some coveted goal or El Maga, their mythical patron(ess) appears online to chat. The only constraint on noise level (as in the Fifth Dimension at the *BGC*) is that children not make so much noise it disturbs the playful problem solving of others in the room.

Yet in one respect, the common relationship of La Clase Mágica to its surroundings has a marked *common* effect on children's participation. Because the idioculture in each case is, so to speak, the only game in town, children typically come and stay for the full time the activity is running. This contrasts strongly with the Fifth Dimension at the BGC where children come and go with such high frequency that merely keeping track of how many children have participated at the site on a given day requires special attention and even is a difficult and uncertain task. This commonality with the Library and contrast with the BGC is closely related to a second one: there is stronger evidence of intellectual gains by children who attended either the Library or La Clase Mágica Fifth Dimensions than there is for the BGC.

This is not to say that no intellectual development occurs at the BGC, but it is extraordinarily difficult to document by a test or common task because children come and go on schedules that make long term assessment of groups of children very difficult. In the one case where this was accomplished by Ageliki Nicolopoulou with respect to a particular problem solving game, there was little evidence of accumulating knowledge at the BGC, but clear evidence at the Library. Such evidence for La Clase Mágica can also be found in Vasquez (2003).

Cautions and expectations

Over the 15 years when I first began this work, the Fifth Dimension has been taken up by a large number of institutions in various parts of the United States and in other countries (for relevant information, see www.uclinks.org). This proliferation has allowed us to extend greatly the potential for cross-cultural comparisons of various kinds. One of particular interest has been cases where Fifth Dimensions have been placed in schools, either as part of the school day or afterschool using school facilities (for reports of these various efforts, the reader is directed to the webpage given above).

Although the variety of idiocultures that has developed from these efforts is enormous, some regularities already anticipatable on the basis of the examples given here are obvious. For example, when a Fifth Dimension occurs in school, and especially if it occurs during school hours, the struggle is to keep its play element alive and to make possible the higher noise levels and degrees of independent child movement and choice that are necessary for the core features of the idioculture to emerge. Or, when a Fifth Dimension in a playful afterschool setting like a BGC begins to get too academic, or to include activities identifiable by the children as tests, the life goes out of the culture and it has to change or die.

Overall, while one cannot pre-scribe, let alone pre-dict(ate) the exact combination of play, education, and peer interaction, that will produce a viable and vibrant Fifth Dimension, the relational view embodied in our comparisons of many Fifth Dimensions in relation to their institutional contexts enables us to identify likely mistakes that newcomers interested in starting up such activities should try to avoid and a huge toolkit of resources that they can call upon to bring such idiocultures into being.

The Importance of Taking Sustainability as the Central Research Question

When I first began to create and compare different instantiations of the Fifth Dimension, I did not do so prove to myself that it is possible to create activities which are both educational and attractive to children during the afterschool hours. From my work with the original Fifth Dimension several years earlier (see Cole, 1996, for a description) I was convinced that this activity was both attractive to children and a good environment in which to promote their development, as well as the academic development of undergraduates. My major foci were two: Under what conditions would it be possible to conduct analysis of cognitive development in such systems and what factors were associated with the failure of successful educational innovations (of which I assumed the Fifth Dimension to be an example) to be sustained, even though they were valued by those who participated in them and their institutional sponsors?

I have touched lightly on the first issue here, and do not plan to pursue it further owing to lack space, although it is a question of considerable theoretical as well as practical importance (see information provided under "references" at www.uclinks.org for a plethora of writing on this topic). But the second point requires special emphasis because it turns out that in taking sustainability as a focus of inquiry, I unwittingly committed myself to the longitudinal study of culture and cognitive development over a period that has thus far spanned 16 years.

I would like to be able to claim that I foresaw the virtues of such longitudinal research on individuals related to idiocultures, but I did not. I actually assumed that within three to four years, all of the original Fifth Dimensions would disappear. Their failure would allow me to study the dynamics of the demise of successful educational innovations, a topic I still consider crucial. But I did not foresee that when three years were up, the BGC would begin to pick up a significant proportion of the costs of running the program. I did not foresee a variety of changes in society that would catapult afterschool into the national consciousness as a means of meeting challenges posed by increased involvement of women in the workforce and demands for higher levels of school achievement. Consequently, I never imagined that 17 years after conceiving of this project, it would have continued at one of the original sites and spread to many parts of the globe.

All of that is interesting in so far as it speaks to the issue of the successful use of the notion of idioculture and Vygotskian theory for purposes of idiocultural design. But I wish to conclude by noting a different benefit that resulted from this emphasis on sustainability, combined with the actual fact of a project involving idioculture design lasting for so long in a number of institutions. This benefit is the ability to observe, participate in, and document the incredible dynamism of change at the cultural, ontogenetic, and micro-genetic levels of analysis, which, with rare exceptions (e.g., Greenfield, 1999), is absent from the cross-cultural literature because of the long time spans involved. In Greenfield's case, she was able to return to southern Mexico after a period of 20 years to document how cultural historical change associated with the coming of roads, modern transportation, and the commodified culture that ensued brought about changes in cultural practices of weaving including not only changes in design and materials, but changes in mother-child interactions surrounding the enculturation of children into weaving practices.

Because they operate at a smaller scale and are accessible in the locales where researchers teach and live, Fifth Dimensions routinely permit the tracing of developmental change at the level of the system as a whole, the cultural practices at the Fifth Dimension sites and university classrooms, as well as the quality of interactions between undergraduates and children and changes in the children and undergraduates over time.

Space permits me only to sketch out one such case, the one I know best, because it is the unique survivor of the original set of Fifth Dimensions that we brought to life in the suburban town near my college campus in 1987, the BGC. I have already contrasted the BGC with similar idiocultures in surrounding institutions, indicating how local context influences the characteristics of the local culture and its impact on the children. What I have not indicated is the constant process of change in the idioculture of the BGC itself over time.

All of the factors that influence synchronic differences between the idiocultures of Fifth Dimension can be seen at work in the diachronic changes in the idioculture as part of the ongoing relationship between the activity system and its institutional environment which is ever changing along multiple dimensions. So, for example, when the Fifth Dimension was first opened at the Club, it occupied a spacious, well lit room that afforded easy movement, plenty of room to place tables where children could draw and play non-computer games, and had a light, airy feel to it. But economic recession induced the Club to combine the Fifth Dimension space with space for its library/homework room in order to raise money by renting out the library room. With its space cut in half (bookshelves were used as dividers between the two different activity systems) the Fifth Dimension became cramped. No tables were available for joint activity away from the computers and the computers themselves were crammed so close together that easy going interaction around them was difficult. The culture of the Fifth Dimension took on a cramped, somewhat strained feeling, and fewer children or undergraduates could participate, changing the overall feel of the activity.

Constant turnover of personnel has provided a constant challenge to maintaining cultural continuity across generations within the Club while the use of temporary faculty to keep the cost of running the activity at the University to a minimum provided a similar challenge from the University side. And of course, the fact that my university runs on a quarter system means an influx of new undergraduates every three months, so that personnel from the research group, aided by a variety of specially designed artifacts (handbooks for the instructor, a book full of hints about how to play the various games at the site, etc.) were in constant production. Mention should also be made of the unexpectedly rapid change in computer technologies, which meant that new games needed to be introduced into the idioculture as the means for implementing them changed.

By Way of a Summary

It is the nature of chapters such as these that the author can do little more than convey to the reader a general sense of the focal topic, especially when that topic is a deviant practice such as the use of theories of culture in development to design environments for children and study their dynamics over time. Clearly, such an enterprise cannot be a general substitute for the continued effort to understand cultural differences as they occur in historical time on national and international levels. But perhaps some of the principles which are naturally highlighted by the comparative study of idiocultures over time can be of use to those operating at more macro scales, providing first hand experience of the dynamics of culturally mediated change while at the same time providing useful tools for cultural psychologists to contribute to the well being of their local communities.

References

Berry, J. W., Poortinga, Y. H., & Pandey, J. (Eds). (1997). *Handbook of cross-cultural psychology: Theory and method* (Vol. 1, 2nd ed.). Boston: Allyn and Bacon.

Boesch, E. E. (1997). The sound of the violin. In M. Cole, Y. Engestrom, & O. Vasquez (Eds.), *Mind, culture, and activity: Seminal papers from the Laboratory of Comparative human cognition* (pp. 164-184). New York: Cambridge University Press.

Cole, M. (1996). *Cultural psychology*. Cambridge, MA: Harvard University Press.

Fine, G. A. (1989). *With the boys: Little baseball and preadolescent culture* (3rd ed.). Chicago, IL: University of Chicago Press.

Greenfield, P. M. (1999). Historical change and cognitive change: A two-decade follow-up study in Zinacantan, a Maya community in Chiapas, Mexico. *Mind, Culture, & Activity, 6*, 92-108.

Hutchins, E. (1995). *Cognition in the wild*. Cambridge, MA: MIT Press.

Jahoda, G. (1993). *Crossroads between culture and mind: Continuities and change in theories of human nature*. Cambridge, MA: Harvard University Press.

Kroeber, A. L., & Kluckhohn, C. (1952). *Culture: A critical review of concepts and definitions*. Cambridge, MA: Harvard University Press.

Nicolopoulou, A., & Cole, M. (1993). Generation and transmission of shared knowledge in the culture of collaborative learning: The Fifth Dimension, its play-world, and its institutional contexts. In E. A. Forman & N. Minick (Eds.), *Contexts for learning: Sociocultural dynamics in children's development* (pp. 283-314). London: Oxford University Press.

Rose, E. & Felton, W. (1955). Experimental histories of culture. *American Sociological Review, 20*, 383-392.

Vasquez, O. (2003). *La Clase Mágica: Imagining optimal possibilities in a bilingual community of learners*. Mahwah, NJ: Erlbaum.

Vygotsky, L. S. (1978). *Mind in society*. Cambridge, MA: Harvard University Press.

Williams, R. (1973). *Keywords*. Oxford, UK: Oxford University Press.

Part II

On the Development of

Developmental Theories

4

Universal and Culture-Specific Aspects of Human Behavior: The Case of Attachment

Klaus E. Grossmann, Karin Grossmann, and Anika Keppler

Attachment in an Evolutionary and Ontogenetic Perspective

This chapter, presenting *attachment* and *caregiving* as universal human behavioral systems that may be expressed differently in various human cultures, will highlight the importance of cross-cultural research in the social sciences. We are looking at attachment from an evolutionary and ontogenetic perspective to show the intricate entwinement of ultimate evolutionary adaptation and proximate ontogenetic appearance by presenting the five core concepts or hypotheses of attachment theory in a cross-cultural perspective. As an example of the interrelatedness between universal traits and cultural specificity in the case of attachment, some of our own data from field observations as well as an experimental analysis of one- to three-year-old children from a small village on the Trobriand Islands will be presented subsequently[1]. In this very traditional society, it could be shown that the underlying biological principles of the attachment and exploratory behavioral systems have the same function as in other cultures although the ecological and historical conditions of the Trobrianders are quite different from those of many other cultures (Schiefenhövel, Uher, & Krell, 1993).

[1] We thank the families of Tauwema village for their cooperation and patience with us. Prof. Dr. Wulf Schiefenhövel of the Research Unit of Human Ethology in the Max-Planck Society was our guide and secure base during our two visits to Papua New-Guinea in 1990 and 1995. The Deutsche Forschungsgemeinschaft has financed our fieldwork in Tauwema.

The phylogenetic perspective on cultural development of man posits that man is a cultural being by biological necessity. Specific cultural aspects are seen as an expression of open genetic programs that are designed to serve the survival of human genes. Man has to survive in his present social and cultural environment with the genetic dispositions acquired in past evolutionary environments. Man's preprogrammed abilities to express and understand emotions are the precursors and foundations of his adaptive propensities that include the need for creating specific familial, social, and cultural ties. Given sufficiently "normal" conditions, a human child develops from a biologically preadapted newborn into a socially and culturally participating individual. For the biological necessity of becoming a successful member of the society of man, humans are genetically equipped to become socialized, to express and understand emotions, to organize their behaviors towards goals, to develop a language that enables a person to relate symbolically his experiences, thoughts, motivations, and intentions, and to understand the mindful conspecifics (Buss, 1999). Thus a young child's complex emotions acquire cultural meanings ranging from highly aversive and despised by his culture to very positive, highly praised, and valued.

The dominant selection principle during man's natural history of evolution, as in any other species, is on the individual to maximize the frequency of his/her own genes in the gene pool of the generations to come. A person endowed with optimal psychological and material resources outperforms genetically those without resources. Good genes and high quality of parental investment together create adaptive human beings (Buss, 1999). Practically all human beings living today, with only a few exceptions of proximate genetic malfunctioning have potentially "good" genes for proper socialization and enculturation. Humans carrying genes incompatible with social and cultural propensities presumably did not survive. For example, by being unable to fend off predators and enemies by himself and without being able to ensure protection from related individuals, the one carrying incompatible genes would surely not live long enough to reproduce them. This development progressed rapidly when man's larger brain evolved within the selection process of creating cultures as his new "natural" environment (Donald, 1991).

The evolutionary perspective is well represented in attachment theory and research. Attachment reflects two biological complementary behavioral systems: the infants' needs to be protected and cared for, and parents' propensity for caregiving, i.e., their readiness to invest resources into their offspring. This is universal in all cultures. At the individual level, a certain range of variety is possible given man's open genetic programs. Within this range, cultures must provide environments suitable for attachment development. Despite large differences between cultures they can only survive if they provide for the basic biological needs of the human species and vice versa: Humans have to adapt to the cultural necessities and demands within their individual lifetimes if they want to increase their probability for having their genes represented in the next generations.

Attachment research is well suited for comparing universal and cultural specifics of human needs. An infant's basic need – among other needs – is an individual relationship to another "stronger and wiser" human. There have been reports about epochs in which parents rather carelessly delegated the care of their infants to others even at the risk of losing their children (Badinter, 1984). However, such temporary carelessness may perhaps be misleading evidence for claims that parental love had to be invented by more humane cultures. Human evolution would not have been successful if early humans did not have the propensity to care for their young. Of course, ignorance such as the inability to limit the number of offspring born into a family of limited resources, as was the case at the onset of the 18th century in Europe when the population explosion started, is an example of cultural limits to human adaptability. It leads to devaluation of individual lives and attachments (K. E. Grossmann, 1995). Under such extreme circumstances, the attachment and caregiving behavioral systems were no longer properly functioning and many infants were neglected and "sent to heaven" ("gehimmelt") on purpose (Imhof, 1984).

Despite such epochal derailments, attachment theory deals with the special relationships between human infants and their parents or close caregivers. It is understood as a genetically predisposed emotional and behavioral organization on the part of an infant to express its needs, and a corresponding complementary program on the part of the parent to understand and to respond properly to the expression of emotions of the infant (Bowlby, 1973; Trevarthen, 1987). The open programs allow cultures to provide a somewhat variable, but not unlimited, range of individual acquisition of best fitting adaptive behavioral strategies that satisfy the underlying emotions.

There are, of course, mutual influences: biological constraints on cultures, as well as cultural constraints on the multitude of individual pathways toward proximate, phenotypic expression of ultimate genetic programs (see earlier contributions of such insights in Hinde, 1974).

The human infant, in comparison to non-human primates, is born prematurely (Portmann, 1956). The infant relies on external organization of his emotions, motives, behaviors, and communications, in addition to "expecting" understanding attachment figures that are designed to be more or less sensitive and responsive (Ainsworth, Bell, & Stayton, 1974; Sander, 1975). Different qualities of attachment develop from different qualities of sensitive responsiveness. Attachment figures become highly individualized, with mostly mothers being preferred when the infants' attachment system is aroused.

Man's biological programs necessitate cultural development. The human infant's brain is already well prepared for those features, which underlie cultural development, particularly those centers for language understanding and language production. The polymodal association areas of the human brain make up 95% of the interneurons (Trevarthen, 1987). Brain growth does not occur by the neocortex covering up older brain parts, but rather, as the human brain grows, it creates a completely rearranged system of connections between the older subcortical parts, particularly the limbic system, and the neocortical parts (Armstrong, 1991).

The evolutionary, cultural interdisciplinary, anthropologically, and developmentally oriented attachment theory favors species-specific, qualitative complexities of human social development in the tradition of Charles Darwin's "The Origin of Species by Means of Natural Selection [...]." It rests on ultimate developments determined by natural selection and inclusive fitness as conceptualized in neo-Darwinian theories by Hamilton, Wilson, Trivers, Dawkins, and others (see Buss, 1999). Attachment research investigates and analyzes proximate mechanisms, which reenact ultimate adaptive emotional systems at the individual level. Whereas attachment formation is a human propensity that is ultimate and theoretically inferred, attachment quality in individual ontogenesis is proximate, observable, and reveals its underlying developmental processes. Attachment quality in conjunction with experienced parenting in any culture affects individual personalities (Ainsworth & Bowlby, 1991). In infancy, the interactive processes have been investigated by systematic observations and qualitative descriptions as developed by behavioral biologists and ethologists.

Relevant species-specific endowments for attachment as well as cultural development are seen in emotion programs (Cosmides & Tooby, 2000), joint attention (Tomasello, 1999), language, and the creation of meaning (Bruner, 1982, 1990), the ability to see events from the perspective of another person (Ainsworth, Bell, & Stayton, 1974; Meins, 1999), the ability to consider another person's wishes and goals when pursuing own goals ("goal-corrected partnership," Bowlby, 1982), and self-cognition (Bischof-Köhler, 1998). These universal mental and representational qualities become increasingly tied to special individuals, whether they are attachment figures or not, who are transmitters of cultural meanings as emphasized by cultural anthropology.

On the basis of frequent and daily dyadic interactions with attachment figures, internal working models of attachment relationships develop in each individual. The experience of attachment persons as being available and responsive when called upon and a picture of the self as worthy of help and attention are conceptualized as filters of perceptions, actions, and motives in the context of interpersonal expectations that occur within culturally "meaningful" situations. Attachment theory holds that a mentally healthy person in any culture is able to organize his emotions around adaptive strategies within personal relationships. An emotionally secure person is neither afraid of loosing contact with significant others when in distress, nor is he afraid of being rejected by others in critical situations (Bowlby, 1991). Psychologically adaptive or "secure" behavior strategies are the result of undistorted perceptions of situations, events, and challenges that demand well planned goal- corrected actions. Robert Sternberg (1997), an intelligence researcher, sees adaptive intelligence as a correspondence between a complex outside reality and its coherent representation in the human mind ("internal coherence and external correspondence").

These ultimate adaptive strategies are universal because of the evolutionary ultimate implications of the attachment system as being in the service of protection of the weaker and younger individual. Research within cultures or subcultures, in turn, highlights the various ways in which universal attachment and caregiving behaviors, as well as their antecedents and consequences, are embedded within a variety of cultural contexts.

The next section provides some empirical evidence for the ultimate adaptive program of attachment by highlighting the five universal core concepts or hypotheses of attachment theory. Chao (2001), Gjerde (2001), Kondo-Ikemura (2001), Posada and Jacobs (2001), van IJzendoorn and Sagi (2001) all respond (alas in undue brevity imposed on their responses by the journal) to seemingly ill researched claims that the attachment behavioral system is not a universal human predisposition (Rothbaum, Weisz, Pott, Miyake, & Morelli, 2000). Rothbaum (this volume) seems to have revised his previous untenable position and now also agrees that there are indeed basic biological pre-dispositions underlying attachment. Undoubtedly, each culture strongly influences the proximate behavioral expressions and attitudes that will serve the ultimate goals of caring and protecting the infant, of ministering to the child's motivation to become socialized and enculturated, and of socializing the child into a competent adult in that specific culture. For example, Gisela Trommsdorff demonstrates in her comparative studies of mother-child interactions in Japan and Germany how culture-specific socialization goals evoke culture-specific modes of interaction that are, in turn, related to culture-specific phenomena in intimate relations (Trommsdorff & Friedlmeier, 1993).

The Five Core Hypotheses of Attachment Theory

From its very beginning, empirical attachment *research* was conducted cross-culturally. The basic principles or hypotheses of attachment theory as stated by Bowlby (1973, 1980, 1982) were first tested through extended field observations in Uganda, a non-western society (Ainsworth, 1967). Subsequently, research in many cultures in Europe, Africa, and Asia was conducted to explore the influence of child-rearing practices on patterns of attachment and the influence of patterns of attachment on the child's further development. From these research results, five core hypotheses emerged that have been supported by a wide variety of attachment studies in many cultures (van IJzendoorn & Sagi, 1999). These five core hypotheses of attachment theory will be presented in the next section.

The universality hypothesis of attachment
It posits that all infants become attached to at least one primary caregiver. Depending on the cultural and social caregiving context, infants may become attached to more than one person but not to many. Many cultures provide mothers with "helpers at the nest" (Hrdy, 1999). However, a hierarchy of attachment figures emerges when

an infant is observed during various intensities of distress with the primary attachment figure being preferred with increasing distress. Attachment formation is independent of the genetic relationship between infant and adult caregiver. Usually,
caregiving behaviors are at the roots of an attachment bond, but often affectionate
responsiveness, attentive protection, and sensitive challenges during joint play as
seen in fathers suffices (K. Grossmann, K. E. Grossmann, Fremmer-Bombik, Kindler, Scheuerer-Englisch, & Zimmermann, 2002).

In all cultures, the primary caregiver for most infants is the biological mother.
The three universal criteria for an attachment bond are (a) seeking closeness to and
protection from the attachment figure when in danger or distressed (the "haven of
safety" function), (b) the use of the attachment figure as a "secure base" from which
to explore the environment safely, and (c) emotional as well as physiological distress
when separated from the attachment figure (separation distress).

The hypothesis of the attachment-exploration balance

It posits that when the attachment behavioral system is active or aroused the exploration behavioral system is inactive and vice versa. The attachment and the exploratory behavioral systems are considered by attachment theory to be separate behavioral systems within the multitude of behavioral systems of individuals. However,
they are inseparably linked to each other such that when one system is active the
other is deactivated (see Figure 1) (Ainsworth, Blehar, Waters, & Wall, 1978). This
activation and deactivation is not complete, however, to the degree of closing down
one or the other system completely. Environmental clues concerning the safety of
the individual are continuously monitored attentively as are events stimulating the
individual's curiosity.

Arousal of the attachment system is best calmed by close bodily proximity ("ten-
der loving care"). Non-arousal of the attachment system can be taken as an index of
emotional security, which favors playful exploration in the service of competent
social and cultural adaptation to the complexities of human life.

The normativity hypothesis

It posits that the secure pattern of attachment is – with very few exceptions – the
most frequent pattern in all samples of uncompromised infants observed in all cultures.

Ainsworth (1979), who first observed the lawful organization of infant attachment and exploratory behaviors in response to the mild stress, later devised a standardized procedure, the "Strange Situation" to analyze systematically infants' behavioral strategies in dealing with mild stress with or without the mother.

The episodes are staged as follows: (1) introduction of mother and baby by researcher, (2) mother and baby alone, (3) stranger enters, (4) mother leaves, (5)
mother returns and stranger leaves, (6) mother leaves and baby stays by himself, (7)
stranger returns, (8) mother returns and stranger leaves. The critical moments are the

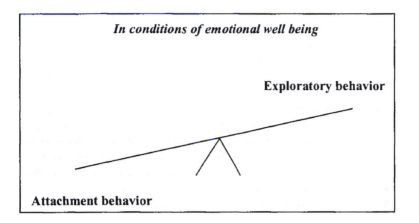

In conditions of emotional well being

Exploratory behavior

Attachment behavior

Figure 1. The Concept of the Attachment-Exploration Balance. The attachment and exploratory behavioral systems are linked to each other such that when one system is activated the other is deactivated.

mother's returns that highlight the infant's expectation of the mother's availability when the infant feels distressed. Classification of quality and pattern of attachment is based on the infant's use of the attachment figure as a secure base and haven of safety. The three main patterns were labeled secure (Group "B"), insecure-avoidant (Group "A"), and insecure-resistant or ambivalent (Group "C"). A child with a secure attachment tends not to be conflicted in her approaches to her attachment figure for comfort when stressed, whereas a young child with an anxious attachment demonstrates moderate to high levels of avoidance or ambivalence toward the attachment figure during times of distress.

After her studies in Uganda and Baltimore, USA, Ainsworth proposed that the secure pattern is to be considered as normative and the optimal adaptive developmental outcome for human infants (Ainsworth, 1979, p. 44). Subsequently, over 100 studies of infant patterns of attachment to mother, father, and sometimes to a permanent non-parental caregiver have been conducted. The "Strange Situation" has been applied to infants from many cultural backgrounds from the western to the eastern hemisphere, from agriculturally oriented to industrialized peoples (van IJzendoorn & Sagi, 1999). Almost all confirmed this proposition (Thompson, 1998).

Only two exceptions from this norm have been published. In our North German sample – but not in our several South German samples –, the insecure-avoidant pattern was found to be dominant (K. Grossmann, K. E. Grossmann, Spangler, Suess, & Unzner, 1985; Spangler & K. Grossmann, 1995), and in an Israeli sample of infants with communal sleeping arrangements the insecure-ambivalent pattern was predominant (Sagi, van IJzendoorn, Aviezer, Donnell, & Mayseless, 1994).

The sensitivity hypothesis
It posits that the quality of attachment depends on the attachment figure's sensitivity to the child's attachment and exploratory behaviors.

As different environments tend to produce different phenotypes of comparable genetic material, secure or insecure patterns of attachment depend on the quality of received care even to the extent of not being given enough food (Valenzuela, 1997). Particularly sensitive responsiveness and cooperation of the attachment figures to the infants' attachment and exploratory needs and behaviors have been identified as the crucial environmental inputs. Those studies conducted in the USA, Europe, and in other cultures investigating antecedents of security of attachment all demonstrated a significant relationship between maternal sensitivity and a secure pattern of infant attachment. Although almost each research team defined maternal sensitivity in a somewhat different way, and many did not even include maternal reactions to infant distress or attachment signals, no study yielded contradictory evidence (De Wolff & van IJzendoorn, 1997; van IJzendoorn & Sagi, 1999).

Some cultural conditions, however, are clearly hindering parents to provide sensitive and cooperative care. A general cultural belief that "crying strengthens the lungs," or "responding is spoiling the child" that predominated in child-rearing customs in Germany for some time have kept mothers from responding to her crying infant. Such misbelieves have even been asserted by some extreme learning theorists (Ainsworth & Bell, 1977). The predominance of insecure-avoidant attachments in North Germany may have been the result of the fear of spoiling the child and rearing a demanding, clinging, dependent tyrant that would put the parents outside the cultural norms (K. Grossmann et al., 1985). A child made obedient by discipline was the ideal in Germany but not an accepting, cooperative child rearing mode that would support the development of compliance in the child (Ainsworth & Bell, 1974; K. E. Grossmann & K. Grossmann, 1981). Furthermore and at the individual level, a history of institutional care, socioeconomic stress, adverse family relations, and maternal mental ill health may all limit a mother's ability to attend appropriately to her infant's needs (Bornstein, 1995).

Some social groups may even limit parents' access to their children. This was the case in a number of traditional Israeli kibbutzim, where parents were allowed to spend only a few hours in the afternoon with each of their children. Professional caregivers provided caregiving, and the children slept in a communal dormitory at night. Under such conditions, the secure pattern of attachment was found only in less than half of the children, although this arrangement was supported by the whole community (Sagi et al., 1995; Sagi, van IJzendoorn, Aviezer, Donnell, & Mayseless, 1994). Being able to rule out other influencing factors, it was concluded that collective sleeping, experienced by infants as a time during which mothers were largely unavailable and inaccessible, was responsible for the greater insecurity found in this group (Aviezer & Sagi, 1999). Intriguingly, during the Gulf War, a time of threat to the survival of Israeli people, all families retrieved their infants to their homes and communal sleeping was never reestablished (Sagi, personal communication).

A significant association between maternal sensitivity and attachment security was found by German Posada in Colombia (Posada, Jacobs, Carbonell, Alzate, Bustamante, & Arenas, 1999), by Martha Valenzuela in Chile (Valenzuela, 1997), and by Mary True in rural Mali (True, Pisani, & Oumar, 2001). Jolien Zevalkink also found in Bandung, Indonesia, that the quality of maternal support was highest for secure dyads, which in turn was related to maternal sensitivity at home (Zevalkink, Riksen-Walraven, & Lieshout, 1999). Van IJzendoorn and Sagi (1999) provide still additional studies that support this hypothesis.

The competence hypothesis
It posits that the secure attachment is related to higher competence in dealing with developmental, social, and cultural challenges.

Ainsworth and Bell (1974) were the first to provide convincing empirical and theoretical evidence for this hypothesis. In view of the diverse customs, goals, and competencies valued in different cultural groups, a definition of competence has to be adopted by researchers in accordance to each specific cultural group. In studies of children in Europe and the USA, qualities of attachment were strongly related to competencies valued in these cultures, i.e., the organization of negative emotions and behaviors in infancy and childhood in response to challenging situations experienced with or without the mother. Insecure patterns of attachment to mother were associated with less readiness to cooperate with parents, peers, and teachers, with dysfunctional aggression, poor ego-control, and behavior problems and with a weak self-confidence and lower ego resilience (Carlson & Sroufe, 1995). However, in Japan, maternal sensitivity was related to cooperative child behavior, a behavioral style highly valued in Japan (Trommsdorff & Friedlmeier, 1993).

Bretherton concludes from her overview of the relation between security of attachment and social competence: "Secure attachment relationships emerge time and again as central in the development of children's cooperative, empathic behavior and 'committed compliance' with parents who, as attachment figures, offer emotional support and protection and, as authority figures, provide flexible, understanding guidance" (Bretherton, Golby, & Cho, 1997, p. 129). They posit further that such parenting abilities are best fostered when the social group acknowledges and respects the values underlying secure attachment relations. Under such conditions, we conclude, children will grow up to value their parents' values.

Thus, this hypothesis has received ample support from studies of the western world (Thompson, 1998). However, only a few studies on this topic conducted in traditional societies have been published in journals of the English language (van IJzendoorn & Sagi, 1999). Nevertheless, support for the competence hypothesis has come from such diverse cultures as Israel, Japan, the Dogon of Mali (van IJzendoorn & Sagi, 1999) and from the Trobriand Islands, as will be shown later.

In our cooperative and comparative German-Japanese study[2] we found that Japanese infants with a secure pattern were, even in comparison to German infants with secure attachments, more competent in mastering the strange situation procedure: they cried less upon mother's leaving the room, they showed more concentrated play, and they were more friendly and trusting toward the stranger than German infants (K. Grossmann & K. E. Grossmann, 1996). In another Japanese study, infants with a secure pattern of attachment were more compliant, curious about objects, and more competent with peers one year later (Takahashi, 1990). Thus, when developmentally and culturally appropriate challenges are properly tested, all evidence points in the direction that emotional security is associated with that type of higher behavioral competence that is valued in that culture.

An Attachment Study on the Trobriand Islands, Papua New Guinea

In cooperation with Wulf Schiefenhövel from the Research Unit of Human Ethology in the Max-Planck Society, we conducted an attachment study in the traditional society of the Trobrianders (K. E. Grossmann & K. Grossmann, 1996). Schiefenhövel speaks the Lingua Franca (Motu) of the people in that region. The Trobriand Islands are off the South Eastern Coast of mainland Papua New Guinea. The field station was in the small village of Tauwema on the island of Kaileuna. The majority of the Austronesian-speaking Trobrianders are horticulturists and gathers of marine resources. The first description of the people was provided by Malinowski between 1922 and 1935. The Trobrianders have a matrilineal descent system. The children of a couple belong to the clan of their mother, and through this clan they receive most of their rights (Schiefenhövel & Bell-Krannhals, 1996).

Our research project focused on the universal, cultural as well as individual aspects of young children's attachment and exploratory behaviors. In 1995, all families with mobile children under 3½ years in this village were asked to participate. Three women of the village spoke English sufficiently well to convey our research goals to the families. Twenty toddlers were available, 13 girls and 7 boys, ranging from 16 to 41 months of age. Security of attachment was assessed for each toddler to her or his mother with the standardized procedure of the "Strange Situation" conducted in the public meetinghouse of the village. Sessions were videotaped. Subsequently, spontaneously occurring attachment and exploratory behaviors of each toddler was openly observed in the village, written into narrative protocols or filmed. The toddlers played mostly around their homes. One full morning and one full afternoon was documented. Occasional observations of the focal toddlers' behaviors on other days were also noted.

---

[2] The scientific cooperation with Prof. Kazuo Miyake, then at the Research and Clinical Center for Child Development at the Hokkaido University, Sapporo, is gratefully acknowledged. Kazuo Miyake and S. Y. Chen provided facilities to reanalyze the videotapes of the "Strange Situations" conducted in Sapporo and also provided the financial support.

Analyses of the "Strange Situations" focused on three aspects: First, patterns of attachment to mothers were classified. Second, the exploratory behaviors were analyzed by coding the kind of object the toddler explored and by rating the play intensity with that object. Play objects in the "Strange Situation" were selected from a variety of household items that were familiar to the toddlers such as cans, shells, and small balls. Our informant insisted that a "doba-set" (a small scraping board, a small metal scraper and fresh pieces of banana leaves) were included in the array of play objects. These utensils – in their large size for adults – are the tools for making "doba." Doba is a bundle of scraped off fibers from banana leaves, dried, bound together, and often dyed to make fiber skirts. These fiber skirts represent women's wealth (K. Grossmann, 1995; Weiner, 1976). Thus, "making doba" is a highly valued activity for women in this society. As long as infant boys sit close to their mothers, they also like to imitate this activity (K. Grossmann, K. E. Grossmann, Keppler, Liegel, & Schiefenhövel, 2003). A number of unfamiliar objects, items selected from the household of the researchers, were added to the familiar items, e.g., a chain of safety pins, a small bag filled with clothespins, and other items. Third, mother's support of the infant's explorations was rated differentiating between supporting exploration of familiar or unfamiliar objects (Keppler, 2000).

The field observations of these toddlers were analyzed for several aspects of the children's attachment and exploratory behavioral systems. First, the toddlers' activities were categorized along a scale representing the attachment exploration balance ranging from showing exclusively attachment behaviors in a given episode to showing exclusively exploratory behaviors with various degrees of a mixture of the two in between. Second, the objects and quality of exploration was coded and rated, again differentiating between familiar and unfamiliar objects for the toddlers. Third, the blood relationship of the person who was with the toddler was noted. This identification was done to determine the degree of kin-investment into child rearing. Fourth, supportive or inhibiting interventions of exploration by the responsible adult were coded, differentiating again between familiar and novel objects. Thus, support of curiosity versus creating anxiety in response to novelty was assessed (Liegel, 2001; K. Grossmann et al., 2003).

Attachment and its behavioral patterns in young Trobriand children
In the mildly distressing "Strange Situation" as well as when distressed during the field observations, all 20 toddlers showed attachment behaviors and fled to their mothers as a haven of safety. All young children exhibited separation distress when separated involuntarily from their mothers. Thus, in support of the universality hypotheses, attachment behavior to mother was clearly observed in all toddlers of this Trobriand village. However, individual differences between the toddlers in their intensity and timing of attachment and exploratory behaviors were also evident. Patterns of attachment were easily classifiable according to Ainsworth's classification scheme (Ainsworth et al., 1978). Each of the three major patterns of attachment

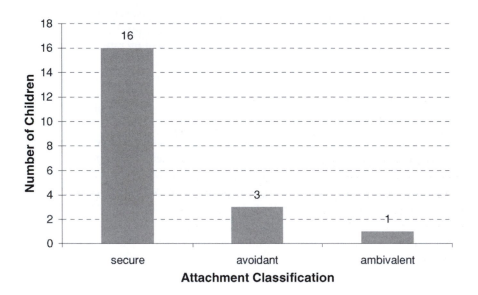

Figure 2. Distribution of Attachment Patterns Among Toddlers in the Village of Tauwema, Papua New Guinea

was reliably identified, the secure pattern, the insecure-avoidant, and the insecure-ambivalent pattern. Thus, individual differences in the organization of the attachment and exploratory behavioral systems of the Tauwema toddlers towards their mothers in response to strangeness and separation distress were clearly comparable to that of toddlers in many other cultures (van IJzendoorn & Sagi, 1999).

Supportive evidence for the normativity hypothesis is shown in Figure 2 documenting the distribution of patterns of attachment among the 20 one- to three-year-olds in Tauwema. Sixteen (80%) toddlers showed a secure pattern, three an insecure-avoidant pattern, and one an insecure-ambivalent pattern. As expected, the percentage of secure children in this group was high.

However, we were surprised to find the avoidant pattern of attachment at all among the Trobriand toddlers. An avoidant pattern implies that the young child will show no or very little attachment behaviors during reunions with the mother but will divert her or his attention from her and keep her- or himself busy with objects. In this society, infants are carried or nested in the lap of the mother or a member of the family most of the day. For the mobile toddler, the mother or a familiar person will be available and easily accessible should she or he experience distress during his explorations. Our findings show that this condition in itself does not seem to be sufficient for the development of a secure attachment to the caregiver.

During our visit to the village, we could not gather sufficient data on individual differences in sensitivity of these mothers. Thus, we can only speculate on the basis of frequent but unsystematic observations in addition to the official observation times. Mothers of infants with an insecure pattern of attachment occasionally behaved in ways as to make bodily proximity and contact with her less enjoyable for the toddler, by responding very slowly, by being harsher in their pick-ups or by handing the infant over quickly to some other caregiver. If a mother dislikes her child or the mothering role within this quite indulgent society, she has the option of leaving the child much of the time in the care of other members of the family who readily provide the infant with bodily contact and protection.

The attachment-exploration balance in young Trobriand children
For the analysis of toddler exploration, each episode of the "Strange Situations" was divided into 15 sec. intervals. The number of 15 sec. intervals in which exploration dominated over other behaviors in the Trobriand toddlers is shown in the upper curve in Figure 3a. This pattern of increasing or decreasing exploratory intensity over the course of the episodes was observable in many toddlers from many cultures. Figures 3a and 3b show comparable results of four studies from four continents.

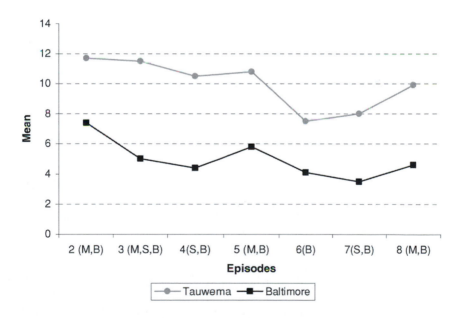

Figure 3a. Exploration Over the Course of the 8 Episodes in the Strange Situation of Toddlers from the Village of Tauwema, Trobriand Islands, Papua New Guinea (Grossmann study of 1995), and of Toddlers in Baltimore, USA, in 1969 (Ainsworth et al., 1978). Mean number of 15 sec intervals in which exploration dominates are indicated; M: Mother; B: Baby; S: Stranger.

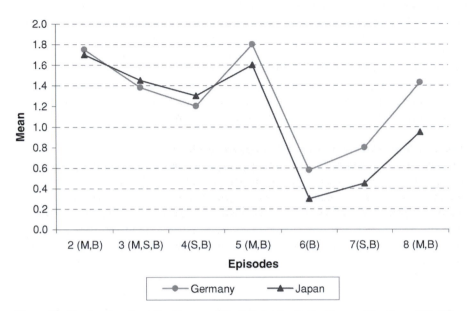

Figure 3b. Exploration Over the Course of the 8 Episodes in the Strange Situation of Toddlers in Various Studies in Germany (K. Grossmann et al., 1985; Spangler, Grossmann, & Schieche, 2002) and in Sapporo, Japan (Miyake et al., 1981). Mean scores on a 3-point scale for intensity of exploration are indicated. M: Mother; B: Baby: S: Stranger.

The absolute levels of exploration depicted in Figures 3a and b is of no concern, they may be a matter of the definition of exploratory behavior in any given study. The lower curve in Figure 3a shows the results of Ainsworth's Baltimore study of forty years ago (Ainsworth et al., 1978, p. 82). The upper curve in Figure 3b represents the course of exploratory behaviors of Japanese toddlers (K. Grossmann & K. E. Grossmann, 1996), and the lower curve in Figure 3b does the same for toddlers from various samples of German infants (K. Grossmann et al., 1985; Spangler, K. E. Grossmann, & Schieche, 2002).

All four curves show, that exploratory intensity followed a very similar course throughout the "Strange Situation" in samples of toddlers from such diverse cultures as the Trobriand Islands, the USA, Japan, and Germany. In Episode 2 (Ep. 2), when the infant was alone with his mother, exploration was most frequent as compared to all other episodes. The stranger's entrance in Ep. 3 reduced exploration more or less, and it declined further or remained at a low level in Ep. 4 after the mother has departed. The mother's return in Ep. 5 activated some increase in exploratory activity, although not nearly to the level of Ep. 2. The second separation, beginning in Ep. 6 and continuing through Ep. 7, lead to another decrease. In none of the samples does the relative recovery in Ep. 8 regain the level of exploratory activity in Ep. 2.

Several propensities seem to be universal and function across all observed cultures: (a) stranger anxiety in young children, (b) proximity seeking to the attachment figure when distressed, (c) separation anxiety, (d) relaxation derived from bodily contact with the attachment figure, and (e) secure base behavior during exploration when not distressed. Thus, the functioning of the attachment-exploration balance in the behavior of young children can be observed in quite diverse cultures. Universally, caregivers offer protection that the child needs to be able to explore his environment safely in the service of adaptation everywhere.

Security and curiosity in young Trobriand children
The competence hypothesis posits that secure attachment is related to higher competence in dealing with developmental, social, and other challenging situations (Ainsworth & Bell, 1974). A central component of competence is open curiosity. It is at the basis for the motivation to meet new challenges. However, curiosity can give rise to wariness and fear. The ability to be curious and to concentrate during exploration seems to rest (a) on the ability to organize emotions and behaviors open-mindedly to "curious" events, and to do so "carefully"; and (b) on the confidence in the attachment figure's availability if help should be needed. Within secure attachment relationships, we see successful external regulation and negotiation of these negative emotions by the attachment figure, alleviating their distracting effects (K. E. Grossmann, K. Grossmann, & Zimmermann, 1999).

In our Trobriand study, we took the strangeness of the object that the child played with as an index of curiosity. The major activity of all toddlers was "making doba," i.e., trying to scrape bananas leaves, an activity that is highly valued in their culture. The next best-liked activity was playing ball, especially by the boys. However, the toddlers showed large individual differences in their play with the new and strange objects that were also available on the floor. Analyses of the relative amount of exploration of these unfamiliar objects as compared to playing with familiar objects revealed a significant difference between attachment statuses of the toddlers (see Figure 4). In the "Strange Situation," securely attached toddlers explored unfamiliar objects significantly more often than toddlers with an insecure attachment pattern. This finding could be replicated in part in our field observations of the same toddlers. Securely attached toddlers were found to play significantly more often with familiar and unfamiliar objects than insecurely attached toddlers while, at the same time, communicating more with their mothers during exploration (K. Grossmann et al., 2003). Thus, attachment security was related to curiosity and exploration in the young children of Tauwema in support of the competence hypothesis.
The analysis of maternal support of the exploration of their toddlers provided additional support for the competence hypothesis. In the "Strange Situations," securely attached children were significantly more frequently supported by their mothers when they played with the new objects (Keppler, 2000) and likewise, during the field observations, securely attached toddlers were supported by their mothers or

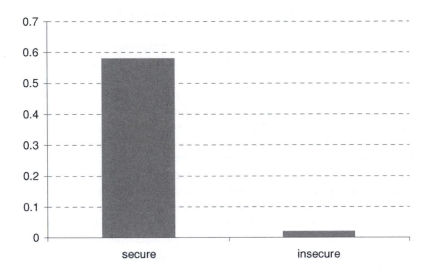

Figure 4. Relative Differences in Mean Frequency of Exploration of New Objects between Securely and Insecurely Attached Toddlers of Tauwema in the Strange Situation

other relatives during their exploration and especially during their exploration of new objects significantly more often than were insecurely attached toddlers (Liegel, 2001; K. Grossmann et al., 2003).

In summary, our observations of young children in the traditional culture of the Trobriand Islands supported the validity of four of the five fundamental hypotheses of attachment theory. All Tauwema toddlers were attached (universality) and the organization of their attachment and exploratory behaviors (attachment-exploration balance) expressed itself in three attachment patterns with the secure pattern being highly predominant (normativity). Tauwema toddlers secure in their attachment to mother were more curious when exploring unfamiliar objects of their environment than their insecurely attached peers (competence). Our observations did not provide enough detailed material to rate maternal sensitivity to all infant signals, but individual differences in maternal support of child exploration was obvious and related to attachment security.

However, the universality of the functioning of the attachment and exploratory behavioral systems does imply that it develops independent of various cultural influences. In contrast to customs in our society or western societies in general, Tauwema toddlers had almost constant access to their mother's breast and were cared for and looked after exclusively by relatives. Tauwema mothers rarely inhibited any activity of their toddlers except showing an interest in the objects that belonged to the researchers but, instead, strongly supported activities valued by their culture such as "making doba."

Conclusion: Attachment, Emotional Security, and Exploration across Cultures

Nature has programmed human beings as cultural beings. Proximate attachment development is the beginning of the ultimate necessity of cultural learning. Attachments are not an option free for any culture to "play" with, but a universal necessity for individual human development. There are definite limits of human adaptability to "inhumane" child rearing conditions as seen in the legendary sad outcomes of infants who were raised in large deindividualized groups as described by René Spitz (1945) and more recently by Kim Chisholm and her team for Romanian orphanages (Chisholm, Carter, Ames, & Morrison, 1995).

In all observed cultures, parents who protect and care for their children are not only the "havens of safety" to their children in situations of perceived danger and "secure bases" from which to explore when feeling safe but all of them also socialize their children into their culture, intentionally or not. Cultures define to a large extent what children should explore and in what skills they should become competent. Attachment theory posits that caring by committed parents who understand the child's needs, and who respond appropriately to the child's emotional expressions of needs and desires will have children who comply with their goals as individuals and members of the culture. Appropriateness will be determined in part by the socialization goals of the cultural group. Furthermore, there is sufficient evidence that committed compliance in childhood will develop into a caring, partnership-oriented commitment in adulthood (Egeland & Erickson, 1999; K. E. Grossmann, K. Grossmann, Winter, & Zimmermann, 2002).

In our conceptualization, emotional security depends on secure attachment that fosters emotionally secure exploration especially of unfamiliar and challenging aspects of the physical and social environment within the respective culture. This concept may lead to further validation of the ultimate perspective of attachment theory for individual emotional development within any culture. Healthy emotional development may be prevented or suffocated by overriding adverse conditions. Such conditions are apt to violate the enormous biological potential of man for successful and secure psychological development, even beyond attachment in the narrow sense but not without it. We propose: The five core hypotheses of attachment theory form the universal basis for psychologically adaptive, secure, and competent development of individuals in any culture, as long as the individual fulfills the ultimate genetic program within its biological boundaries.

References

Ainsworth, M. D. S. (1967). *Infancy in Uganda: Infant care and the growth of love.* Baltimore: Johns Hopkins University Press.

Ainsworth, M. D. S. (1979). Attachment as related to mother-infant interaction. In D. S. Lehrmann & R. A. Hinde (Eds.), *Advances in the study of behavior* (Vol. 9, pp. 2-51). New York: Academic Press.

Ainsworth, M. D. S., & Bell, S. M. (1974). Mother-infant interaction and the development of competence. In K. J. Connolly & J. Bruner (Eds.), *The growth of competence* (pp. 97-118). London: Academic Press.

Ainsworth, M. D. S., & Bell, S. M. (1977). Infant crying and maternal responsiveness: A rejoinder to Gewirtz and Boyd. *Child Development, 48,* 1208-1216.

Ainsworth, M. D. S., Bell, S. M., & Stayton, D. J. (1974). Infant-mother attachment and social development: "Socialization" as a product of reciprocal responsiveness to signals. In P. M. Richards (Ed.), *The integration of a child into a social world* (pp. 99-135). Cambridge, UK: Cambridge University Press.

Ainsworth, M. D. S., Blehar, M. C., Waters, E., & Wall, S. (1978). *Patterns of attachment. A psychological study of the strange situation.* Hillsdale, NJ: Erlbaum.

Ainsworth, M. D. S., & Bowlby, J. (1991). 1989 APA award recipient address. An ethological approach to personality development. *American Psychologist, 46,* 333-341.

Armstrong, E. (1991). The limbic system and culture: An allometric analysis of the neocortex and limbic nuclei. *Human Nature, 2,* 117-136.

Aviezer, O., & Sagi, A. (1999). The rise and fall of collective sleeping and its impact on the relationships of kibbutz children and parents. In W. Fölling & M. Fölling-Albers (Eds.), *The transformation of collective education in the kibbutz. The end of utopia?* (pp. 192-211). Frankfurt/M., Germany: Peter Lang.

Badinter, E. (1984). *Die Mutterliebe. Geschichte eines Gefühls vom 17. Jahrhundert bis heute.* Munich, Germany: Deutscher Taschenbuch Verlag. (Orig.: L'amour en plus, 1980; Motherlove. History of a feeling from the 17th century until today.)

Bischof-Köhler, D. (1998). Zusammenhänge zwischen kognitiver, motivationaler und emotionaler Entwicklung in der frühen Kindheit und im Vorschulalter [Relations between cognitive, motivational, and emotional development in early childhood]. In H. Keller (Ed.), *Lehrbuch Entwicklungspsychologie* (pp. 319-376). Bern, Switzerland: Verlag Hans Huber.

Bornstein, M. H. (Ed.). (1995). *Handbook of parenting.* Hillsdale, NJ: Erlbaum.

Bowlby, J. (1973). *Attachment and loss: Vol. 2. Separation: Anxiety and anger.* New York: Basic Books.

Bowlby, J. (1980). *Attachment and loss: Vol. 3. Loss: Sadness and depression.* New York: Basic Books.

Bowlby, J. (1982). *Attachment and loss: Vol. 1. Attachment.* (2nd rev. ed.). New York: Basic Books.

Bowlby, J. (1991). Postscript. In C. M. Parkes, J. Stevenson-Hinde, & P. Marris (Eds.), *Attachment across the life cycle* (pp. 293-297). New York: Routledge.

Bretherton, I., Golby, B., & Cho, E. (1997). Attachment and the transmission of values. In J. E. Grusec & L. Kuczynski (Eds.), *Parenting and children's internalization of values. A handbook of contemporary theory* (pp. 103-134). New York: Wiley.

Bruner, J. S. (1982). The organization of action and the nature of adult-infant transaction. In M. von Cranach & R. Harre (Eds.), *Analysis of action* (pp. 313-327). Cambridge, UK: Cambridge University Press.

Bruner, J. S. (1990). *Acts of meaning.* Cambridge, MA: Harvard University Press.

Buss, D. M. (1999). *Evolutionary psychology.* Boston: Allyn & Bacon.

Carlson, E., & Sroufe, L. A. (1995). Contribution of attachment theory to developmental psychology. In D. Cicchetti & D. Cohen (Eds.), *Developmental processes and psychopathology: Vol. 1. Theoretical perspectives and methodological approaches* (pp. 581-617). New York: Cambridge University Press.

Chao, R. (2001). Integrating culture and attachment. *American Psychologist, 56,* 822-823.

Chisholm, K. M., Carter, M. C., Ames, E. W., & Morrison, S. J. (1995). Attachment security and indiscriminately friendly behavior in children adopted from Romanian orphanages. *Development and Psychopathology, 7,* 283-294.

Cosmides, L., & Tooby, J. (2000). Evolutionary psychology and the emotions. In M. Lewis & J. M. Haviland-Jones (Eds.), *Handbook of emotions* (2nd ed., pp. 91-115). New York: The Guilford Press.

De Wolff, M. S., & van IJzendoorn, M. H. (1997). Sensitivity and attachment: A meta-analysis on parental antecedents of infant attachment. *Child Development, 68,* 571-746.

Donald, M. (1991). *Origins of the modern mind: Three stages in the evolution of culture and cognition.* Cambridge, MA: Harvard University Press.

Egeland, B., & Erickson, M. (1999). Findings from the parent-child project and implications for early intervention. *Zero to Three, 20,* 3-10.

Gjerde, P. (2001). Attachment, culture and amae. *American Psychologist, 56,* 826-827.

Grossmann, K. (1995). Eigene Werte und eigener Reichtum der Frauen von den Trobriand-Inseln (Papua-Newguinea) [Values and wealth of the women of the Trobriand Islands]. In H. Helfrich (Ed.), *Frauen zwischen Eigen- und Fremdkultur* (pp. 198-215). Münster, Germany: Daedalus Verlag.

Grossmann, K., & Grossmann, K. E. (1996). Kulturelle Perspektiven der Bindungsentwicklung in Japan und Deutschland [Cultural perspectives of attachment development in Japan and Germany]. In G. Trommsdorff & H.-J. Kornadt (Eds.), *Gesellschaftliche und individuelle Entwicklung in Japan und Deutschland* (pp. 215-235). Konstanz, Germany: Universitätsverlag Konstanz.

Grossmann, K., Grossmann, K. E., Fremmer-Bombik, E., Kindler, H., Scheuerer-Englisch, H., & Zimmermann, P. (2002). The uniqueness of the child-father attachment relationship: Fathers' sensitive and challenging play as the pivotal variable in a 16-year longitudinal study. *Social Development, 11*, 307-331.

Grossmann, K., Grossmann, K. E., Keppler, A., Liegel, M., & Schiefenhövel, W. (2003). Exploration, Spiel und die Anfänge kultureller Entwicklung beim Kind: Die Rolle der psychischen Sicherheit [Exploration, play, and the beginnings of cultural development in the child. The role of emotional security]. In M. Papousek & A. von Gontard (Eds.), *Spiel und Kreativität in der frühen Kindheit* (pp. 112-137). Stuttgart, Germany: Pfeiffer bei Klett-Cotta.

Grossmann, K., Grossmann, K. E., Spangler, G., Suess, G., & Unzner, L. (1985). Maternal sensitivity and newborns' orientation responses as related to quality of attachment in northern Germany. In I. Bretherton & E. Waters (Eds.), *Growing points in attachment theory and research. Monographs of the Society for Research in Child Development, 50* (1-2, Serial No. 209), 233-256.

Grossmann, K. E. (1995). The evolution and history of attachment research and theory. In S. Goldberg, R. Muir, & J. Kerr (Eds.), *Attachment theory: Social, developmental and clinical perspectives* (pp. 85-102). Hillsdale, NJ: The Analytic Press.

Grossmann, K. E., & Grossmann, K. (1981). Parent-infant attachment relationship in Bielefeld: A research note. In K. Immelmann, G. W. Barlow, L. Petrinovich, & M. Main (Eds.), *Behavioral development: The Bielefeld interdisciplinary project* (pp. 694-699). London: Cambridge University Press.

Grossmann, K. E., & Grossmann, K. (1996). Kindsein auf einer Südseeinsel. Kindliche Bindungen in kulturvergleichender Sicht [Being a child on a South See island. Childrens' attachments from a cultural-comparison perspective]. In C. E. Gottschalk-Batschkus & J. Schuler (Eds.), *Ethnomedizinische Perspektiven zur frühen Kindheit* (pp. 283-292). Berlin: Verlag für Wissenschaft und Bildung.

Grossmann, K. E., Grossmann, K., Winter, M., & Zimmermann, P. (2002). Attachment relationships and appraisal of partnership: From early experience of sensitive support to later relationship representation. In L. Pulkkinen & A. Caspi (Eds.), *Paths to successful development* (pp. 73-105). Cambridge, UK: Cambridge University Press.

Grossmann, K. E., Grossmann, K., & Zimmermann, P. (1999). A wider view of attachment and exploration: Stability and change during the years of immaturity. In J. Cassidy & P. R. Shaver (Eds.), *Handbook of attachment: Theory, research, and clinical applications* (pp. 760-786). New York: The Guilford Press.

Hinde, R. A. (1974). *Biological bases of human social behavior*. New York: McGraw Hill.

Hrdy, S. B. (1999). *Mother nature. A history of mothers, infants, and natural selection*. New York: Pantheon Books.

Imhof, A. E. (1984). Wandel der Säuglingssterblichkeit vom 18. bis 20. Jahrhundert [Changes in infant mortality from the 18th to the 20th century]. In H. Schaefer, H. Schipperges, & G. Wagner (Eds.), *Gesundheitspolitik. Historische und zeitkritische Analyse* (pp. 1-35). Cologne, Germany: Deutscher Ärzte-Verlag.

Keppler, A. (2000). *Bindungs- und Explorationsverhalten von 20 Kindern aus Tauwema, Papua-Neuguinea, in einer standardisierten Situation* [Attachment and exploration of 20 children from Tauwema, PNG, in a standardized situation]. Unpublished diploma thesis, Institut für Psychologie, Universität Regensburg, Germany.

Kondo-Ikemura, K. (2001). Insufficient evidence. *American Psychologist, 56,* 825-826.

Liegel, M. (2001). *Beobachtungen zum Explorations- und Bindungsverhalten einbis dreijähriger Trobriand Kinder* [Observations of exploratory and attachment behavior of one-to-three-year-old Trobriand children]. Unpublished diploma thesis, Institut für Psychologie, Universität Regensburg, Germany.

Malinowski, B. (1922-1935). *Argonauts of the Western Pacific. The sexual life of savages in North Western Melanesia. Coral gardens and their magic.* London: Routledge.

Meins, E. (1999). Sensitivity, security, and internal working models: Bridging the transmission gap. *Attachment and Human Development, 1,* 325-342.

Miyake, K., Chen, S.-J., Ujiie, T., Tajima, N., Satoh, K., & Takahashi, K. (1981). *Infant's temperamental disposition, mother's mode of interaction, quality of attachment, and infant's receptivity to sozialization.* Interim Progress Report, Research and Clinical Center for Child Development of the Hokkaido University, at Sapporo, Japan.

Portmann, A. (1956). *Zoologie und das neue Bild des Menschen. Biologische Fragmente zu einer Lehre vom Menschen* [Zoology and the new picture of man. Biological fragments for a theory of man]. Hamburg, Germany: Rowohlt.

Posada, G., & Jacobs, A. (2001). Child-mother attachment relationship and culture. *American Psychologist, 56,* 821-822.

Posada, G., Jacobs, A., Carbonell, O. A., Alzate, G., Bustamante, M. R., & Arenas, A. (1999). Maternal care and attachment security in ordinary and emergency contexts. *Developmental Psychology, 35,* 1379-1388.

Rothbaum, F., Weisz, J., Pott, M., Miyake, K., & Morelli, G. (2000). Attachment and Culture. Security in the United States and Japan. *American Psychologist, 55,* 1093-1104.

Sagi, A., van IJzendoorn, M. H., Aviezer, O., Donnell, F., Koren-Karie, N., Joels, T., & Havel, Y. (1995). Attachments in a multiple-caregiver and multiple-infant environment: The case of the Israeli Kibbutzim. In E. Waters, B. E. Vaughn, G. Posada, & K. Kondo-Ikemura (Eds.), *Caregiving, cultural, and cognitive perspectives on secure-base behavior and working models: New growing points of attachment theory and research. Monographs of the Society for Research in Child Development, 60* (2-3, Serial No. 244, pp. 71-91).

Sagi, A., van IJzendoorn, M. H., Aviezer, O., Donnell, F., & Mayseless, O. (1994). Sleeping out of home in a Kibbutz communal arrangement: It makes a difference for infant-mother attachment. *Child Development, 65,* 902-1004.

Sander, L. (1975). Infant and caretaking environment. In E. J. Anthony (Ed.), *Explorations in child psychiatry* (pp. 129-165). New York: Plenum.

Schiefenhövel, W., & Bell-Krannhals, I. (1996). Of harvest and hierarchies: Securing staple food and social position in the Trobriand Islands. In P. Wiesauer & W. Schiefenhövel (Eds.), *Food and the status quest. An interdisciplinary perspective* (pp. 235-251). Providence, UK: Berghan.

Schiefenhövel, W., Uher, J., & Krell, R. (Eds.). (1996). Im Spiegel der Anderen [In the mirror of the others]. München, Germany: Realis Verlags-GmbH.

Spangler, G., & Grossmann, K. (1995). Zwanzig Jahre Bindungsforschung in Bielefeld und Regensburg [Twenty years of attachment research in Bielefeld and Regensburg]. In G. Spangler & P. Zimmermann (Eds.), *Die Bindungstheorie. Grundlagen, Forschung und Anwendung* (pp. 50-63). Stuttgart, Germany: Klett-Cotta.

Spangler, G., Grossmann, K. E., & Schieche, M. (2002). Psychobiologische Grundlagen der Organisation des Bindungsverhaltenssystems im Kleinkindalter [Psychobiological bases of the organization of the attachment behavioral system in infancy]. *Psychologie in Erziehung und Unterricht, 49,* 102-120.

Spitz, R. A. (1945). Hospitalism. *Psychoanalytic Study of the Child, 1,* 53-74.

Sternberg, R. J. (1997). The concept of intelligence and its role in lifelong learning and success. *American Psychologist, 52,* 1030-1037.

Takahashi, K. (1990). Are the key assumptions of the "Strange Situation" procedure universal? A view from Japanese research. *Human Development, 33,* 23 - 30.

Thompson, R. A. (1998). Early sociopersonality development. In W. Damon (Series Ed.) & N. Eisenberg, (Vol. Ed.), *Handbook of Child Psychology: Vol. 3. Social, Emotional, and Personality Development* (pp. 25-104). New York: Wiley.

Tomasello, M. (1999). *The cultural origins of human cognition.* London: Harvard University Press.

Trevarthen, C. (1987). Brain development. In R. L. Gregory (Ed.), *The Oxford companion to the mind* (pp. 101-110). Oxford, UK: Oxford University Press.

Trommsdorff, G., & Friedlmeier, W. (1993). Control and responsiveness in Japanese and German mother-child interactions. *Early Development and Parenting, 2,* 65-78.

True, M. M., Pisani, L., & Oumar, F. (2001). Infant-mother attachment among the Dogon of Mali. *Child Development, 72,* 1451-1466.

Valenzuela, M. (1997). Maternal sensitivity in a developing society: The context of urban poverty and infant chronic under nutrition. *Developmental Psychology, 33,* 845-855.

van IJzendoorn, M. H., & Sagi, A. (1999). Cross-cultural patterns of attachment: Universal and contextual determinants. In J. Cassidy & P. R. Shaver (Eds.), *Handbook of attachment theory and research* (pp. 713-734). New York: The Guilford Press.

van IJzendoorn, M. H., & Sagi, A. (2001). Cultural blindness or selective inattention? *American Psychologist, 56,* 824-825.

Weiner, A. B. (1976). *Women of value, men of renown: New perspectives in Trobriand exchange.* Austin, TX: University of Texas Press.

Zevalkink, J., Riksen-Walraven, J. M., & van Lieshout, C. F. M. (1999). Attachment in the Indonesian caregiving context. *Social Development, 8*, 21-40.

5

Attachment and Culture: Bridging Relativism and Universalism

Fred Rothbaum and Gilda Morelli

"...a deeper understanding of human psychology will develop when the same or parallel phenomena are observed and interpreted by researchers from different cultures." (Azuma, 1996, p. 221)

Introduction

In the millennial edition of Child Development (January, 2000), Everett Waters and Marc Cummings highlight an extremely fertile but largely uncharted territory for attachment research in the 21st century: "Cross-cultural research on key issues in attachment theory is one of the most exciting prospects for the next generation of attachment research" (Waters & Cummings, 2000, p. 169).

In this chapter we ask *why* cultural research on attachment is exciting – what can it teach us about human development? We question whether the value of such research lies primarily in its ability to confirm or deny the universality of attachment theory claims. While the identification of universals is a valuable research goal, our underlying assumption is that cultural studies can accomplish much more (see also Chakkarath, this volume; Friedlmeier, this volume).

We view cultural studies as the "royal road" to understanding the co-mingling of variability and universality in attachment behavior. Studies on the ways cultures vary are important because they provide texture to our understanding of key attachment theory phenomena such as sensitive caregiving and social competence presumed to be a consequence of secure attachment. Attachment theorists acknowledge that there are differences between cultures in the ways that these phenomena are manifested, but they neither focus on nor describe the variation. As a result, we are left with overly abstract descriptions of key attachment phenomena or with specific descriptions that have a western slant. For example, sensitivity is defined in terms of vague modifiers such as "timely" and "appropriate" responsiveness; we know little about what timeliness or appropriateness mean – except in a western context. When descriptions of key attachment theory phenomena are designed to fit the western case, they do not do justice to the richness, complexity and myriad manifestations of those phenomena elsewhere.

In seeking to understand how cultural processes are involved in the similarities and variations in human attachment, we adopt a sociocultural perspective. A major assumption underlying this perspective is that biological and social processes co-evolved (Bruner, 1990; Rogoff, 1990, 2003; Valsiner, 2000). A sociocultural approach to studying attachment would enable us to flesh out concepts like timeliness and appropriate responsiveness in contextually meaningful ways. This is because it uses activity as the unit of analysis. Activity is constituted by the child and her social partners as well as by the local values, beliefs, traditions, and settings in which it is embedded. Aspects of activity do not exist separate from each other; it is not possible to understand the child's activity, for example, without considering the partner's contributions. Research may focus on one aspect of activity as an analytic strategy, but must consider findings in light of other aspects, or risk destroying the reality of the phenomenon under study (see Friedlmeier, this volume; Rogoff & Angelillo, 2002).

A sociocultural approach can do more than flesh out our descriptions of key attachment theory constructs. It can also lead to important modifications in these constructs. For example, sensitivity is often equated with responsiveness; yet we believe that the study of other cultures will lead to increasing emphasis on proactive/anticipatory (as contrasted with reactive/responsive) forms of sensitivity (evidence for this is provided later). Moreover, we believe that the construct of secure base, which lies even nearer the heart of attachment theory, may be recast as a result of studies adopting a sociocultural approach: We expect there will be less emphasis on exploration of the physical environment and more emphasis on social forms of engaging and learning about the environment. A recasting of attachment theory along these lines highlights the co-mingling of variability and universality in attachment behavior.

It is important to clarify what our disagreement with attachment theorists is *not* about: We do *not* disagree with attachment theorists' claim that there are basic biological predispositions underlying attachment. And the debate is *not* primarily about the fact that we are assigning a greater role to culture. Rather the debate is about the relationship between culture and biology. We argue that biology and culture are inseparable and fused. We believe that the study of attachment should be always mindful of the particular cultural context. Until very recently, this has not been the case – cross-cultural attachment research has been overwhelmingly focused on proving the universality of the theory. Cultural variation is acknowledged in theory, but it is not a focus of research (e.g., K. Grossmann, K. E. Grossmann, & Keppler, this volume; van IJzendoorn & Sagi, 1999).

We believe that attachment theory has much to tell us about human development across cultures, both because of Bowlby's conceptual foundation (in evolutionary theory and ethology) and Ainsworth's early cultural studies in Uganda. As we noted elsewhere, "there is much to admire about attachment theory, not least of which is its remarkable generativity and empirical orientation;" moreover, we suggested that increased cultural research "may, in fact, reveal what an intellectual treasure chest attachment theory truly is" (Rothbaum, Weisz, Pott, Miyake, & Morelli, 2000, p. 1102).

Recent efforts to apply core attachment theory constructs to other peoples (including but not limited to Chileans, Columbians, the Dogon of Mali, and Trobriand Islanders) have not raised alarms about the relevance of the theory in these varied contexts and in fact have led to findings predicted by the theory. These successes strongly suggest that there are basic aspects of the theory that are relevant in very different contexts.

In the long run, we suspect that the cultural studies conducted by attachment researchers will be seen as having played a critical role in illuminating the interplay of culture and attachment. While most of the studies to date are limited by both their parochial intent (to find evidence of universality, rather than to examine the co-mingling of variation and universality), and methodology (almost exclusive use of western measures; failure to focus on indigenous concepts and hypotheses), they have ushered in a new era of attachment research. These early studies on culture and attachment raised fundamental questions about universality and they provided relevant data. Without this groundbreaking research there would not be the kind of healthy tension between approaches and between views of attachment that are the focus of this chapter.

In the sections that follow, we examine research on variations and similarities in attachment relationships across cultures. In the first section, we review evidence that calls into question the universality of core hypotheses of attachment theory. This section is primarily concerned with research by investigators focused on *variation* in attachment behavior. In the second section, we provide a brief review of recent evidence from cultural studies on attachment that focus on *universal* processes. We highlight findings that are most strongly supported by these studies. In the third section, we propose a shift in paradigms for thinking about and investigating attachment. We claim that other theorists, including attachment theorists, have already laid the foundation for this shift. The final section provides guidelines for future cultural research – methods that are needed to further our understanding of cultural variation as well as cultural similarities. We end with a brief conclusion.

Studies Highlighting Cultural Variation in Attachment

This section begins with a brief mention of Mary Ainsworth's (1967) early research in Uganda and a summary of our own review of Japanese-US differences in attachment. Most of this section, however, is devoted to a description of other emic and derived etic research on attachment, examining its antecedents, consequences and nature (i.e., the notion of secure base).

In an emic approach, the researcher attempts to represent cultural processes as an "insider." In a derived etic approach, the researcher adapts tools, concepts, and interpretations developed in one culture (usually the US) in ways that make sense to the local community. While an emic approach is optimal in terms of capturing local conditions and the particulars of a community, a derived etic approach enables researchers to make comparisons and contrasts between cultures, an important step in building a theory of attachment. We feature emic and derived etic approaches to research because they take into consideration local values and practices of the people studied, which is essential to understanding developmental processes. Ainsworth expressed this view as well when she noted, "Let us not blind ourselves to the unusual features of the unfamiliar society by limiting ourselves to variables or to procedures based on the familiar society – our own" (Ainsworth, 1976, p. 145).

Ainsworth's work in Uganda
Even though Ainsworth's (1967) systematic observations in Uganda are often cited as evidence of universal processes, she was very mindful of the role of context. In her conclusions she stated: "Attachment does not develop willy nilly according to some inner, genetic, regulating mechanism, but rather is influenced by conditions in the baby's environment" (p. 387).

Ainsworth's work in Uganda led her to look more closely at aspects of infants' relationship with their caregivers that were considered universal. For example, she commented that stranger anxiety in part "... depends on accidents of individual experience" (pp. 440-441) and she cites culture-laden factors, such as familiarity with strangers, as critical determinants. Based on her Uganda findings, she also placed more emphasis on multiple caregivers ("substitute mothers") than she did in

her later US studies. And her observations regarding the relationship between weaning and attachment led her to conclude, "one must evaluate an infant care practice in
its context" (p. 457).

We include Mary Ainsworth's Uganda research in this section because of her
emphasis on the degree to which context is critical in understanding a number of
attachment related phenomena. However, there is little doubt that Ainsworth was
more focused on cultural similarities than cultural variation. Perhaps because of this
focus, her early cultural perspective was relied on less often to guide research.

Cross-cultural evidence from Japan and the US
We view our own work on attachment theory as an effort to underscore Mary Ainsworth's emphasis on context. In one paper, our colleagues – John Weisz, Martha
Pott, and Kazuo Miyake – and we called into question the universality of attachment
theory on the grounds that it was rooted in western ideas and assumptions and was
based primarily on western samples (Rothbaum et al., 2000). We maintained that
three core hypotheses of attachment theory, involving the antecedents (sensitivity),
consequences (social competence), and nature (secure base) of secure attachment,
are biased toward western ways of thinking and acting. These hypotheses emphasize
values such as autonomy, exploration and other forms of individuation. Our review
of the evidence leads us to believe that, in Japan, the antecedents, consequences, and
nature of secure attachment have more to do with Eastern values such as interdependence, harmony, and other forms of accommodation. To understand better these
cultural differences, we advocate an approach that is grounded in concepts that are
most meaningful to the peoples being examined.

In support of our claim that attachment theorists' descriptions of antecedents of
security reflect western values, we highlight biases in their measures of sensitive
caregiving. For example, Ainsworth (1976) describes high level sensitivity as follows: "[the mother] values the fact that the baby has a will of its own ... finds his
anger worthy of respect ... respects the baby as a separate autonomous person" (p.
4). This description clearly reflects a bias toward individuation.

With respect to consequences of security, attachment theorists emphasize western values such as autonomy, self-esteem, exploration, self-assertion, and low dependence. By contrast, "From [an East Asian] perspective, an assertive, autonomous...person is immature and uncultivated" (Fiske, Kitayama, Markus, & Nisbett,
1998, p. 923).

If there are cultural differences in the antecedents and consequences of security,
it stands to reason there may be cultural differences in the nature of security. Support
for this idea comes from research showing that Japanese babies are especially oriented to their mothers in stressful situations (Bornstein, Azuma, Tamis-LeMonda, &
Ogino, 1990; Friedlmeier & Trommsdorff, 1999; Miyake, Chen, & Campos, 1985).

Moreover, these children experience more sadness and dependent behaviors [amae] when separated from their mothers (Mizuta, Zahn-Waxler, Cole, & Hiruma, 1996), and they explore less, especially in the strange situation, than western babies (Takahashi, 1990). Mizuta et al. (1996) suggest that attachment for the Japanese "... is aroused by loss more than by exploratory risk" (p. 156).

Other emic and derived etic studies on attachment

As illustrated by the above studies, a sociocultural perspective emphasizes the importance of local values and practices of the people studied. Several other studies have adopted this approach to learn more about differences in the antecedents, consequences and the nature of attachment relationships across cultures. We review these studies below.

Antecedents of security

There is evidence that aspects of caregiving that relate to security of attachment are not the same across cultures. For example Carlson and Harwood (2003) found that, as predicted, mothers' physical control relates to insecure attachment in Anglo-American families, but not in Puerto Rican families: "The highest ratings of physical control were associated with secure 12-month attachment status for these middle-class Puerto Rican dyads. This apparently paradoxical finding highlights the need for culturally-specific definitions of sensitive caregiving" (p. 17).

This finding is understood when physical control is considered as part of a larger system of practices and beliefs among the Puerto Rican mothers. According to Carlson and Harwood:

> Teaching infants to be attentive, calm, and well behaved requires considerable more physical prompting and control than teaching infants to be assertive and self-confident. Thus it appears that maternal use of physical control may be regulated by maternal socialization goals. (p. 18)

Interestingly, parental control, directiveness, and strictness are more valued and emphasized in many cultural and ethnic communities – including African-American, Korean, Chinese and Iranian – than they are among Euro-Americans (Carlson & Harwood, 2003). Future research may show an association between parental control and security in all of these cultural groups.

By contrast, attachment theorists maintain that efforts to physically control, shape or interfere with infants' activity are associated with insensitivity and insecurity. The cultural evidence suggests that an association between autonomy fostering and security – which is assumed to be universal by attachment theorists (Allen &

Land, 1999; Belsky, Rosenberger, & Crnic, 1995) – may be a predominantly western phenomenon.

The circumstances associated with contingent responsiveness also vary across cultures, and this may have implications for security of attachment. Cameroonian and German mothers, for example, differ in their responsiveness to positive and negative infant signals – Cameroonian mothers are more likely to respond to infants' signs of distress, German mothers to infants' positive signals (Völker, Yovsi, & Keller, 1998). Friedlmeier and Trommsdorff (1999) and LeVine (2004) reported similar differences between non-western and western mothers. LeVine's findings indicate that Gusii mothers of Kenya are more responsive to their babies' distressed vocalizations than are middle-class US mothers, and that Gusii babies cry less than the US babies. Gusii mothers' practice of maintaining nearly constant contact with babies in the first year of life allows them to respond quickly to their infants' distress. Gusii mothers are shocked by videos of American mothers allowing infants to cry, even momentarily. For Gusii mothers, prevention of crying through continuous contact is morally mandated. Yet, Gusii moms show little responsiveness to positive signals. Unlike middle-class US mothers, they do not amplify interactive excitement but turn away from infants who are getting positively excited so as to calm and soothe their babies (LeVine, 2004).

Cultural studies suggest as well that the timing of caregivers' response to babies' signals may not be the same across cultures. Western investigators evaluate caregiver's behavior in terms of its *responsiveness* – how soon *after* the child's overt signal the response occurs. However, studies in other cultures emphasize the ways in which caregivers *anticipate* shifts in a baby's emotional state, and respond proactively (or respond to very subtle and covert signals). Anticipatory responsiveness is reported among the Japanese (Friedlmeier & Trommsdorff, 2004), Nso of Cameroon (Völker et al., 1998), and Puerto Ricans and Central American immigrants in the US (Harwood, 1992).

Cultural differences in proactive compared to reactive response to babies signals may reflect different cultural priorities regarding the development of independent/individualistic or interdependent/symbiotic forms of competence (Keller et al., 2003). Findings from a recent pilot interview study of Japanese and US mothers (n = 30) support this speculation (Rothbaum & Yamaguchi, 2004). Most mothers in both countries (79% and 90% respectively) maintain that anticipating children's needs is more likely to foster accommodative behaviors in their children (i.e., empathy, propriety, compliance) than individualistic behaviors (i.e., exploration, autonomy, self assertion). At the same time, these mothers (93% of the Japanese and 100% of the Americans) maintain that responsiveness (waiting until the child signals a need before responding) is more likely to foster individualistic than accommodative behaviors (cf. Trommsdorff & Friedlmeier, 1993). That is, mothers in both cultures agree that anticipating and responding to needs lead to different developmental out-comes. These findings suggest one reason why mothers from non-western cultures may be more predisposed to anticipating needs – because it is especially effective in fostering outcomes that they value highly.

Other studies support this view by showing that sensitivity to children's auton-omy varies across cultures. For example, preliminary findings from Dennis, Cole, Zahn-Waxler, and Mizuta (2003), who examined the contingent responsiveness of mothers to children's bids for autonomy or relatedness, indicate that US mothers exhibit greater autonomy (e.g., discussing one's own separate experience, wants, feelings) and positivity than Japanese mothers when responding to child autonomy. Keller et al. (2003) also reported cultural differences in responsiveness to autonomy. The latter investigators found that urban, formally educated (Germany and Greek) mothers as compared to traditional, rural, not formally educated (Cameroonian Nso, Indian Gujarati, and Costa Rican Carer) mothers place more emphasis on face-to-face communication and object stimulation – caregiving practices that, according to Keller et al. (2003), foster greater autonomy. Taken together, these findings show that circumstances associated with sensitivity vary across cultures, and cast doubt on Ainsworth's assumption that there is a universal relationship between sensitive care-giving and encouragement of autonomy (Ainsworth, 1976).

Consequences of security
Conceptions of competence are not the same across cultures. Keller (2003) notes that western-based ideas of competence – which emphasize individual ability, culti-vation of the individual mind, exploration, discovery and personal achievement – are fundamentally different from conceptions seen in many other societies, like the Baolue of Ivory Coast; A-Chew of Zambia; Nso of Cameroon; Cree of Alaska; Hindu of India; and Chinese of mainland China and Taiwan. In these non-western societies, competence is considered as "moral self cultivation, a social contribution, discouraging individual celebration of achievement [and] the ability to maintain social harmony" (p. 2) as well as respect of elders and acceptance of social roles.

Other cultural studies support Keller's view. In their conversations with mothers, Harwood and her colleagues found that while Anglo-American mothers' views of social competence centered on self maximization and independence, as seen in their emphasis on autonomy, happiness, confidence and exploration, Puerto Rican moth-ers' views did not (Harwood, Miller, & Irizarry, 1995). Instead, for these Puerto Rican mothers, social competence involved "proper demeanor" and interdepend-ence, as seen in their emphasis on respect, obedience, calmness, politeness, gentle-ness, and kindness. Proper demeanor refers to more than appropriate ways of relat-ing to others; it also refers to what is described in English as "teachable." In addition to the characteristics described above, it involves a receptivity to one's elders "… in order to become skilled in the interpersonal and rhetorical competencies that will someday be expected of the well-socialized adult" (p. 98).

Interestingly there is a Japanese concept that parallels the Puerto Rican notion of proper demeanor. *Sunao*, which is difficult to translate in English, refers to an array of characteristics including but not limited to open mindedness, nonresistance, and obedience (White & LeVine, 1986). If attachment research had its origins in non-western cultures, we suspect that qualities like proper demeanor and sunao would be considered universal consequences of security.

Taken together, these findings suggest that a pre-condition for understanding the association between attachment security and social competence is awareness of cultural differences in the meaning of social competence.

The nature of security

There are few cultural studies examining the nature of security. To our knowledge, Harwood and her colleagues are the only ones who have used open-ended methods to explore indigenous concepts pertaining to the nature of the secure base (Harwood et al., 1995). These investigators focused on the key attachment theory concept of optimal balance (alternating between exploration/autonomy and attach-ment/relatedness). They found that "Puerto Rican mothers conceptualized optimal balance in terms of ... a contextually appropriate balancing of calm, respectful atten-tiveness with positive engagement in interpersonal relationships" (rather than) "[...] in terms of autonomy and relatedness" (p. 112).

As expected, the balance of autonomy and relatedness was the primary theme emerging from the interviews with the Anglo-American mothers. In summarizing their findings, Harwood et al. (1995) comment: "The construct of security versus insecurity has become equated in US psychology with a host of culturally valued qualities that are specific to the socialization goals of our highly individualistic soci-ety, thus limiting their cross-cultural meaningfulness" (p. 114). This captures well our concerns about current conceptualizations of security.

Studies Highlighting Cultural Similarities in Attachment

In our earlier paper (Rothbaum et al., 2000) we dealt very briefly with evidence of universals. Our goal was to highlight cultural differences that had not been ade-quately considered "to foster an enriched understanding of what is culturally specific about human attachment" (p. 1094). We focused on limitations in prior studies that claim to demonstrate universals because we believe that their *conclusions* about universality were premature. The universals we criticized were ones which conflated abstract constructs, like sensitivity, with operational definitions of those constructs that reflected western views about appropriate ways of acting.

We firmly believe that there *are* universal predispositions to form attachment relationships, including universals involving the antecedents, consequences and nature of security, even though our earlier work did not focus on them. It would be silly to expect otherwise, given what we have learned about so many other psychological processes, from those far removed from attachment (color perception and language) to those that are closely related (emotional expression). However, at this point we can only guess what those universal predispositions are. We believe that descriptions of universals are necessarily tied to descriptions of the diverse ways in which biological predispositions are manifested in different settings, and that we have only begun to identify that diversity.

In this section we consider the merits of the universalist position and pay closer attention to evidence from the studies that champion it. Our goal here is to move beyond a focus on cultural differences and to join forces with "authors (who) have argued for the importance of taking into consideration both a universal and a culture-specific perspective" (Posada et al., 2002, p. 69). For the most part, the studies reviewed below adopt an imposed etic approach in studying attachment. That is, measures developed in one culture (typically the US) were used in other cultures in order to provide comparisons between the cultures. To a limited extent these studies also employed a derived etic approach, i.e., they used standardized measures originating in one culture, but adapted the measures so as to make them more meaningful to the people studied. It is this adaptation that offers the greatest promise for integrating what we know about cultural similarities and differences, and for advancing attachment theory.

Evidence of cultural similarities in antecedents of attachment

In the earlier review we complained that "there is remarkably little cross-cultural research in the attachment field" (p. 1094), and noted that a recent review on culture and attachment (van IJzendoorn & Sagi, 1999) identified only 14 studies. We criticized the research on sensitivity, arguing that the evidence of universals was not compelling and that prior studies had relied on indirect measures of sensitivity.

However, the evidence regarding the sensitivity-security association is increasingly compelling. The one highly relevant study that we were aware of at the time of our earlier review (Vereijken, Riksen-Walraven, & Kondo-Ikemura, 1997) was mentioned by us in a footnote. We were concerned that the methods employed were problematic and that the findings were much stronger than what could reasonably be expected given the findings reported by the majority of studies, thus increasing doubts about the methods (Rothbaum, Weisz, Pott, Miyake, & Morelli, 2001). Now there are several studies from non-western communities – including Bogota, Columbia (Posada, Jacobs, Carbonell, Alzate, Bustamante, & Arenas, 1999; Posada et al., 2002), the Dogon of Mali (True, Pisani, & Oumar, 2001), and Chile (Valenzuela, 1997) – showing significant associations between sensitivity and security. The evidence indicates that sensitivity predicts attachment security in diverse cultural contexts, even when the two constructs are assessed at different times and in different situations (Posada et al., 2002), and when they are coded by different observers (Posada et al., 2002; Valenzuela, 1997). This constitutes important evidence in support of the sensitivity hypothesis.

The fact that these studies relied on measures of caregiving that were similar or identical to those developed by Ainsworth suggests that her measures are valid in many cultures. It seems that her broad constructs – especially sensitivity to signals, but also accessibility, cooperation with ongoing behavior, and acceptance of the child – tap into important qualities of human caregiving, even though Ainsworth's descriptions of these constructs are grounded in western values. As noted by advocates of the universalist position, this is not surprising given that it was Ainsworth's observations in a non-western culture, Uganda, that provided the foundation for her later work on caregiving.

While the recent evidence of universals is of substantial value, we must be mindful of local variation in conceptions of sensitivity, including the circumstances related to its expression. Moreover, we must develop ways to evaluate sensitivity that make sense to the community studied. Since the concept of sensitivity is grounded in the concept of "appropriateness" it can never be divorced from local contexts and meanings. Until recently, this view was championed by only a handful of researchers (Harwood et al., 1995; Lamb, Thompson, Gardner, & Charnov, 1985: LeVine & Miller, 1990); however, it is now becoming widespread. For example, Posada et al. (2002), major spokespersons for the universalist position, recently wrote: "Ideally, naturalistic observations of caregiving behavior ... in different situations and in different cultures would be key in documenting specific ways in which caregiving behavior is implemented (e.g., LeVine, 1974). This kind of research can only enrich attachment theory and is needed" (p. 76). We agree.

Despite the value of the etic research cited above, we see limitations. Since observers have had to rely on western measures – with little or no adaptation – they may have forced observations of indigenous phenomena into categories that do not quite fit but are the only ones available. For example, if an observer believes that a mother is anticipating her child's signals, but there is no category for anticipating signals, the observer may be forced to code the mother's behavior as "responsive." Research in a variety of cultural contexts involving naturalistic and ethnographic measures is needed to address these concerns.

Particularly exciting to us are suggestions from the aforementioned studies of cultural differences amidst the cultural similarities. For example, in their investigation of the Dogon of Mali, True et al. (2001) found that maternal frightened or frightening behavior predicts attachment insecurity far better than do more general measures of maternal insensitivity. These maternal variables have only rarely been a focus of research in the West (primarily in studies of disorganized attachment). It is possible that, in cultures where physical dangers are common, sensitivity may more often be expressed in ways that protect the infant from harm. Given that one of the unique features of primate attachment is the ability of the mother to reduce the infant's fear and associated physiological arousal via direct contact and soothing behavior (Suomi, 1999), these findings are not surprising. The failure to focus on the regulation of fear may again reflect the bias toward studying western samples.

As another example, the findings of Posada et al. (2002) indicate that maternal interference predicts (inversely) attachment security in the US, but not in Bogota Columbia, and that active-animated behavior by mothers predicts security in Bogota but not in the US. The authors suggest that their findings may be partly due to cultural differences in the emphasis on and/or frequency of the behaviors at issue (e.g., active animated behavior is more valued and common in Bogota). Since low levels of maternal interference/intrusion have in the past been regarded as universal features of sensitivity, the Posada et al. (2002) findings underscore the need for more research on cultural variation in sensitivity. Posada et al. (2002) conclude "there may be unique domains of maternal behavior in different contexts [and] their associations with security may vary by context" (p. 76). That is, there may be aspects of maternal behavior that are both more common and more associated with security in certain communities or settings.

While we are encouraged by research like this that considers local views relevant to attachment, we believe that an emic approach to research can lead to much more than the identification of "unique domains." Cultural practices do not exist independent of one another but are part of an integrated and coordinated system that help to create regularities in children's experiences over time and place. The search for regularities and exceptions to regularities relates to Waters and Valenzuela's (1999) quest to understand underlying processes – processes that they suggest constitute the next great frontier for attachment theory. These investigators further suggest that cultural studies can play a pivotal role in illuminating underlying processes. We agree that the study of cultural variations and similarities is likely to lead the way to this new frontier, much as Ainsworth's study in Uganda paved the way for so many early attachment theory insights.

Evidence of cultural similarities in consequences of attachment

In our earlier paper (Rothbaum et al., 2000) we highlighted cultural differences in social competence. These differences have not been a focus of attachment theorists, leading to the mistaken conclusion that secure attachment universally leads to outcomes that are valued and regarded as competent in the West, such as exploration independence, self esteem, and mastery of the environment.

What we did not highlight in the earlier paper is that, when competence is defined as health and nutrition, there *is* cross-cultural evidence of an association between security and competence (evidence reviewed in van IJzendoorn & Sagi, 1999). In retrospect, this is an important finding that clarifies the complex interplay between universal predisposition and cultural context. Most studies in the West focus on social forms of competence because good health (relative to children growing up in poor countries) is taken for granted. The notion that there are cultural differences in the form that competence takes is consistent with LeVine's analysis of factors that guide parenting practices (LeVine, 1974, 1988). He posits that, first and foremost, parents are concerned with promoting the survival and health of their children. Even though they may do this in ways that foster the development of valued ways of thinking and acting, he suggests that practices concerned with fostering other cultural values come to the foreground only when this first goal – ensuring survival and health – is met with relative certainty.*

We also did not acknowledge in our earlier review the very exciting possibility that certain forms of social competence universally follow from secure attachment. There is evidence of an association between security and social competence in non-human primates. Infant rhesus monkeys exhibiting secure behavior grow up to become adolescents and adults who have higher status and raise offspring who are themselves secure, even when they are not the biological parents (Suomi, 1999). The primate evidence complements evidence of cross-generational transmission of attachment security in humans – at least among humans from western cultures (van IJzendoorn, 1995). An important next step is to determine if cross-generational transmission is widespread among humans, and at the same time to examine differences in the way it is manifested.

Evidence of cultural similarities in the nature of the secure base

Because our earlier report (Rothbaum et al., 2000) was intended to highlight human variation in the manifestation of security, we did not sufficiently acknowledge important ways in which humans were similar. Human infants throughout the world, and closely related non-human primate infants, exhibit predictable forms of behavior – including sucking, clinging, crying and following – in their effort to obtain and maintain physical contact with and proximity to their primary caregivers, and their caregivers manifest complementary behaviors (Suomi, 1999). Moreover it is clear

---

* We do not mean to suggest that there is a linear pathway from maternal sensitivity and care to children's health status. There are many reasons why a child's health may be compromised; we suspect that maternal sensitivity plays a role only sometimes and that sensitivity can be a consequence or correlate as well as a cause of health outcomes.

that these attachment behaviors are activated by perceived dangers in the environment. The numerous naturalistic and controlled observations of these behaviors by attachment researchers in cultures throughout the world provide a great deal of support that this "safe haven" phenomenon is indeed widespread if not universal.

Similarly, we did not emphasize enough the widespread nature of the secure base phenomenon (of which safe haven is one component). While we did acknowledge that "observations of infants in different cultures [and different species] suggest that there may be a biological basis to the link between attachment and exploration" (Rothbaum et al., 2000; p. 1099), there were more qualifications of this statement than elaborations of it. Attachment theorists highlight the secure base because they believe that the attachment system and the exploration system are very closely linked. As with the safe haven phenomenon, there are ample naturalistic and controlled laboratory observations of this phenomenon in diverse settings to conclude that there is something about it that is widespread. The work by Posada et al. (1995) on parents' beliefs about secure base behavior in seven cultures provides further evidence of the cultural similarities as does the chapter by Grossmann, Grossmann, and Keppler. (2003, this volume), which summarizes evidence of predictable variation in exploration behavior across the strange situation episodes in different cultures.

Why did we not more enthusiastically embrace the conclusion that the secure base is universal? First, we believed – and continue to be believe – that there are other important behavioral systems that are closely linked to attachment (e.g., interdependence) and that cultural study will illuminate these other systems. Interestingly, it was Ainsworth's research in Uganda that led her to conclude that the attachment system can be closely linked to the feeding system in certain cultures – a conclusion recently echoed by True et al. (2001). Researchers who rely on western measures, as did the one of Posada et al. (1995), are unlikely to unveil these other behavioral systems.

There is another reason why we question the centrality of the attachment-exploration balance. It has to do with the notion of *exploration*, which has connotations of independent if not solitary activity, mastery of the environment, and a penchant for the unknown. While we believe there is a secure base of the type described by attachment theorists, we would depict it as a balance between contact with the attachment figure and re-*engaging* the wider social world. That is, the balance is a means of regulating the scope of social involvements – when threats are salient children focus attention, proximity and contact on the attachment figure; when children feel secure they broaden their social involvements to include other partners and activities (i.e., exploration).

Viewed from this perspective, social partners guide the child's participation in the outside world and they do so in ways that reflect current circumstances, and cultural values and traditions. Their guidance fosters the child's understanding of appropriate ways of acting and thinking (Bruner, 1990; Rogoff, Mistry, Goncu, & Mosier, 1993). In some contexts, social partners may encourage the child to engage in activities that are relatively passive and staid rather than active and adventurous. Observations by Keller and her colleagues of Indian mothers' discouragement of exploration illustrate this point. They observed Indian infants and toddlers who were immediately grabbed by older siblings or other relatives, when they made the slightest effort to engage in locomotor exploration. Safety could not be the reason, because the children were in a fenced area of the compound (Keller, personal communication, 2003).

This perspective reconceptualizes exploration as a social, not solitary, process and it downplays other western connotations of exploration. Such differences in meaning hopefully highlight the potential of cultural studies to enrich our understanding of the universality of attachment.

Other attachment theory concepts that may be relevant in diverse cultures

There are other extremely important aspects of attachment theory that, surprisingly, have not been a focus of recent publications on culture and attachment (Grossmann et al., in this volume; van IJzendoorn & Sagi, 1999). One of these involves the relationship between loss and bereavement. We think that the neglect of this phenomenon is unfortunate. Previously, we speculated that "suffering resulting from loss" is especially likely to emerge as a universal aspect of attachment theory (Rothbaum et al., 2000; p. 1099). Our speculation was fueled by the fact that much of Bowlby's early work was on loss and that his conclusions were based in large part on colleagues' findings regarding other primates (Kondo-Ikemura & Waters, 1995).

Here again, we suspect that our richest understanding will entail a contextualized understanding of universal processes. For example, the availability of alternative caregivers, as well as the prevalence of loss in the community – which is likely to influence the meaning of loss to children and adults – may play a critical role in the bereavement process. Cultural studies are likely to enrich our understanding of when and how loss leads to disturbances in (disorganized forms of) attachment. For example, True et al. (2001) suggest that the pervasive experience of loss and grief by Dogon mothers – most of the mothers in their study had lost one or more children – and cultural beliefs that inhibit self blame, play a critical role in mothers' ability to resolve their grief in a way that does not affect the attachment security of their children. Clearly, the study of cultural variation can contribute much to our understanding of universal associations between loss of attachment figures on one hand and grief and disorganization on the other.

A Paradigm Shift: From Behavior to Behavior-Context Interactions

Why context matters: Issues involving parental sensitivity

To address the conceptual and methodological issues raised above, we recommend an approach that is informed by a sociocultural perspective as well as by the perspective of classic attachment theory. Attachment theorists are concerned primarily with identifying regularities in behavior, and socioculturalists with identifying the mixture of regularities and variation. A key characteristic of sociocultural theory is attention to the context in which activities occur. Contextual factors that must be considered include locality (e.g., urban-rural), setting (home, fields, school, or neighborhood), and available people (grandmother, day care provider, sibling) (Super & Harkness, 2002; Valsiner, 2000).

We believe that the shift in paradigms we are advocating is long overdue. The need for greater attention to context was evident even before the recent increased focus on cultural variation. Research on parental sensitivity, for example, has for many years highlighted the limitations of research that fails to consider contextual factors. In a review of the western evidence, De Wolff and van IJzendoorn (1997) found that sensitivity *per se* only accounts for a modest portion of the variance in security. The processes by which the caregivers' sensitivity contributes to security are not well understood, which may help explain the modest associations reported. The association depends on the group studied – there are weaker associations for clinical and low SES samples than for non-clinical and middle SES samples. They call for "a move to the contextual level" (De Wolff & van IJzendoorn, 1997, p. 571). We believe that there are many aspects of the context besides the group studied that will contribute to a better understanding of caregiver effects on attachment.

A broader view of context as it pertains to attachment has been championed by Claussen and Crittenden (2000). These authors emphasize the ways in which cultural roles and values influence the meaning of sensitivity, how sensitivity involves fit of the child to the context as well as fit of the parent to the child's signals and needs, and the fact that danger varies across context and so too must sensitivity to danger. They conclude,

> sensitivity must be defined explicitly within the social and cultural context .... If it is not defined contextually, some cultures will look very insensitive, even when their children are well adapted and made safer (in that context) by the parents' 'insensitive' behavior. (p. 122)

One relatively ignored contextual factor is the child-caregiver interaction. We refer to this interaction as a contextual factor to highlight attachment theorists' very narrow view of the caregiver's contribution, i.e., attachment theorists typically focus on caregiver behavior as opposed to caregiver-child interaction. Interpersonal dynamics constitute a larger whole of which caregiving is a part. It is surprising that attachment theorists have so seldom considered the interaction between child characteristics and caregiver behavior like sensitivity. The case for interaction is persuasively argued by Ainsworth (1967) in her description of insecure children in Uganda: "There seemed to be a vicious cycle in which the baby's fussy demands exasperated the mother, who then overtly or covertly rejected the baby, who in turn responded by anxiety and by increasing his demands" (p. 392). The importance of caregiver-child interaction may explain why mutuality and synchrony predict security at least as well as does sensitivity (De Wolff & van IJzendoorn, 1997; see also Claussen & Crittenden, 2000).

There are many other contextual factors that play a role in the relationship between caregiver behavior and attachment security. In a number of instances, caregivers influence the child via their affects on the child's environment. For example, how parents negotiate the spousal relationship influences the quality of that relationship which in turns affects the security of attachment (Davies, Harold, Goeke-Morey, & Cummings, 2002). By the same token, the ways in which parents negotiate sibling relationships, as well as relationships with grandparents and extended family members, are likely to influence the child's security. Other aspects of the environment over which primary caregivers have considerable influence are arranging for a safe setting, selection and supervision of alternative caregivers, and the organization of the home environment; all of these may influence the child's security.

In addition to increasing our understanding of caregiver influences, a focus on context also heightens our awareness of ways in which different settings place different demands on children and thereby influence children's needs. Among the contextual factors that are likely to influence children's needs are: (a) protection from vs. exposure to threats and dangers in the environment; (b) opportunities and rewards vs. restrictions and punishments for exploration; and (c) encouragement to individuate from others vs. pressure to accommodate to others. We think these contextual factors are worthy of future study in part because western cultures tend to score at an extreme end of all of them.

How context explains prior findings involving parental sensitivity

Differences in demands may explain why caregivers in some cultures place more emphasis on responsiveness to positive signals whereas caregivers in other cultures place more emphasis on responsiveness to negative signals. In environments where children are expected to be autonomous, self assertive, and to have high self-esteem, it may be more important that their primary caregivers are responsive to their positive signals (i.e., their curiosity, interests, and personal preferences). In environments where children face more health and nutritional challenges, it may be more important that their primary caregivers are responsive to their negative/distress signals. Understanding the complex interplay between caregiver behavior, cultural and contextual factors, and children's needs is an important new frontier in research on attachment.

Differences in demands may also explain cultural differences in whether parental control is part of the sensitive caregiving profile. When mother and child are required to maintain symbiotic/harmonious relations with one another, caregivers will not risk being controlling unless they and their child are secure (Azuma, 1996). In such cases, willingness to exercise control reflects security about the relationship. Sensitive parents, who are better able to cultivate symbiotic and secure relations, are the ones most likely to be controlling. By contrast, in western cultures, where symbiosis is rare, parents who are controlling are placing their relationship at risk. Even if the parents are sensitive, their children are likely to resist their control and to seek less closeness (see also Carlson & Harwood, 2003). In the West, parents who would place their relationship at risk – by being controlling – are the ones most likely to be insensitive toward their children.

Guidelines for Future Cross-Cultural Research on Attachment

In this section we highlight four key components of effective cultural research: (a) an array of methods; (b) a partnership between investigators from different cultures; (c) a description of the demographic, social, economic and philosophical context; and (d) receptivity to new questions and methods.

An array of methods
To move beyond current debates about whether cultural differences are broad and fundamental or are minor and superficial we need an array of methodologies. While multi-method approaches are generally regarded as optimal, they are especially needed in cultural research. One theorist who has eloquently argued and demonstrated the merits of combining emic and etic approaches (imposed and derived) is Trommsdorff (1995). The advantage of an emic approach, which focuses on indigenous beliefs and practices that are most meaningful to the people being studied, is the picture it provides about behavior in context and the meaning of variations in human functioning. The advantage of etic approaches, which focus on widely used, well validated measures that are grounded in established theories about human functioning, are their ability to provide data about critical processes relevant to all humans.

In the case of attachment theory, there have been too few efforts to integrate these complementary approaches. Prior cultural studies of attachment have almost always employed an imposed etic approach – the measures have been borrowed from prior western studies and have not been substantially adapted (van IJzendoorn & Sagi, 1999). Only by including an emic or derived etic approach will we be able to test whether there are biases in attachment theory. Fortunately attachment theorists are increasingly recognizing the value of these other approaches. For example, True et al. (2001) observe, "The major limitation of the present study was the lack of insider (emic) information on how mothering, alternate caregiving, and attachment were conceived by the participants and the community" (p. 1463).

A multi-method approach should include ethnographic, naturalistic and qualitative methods as well as highly controlled, laboratory and quantitative methods. Most investigators studying attachment and culture have relied almost exclusively on the latter methods. Yet there are signs that the former methods are increasingly appreciated. For example, Posada et al. (2002) acknowledge that an "ideal" assessment of mothers would include "open naturalistic observations and ethnographic descriptions" (p. 69).

One suite of methodologies we find particularly valuable is participant observations, structured observations and interviews. Interestingly, Ainsworth made excellent use of these methods in her Uganda study and relied heavily on the triangulation of data to draw her conclusions. Tobin, Wu, and Davidson (1989) have developed more sophisticated ways of capitalizing on observations and interviews by showing informants tapes of their own behavior as well as the behavior of adults and children from the "other culture(s)" and recording their responses to the tapes. In this way, they are able to sharpen their understanding of cultural differences in behavior as well as in the meaning of behavior.

A partnership between investigators

As part of an emic or derived etic approach, it is critical that the research team rely heavily on reports from informants from the culture under investigation. Ainsworth relied heavily on a local informant in her Uganda study. She describes her as a "valued assistant" because she was fluent in English, had toured for a year in the US, and was herself a mother. Ideally these informants should be full partners in the research process. While inequities between western principal investigators and informants from developing countries are not easily overcome, the goal should be to minimize them – when deciding the issues to explore, the measures to employ, and how to interpret the findings.

These methodological issues have been candidly and thoughtfully addressed by Azuma (1996) in a retrospective account of his groundbreaking cross-national collaboration with Robert Hess. Azuma highlights the need for an "open-minded team of researchers to fully realize the potential of cross-cultural psychology" (p. 223). Like Harwood and Ainsworth, Azuma explains how demographic, political, economic, and religious/philosophical differences spanning several centuries have set the stage for the cultural differences in parenting on which his research centered.

Working collaboratively, however, is difficult. Azuma (1996) identifies numerous factors that make non-western investigators less than equal partners in the research process. First, their lower level of status and resources, as well as the lower educational and living standards of their own culture as compared to the West, may create or accentuate differences in assertiveness, thereby muting the voices of the non-western "partners." Second, funding is usually obtained by western collaborators, making the latter responsible for final decisions over methods, instrumentation, analyses and conclusions. Third, the fact that many non-western investigators are trained in the West and have internalized a western bias is a further obstacle to fair collaboration. Azuma (1996) was struck by the difficulty of resolving these differences, as evident in his comment "in working with researchers from another culture one must assert oneself tenaciously in order to achieve satisfying results" (p. 233).

Descriptions of the broader context
To make cross-cultural research more ecologically valid, we need ethnographic accounts of the people being studied and the settings in which they live. Harwood et al. (1995) do an excellent job of briefly describing historical, institutional and everyday aspects of life in Puerto Rico that are relevant to attachment relationships in that culture. Ainsworth does the same in her study of Uganda – providing a valuable albeit "very sketchy account of Ganda life, including only what seemed essential as a background" (p. viii) for studying attachment. Recently, even brief research reports have included meaningful descriptions of the cultural context (e.g., True et al., 2001). Addressing the broader context does not entail a major shift in scientific reporting; the descriptions provided by Harwood, Ainsworth, and True constitute a very small percentage of their total research report.

Receptivity to new questions and methods
Especially in the first stages of research, descriptive "field study" is required (Ainsworth, 1967, p. vii). Descriptive field study entails measures that are open ended; tightly controlled designs are not optimal when initially studying new settings. In recent years attachment researchers have demonstrated an increasing receptivity to new measures and methods (Posada et al., 2002, True et al., 2001; Valenzuela, 1997). Waters (2002), for example, notes that it is appropriate to abandon the strange situation in cases where it is not ecologically valid (e.g., in cultures where children are not separated from caregivers). Waters further comments that Bowlby

would be delighted to have attachment theory challenged in much the way that he (Bowlby) challenged psychoanalytic theory.

As the last comment indicates, openness in research is an attitude that transcends particular methodologies. Ainsworth's openness was evident in her acknowledgement that, "not infrequently, a project that sets out to explore one problem becomes transformed into an investigation of a related problem. Such was the case with this [Uganda] project" (Ainsworth, 1967; p. 3).

Conclusion

The bottom line is that we need to better understand the myriad ways in which biological dispositions to develop attachments and real environments in which these attachments occur are co-mingled. We suggest that a multi-method approach to the study of cultural variation is especially likely to shed light on attachment processes. A greater understanding of these processes, in turn, will allow us to account for a greater portion of the variance in critical attachment associations – such as that between caregiver behavior and child security. The extreme generativity of attachment theory in its early stages was partly due to Bowlby's understanding of ethology and Ainsworth's observations in Uganda. Work with other species and cultures is not something that can be performed at one point in time and completed; as attachment theory and methods evolve it is essential that they be continuously challenged by observations involving human and non-human primate variation. We trust that this is the "exciting prospect" to which Waters and Cummings were referring in the first paragraph of this chapter.

References

Ainsworth, M. D. S. (1967). *Infancy in Uganda: Infant care and the growth of love.* Baltimore: John Hopkins University Press.

Ainsworth, M. D. S. (1976). *System for rating maternal care behavior.* Princeton, NJ: ETS Test Collection.

Allen, J. P., & Land, D. (1999). Attachment in adolescence. In J. Cassidy & P. R. Shaver (Eds.), *Handbook of attachment: Theory, research, and clinical applications* (pp. 319-335). New York: The Guilford Press.

Azuma, H. (1996). Cross-national research on child development: The Hess-Azuma collaboration in retrospect. In D. W. Shwalb & B. J. Shwalb (Eds.), *Japanese childrearing: Two generations of scholarship* (pp. 220-240). New York: The Guilford Press.

Belsky, J., Rosenberger, K., & Crnic, K. (1995). The origins of attachment security: "Classical" and contextual determinants. In S. Goldberg, R. Muir, & J. Kerr (Eds.), *Attachment theory: Social, developmental, and clinical perspectives* (pp. 153-83). Hillsdale, NJ: The Analytic Press.

Bornstein, M. H., Azuma, H., Tamis-LeMonda, C. S., & Ogino, M. (1990). Mother and infant activity and interaction in Japan and in the United States: I. A comparative macroanalysis of naturalistic exchanges. *International Journal of Behavioral Development, 13*, 267-287.

Bruner, J. (1990). *Acts of meaning.* Cambridge, MA: Harvard University Press.

Carlson, V., & Harwood, R. (2003). Attachment, culture, and the caregiving system: The cultural patterning of everyday experiences among Anglo and Puerto Rican mother-infant pairs. *Infant Mental Health Journal, 24*, 53-73.

Claussen, H. A., & Crittenden, P. M. (2000). Maternal sensitivity. In A. H. Claussen & P. M. Crittenden, P. (Eds.), *The organization of attachment relationships* (pp. 115-122). Cambridge, UK: Cambridge University Press.

Davies, P. T., Harold, G. T., Goeke-Morey, M. C., & Cummings, E. M. (2002). Child emotional security and interparental conflict. *Monographs of the Society for Research in Child Development, 67*, (Serial No. 270).

Dennis, T. A., Cole, P. M., Zahn-Waxler, C, & Mizuta, I. (2003, June). Process versus content: Patterns of contingent responsiveness during play in Japanese and U.S. mother-preschooler dyads. *Paper presented at Play and Development, the Annual Meeting of the Jean Piaget Society*, Chicago.

De Wolff, M. S., & van IJzendoorn, M. H. (1997). Sensitivity and attachment: A meta-analysis on parental antecedents of infant attachment. *Child Development, 68*, 571-591.

Fiske, A. P., Kitayama, S., Markus, H. R., & Nisbett, R. E. (1998). The cultural matrix of social psychology. In D. Gilbert, S. T. Fiske, & G. Lindzey (Eds.), *The handbook of social psychology* (Vol. 2, 4th ed., pp. 915-981). Boston: McGraw-Hill.

Friedlmeier, W., & Trommsdorff, G. (1999). Emotion regulation in early childhood: A cross-cultural comparison between German and Japanese toddlers. *Journal of Cross-Cultural Psychology, 30*, 684-711.

Friedlmeier, W., & Trommsdorff, G. (2004). *Maternal sensitivity and preschool children's emotion regulation in Japan and Germany.* Manuscript submitted for publication.

Harwood, R. L. (1992). The influence of culturally derived values on Anglo and Puerto Rican mothers' perceptions of attachment behavior. *Child Development, 63*, 822-839.

Harwood, R. L., Miller, J. G., & Irizarry, N. L. (1995). *Culture and attachment: Perceptions of the child in context.* New York: The Guilford Press.

Keller, H. (2003). *Socialization for competence: Cultural models of infancy.* Manuscript in preparation.

Keller, H., Künsemüller, P., Abels, M., Völker, S., Yovsi, R. D., Jensen, H., Papaligoura, Z., Lohaus, A., Rosabal-Coto, M., Kulks, D., & Mohite, P. (2003). The bio-culture of parenting. Evidence from five cultural communities. *Human Development, 46,* 288-311.

Kondo-Ikemura, K., & Waters, E. (1995). Maternal behavior and infant security in old world monkeys: conceptual issues and a methodological bridge between human and nonhuman primate research. In Kondo-Ikemura, K., Posada, G., Vaughn B. E., & Waters, E. (Eds.), *Caregiving, cultural, and cognitive perspectives on secure-base behavior and working models* (pp. 97-110). Chicago: Society for Research in Child Development, Inc.

Lamb, M. E., Thompson, R. A., Gardner, W., & Charnov, E. L. (1985) *Infant mother attachment: The origins and developmental significance of individual differences in strange situation behavior.* Hillsdale, NJ: Erlbaum.

LeVine, R. A. (1974). Parental goals: A cross-cultural review. *Teachers College Record, 76,* 226-239.

LeVine, R. A. (2004). Challenging expert knowledge: Findings from an African study of infant care and development. In U. P. Gielen & J. L. Roopnarine (Eds.), *Childhood and adolescence: Cross-cultural perspectives and applications.*

LeVine, R. A., & Miller, P. M. (1990). Commentary. *Human Development, 33,* 73-80

Miyake, K., Chen, S.-J., & Campos, J. (1985). Infant temperament, mother's mode of interaction, and attachment in Japan: An interim report. In I. Bretherton & E. Waters (Eds.), Growing points of attachment theory and research. *Monographs of the Society for Research in Child Development, 50* (Serial No. 209).

Mizuta, I., Zahn-Waxler, C., Cole, P. M., & Hiruma, N. (1996). A cross-cultural study of preschoolers' attachment: Security and sensitivity in Japanese and US dyads. *International Journal of Behavioral Development, 19,* 141-159.

Posada, G., Jacobs, A., Carbonell, O. A., Alzate, G., Bustamante, M., & Arenas, A. (1999). Maternal care and attachment security in ordinary and emergency contexts. *Developmental Psychology, 35,* 1379-1388.

Posada, G., Jacobs, A., Richmond, M. K., Carbonell, O. A., Alzate, G., Bustamante, M. R., & Quiceno, J. (2002). Maternal caregiving and infant security in two cultures. *Developmental Psychology, 38,* 67-78.

Rogoff, B. (1990). *Apprenticeship in thinking.* New York: Oxford University Press.

Rogoff, B. (2003). *The cultural nature of human development.* New York: Oxford University Press.

Rogoff, B., & Angelillo, C. (2002). Investigating the coordinated functioning of multifaceted cultural practices in human development. *Human Development, 45,* 211-225.

Rogoff, B., Mistry, J., Goncu, A., & Mosier, C. (1993). Guided participation in cultural activity by toddlers and caregivers. *Monographs of the Society for Research in Child Development, 58,* (Serial No. 236).

Rothbaum, F., Weisz, J., Pott, M., Miyake, K., & Morelli, G. (2000). Attachment and culture: Security in the United States and Japan. *American Psychologist, 55,* 1093-1104.

Rothbaum, F., Weisz, J., Pott, M., Miyake, K., & Morelli, G. (2001). Deeper into attachment and culture. *American Psychologist, 56,* 827-829.

Rothbaum, F., & Yamaguchi, S. (2004*). Attachment and amae in the United States and Japan.* Manuscript in preparation.

Suomi, S. J. (1999). Attachment in rhesus monkeys. In J. Cassidy & P. R. Shaver (Eds.), *Handbook of attachment: Theory, research, and clinical applications* (pp. 181-197). New York: The Guilford Press.

Super, C. M., & Harkness, S. (2002). Culture structures the environment for development. *Human Development, 45,* 270-274.

Takahashi, K. (1990). Are the key assumptions of the 'Strange Situation' procedure universal? A view from Japanese research. *Human Development, 33,* 23-30.

Tobin, J., Wu, D., & Davidson, D. (1989). *Preschool in three cultures.* New Haven, CT: Yale University Press.

Trommsdorff, G. (1995). Parent-adolescent relations in changing societies: A cross-cultural study. In P. Noack, M. Hofer, & J. Youniss (Eds.), *Psychological responses to social change* (pp. 189-218). Berlin, Germany: Walter de Gruyter.

Trommsdorff, G., & Friedlmeier, W. (1993). Control and responsiveness in Japanese and German mother-child interactions. *Early Development and Parenting, 2,* 65-78.

True, M. M., Pisani, L., & Oumar, F. (2001). Infant-mother attachment among the Dogon of Mali. *Child Development, 72,* 1451-1466.

Valenzuela, M. (1997). Maternal sensitivity in a developing society: The context of urban poverty and infant chronic under nutrition. *Developmental Psychology, 33,* 845-855.

Valsiner, J. (2000). *Culture and human development.* Thousand Oaks, CA: Sage.

van IJzendoorn, M. H. (1995). Adult attachment representations, parental responsiveness, and infant attachment: A meta-analysis on the predictive validity of the adult attachment interview. *Psychological Bulletin, 117,* 387-403

van IJzendoorn, M. H., & Sagi, A. (1999). Cross-cultural patterns of attachment: Universal and contextual dimensions. In J. Cassidy & P. R. Shaver (Eds.), *Hand-*

book of attachment: Theory, research, and clinical applications (pp. 713-734). New York: Guilford.

Vereijken, C. M. J. L., Riksen-Walraven, J. M., & Kondo-Ikemura, K. (1997). Maternal sensitivity and infant attachment security in Japan: A longitudinal study. *International Journal of Behavioral Development, 21*, 35-50.

Völker, S., Yovsi, R., & Keller, H. (1998, July). *Maternal interactional quality as assessed by non-trained raters from different cultural backgrounds.* Paper presented at the XVth Biennial ISSBD Meetings, Bern, Switzerland.

Waters, E. (2002, April). *Attachment theory – is it relevant universally?* Paper presented at the International Society of Infant Studies, Toronto, Canada.

Waters, E., & Cummings, E. M. (2000). A secure base from which to explore the environment. *Child Development, 71*, 164-172.

Waters, E., & Valenzuela, M. (1999). Explaining disorganized attachment: Clues from research on mild-to-moderately undernourished children in Chile. In C. George & J. Solomon (Eds.), *Attachment disorganization (pp. 265-287).* New York: The Guilford Press.

White, M. I., & LeVine, R. A. (1986). What is an "ii ko" (good child)? In H. W. Stevenson & H. Azuma (Eds.), *Child development and education in Japan* (pp. 55-62). New York: Freeman.

6

Emotional Development and Culture: Reciprocal Contributions of Cross-Cultural Research and Developmental Psychology

Wolfgang Friedlmeier

Introduction

This volume focuses on the importance of cross-cultural psychology to social sciences. This perspective would not be complete if the opposite influence is not taken into account, namely the contribution of knowledge and findings in social sciences to cross-cultural psychology. Here, developmental psychology is chosen as a specific domain of social sciences. The aim of this chapter is to describe contributions of developmental psychology to conceptualization of culture and to cross-cultural research designs and vice versa. The domain of emotions will be used as an example for demonstrating such reciprocal effects.

Cross-cultural research is mainly driven by describing universal phenomena or culture-specific differences with regard to psychological aspects, and to explain (and predict) differences by referring to general aspects of the cultural settings. Developmental research takes a different perspective as explanations refer to questions of transmission of cultural knowledge through child rearing and processes of person's internalization, which are relevant to understanding personality development in cultural context.

Cross-cultural studies can be differentiated as to whether they aim to study universals or psychological differences (van de Vijver & Leung, 1997; see also Lonner, this volume). Theory-driven studies, which test the universality of psychological phenomena, often neglect culture-specific characteristics. The recent research of emotions in cultural perspective can be described as a shift from universal to culture-sensitive studies. It will be argued here that taking a developmental perspective may lead to a clearer specification of the relationships between culture and emotion.

The structure of this chapter is as follows: First, cross-cultural studies of emotions that tested the universality hypothesis will be described. Thereby, studies can be differentiated according to their perspective on the concept of emotion (structuralistic vs. functionalistic perspective). Second, I will present several studies based on a culture-sensitive approach. Especially the differentiation between cultural norms and the individual's representation of such norms were important steps. By drawing upon the sociohistorical approach (Vygotsky, 1994), I will show that even more prerequisites of a developmental culture-sensitive approach are necessary. Finally, two cross-cultural studies will be described in more detail, in order to illustrate the developmental framework. A general discussion will close the chapter.

Universal Approaches on Emotions

Universal studies on emotions in structuralistic perspective

According to a structuralistic perspective, emotions are *defined by structural features* as subjective experience (feeling), expression, and physiological processes (Schmidt-Atzert, 1997). Emotions, especially basic emotions such as joy, fear, anger, and surprise are defined as inborn affect programs (Ekman, 1972; Izard, 1977). Based on evolution theoretical argumentation in following Darwin (1872/2000), it is assumed that these basic emotions show phylogenetic continuity and occur in all human beings. The goal of this research was to demonstrate the *universality of these basic emotions*. Except for some studies about the psycho-physiological reaction, e.g., activation of vegetative nerve system (Levenson, Ekman, Heider, & Friesen, 1992), mainly expressive characteristics were studied, e.g., posture (Kudoh & Matsumoto, 1985; Sogon & Masutani, 1989) and nonverbal vocal characteristics of emotional expression (Albas, McCluskey, & Albas, 1976). However, the main focus was on *facial expression* because the basic emotions could be differentiated best.

The method used was the recognition of pictures of facial expressions and photographs. The analysis was done by testing the recognition rate against the chance level. Ekman, Friesen and Ellsworth (1982) were able to show that members of very different cultures, e.g., members of the Fore, an ethnic group in New Guinea that had no contact with western culture before, could identify the whole set of expressions of western faces, namely for joy, anger, fear, surprise, disgust, and sadness beyond chance level.

It is assumed that emotional experience (feeling) of basic emotions is universal because emotional experience is inborn and cannot be learned (Izard & Ackerman, 2000). Cultural differences are explained by *varying display rules* (e.g., Ekman, Friesen, & Ellsworth, 1982). Display rules determine when, where, and how the expression of a certain emotion should be consciously regulated, e.g., by neutralizing, masking, or emphasizing the expression.

Several critical points can be mentioned. First, the recognition of facial expressions is sometimes far from being perfect and culture-dependent. For example, American subjects only recognized four of the six facial expressions displayed by the Fore people (Mesquita, 2001a). Second, the analysis beyond chance does not take differences of recognition rates between cultures into account. Even if the recognition is beyond chance, the percentages of recognition between groups from different cultures may still differ significantly. A third critical point is related to a more central issue: it remains unclear why the emotions are recognized at all. Russell (1994) argued that basic emotions are not recognized due to the corresponding expression but based on the action readiness or situational meaning. The translation of the terms also might contain different levels of salience that lead to different levels of recognition.

Universal studies on emotions in functionalistic perspective

In a functionalistic perspective emotions are not defined as a specific configuration of a structure (feeling, expression, physiological state) but rather as *processes* that indicate the relationship between the person and the social/physical environment (Frijda, 1986; Lazarus, 1991; Leventhal & Scherer, 1987). Emotions are seen as being embedded in the person's action and having regulative functions. On the one hand, emotions are caused by appraisals (a person's evaluation of a situation), and on the other hand, emotions contain an action readiness, i.e. emotions imply a tendency of a spontaneous reaction as the physiological processes also prepare the body to react, e.g., to flee in case of fear or to attack in case of anger (Frijda, 1994). Furthermore, *feeling (subjective experience)* is more important than expression. Cross-cultural studies focused on the analysis of these single processes (appraisals, experience, action readiness, and regulation behavior) and also aimed to test their universality. Scherer and his colleagues (Scherer, Matsumoto, Wallbott, & Kudoh, 1988; Scherer, Summerfield & Wallbott, 1983; Scherer & Wallbott, 1994) studied these components in 37 countries over four continents. The subjects were asked to describe a situation in which a specific emotion occurs (joy, anger, sadness, fear, shame, guilt, and disgust) and to rate components like appraisal, experience, expressive behavior, and action readiness. It was analyzed whether the variance of the answer patterns between the emotions is higher than the variance between the cultures. The authors showed a high cross-cultural convergence that speaks in favor of universal features. For example, the descriptions of experience were similar over cultures: A joyful event is experienced as desired, very pleasant, and strengthening the self-esteem, a threatening event as unpleasant, goal preventing and difficult to overcome. Such common features were also confirmed in other studies (Frijda et al., 1995; Mesquita, 2001b; Roseman et al. 1995). The subjects' evaluation of action readiness also showed cross-cultural similarities (Frijda, Markam, Sato, & Wiers, 1995; Mesquita, 2001b).

At the same time, clear differences were found, especially with regard to the endurance, experienced intensity and regulation of the single emotions. Furthermore, the explained variance of appraisal dimensions (e.g., level of attention, controllability) over the cultures was not higher than 40% for single emotions (e.g., Frijda et al., 1995). Such culture-specific variations are not explained further because culture is used as an independent variable without specific contents.

The methodological approaches of the studies also created some problems. First of all, the questionnaires used did not allow the researchers to differentiate between how people in different cultures think about emotions and how they experience them. Second, the cultural variance was restricted due to two reasons: (a) only students were tested, and (b) only western concepts were taken into account while features within other cultures were not. For example, Japanese emotions like "tanomi" (feeling like relying on someone) or "oime" (feeling of indebtedness) that represent other-focussed emotions (see Markus & Kitayama, 1991) can also be experienced in other cultures. However, they were never studied cross-culturally probably because their salience is low in western cultures.

Both approaches aimed at testing universality. Such a research design impedes the construction of hypotheses about possible cultural differences. Without theoretical assumptions about culture-specific characteristics, differences – when they appear – can only be described and explained post-hoc. Mesquita (2001a) speculates that the appraisals about the influence of the emotion on the relation with the interaction partner may vary culturally. Shame might be seen in some countries as more important for social relations whereas in other countries anger may be evaluated higher.

Culture-Sensitive Approaches on Emotions

Culture-sensitive approach on emotions at the cultural level
In more recent cross-cultural studies on emotions, the concept of culture is worked out as an explanation variable. Hofstede (1980, 2001) constructed five dimensions

based on extended cross-cultural studies. Especially two of his dimensions have been applied for cultural studies on emotions, namely individualism and power distance. Individualism represents the extent in which a culture gives priority to motives, goals, and values of an autonomous and unique individual in relation to the group. In spite of critics of this dimension (Kagitçibasi, 1994, 1996; this volume; Klages, this volume; Oysermann, Coon, & Kemmelmeier, 2002) these concepts were proved successfully for emotion research (Matsumoto, 2001). The comprehensive descriptions of this dimension by Hofstede (2001) picture individualism and collectivism as cultural syndromes. Thereby, consequences for the individual and the diverse social relationships (family, friendship, work) are also discussed. Power distance describes the extent to which people accept and expect that power is distributed unequally in society. In cultures with low power distance, hierarchy is seen as an inequality of roles that is established for convenience and superiors or subordinates are perceived as people like oneself. In contrast, in cultures with high power distance, hierarchy means existential inequality and superiors and subordinates are beings of a different kind. Therefore, in the latter case, the person has to adapt his/her interaction behavior to the status of the interaction partner.

The results from a large number of different countries can be ranked according to these dimensions and an analysis of relations at the cultural level can be done, e.g., by correlation analysis. Studies were carried out about *recognition of emotion* and *intensity ratings of experiences.*

Schimmack (1996) reported in a Meta analysis on emotion recognition that individualism was a better predictor for recognition of "happiness" than the ethnicity of Caucasian and Non-Caucasian persons. With regard to intensity ratings of experiences, Matsumoto (1989) reported a negative correlation between power distance and intensity of anger, fear, and sadness. *The higher a culture is in power distance the less intensive these emotions are experienced.* This result questions the structuralists' hypothesis that cultural differences only occur at the expression level due to display rules.

The importance of such approaches relates to the fact that they allow the categorization of cultural groups according to dimensions at the cultural level. This strategy is a first fruitful approach for explicative studies. However, this approach does not allow the testing of individual preferences. On the contrary, it includes the implicit assumption that all cultural members share the same value orientation and this neglects intracultural variations and interindividual differences.

Culture-sensitive approaches on emotions at the individual level
An important step to overcome this implicit sociodeterministic conceptualization was contributed by Triandis (1995) who introduced the concepts of "idiocentrism" and "allocentrism" in order to measure individualistic and collectivistic attitudes at

the individual level. Persons who share the same attitude can be compared independently of their cultural membership. However, the relationship between cultural dimensions and individual attitudes is not completely clear. According to Triandis (1995) individual attitudes towards individualism vs. collectivism represent group-related cultural phenomena at the same time. Heine, Lehmann, Peng, and Greenholtz (2002) argue that individual attitudes destroy group differences at the cultural level because the individuals do not evaluate themselves with regard to other cultures but rather to in-group members. According to the latter argument, the use of detailed descriptions of cultural syndromes as discussed above cannot be neglected completely, and the individual level may rather complete the picture.

In recent cross-cultural studies on emotions, cultural dimensions are taken into account at the individual level (e.g., Matsumoto & Kupperbusch, 2001). Matsumoto et al. (2002) studied the relation between expression and experience of emotions with Japanese and American subjects. The intensity of expression of a computer-animated face was varied by modifying the expression criteria according to the Facial Action Coding System developed by Ekman and Friesen (1978). In case of full intensity (100%), American subjects evaluated the expression stronger than the supposed targets' experience, whereas Japanese subjects did not see any difference. In case of 50% of intensity, the results showed inverse patterns. Japanese subjects evaluated experience stronger than expression and American subjects did not see any difference. A weaker expression is a sign for display rules for Japanese subjects. A strong expression is seen as being identical to the experience for Japanese because the person lost his/her control of the expression, whereas Americans evaluate such strong expression as an exaggeration, i.e., a display rule is applied. The individual characteristic in individualism and power distance explained 90% of the variance of the differences.

These studies measured the cultural values and characteristics at the individual level and overcame the sociodeterministic assumption. So they could also analyze *interindividual differences within the cultural samples*. Here, we already reach a perspective that differentiates between a cultural level and the representation of cultural aspects at the individual level. However, several questions still need to be answered. When the relation between cultural and individual values as well as between values and emotions exist, how does an individual acquire these values and abilities in the course of development? How are the cultural characteristics of emotions transmitted to children? Such questions are neglected in cross-cultural research that focuses on a general or social psychological thinking, but they are highly relevant within a developmental perspective. Therefore, it is necessary to describe a theoretical framework that includes a developmental perspective on emotions by paying tribute to sociocultural variations.

Developmental Framework for a Culture-Sensitive Approach on Emotions

A developmental framework for cross-cultural studies in the domain of emotions requires three prerequisites: (1) The conceptualization of human being as a cultural being, (2) the conceptualization of emotions as a culturally mediated construct, and as a consequence, (3) the explanation of transmission of cultural knowledge.

The sociohistorical approach of Vygotsky (1978) can serve as a theoretical framework for cross-cultural research in developmental psychology because his approach provides an integration of the first and the third prerequisite, offering a twofold dialectic perspective on development: an intrapersonal and an interpersonal perspective. The second point can be derived as a consequence of Vygotsky's model.

Conceptualization of the human being as a cultural being
The first perspective in Vygotsky's theoretical approach is *intrapersonal*. A person's psychological processes and functions are based on different hierarchical levels (see Figure 1): (a) inborn behavioral reactions (e.g., reflexes); (b) abilities and conditional reflexes, i.e. learning by experience; (c) mental abilities, i.e. organized hierarchy of competencies oriented towards solving new problems; and (d) cultural-historical abilities. Thereby, the higher psychological functions (c) and (d) do not eliminate the lower levels but rather the lower ones are embedded in the higher ones and are transcended by being organized and used in new ways (see Figure 1). In other words, a person's behavior operates at different levels: automatic reactions, emotional behavior regulation, volitional behavior regulation, and reflective behavior regulation (Holodynski & Friedlmeier, in press).

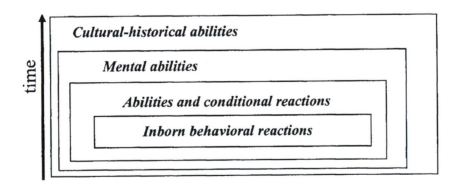

Figure 1. The First Dialectic Process: Intrapersonal

On each level, a new qualitative structure emerges. The cultural-historical abilities refer to the assumption that culture is an inherent part of the person's psychic functioning. The biological relevance of cues for behavior is reduced. Human behavior is not direct but indirect, i.e., it is mediated by the construction of meaning (Valsiner, 1989). This means that actions depend on one's attribution of the meaning given to situational cues. And these meanings are culturally shared and mediated. The idea that culture is a necessary prerequisite of individual development is also expressed by Geertz (1973) who emphasizes that "(...) man is precisely the animal most desperately dependent upon such extragenetic, outside the skin control mechanisms, such cultural programs, for ordering his behaviour" (p. 44). According to Vygotsky, language as a sign system plays a central role. The use of signs and symbolic activity requires higher psychological functions like consciousness. In contrast to other tools, which have effects on objects in the outer world, language is a medium that has effects on behavior and experience, namely the others' and one's own behavior (see Vygotski, 1978).

Explanation of the transmission of cultural knowledge

The second dialectic process according to Vygotsky is related to the *relationship between person and social environment*. The development of higher psychological functions (level c and especially d) takes place by means of internalization of cultural knowledge, values, and actions. Thereby, the inner symbols are internalizations of the outer symbols. According to Vygotsky, (higher) psychological functions are socially constituted and variable. The *zone of proximal development*, i.e. the discrepancy between a child's abilities with and without support of a caregiver, describes this process of internalization. The caregiver's support is the condition for later self-guided action. This developmental path *from interactive to self-regulated actions* stands in contrast to most cognitive theories. These assume that psychological functions are ends of universal and primarily natural processes.

Conceptualization of emotions as culturally mediated constructs

The application of the intrapersonal perspective has three important implications, namely for the conceptualization of expression of emotions, of experience of emotions, and of emotion regulation.

Expression of emotions

The embeddedness of emotional behavior in hierarchical levels of behavior organisation leads to the recognition that emotional expression has a symbolic meaning and, thus, is part of human symbolic activity. Human emotional expressions represent a sign system analogous to human language. Therefore, expressive signs play a similar role for emotional development as do speech signs for cognitive development (Holodynski & Friedlmeier, 2004). The expressive signs are used as symbols because they do not possess naturally inborn signal character but can be removed from the referent. The symbol function of emotional expression is evident in the variety of interpretations of expressive signs, and especially in the ability to dissociate expression and experience. People know that the expression does not necessarily correspond with the experience. The reaction of another person to one's emotional expression primarily depends on the meaning that he/she gives to the expressive signs in a specific context. The symbol function is also evident in the display rules, i.e. regulating expressive signs according to certain conventions. There are societal norms that regulate certain expressions independent of the individual's inner experience of that expression (Ekman & Friesen, 1972; Matsumoto, 2001). For example, it is expected that one not express one's disappointment about a gift. Starting from unspecific distress reactions, a child has to learn the symbolic use of expressive signs that are mediated in interactions with the caregivers.

Experience of emotions
The dissociation between expression and experience is possible because the individual becomes *conscious of his/her feelings*. Damasio (1999) calls it "feeling of feelings." And by this, emotional experience as "felt feeling" includes a conscious process that requires a learning history for children. The person perceives the arousal of the vegetative nerve system (e.g., increase of heartbeat or change of skin conductance) as well as proprioceptive reactions, i.e. the feedback of the facial and body expression. This flux of processes has to be structured by the subject. Moreover, according to Gergely and Watson (1999) the experience of emotions is mediated through interactions with the caregivers as they mirror the child's emotion. This is a necessary condition for the child to learn to *recognize and structure this arousal as discrete qualities in a categorical way* and to learn to label it with specific verbal terms like "anger," "joy," or "sadness."

Regulation of emotions
The hierarchical levels of behavior regulation can explain that emotions are not only regulators of one's behavior. Emotions are also *regulated by voluntary inhibition processes*. The latter is called *reflexive emotion regulation*. The importance of emotion regulation was studied intensively in the last years (see Friedlmeier, 1999a, 1999b; Friedlmeier & Trommsdorff, 1999; Stansbury & Sigman, 2000; Thompson, 1990).

The action readiness that is inherent in emotions represents the *instrumental level of emotion regulation*. When one experiences fear then one has the tendency to flee. When one gets angry one has the tendency to remove the barrier or to attack the person who evoked the anger reaction. When one experiences shame one wants to "disappear." When one feels guilty, one wants to repair. These strategies lead to a change in the emotion by fulfilling the related goals/motives. According to coping research, those actions that aim to change the situation can be characterized as *problem-focused regulation* (Holodynski & Friedlmeier, in press; Lazarus, 1991).

However, there are many situations in which it is not possible to act according to the emotion inherent strategy. One may feel fear but cannot escape the situation. One may feel guilty but thinks that the other earns this treatment. One is angry with someone but does not want to confront the other with his or her anger. Therefore, motive conflicts due to one-self, due to the situational context (e.g., the child has other goals than the caregiver), or situation-specific constellations arise that hinder the direct execution of the inherent strategy. The instrumental strategies cannot be realized. The fulfillment of the motive or of the goal has at least to be postponed.

Nevertheless, the negative state of feeling has to be regulated and changed. There is a group of strategies that are not goal-oriented but rather are directly oriented to changing the actual emotion. Self-soothing strategies (e.g., calming down, inner speech, e.g., "it is not that dramatic"), distraction (e.g., focusing one's attention on other things, thinking of something different), and reappraisal of the event (excusing the other's behavior, redefining the situation and/or the relevance of one's own goal) are the most prominent strategies in adulthood. Such strategies represent the reflexive level of emotion regulation as they afford the consciousness of emotions (Damasio, 1999). In contrast to problem-focused regulation, these actions aim to change the internal state and can be seen as *emotion-focused regulation* (Lazarus, 1991).

The preference for problem- versus emotion-focused regulation may not only be related to the specific situation but also to a person's general style of control. Preferences for either primary control, understood as an attempt to gain control by influencing existing realities, or for secondary control, the attempt to align oneself with existing realities by controlling the personal psychological impact (Weisz, 1990), can be seen as personality traits that may affect the preference for problem- or emotion-focused regulation. As secondary control is more prevalent in many Asian cultures and primary control is more dominant in western cultures (e.g., Seginer, Trommsdorff, & Essau, 1993; Rothbaum, Weisz, & Snyder, 1982), it can be expected that emotion-focused regulation is more important in the Asian cultures.

Culture-Inherent Developmental Approach

It was argued above, that central components of emotions – expression, feeling, and emotion regulation – are to a large extent culturally defined. The relevant question is how this knowledge is transmitted through socialization processes. According to a developmental approach, this knowledge is transmitted in the daily interactions between the child and its caregivers. Despite some inborn emotion regulation strategies like self-soothing (sucking) and distraction (gaze aversion), infants can only apply such strategies in cases of moderate negative emotions. In most other cases, caregivers are the vicarious regulators of infants' emotions in the first years of life.

Furthermore, the development of discrete emotions relies upon interactive experiences with caregivers (Friedlmeier, 1999a; Sroufe, 1996). The caregiver's affect-reflecting mirroring of infants' expressions (Gergely & Watson, 1999) and infant's motor mimicry (Field & Walden, 1982; Meltzoff & Moore, 1983) are the most important mechanisms for development of discrete emotions. They lead to the differentiation of context- and emotion-specific expressive signs (Holodynski & Friedlmeier, in press). Therefore, in all these interactions, cultural specificities like linguistic conventions, socialization practices, prescriptions for daily behavior as well as religious, ideological and educational beliefs are actualized (Nussbaum, 2000) by the caregiver and affect the child's emotional development.

The developmental framework goes beyond the culture-sensitive approaches described above since it conceives of culture not only as represented in general norms but also represented by the subjective beliefs of socialization agents. Culture also determines the frame of the specific course and content of the interactions as a learning field for the child. The growing capacities and abilities of a child *are culturally-based capacities* rather than inborn capacities. We have to understand these specific interactive processes and the child's related internalizations of social mediated knowledge and messages as well as the externalizations, in order to understand the effects of culture (Friedlmeier, in press). This perspective leads to the *claim of the immediacy of culture* that is also made by anthropologists (Super & Harkness, 1997) and cultural psychologists who emphasize a developmental perspective (e.g., Valsiner, 2003). It is in line with the requirements that Rothbaum and Morelli (see this volume) formulated for studying attachment, especially when they emphasize that "aspects of activity do not exist separate from each other; it is not possible to understand the child's activity, for example, without considering the partner's contributions. Research may focus on one aspect of activity as an analytic strategy, but must consider findings in light of other aspects, or risk destroying the reality of the phenomenon under study" (p. 100).

Developmental studies in cross-cultural psychology are still rare and they mostly follow the general framework of cross-cultural research. Some studies focus on socialization practices like caregivers' developmental goals and practices. For example, Japanese mothers are more indulgent in the first years of life than American mothers and less interested in independence training (Caudill & Weinstein, 1969; Chao, 1995; Miyake, Campos, Kagan, & Bradshaw, 1986). They rarely show expressions of anger in front of their child and try to hide crying (Doi, 1973; Lebra, 1976; Miyake et al., 1986). However, the specific effects on the child's development remain unclear. Other studies only focus on developmental outcomes. Camras et al. (1998) studied cultural differences in expressions of emotions in young children, and Choy and Mohay (2001) investigated display rules of Australian and Chinese children. The specific interaction behavior of the mothers and their socialization practices are not included, and it remains an open question which practices may cause the commonalities and differences observed in children's reactions. Therefore, we do not know well how parents or other socialization agents mediate cultural characteristics of emotions, and in which ways children's development is affected. There is still a lack of specific reports on culture-based rules of emotion socialization (Friedlmeier & Matsumoto, in prep).

In the following section, two cross-cultural studies about children's emotions and emotion regulation will serve as examples as how to go beyond such limitations by relying on the developmental framework outlined above. In the first study, a careful and intensive description of the cultural background and culture-specific rules about expression of emotions and its regulation is given. The argumentation and testing remain at the cultural level. The second study then argues and tests at the inter- and intraindividual levels.

Culture-inherent developmental approach at the cultural level

Cole, Bruschi, and Tamang (2002) carried out a comprehensive study in rural Nepal. They studied emotions and emotion regulation of children in the second and fourth or fifth grade in two different ethnic groups: the Brahman and the Tamang. US-American children were also studied as a comparison group. The Nepali subjects lived in Brahman and Tamang villages located in comparably hilly surrounding, with a similar number of inhabitants, and within family groups in which, members work, ate, and slept together.

In spite of these commonalities there were also remarkable differences. Brahmans represent a very high caste related with *pride* and *status*. There is a big difference with regard to the behavior towards in- and out-group members. It is adequate *to show anger towards out-group members*. Respect for authority is expected within the in-group, since dominance would threaten the harmony. In contrast, the Tamang, an indigenous group in Nepal of Mongolic origin, have a low societal status. Equality is a central value. Material possession is shared, being unselfish is an ideal, and showing *anger to either in- or out-group members is generally avoided*.

Based on these cultural backgrounds, the authors derive hypotheses about children's descriptions of their emotional reactions in different interpersonal situations: (1) It was expected that the Nepali children would report that they experience less anger and more shame than the American children who grow up in a culture that highly values self-assertion. Due to the differences in social status, it was supposed that Brahman children would experience more anger as compared to the Tamang. In the latter group, *anger expression is discouraged and shame feeling is encouraged.* (2) It was also expected that the control of expression of emotions would differ: American children were expected to express anger strongly as it supports self-assertion, and Brahman children were expected to report a stronger control similar to Tamang children. In respect to shame, it was expected that only Tamang would report expressing shame. (3) Concerning the reasons for hiding or expressing an emotion, it was expected that U.S. children would argue from a problem-focused point of view by aiming to alter the situation, whereas Nepali children would rely on emotion-focused reasons by accepting difficult situations. (4) This difference in justifications was expected to correspond to similar differences in relation to the emotion regulation behavior that the children would display in such situations.

Sample and instruments
62 Brahman, 62 Tamang, and 99 American children between the ages of 9 and 12 participated in this study. The children listened to nine stories that contained six difficult and three pleasant situations. Stories were told in the second person to help the child imagine being in the situation. After each story the children were asked five questions. The questions aimed to assess the experienced emotion, the regulation of their feeling (expressing or hiding), the reason for the chosen form of regulation and the possible regulation behavior.

Variables
Emotion. The frequency of experienced emotions over the nine stories was used to measure the described feeling.
Emotion regulation. The frequency of hiding was used to measure the intensity of control.
Justifications of hiding or revealing the emotion. The answers were coded into four categories. Self-evident justification when facts of the situation were mentioned, emotion-focused justification by reappraisal (e.g., "I am angry but I do not want this thing that much anyway"), problem-focused justification by giving instrumental arguments (e.g., "if I do not look angry, they will not tease me longer"), and uncodable justifications.
Emotion regulation behavior. Two main categories were used: Emotion-focused regulations, i.e., the children change the internal state of experience, and problem-focused regulations, i.e., the children change the situation in order to reach the intended goal.

Results
The Tamang children reported shame in negative emotional situations significantly more often, whereas the U.S. children reported more anger reactions.

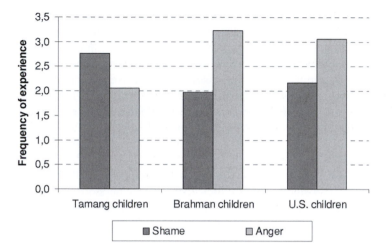

Figure 2. Mean Frequency of Reported Experience of Shame and Anger

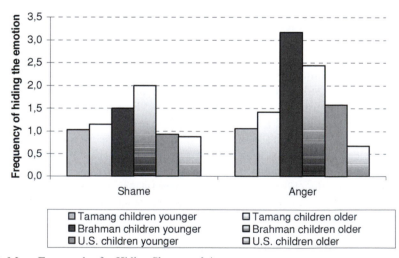

Figure 3. Mean Frequencies for Hiding Shame and Anger

In contrast to the assumptions, Brahman children showed a similar frequency as the U.S. children did and clearly different from the pattern of the Tamang children (see Figure 2). Concerning the control of emotions, Brahman children indicated that they controlled the expression of anger and shame significantly stronger than the other two groups (see Figure 3). Age-specific differences occurred with regard to controlling for anger. The older Tamang children mentioned controlling anger more often than younger children, and the inverse result occurred for U.S. children (see Figure 3).

Furthermore, Tamang children reported that they would communicate shame more often than Brahman children. Tamang children used self-evident justifications more often than the Brahman and U.S. children did. They did not see any reasons to hide the feeling. This openness and tolerance of expression of emotions fits with the observation that the Tamang are generally perceived as direct and without artificiality (Cole, Bruschi & Tamang, 2002). As expected, Nepali children gave more emotion-focused justifications and applied more emotion-focused regulation by reappraisal as compared to the U.S. children who reported more problem-focused justifications, and related regulation behavior by changing the situation.

Discussion
To summarize, this study shows that clear culture-specific patterns with regard to feeling and emotion regulation already occur in school-age children, reflecting cultural expectations of their cultural group. Tamang children indicated displaying more shame and less control, Brahman children more anger and higher control. Cole et al. (2002) interpret the result that older Tamang children controlled anger more than the younger Tamang as follows. It may be that Tamang children have learnt this rule – to not reveal anger – in the school setting where Brahman teachers are working. Compared to U.S. children, both groups of Nepali children showed a higher preference for emotion-focused regulation strategies that aimed at changing their own internal state. This means that they prefered secondary control strategies. In the long run, such regulation strategies relying on secondary control behavior may lead to a decrease of negative feeling in future similar situations, a consequence that again fits in with cultural expectations.

Culture-inherent developmental approach at the individual level
The second study was carried out by Trommsdorff and her research team who observed 2- and 5-year-old Japanese and German girls, and their mothers (Friedlmeier & Trommsdorff, 2002; Friedlmeier & Trommsdorff, 1999; Trommsdorff & Friedlmeier, 1999). The objective was to test the extent of distress reactions in a disappointment situation, as well as the relationship between the course of emotions and interactive regulation with the mother.

We based our study on the following assumptions: The interactive regulation of a child's distress through a caregiver's support is a universal feature. Thereby, emotion regulation develops as an inherently cultural process because the caregivers interact with their children according to their own subjective meaning system that they share with the social and cultural environment. Cultural differences with regard to emotions and emotion socialization between Japan and Germany are expected due to the different cultural evaluations of emotional behavior in both countries. Whereas in Germany the child's expression of negative emotion is seen as indicating authenticity, individuality, and a trustful relationship, in Japan control of emotion is regarded as an indicator of maturity and as serving the value of harmony within the group. Furthermore, the experience of negative emotions is valued differently: Japanese mothers protect their children against the experience of negative emotions more than German mothers (Trommsdorff & Kornadt, 2003).

The process of successful transmission depends on maternal sensitivity. Maternal sensitivity towards the child in a distress situation is seen as a universal factor that influences the child's development of emotion: regulation (see Grossmann, Grossmann, & Keppler, this volume). Here we expected that sensitive mothers to not only foster their child's development, but more specifically, that they transfer the culture-specific aspects of emotion regulation more successfully than less sensitive mothers did.

As emotion regulation develops from interactive to self-guided regulation, stronger differences are expected with regard to older children. Three main research questions were formulated:

1. Do Japanese and German children display a different course of expression of emotions in a disappointment situation?
2. Do culture-specific differences occur in both age groups?
3. Is mothers' sensitivity related to their children's course of expression of emotion in a culture-specific way?

2- year-old Japanese ($n = 20$) and German ($n = 20$), as well as 5-year-old Japanese ($n = 20$) and German girls ($n = 30$) were observed and videotaped in a disappointment situation with their mothers. Selecting an age-specific situation, a negative emotion was induced. The 2-year-olds played with a dollhouse, which was suddenly taken away by a stranger. The 5-year-old girls were asked to paint a picture within a limited time period and a stranger took the picture away before it could be finished. Both situations had in common that an event evoking negative emotion occurred for both age groups in a sudden way.

Variables

Strength of negative expression of emotion. The extent of the girls' expression of negative emotion was evaluated on six-point scales in four time intervals of 10 seconds each: (1) before the disappointing event, (2) immediately after the event, (3) one minute later and (4) two minutes later. After the last sequence the experimenter came back and returned the dollhouse or picture. The children's gestures and facial expressions were used as criteria for evaluating the extent of expression of negative emotion. Japanese and German psychologists rated observations of both samples in order to control for cultural bias of ratings.

Mothers' Sensitivity was also assessed in the disappointment situation. The mothers' warmth and responsiveness was measured on 6-point scales and "sensitivity" was built as an aggregated variable of these two 6-point scales (warmth, responsiveness). This was viable step as these two measures were highly correlated in all four groups: $r(82) = .78$, $p < .001$ with a range from $r(14) = .74$, $p < .001$ to $r(28) = .79$, $p < .001$ for the subgroups. A median split was carried out for each age group within each culture in order to differentiate between high and low sensitive mothers.

Maternal Interactive Regulation Behavior. Problem-focused regulation, e.g., verbal comments that focus on the emotional event or the child's feeling, and emotion-focused regulation strategies like *comforting*, e.g., smiling at the child, *reappraisal*, e.g., giving explanations why they need this object, and *distraction*, e.g., initiating another activity or asking for playing were constructed as categories. A German and a Japanese rater coded each strategy in a dichotomous way (0 – does not appear, 1 – appears). The interrater reliability reached satisfying levels.

Results

The 2 (culture) x 2 (gender) ANOVA yielded a significant effect, $F(3, 80) = 5.58$, $p < .01$, that was based on the two main effects: Culture, $F(1, 82) = 5.49$, $p < .05$, and Age, $F(1, 82) = 6.11$, $p < .05$ (see Figure 4). Japanese mothers ($M = 5.26$, $SD = .79$) were significantly more sensitive than German mothers ($M = 4.57$, $SD = 1.33$) and mothers of 2-year-olds ($M = 5.29$, $SD = .79$) were significantly more sensitive than mothers of 5-year-old children ($M = 4.60$, $SD = 1.30$). The interaction effect was not significant, $F(1, 82) = 1.61$, ns (see Figure 4).

For the total sample the four time point measures of expressions correlated significantly, ranging between $r(83) = .30$, $p < .05$, and $r(83) = .69$, $p < .001$, except the correlation between baseline (time point 1) and the direct reaction to the event (time point 2), $r(83) = .15$, ns. This lacking relationship has to do with the low variation of the baseline measures.

A 2 (Culture) x 2 (Age) ANOVA with the repeated factor of children's expression of negative emotion (4 time points) was computed. The course of expression

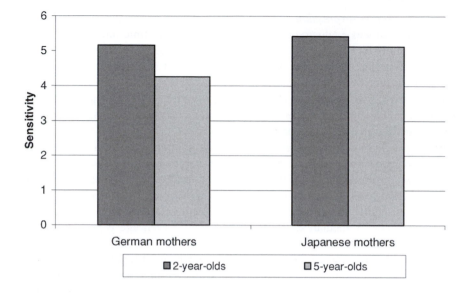

Figure 4. Mean Sensitivity of German and Japanese Mothers

showed no cultural effect, λ = .95, F (3, 78) = 1.28, *ns*, nor an interaction effect between culture and age groups, λ = .97, F (3, 78) = .97, *ns*. However, a significant age-effect resulted, λ = .55 F (3, 78) = 21.14, p < .001. Single comparisons showed that the expression of negative emotion of the 2-year-olds directly after the event was significantly stronger than compared to the 5-year-olds, F (1, 79) = 62.94, p < .001. At the same time the 2-year-olds also showed a tendency to recover more after one minute, F (1, 79) = 2.98, p < .10, and significantly more after two minutes, F (1, 79) = 5.94, p < .95. Therefore, the differences between 2- and 5-year-olds disappeared at the end of the situation.

The analysis of the relationship between mothers' sensitivity and the children's expression of negative emotion showed a nearly significant three-way interaction between culture and sensitivity, λ = .92, F (3, 76) = 2.23, p = .06. Single analysis showed that the culture-specific differences occurred in relation to the last time point. 2- and 5-year-old German girls of sensitive mothers displayed higher negative emotion at the end and recovered less than those of less sensitive mothers, whereas the girls of sensitive Japanese mothers recovered more compared to girls of less sensitive mothers. Therefore, the German girls of sensitive mothers were at the end more negative compared to the baseline and the Japanese more positive, F (1, 78) =

6.24, $p < .05$; they recovered less in relation to the spontaneous reaction after the event, $F(1, 78) = 2.81$, $p < .10$, and they recovered even less in relation to the third time point, $F(1, 78) = 2.94$, $p < .10$.

A separate analysis for both age groups showed that the course of negative emotion for the 2-year-olds was not affected by the maternal sensitivity in either cultural group, $\lambda = .92$, $F(3, 28) = .81$, $ns.$, but in the 5-year-old group, $\lambda = .85$, $F(3, 44) = 2.75$, $p < .05$. Sensitivity led to an inverse relation of the 5-year-old girls' course of negative emotion with regard to sensitivity (see Figure 5). Single analysis yielded that the German 5-year-old girls of sensitive mothers showed a stronger reaction directly after the event, whereas the pattern was inverse for the Japanese group, $F(1, 46) = 3.49$, $p < .10$. The former recovered less after one minute compared to the girls of less sensitive mothers, $F(1, 46) = 4.24$, $p < .05$, and whereas the girls of less sensitive German mothers came back to the baseline, girls of sensitive mothers stayed more negative, and the Japanese girls showed an inverse position, $F(1, 46) = 6.72$, $p < .01$ (see Figure 5). In other words: whereas Japanese girls of sensitive mothers showed lower strength of reaction compared to the girls with less sensitive mothers, the pattern for the German dyads was inverse. The girls whose mothers were sensitive displayed a much stronger reaction and they recovered less compared to the German girls with less sensitive mothers.

In a next step we analyzed the differences of mothers' emotion regulation behavior of the 5-year-old girls by using loglinear analysis. Both the German and the Japanese sensitive mothers displayed more comforting compared to less sensitive mothers. They showed a calming smiling more often (German mothers 46.67%; Japanese mothers: 70.00%) than less sensitive mothers (German mothers: 13.33%, Japanese mothers: 10.00%), $\chi^2(1) = 9.27$, $p < .01$. The Japanese mothers encouraged their child to continue with the task (sensitive mothers: 70.00%, less sensitive mothers: 78.00%) more than the German mothers did (sensitive mothers: 33.00%, less sensitive mothers: 20.00%), $\chi^2(1) = 9.40$, $p < .01$. In contrast to German mothers (sensitive mothers: 73.33%; less sensitive mothers: 53.33%), no Japanese mother commented on the child's emotion or the cause of the negative emotion. Due to the lack of variance of Japanese mothers, no statistical value could be computed but the difference is apparent as no Japanese mother showed a problem-focused regulation.

Finally, body contact between mother and child occurred more often in Japanese dyads (74.50%) than in German dyads (33.33%), $\chi^2(1) = 5.54$, $p < .05$ and more often in dyads with sensitive mothers (77.70%) than with less sensitive mothers (30.00%), $\chi^2(1) = 6.56$, $p < .05$.

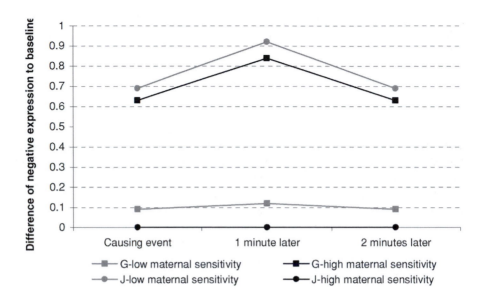

Figure 5. Relations between Maternal Sensitivity and Course of Negative Emotional Reactions for Japanese and German 5-Year-Old Girls

Discussion

The aim of this study was to test commonalities and differences of children's negative emotions in relation to mothers' sensitivity and interactive regulation behavior by taking two cultural groups and two age groups into account. The results cannot be interpreted for both genders as we tested only girls. The sample had to be restricted for economic reasons. The age-specific differences point to the question whether the situations were equivalent for both age groups. The analysis of specific differences in mothers' regulation behavior did not lead to a clear pattern that differentiated between German and Japanese, as well as between sensitive and less sensitive mothers, in order to explain the specific differences that occurred with regard to the girls' reactions. Nevertheless, and in spite of such limitation, several interesting results were found.

2-year-old Japanese and German girls' course of negative emotion did not differ but the 5-year-olds' did. It seems that different developmental paths concerning the expression and regulation become more apparent in preschool age. 5-year-old girls' expressions showed a culturally inverse pattern in relation to the mothers' sensitivity. Whereas the German girls of sensitive mothers displayed a stronger negative expression and did not recover over the observed period as compared to the girls of

less sensitive mothers, the Japanese girls demonstrated an inverse pattern. By looking at the interactive regulation strategies, Japanese mothers showed a preference for
emotion-focused regulation. They comforted and distracted the child more often
than the German mothers did. They ignored the cause and created a situation for the
child "as if" nothing had happened, i.e. the child's focus was not oriented towards
her own feeling. In contrast, German mothers showed strong problem-focused regulation. They commented on the cause directly and verbally, talked about solutions
and the child's emotion, i.e., the child's focus was oriented to her own inner experience. This is in line with the finding that Japanese as compared to German mothers
also show more secondary control towards their children when facing stressful situations (Trommsdorff & Friedlmeier, 1993).

The child's experience of interactive regulation may lead to an internalization of
such strategies, which can be used later on for self-regulation. Moreover, the cultural
models of emotion are transferred within these interactive regulation processes and
the child acquires these cultural standards. Similar former experiences of such interactions can be assumed and these former experiences may explain the observed
cultural differences of children's expression of negative emotion and its course.
Similar experiences will occur in the future and it can be expected that the German
children will strengthen the experience of a negative emotion as a personal cue to act
out and to act upon it, whereas the Japanese children will decrease the experiences
of negative emotions and reevaluate the meaning of this cue – if it occurs. This
means that interactive regulation behavior mediates the child's feeling and leads to
different focus of attention. This interpretation may also help to understand the findings that persons in collectivistic as compared to individualistic contexts perceive
emotions as reflecting reality rather than the inner world of the individual, and that
these emotions belong to self-other relationships rather than to the subjectivity of the
self (Mesquita, 2001b). And finally, based on the specific experiences with the caregiver, emotional processes become individualized.

Conclusions

The aim of this chapter was to argue for the necessity of conceptualizing a theoretical framework that takes cultural diversity as well as developmental processes into
account. The two more extensively described studies were used as examples to demonstrate two different approaches. The study of Cole, Bruschi, and Tamang (2002)
focused on a broad description of the cultural background. Thereby, the authors
clearly relate culture-specific features to the emotional domain. They include ideas
on child-rearing practices as mediators of such differences and derive specific hypotheses about commonalities and differences in regard to children's experience and

expression of emotions. Nevertheless, the study also has some shortcomings. The authors had difficulty in conceptualising developmental hypotheses as too little is known in this area. Their argumentation of relations between cultural background, child-rearing practices, and children's emotional development remains untested as they only measured the outcome variable. The measurement of expression by interviewing is not a valid measure and observation data are necessary.

The second study tries to overcome some of these mentioned shortcomings. Children's emotional expression was observed and the interaction between mother and child, as the place where cultural knowledge is transmitted, was also taken into account. Furthermore, not only the strength of expression of negative emotion reaction but also its course was observed, in order to evaluate the consequences of regulation strategies for the emotion itself. This study also has its shortcomings. Similar to Cole's study, mothers' general value orientations and ethnotheories about emotion were not taken into account. This could provide important information to help understand the interaction and child's development better. Second, both studies were cross-sectional studies. Longitudinal cross-cultural studies would allow a better insight into developmental questions in a cultural perspective. Such a research design is an ideal quite difficult to realize but as a working ideal it may serve as a motivating force to proceed in this direction as a future task.

By going back to the general question of this chapter, namely the reciprocal relation between social sciences and cross-cultural psychology, I will try and provide a more specific answer.

First, culture-sensitive approaches have demonstrated that culture-specific differences are based on differences with regard to cultural norms and values (Matsumoto, 2001). The results of such studies are a strong argument for psychologists to take culture as an important condition for personality development into account – be it at the group level or at the individual level. Developmental psychology should recognize this starting point in order to construct more culturally valid theories.

Second, it was argued that for questions of developmental psychology most of the models in cross-cultural psychology are not helpful in answering the question of the genesis of psychological phenomena. It is necessary to specify and extend the existing models as exemplified by the use of the topic of emotion and culture. Emotions and emotion regulation develop and become more and more integrated into higher levels of behavior regulation. By this, the emotional behavior may have a universal starting point (similar to language) but is increasingly culturally mediated. A developmental perspective requires the assumption of immediacy of culture in order to describe, explain and predict the processes by which cultural knowledge is transmitted to the developing child. Beside general norms, specific cultural ideas and attitudes on emotions have to be understood. In addition, it is important to comprehend how these aspects become actualized in socialization processes at different levels. It may be that in the long run research in this field may lead to a general revision of models in cross-cultural psychology.

References

Albas, D. C., McCluskey, K. W., & Albas, C. A. (1976). Perception of the emotional content of speech: A comparison of two Canadian groups. *Journal of Cross-Cultural Psychology 7,* 481-490.

Camras, L. A., Campos, J., Campos, R., Miyake, K., Oster, H., Ujiie, T., Wang, L., & Zhaolan, M. (1998). Production of emotional facial expressions in European American, Japanese, and Chinese infants. *Developmental Psychology, 34,* 616-628.

Caudill, W., & Weinstein, H. (1969). Maternal care and infant behavior in Japan and America. *Journal for the Study of Interpersonal Processes, 32,* 12-43.

Chao, R. K. (1995). Chinese and European-American cultural models of the self reflected in mothers' child-rearing beliefs. *Ethos, 23,* 328-354.

Choy, G., & Mohay, H. (2001, April), *A cross-cultural study of Chinese and Australian children's understanding of emotional dissemblance.* Poster presented at the Biennial Meeting of the Society for Research in Child Development, Minneapolis, MN.

Cole, P. M., Bruschi, C. J., & Tamang, B. L. (2002). Cultural differences in children's emotional reactions to difficult situations. *Child Development, 73,* 983-996.

Damasio, A. R. (1999). *The feeling of what happens: Body and emotion in the making of consciousness.* San Diego, CA: Hartcourt.

Darwin, C. (2000/1872). *Der Ausdruck der Gemütsbewegungen bei dem Menschen und den Tieren [The expression of the emotions in men and animals].* Frankfurt a.M., Germany: Eichborn.

Doi, T. (1973). *The anatomy of dependence.* Tokyo: Kodansha.

Ekman, P. (1972). Universals and cultural differences in facial expressions of emotion. In J. K. Cole (Ed.), *Nebraska Symposium on motivation, 1971* (Vol. 19, pp. 207-283). Lincoln, NE: University of Nebraska Press.

Ekman, P., & Friesen, W. V. (1978). *The facial action coding system.* Palo Alto, CA: Consulting Psychologists Press.

Ekman, P., Friesen, W. V., & Ellsworth, P. (1982). What are the similarities and differences in facial behavior across cultures? In P. Ekman (Ed.), *Emotion in the human face* (pp. 128-146). Cambridge, UK: Cambridge University Press.

Essau, C. A., & Trommsdorff, G. (1996). Coping with university-related problems: A cross-cultural comparison. *Journal of Cross-Cultural Psychology, 27,* 315-328.

Field, T., & Walden, T. A. (1982). Production and discrimination of facial expressions by preschool children. *Child Development, 53,* 1299-1311.

Friedlmeier, W. (1999a). Entwicklung der Emotionsregulation in der Kindheit [Development of emotion regulation in childhood]. In W. Friedlmeier & M. Holodynski (Eds.), *Emotionale Entwicklung: Funktion, Regulation und soziokultureller Kontext von Emotionen* (pp. 197-219). Heidelberg, Germany: Spektrum.

Friedlmeier, W. (1999b). Sozialisation der Emotionsregulation [Socialization of emotion regulation]. *Zeitschrift für Soziologie der Erziehung und Sozialisation, 19,* 35-51.

Friedlmeier, W. (in press). Kultur und Emotion. Zur Sozialisation menschlicher Gefühle [Culture and Emotion. On socialization of human emotions]. In B. Kleeberg, T. Walter, & F. Crivellari (Eds.), *Urmensch und Wissenschaftskultur.* Tübingen, Germany: Gunter Narr.

Friedlmeier, W., & Matsumoto, D. (2004). *Emotion und Emotionsregulation im Kulturvergleich [Emotion and emotion regulation in cross-cultural perspective].* Manuscript submitted for publication.

Friedlmeier, W., & Trommsdorff, G. (1999). Emotion regulation in early childhood. A cross-cultural comparison between German and Japanese toddlers. *Journal of Cross-Cultural Psychology 30,* 684-711.

Friedlmeier, W., & Trommsdorff, G. (2002, August). *Negative emotional reaction and interactive regulation in 2- and 5-year-old German and Japanese children with their mothers.* Paper presented at the XVIIth Meetings of the ISSBD in Ottawa, Canada.

Frijda, N. H. (1986). *The emotions.* Cambridge, U.K.: Cambridge University Press.

Frijda, N. H. (1994). Varieties of affect: Emotions and episodes, moods, and sentiments. In P. Ekman & R. J. Davidson (Eds.), *The nature of emotions: Fundamental questions* (pp. 59-67). London: Oxford University Press.

Frijda, N. H., Markam, S., Sato, K., & Wiers, R. (1995). Emotions and emotion words. In J. A. Russell, A. S. R. Manstead, J. C. Wellenkamp, & J. M. Fernández-Dols (Eds.), *Everyday conceptions of emotion: An introduction to the psychology, anthropology, and linguistics of emotion* (pp. 121-143). Dordrecht, The Netherlands: Kluwer.

Geertz, C. (1973). *The interpretation of cultures.* New York: Basic Books.

Gergely, G., & Watson, J. S. (1999). Early socio-emotional development: Contingency perception and the social-biofeedback model. In P. Rochat (Ed.), *Early social cognition: Understanding others in the first months of life* (pp. 101-136). Mahwah, NJ: Erlbaum.

Heine, S. J., Lehman, D. R., Peng, K., & Greenholtz, J. (2002). What's wrong with cross-cultural comparisons of subjective Likert scales?: The reference-group effect. *Journal of Personality and Social Psychology, 82,* 903-918.

Hofstede, G. H. (1980). *Culture's consequences. International differences in work-related values.* London: Sage.

Hofstede, G. H. (2001). *Culture's consequences: Comparing values, behaviors, institutions, and organizations across nations* (2nd ed.). Thousand Oaks, CA: Sage.

Holodynski, M., & Friedlmeier, W. (in press). *Development of emotions and emotion regulation. An internalization model.* New York: Kluwer.

Izard, C. E. (1977). *Human emotions.* New York: Plenum Press.

Izard, C. E., & Ackerman, B. P. (2000). Motivational, organizational, and regulatory functions of discrete emotions. In M. Lewis & J. M. Haviland-Jones (Eds.), *Handbook of emotions (*2nd ed., pp. 253-265). New York: The Guilford Press.

Kagitçibasi, C. (1994). A critical appraisal of individualism and collectivism: Toward a new formulation. In U. Kim, H. C. Triandis, C. Kagitçibasi, S.-C. Choi, & G. Yoon (Eds.), *Individualism and collectivism: Theory, method, and applications* (pp. 52-65). London: Sage.

Kagitçibasi, C. (1996). The autonomous-relational self: A new synthesis. *European Psychologist, 1,* 180-186.

Kudoh, T., & Matsumoto, D. (1985). Cross-cultural examination of the semantic dimensions of body postures. *Journal of Personality & Social Psychology 48,* 1440-1446.

Lazarus, R. S. (1991). *Emotion and adaptation.* New York: Oxford University Press.

Lebra, T. S. (1976). *Japanese patterns of behavior.* Honolulu, HI: University of Hawaii Press.

Levenson, R. W., Ekman, P., Heider, K., & Friesen, W. V. (1992). Emotion and autonomic nervous system activity in the Minangkabau of West Sumatra. *Journal of Personality & Social Psychology, 62,* 972-988.

Leventhal, H., & Scherer, K. (1987). The relationship of emotion to cognition: A functional approach to a semantic controversy. *Cognition and Emotion, 1,* 3-28.

Markus, H. R., & Kitayama, S. (1991). Culture and the self: Implications for cognition, emotion, and motivation. *Psychological Review, 98,* 224–253.

Matsumoto, D. (1989). Cultural influences on the perception of emotion. *Journal of Cross-Cultural Psychology, 20,* 92-105.

Matsumoto, D. (2001). Culture and Emotion. In D. Matsumoto. (Ed.), The handbook of culture and psychology (pp. 171-194). London: Oxford University Press.

Matsumoto, D., Consolacion, T., Yamada, H., Suzuki, R., Franklin, B., Paul, S., Ray, R., & Uchida, H. (2002). American-Japanese cultural differences in judgements of emotional expressions of different intensities. *Cognition & Emotion, 16,* 721-747.

Matsumoto, D., & Kupperbusch, C. (2001). Ideocentric and allocentric differences in emotional expression, experience, and the coherence between expression and experience. *Asian Journal of Social Psychology, 4,* 113-131.

Meltzoff, A. N., & Moore, M. K. (1983). Newborn infants imitate adult facial gestures. *Child Development, 54,* 702–709.

Mesquita, B. (2001a). Emotions in collectivist and individualist contexts. *Journal of Personality & Social Psychology, 80,* 68-74.

Mesquita, B. (2001b). Culture and emotion: Different approaches to the question. In T. J. Mayne & G. A. Bonanno (Eds.). *Emotions: Current issues and future directions. Emotions and social behavior* (pp. 214-250). New York: The Guilford Press.

Miyake, K., Campos, J. J., Kagan, J., & Bradshaw, D. L. (1986). Issues in socioemotional development. In H. Stevenson, H. Azuma, & K. Hakuta (Eds.), *Child development and education in Japan* (pp. 239-261). New York: W. H. Freeman and Company.

Nussbaum, M. C. (2000). Emotions and social norms. In L. P. Nucci, G. B. Saxe, & E. Turiel (Eds.), *Culture, thought, and development. The Jean Piaget Symposium Series* (pp. 41-63). Mahwah, NJ: Erlbaum.

Oyserman, D., Coon, H. M., & Kemmelmeier, M. (2002). Rethinking individualism and collectivism: Evaluation of theoretical assumptions and meta-analyses. *Psychological Bulletin, 128,* 3-72.

Roseman, I. J., Dhawan, N., Rettek, S. I., Naidu, R. K., & Thapa, K. (1995). Cultural differences and cross-cultural similarities in appraisals and emotional responses. *Journal of Cross-Cultural Psychology 26,* 23-48.

Rothbaum, F., Weisz, J. R., & Snyder, S. S. (1982). Changing the world and changing the self: A two-processing model of perceived control. *Journal of Personality & Social Psychology, 42,* 5-37.

Russell, J. A. (1994). Is there universal recognition of emotion from facial expressions? A review of the cross-cultural studies. *Psychological Bulletin, 115,* 102-141.

Scherer, K. R., Matsumoto, D., Wallbott, H. G., & Kudoh, T. (1988). Emotional experience in cultural context: A comparison between Europe, Japan, and the United States. In K. R. Scherer (Ed.), *Facets of emotion: Recent research* (pp. 5-30). Hillsdale, NJ: Erlbaum.

Scherer, K. R., & Wallbott, H. G. (1994). Evidence for universality and cultural variation of differential emotion response patterning. *Journal of Personality & Social Psychology, 66,* 310-328.

Schimmack, U. (1996). Cultural influences on the recognition of emotion by facial expressions: Individualistic or Caucasian cultures? *Journal of Cross-Cultural Psychology, 27,* 37-50.

Scherer, K. R., Summerfield, A. B., & Wallbott, H. G. (1983). Cross-national research on antecedents and components of emotion: A progress report. *Social Science Information, 22,* 355-385.

Schmidt-Atzert, L. (1997). *Lehrbuch der Emotionspsychologie [Textbook of emotion psychology].* Stuttgart, Germany: Kohlhammer.

Seginer, R., Trommsdorff, G., & Essau, C. (1993). Adolescent control beliefs: Cross-cultural variations of primary and secondary orientations. *International Journal of Behavioral Development, 16,* 243-260.

Sogon, S., & Masutani, M. (1989). Identification of emotion from body movements: A cross-cultural study of Americans and Japanese. *Psychological Reports 65,* 35-46.

Sroufe, L. A. (1996). *Emotional development: The organization of emotional life in the early years.* New York: Cambridge University Press.

Stansbury, K., & Sigman, M. (2000). Responses of preschoolers in two frustrating episodes: Emergence of complex strategies for emotion regulation. *Journal of Genetic Psychology, 161,* 182-202.

Super, C. M., & Harkness, S. (1997). The cultural structuring of child development. In J. Berry, P. R. Dasen, & T. S. Saraswathi (Eds.), *Handbook of cross-cultural psychology* (Vol. 2, pp. 1-39). Boston: Allyn & Bacon.

Thompson, R. A. (1990). Emotion and self-regulation. In R. A. Thompson (Ed.), *Socioemotional development: Nebraska Symposium on Motivation, 1988* (Vol. 36, pp. 367-467). Lincoln, NE: University of Nebraska Press.

Triandis, H. C. (1995). *Individualism and collectivism.* Boulder, CO: Westview.

Trommsdorff, G., & Friedlmeier, W. (1993). Control behavior and responsiveness in Japanese and German mothers. *Early Development and Parenting, 2,* 65-78.

Trommsdorff, G., & Friedlmeier, W. (1999). Emotionale Entwicklung im Kulturvergleich [Emotional development in cross-cultural perspective]. In W. Friedlmeier & M. Holodynski (Eds.), *Emotionale Entwicklung. Funktion, Regulation und soziokultureller Kontext von Emotionen* (pp. 275-293). Heidelberg, Germany: Spektrum.

Trommsdorff, G., & Kornadt, H.-J. (2003). Parent-child relations in cross-cultural perspective. In L. Kuczynski (Ed.), *Handbook of dynamics in parent-child relations* (pp. 271-306). London: Sage.

Valsiner, J. (1989). *Human development and culture. The social nature of personality and its study.* Lexington, MA: Lexington Books.

Valsiner, J. (2003). Culture and its transfer: Ways of creating general knowledge through the study of cultural particulars. In W. J. Lonner, D. L. Dinnel, S. A. Hayes, & D. N. Sattler (Eds.). *Online Readings in Psychology and Culture* (Unit 2, Ch. 12, Center for Cross-Cultural Research, Western Washington University, Bellingham, WA, from http://www.ac.wwu.edu/~culture/readings.htm

van de Vijver, F. J. R., & Leung, K. (1997). *Methods and data analysis for cross-cultural research.* Thousand Oaks, CA: Sage.

Vygotsky, L. S. (1978). *Mind in society.* Cambridge, MA: MIT Press.

Vygotsky, L. S. (1994). The problem of the cultural development of the child. In R. van der Veer & J. Valsiner (Eds.), *The Vygotsky Reader* (pp. 57-72). Oxford, UK: Blackwell.

Weisz, J. R. (1990). Development of control-related beliefs, goals, and styles in childhood and adolescence: A clinical perspective. In J. Rodin, C. Schooler, & K. W. Schaie (Eds.), *Self-directedness: Cause and effects throughout the life course* (pp. 103-145). Hillsdale, NJ: Erlbaum.

7

Spatial Language and Cognitive Development in India: An Urban/Rural Comparison[1]

Ramesh C. Mishra and Pierre R. Dasen

Introduction

Within the general framework of cross-cultural research on human development (Berry, Dasen, & Saraswathi, 1997; Trommsdorff, 1993, 1995), this chapter reports on a study of spatial orientation systems in different cultures, the language people use to describe the location of objects in space, how they encode these in memory, and the relationships of these features to cognitive development. An interdisciplinary approach draws on the fields of anthropology, psycholinguistics, and cross-cultural cognitive developmental psychology. We report findings with 4- to 14-year-old children in India ($N = 369$), with a particular focus on the comparison between an urban and a rural group. The field sites were selected taking into consideration how reference to spatial locations is organized in the language as well as in the local cultural practices. In a village in the Ganges plains of India, a geocentric spatial localization system is used mainly with reference to cardinal directions, while in the city of Varanasi, relative references (right/left) are additionally used, although the same language (Hindi) is spoken in both locations. This allows us to test the relationships between ecology, culture, and language, and the encoding of spatial infor-

---

[1] This study was funded by grant 11-54101.98 of the Swiss National Fund for Scientific Research attributed to the second author. Assistance of Dr. A. C. Chaubey in fieldwork is gratefully acknowledged.

mation and performance on some Piagetian spatial tasks, while taking age and schooling into account. The findings support a moderate form of linguistic relativism at the group but not at the individual level.

Theoretical Background

Piaget and Inhelder (1948/1956), and other western developmental psychologists have found that children first build up spatial concepts in relation to their own body, both at the sensori-motor level of action and at the later representational level. Piaget and Inhelder's theory also establishes the developmental sequence of topological, projective, and Euclidean spatial concepts, that has gained wide acceptance in developmental psychology and in linguistics. More recent cognitive development theories use the same typology with different words. For example, Taylor and Tversky (1996) state that theorists of spatial language have distinguished three kinds of reference frames: intrinsic or object-centered, deictic or viewer-centered, and extrinsic or environment-centered. Although there is some controversy about the best terminology, these three frames also correspond, in linguistics, to Levinson's (1996) distinction between relative, intrinsic, and absolute (or extrinsic) frames. Within an intrinsic frame, locations are described in relation to an object's front, back, or sides, and depend on the agreement on the intrinsic orientation of the reference object. In the relative frame, the locations of objects are described in relation to an individual's left, right, front, and back (LRFB); they are viewer-centered and require knowledge of the viewer's orientation. In the absolute or extrinsic frame, objects are located according to a co-ordinate system that is external to the scene, i.e., geocentric. The correspondence between these three schemes is presented in Table 1.

One problem with the area of spatial concept development is that it has almost completely relied on research with western samples. Would the sequence of stages hold up in research in other cultures? Could it be that the very centering on the individual's construction of space on the basis of his or her own body is a bias, due to western individualism (Kagitçibasi, 1997; Wassmann, 1994)?

Table 1

Comparison between Three Typologies of Spatial Frames of Reference in Cognitive Development and in Linguistics

	Object-centered	Viewer-centered	Environment-centered
Piaget and Inhelder (1948/1956)	Topological	Projective	Euclidean
Taylor and Tversky (1996)	Intrinsic	Deictic	Extrinsic
Levinson (1996)	Intrinsic	Relative, egocentric	Absolute, geocentric

While there is some cross-cultural research on spatial cognition, most of it is not directly relevant to our issue. The situation can perhaps best be described as a contrast between the emic and etic approaches (Segall, Dasen, Berry, & Poortinga, 1999). On the emic side, there are a large number of anthropological descriptions of how space is organized in different cultures, yet few say anything about developmental aspects. For example, the very interesting studies on traditional navigational systems (Gladwin, 1970; Hutchins, 1983; Lewis, 1980) that demonstrate culture-specific, extremely complex and abstract thinking, fail to describe the precise cognitive processes that are involved, and are not developmental. On the etic side is the cross-cultural replication of Piaget's theory, using classical "Piagetian" tasks (Dasen & Heron, 1981; Dasen, 1998b). While systematic cultural differences were found in the rates of cognitive development that could be related to eco-cultural factors, there is no indication from this body of research that there could be any reversals in the sequence of stages, nor indeed any culture-specific cognitive processes (Dasen, 1993; Mishra, 1997, 2001). The only hint at a possible reversal of stages in spatial concept development between projective and Euclidean space comes from a study in Bali, to be reviewed presently.

Spatial orientation in Bali

Following previous efforts to combine the methods of anthropology and psychology in fieldwork in Papua-New Guinea (Wassmann & Dasen, 1994a, 1994b), Wassmann and Dasen (1998) studied the Balinese orientation system, this being an essential aspect of Balinese culture. Orientation is based on a geocentric system of two orthogonal axes, somewhat like cardinal directions, except that the main axis is geared to the island's central volcano, the dwelling place of the Hindu gods of Bali; *kaja,* "towards the mountain," is the sacred and pure direction, opposed to *kelod,* "towards the sea." The *kaja-kelod* axis cannot be translated as north-south, because its orientation changes as one proceeds around the island. Similarly, the orthogonal axis *kangin-kauh* corresponds to East and West, or sunrise and sunset, only in the south of Bali. In order to document the use of spatial terms in Balinese, Wassmann and Dasen (1998) carried out an ethnographic and linguistic survey, examining in detail how the inhabitants of various sites on the Eastern peninsula of Bali use the system. They discovered quite some complexity in the local adaptations of the system. This type of topography-dependent geocentric orientation system can also be found in other languages of South-East Asia and Oceania (Barnes, 1993; Ozanne-Rivierre, 1987; Senft, 1997, 2001).

The entire Balinese cosmology is related to this orientation system: from the representation of the human body to the whole of the universe, from the architecture of temples and villages to the social structure. Children learn the use of the orientation system very early in life, although they also learn the ritually important distinction between the left and the right hand. However, left and right are only applied to the body and to objects in contact with the body; all other objects are located with the geocentric orientation system. In other words, while in European languages, a geocentric system (cardinal directions) is applied only to the macro-space (e.g., for maps, for the outline of some cities), in Bali a geocentric system is also applied to the micro-space, i.e., for the localization of objects on a table or in a room.

In previous research, Wassmann and Dasen (1994a, 1994b) had shown how the linguistic and ethnographic parts of the research are absolutely essential before turning to the use of "induced situations" such as psychological tasks. In Bali, Wassmann and Dasen (1996, 1998) used two spatial encoding tasks based on a simple paradigm developed by the Cognitive Anthropology Research Group (CARG) at the Max Planck Institute for Psycholinguistics in Nijmegen, The Netherlands (Levinson, 1997, 2003). Let us suppose, for example, that three toy animals, aligned and all looking to the left are presented on a table in front of you. You are asked to remember this display, then turn around by 180°, and then place the animals in the same way as they were on the first table. If you orient them to the left, you have used an egocentric (relative) encoding, related to your own body. But, if you are encoding space in the geocentric way, you will orient the animals to the right, keeping the same absolute direction.

This simple task called "Animals in a Row," along with another similar task ("Steve's Mazes," to be described later in the method section), was used with 26 Balinese children aged 4 to 15 years, and 12 adults. In the Animals task, most subjects systematically showed absolute (geocentric) reactions similar to those obtained with the Tzeltal of Tenejapa in Mexico, and contrary to those of a sample of Dutch adults who almost exclusively used relative encoding (Brown & Levinson, 1993, 2000). In Steve's Mazes, Balinese informants made both geocentric and egocentric (relative) choices. This showed that the Balinese could use two coding systems, but clearly prefer the geocentric (absolute) system. In the Balinese language, the system of geocentric spatial reference is so strong that it determines not only the manner of speaking, but is also a mode of spatial representation and its commitment to memory. The results support a moderate form of linguistic relativity: while the very young children (4 to 7 years) almost exclusively used the absolute system in their language and in their way of memorizing a spatial device, there seems to be a developmental change towards relative solutions. This age trend is in contradiction with the developmental theories of Piaget and Inhelder, and others. It was therefore essential to continue the research in similar cultural and linguistic contexts using other spatial development tasks, in order to determine if we will really find a reversal of the developmental sequence described for western children.

The research in Bali, based on a very small sample, can be considered as a pilot study that requires replication. What is needed is a study with larger samples, and other tasks assessing not only spatial encoding but also spatial concept development. Also, having been unable to include a sample of unschooled children, Wassmann and Dasen (1996, 1998) were not in a position to separate the confounded factors of schooling and age. Schooling in Bali takes place in Indonesian, which is akin to European languages in its use of relative terms. Hence, we do not know whether the trend from absolute to relative encoding is linked to age or to schooling or, more generally, to acculturation.

While a replication study in Bali is also being undertaken, the present research program in India is geared to answer some of the questions raised by this pilot study in Bali, with much larger samples and better controls over the language spoken and schooling.

Linguistic relativism

Basic cognitive processes have been found to be universal (Segall et al., 1999; Dasen, 1993; Mishra, 1997), and languages themselves have been shown to conform to many universal principles (Holenstein, 1993), though recent research in language acquisition has tended to emphasize differences as well as similarities across languages (Mohanty & Perregaux, 1997). Speakers of European languages are used to egocentric encoding. Other forms of encoding will appear peculiar or even impossible to them. So much, so that in developmental psychology, cognitive sciences and even European philosophical traditions, the conception of space was considered to necessarily emanate from one's own body, standing in an upright position and looking straight ahead; in the so called "canonical position" (Clark, 1973, p. 34). The egocentric conception of space was also considered universal, because it was "more natural and primitive" (Miller & Johnson-Laird, 1976, p. 34). However, there are growing doubts about these basic assumptions as they may well be ethnocentric (Wassmann, 1994).

Does language constrain the way one thinks? In the middle of last century, Whorf's theory of linguistic relativism enjoyed prominence. But in more recent times the answer to this question has become an emphatic "no." Berry, Poortinga, Segall and Dasen (1992/2002) summarized the empirical data in the following fashion: "In general, we can conclude that there is at best limited support for the linguistic relativity hypothesis at the lexical level, but the last word has probably not been spoken on this issue" (p. 105). The issue of linguistic relativity has been revived by Lucy (1992), and by Levinson and his CARG colleagues (Brown & Levinson, 1993, 2000; Gumperz & Levinson, 1996; Levinson, 1996, 2003). The present research is designed to contribute to this topic, with the particularity of observing language and cognition also at the individual rather than only at the group level.

If one has to describe the position of an object or person with respect to another, we accomplish this in English by utilizing the projective notions of right and left, in reference to the speaker's body. For example: "Two men are standing before me side by side, the man on the right is holding a stick." A viewer taking up a position on the other side of the two men would say: "The man on the left is holding the stick." At first sight this seems obvious and natural, also because the linguistic encoding is congruent with the kind of information provided by the visual, auditory, and haptic senses. But it is not so. Some languages do not use the apparently fundamental, body-centered spatial notions of "left/right," "front/back." Instead they rely on fixed, environment-centered (also called geocentric) frames of reference, such as cardinal directions or related terms. For example, "the man on the West side is holding a stick." In this case, the description does not change with the viewer's change of position.

The question arises whether these linguistic differences correspond to conceptual differences. We may assume that spatial representations are influenced either by sensory information (which is egocentric) or by language (which may or may not be egocentric). In European languages, that are egocentric, the two are confounded. Carrying out a study in languages that do not use the egocentric frame of reference, like Balinese or several languages in India and Nepal, will allow us to dissociate the two.

Pederson, Danziger, Levinson, Kita, Senft, and Wilkins (1998) have provided a typology of languages along these lines, distinguishing languages that use exclusively the intrinsic (e.g., Mayan), relative (e.g., Dutch, Japanese), or absolute (e.g., Australian Aboriginal languages; Tzeltal, a Mayan language from Chiapas in Mexico) frames of reference, as well as several mixed cases, such as the Dravidian and Tibeto-Burman languages (Pederson, 1993; Bickel, 1997). However, in several cases, including Balinese and the languages in locations used in our study, the absolute frame is dominant.

CARG members have carried out coordinated research in several locations, working on language acquisition in longitudinal studies with children (León, 1994, 1995), carefully documenting language use in everyday situations and in standardized situations called "space games" (e.g., Levinson, 1991; Ruiter & Wilkins, 1997; Wassmann, 1994, 1997), and by studying the impact of language on spatial encoding through a series of memory tasks (Danziger, 1993), some of which will be described below in more detail. We cannot do justice by any means in this brief review to all of the work carried out by this group (for a summary, see Levinson, 2003).

One study that is directly relevant to our project was carried out by Pederson (1993) in South India. The author provides an interesting classification of subtypes of the absolute, geocentric systems:

- North/south/east/west (NSEW); monsoonwards; towards sunset/sunrise; etc.;
- Uphill/downhill; inland/seaward;
- Conventional landmark, e.g., "towards the headman's house," used to designate distant direction (usually beyond the horizon);
- Situation based local landmark, e.g., "towards the door," used to designate direction in a limited universe of discourse.

Tamil speakers have both a geocentric system (NSEW) and a relative one (LRFB). While both exist in the language, in the rural areas of Tamil Nadu people tend to use the NSEW system and conventional landmarks, while in the urban areas the LRFB system is dominant, with an occasional reference to situation-based local landmarks. However, both groups of speakers have the ability to shift between absolute and relative terminology.

The research reported here is to answer the following research questions, concentrating each time on the urban/rural contrast:

1. What is the spatial language actually used by children of various ages in the two settings?
2. What are the developmental trends in spatial encoding according to the two frames of reference (geocentric and egocentric)? Does this trend confirm the possible reversal found in previous research in Bali? Is there a significant relationship (controlling for age and schooling) between spatial language use and spatial encoding?
3. Is there a significant relationship (controlling for age and schooling) between spatial language use and/or spatial encoding and spatial concept development? In particular, does using more geocentric language and/or more geocentric spatial encoding favor the development of Euclidean spatial concepts?

In the study described here, we take advantage of a similar situation in Northern India with Hindi speaking people: we compare two samples, a rural and an urban one, both speaking the same language, yet using (to some extent) different spatial orientation systems. This situation represents a challenge to any strong linguistic relativism theory, though it does allow us to test the hypothesis that those children who use a geocentric language more will also use more absolute encoding (and of course the reverse should hold true for those who use an egocentric language more). We also set out to test the hypothesis that using a more geocentric language and/or spatial encoding may foster spatial conceptual development, in particular of Euclidean space.

Empirical Study in India

In the present study in India, two locations in Uttar Pradesh were chosen because they clearly represent different eco-cultural settings, with spatial orientation systems (and their corresponding language use) adapted to the ecological contexts. We therefore place our research within the eco-cultural framework developed by Berry (e.g., Berry et al., 1992/2002) that has also guided much of our previous research (Dasen, 1998a; Mishra, Sinha, & Berry, 1996; Niraula, 1998; Niraula & Mishra, 2001). According to this framework, individual psychological characteristics are functionally linked to culture that is itself an adaptation to ecological and sociohistorical contexts. In other words, people develop preferentially those skills that are needed in a particular eco-cultural setting.

Sample description
The people in the city and the village chosen for the study speak the same language, Hindi, containing a rich vocabulary of directional terms. However, the use of these

terms indicates a clear preference on the part of village people: they use cardinal directions (NSEW) in referring to objects and places in their environment, and when speaking of proximal space. Egocentric terms (LRFB) are very rarely used, and only to refer to objects that are either in contact with one's body (e.g., the glass is in the right hand) or placed close to one's body. Children are socialized from early childhood to make a distinction between the right and left hand, because the use of the right (socially accepted) hand for purposes like eating, drinking, and writing is greatly emphasized. The NSEW terms have a functional value for the society because many activities are oriented to different directions. Verbal interactions in the community also involve the use of conventional landmarks (e.g., headman's orchard, pond, road, Kali or Durga temple, mosque) known to all people of the village. Interactions with young children in restricted settings (e.g., in a room) may also involve reference to situation based local landmarks (e.g., door, wall, window, and chair), but people refer to various rooms by using cardinal directions (e.g., Eastern room, Northern room).

In the city of Varanasi[2], while the same language, Hindi, is spoken (with minor dialectical variations), and the same NSEW system may be used, it is frequent to use the LRFB system, both for route descriptions, and object localization. The city is very old, with a complex pattern of small alleys and roads, almost none of which are aligned in a grid pattern. Although the Ganges River and two of its tributaries on each side of the town provide some overall guidance, finding one's way in the city requires a close familiarity with it. Further work is needed to ascertain how children become familiar with these surroundings, and how they are induced to use either the NSEW or the LRFB systems.

Hinduism is the main belief system in both locations, conferring special attention to the four cardinal directions. For example, South is believed to be an inauspicious direction (abode of *Yama,* the god of death). Hence, facing South is avoided while eating, engaging in religious activities, during excretory behaviors and sleeping. Children attending Sanskrit schools even learn to distinguish eight cardinal directions with their attendant symbolism, however there were no such children in the present sample. The two samples correspond to the features summarized in Table 2.

Table 2
Characteristics of the Two Samples

Urban/rural contrast	Name	Ecological features	Language	Spatial orientation system used by adults
Rural	Roopchandpur	Flat Ganges plain	Hindi	NSEW
Urban	Varanasi	Old city	Hindi	Mixed (LRFB and NSEW)

---

[2] Varanasi is also called Banaras or Benares.

Table 3
Design and Number of Children in Each Sample

	India, village				India, city			
	No school		School		No school		School	
Age groups	girls	boys	girls	boys	girls	boys	girls	boys
4- 5	4	5	12	11			16	16
6- 8	16	14	10	13	12	13	13	12
9-11	12	13	13	16	12	12	12	12
12-14	12	11	14	15	12	12	12	12
Total	44	43	49	55	36	37	53	52

In each of the locations, we sampled children from age 4 to 14, boys and girls, schooled or completely unschooled, in about equal numbers. This led to a total number of 369 children. The groups of 4- to 5-year-old children were tested with a reduced range of tasks (Steve's Maze, Perspectives and Route memory tasks were not used). The details of the samples are presented in Table 3.

The present study will concentrate on developmental trends in the urban/rural comparison. The effects of schooling have been examined elsewhere (Mishra & Dasen, 2004), and there were no gender differences to speak of. The study reported here is part of a larger design (Mishra & Dasen, 2004) that also includes a sample in Nepal (Niraula, Mishra, & Dasen, in press).

Tasks
The tasks used in this study were divided into three main categories: Spatial encoding tasks, spatial cognitive development tasks, and language tasks.

All the tasks are presented as games. The child is allowed enough practice to ensure complete understanding of the tasks. If needed, the child is allowed to come back to the display on the tasks that place reliance on memory (i.e., Animals, Chips, Steve's Maze, Rotation of landscapes). The experimenter does not hurry the child, allowing it enough time for each task.

Spatial encoding tasks
These are tasks initially devised by the Cognitive Anthropology Research Group (CARG) at the Max Planck Institute of Psycholinguistics in Nijmegen (Danziger, 1993; Levinson, 2003). Hence, they are referred to as the Nijmegen tasks. These tasks are basically non-verbal, and always start with extensive training to ensure the children's comprehension of the instructions.

Animals in a Row. This task presents the child with three animals (chosen in this study from locally available models of duck, elephant, horse, tiger, and tortoise) aligned on a table, all facing in one direction. The child is asked to remember this display ("just how they are standing and which way they are looking"). No spatial language is used in the instructions. After some training items and being rotated 180°, the child moves to another table approximately 5 meters away. Here it is asked to align another set of the same animals the way they were shown before. Five trials, with the animals oriented to the right or left, are given in the RLLRL sequence; this number of trials is a standard part of the procedures developed by the CARG group, except that they randomize the order of the five trials, which seemed to us unnecessary.

The encoding is deemed "absolute" or geocentric if the animals face in the same geographic direction on table 2 as on table 1, and "relative" or egocentric if the right or left orientation is maintained.

This task is also repeated at the end of the testing (for children aged 6 to 14 years) in order to see if the child can shift from one encoding to the other. Depending on whether the child had previously encoded the display in a geocentric or egocentric manner, instructions are imparted by using appropriate language to encourage an encoding just opposite to the previous one. To induce egocentric encoding, the table on which the animals are displayed is placed 30° of the main direction, so that a geocentric encoding is less obvious.

Chips. For this task, two-dimensional shapes (small or large, red or blue, and yellow or green, circles or squares) are drawn on cards, two at a time. The child is shown five cards of a series all with the same orientation, and is asked to notice that all of them are identical. Then one of the cards is rotated by 90°, and the child is asked to tell how it is now different from the other cards. Following this exercise, the child is presented with a card oriented in a particular direction by the configuration of shapes, and is asked to remember this orientation. Then the child moves on to another table approximately 5 meters away (after a 180° rotation), and is asked to choose from a set of four cards set out as a cross, the one displaying the same spatial orientation as seen before. One of the cards represents a geocentric encoding, another an egocentric encoding, and two other cards function as "distractors." If the child points to one of these, she/he is asked to go back to table 1 and to try again; the second attempt is the one used for scoring. A series of practice trials are given before moving on to the actual testing, which consists of 5 items.

Steve's Maze. This task comprises six maps of landscapes that depict a house, rice fields, trees, and an incomplete pathway. The child is presented with a map and is told a story, thereby being shown the route that can be taken from the end of the drawn path back to the house. The child is asked to remember this route while moving (after a 180° rotation) to another table approximately 5 meters away where three cards are displayed showing three different path segments. One of these represents an egocentric encoding, another a geocentric solution, and the third acts as an irrelevant choice (called distractor). If the child points to one of these, she/he is asked to go back to table 1 and try again; the second attempt is the one used for scoring. One item is used for demonstration; another five items constitute the test series.

The scores consist of the proportion of items out of 5 on which the child uses a geocentric encoding, with D (choice of distractor) counting as ½; following the scheme worked out by Levinson and Nagy (1998), the scores are called R-A gradients. A higher gradient indicates a higher tendency towards geocentric encoding; a gradient below .50 indicates the predominance of egocentric encoding.

Spatial cognitive development tasks
These tasks are used to assess spatial concept development, and are mainly based on Piaget and Inhelder's (1948/1956) theory. Except for the task instructions, accompanied with sufficient training, the tasks are mainly non-verbal. The children are not asked to give extensive explanations of their thinking, and no counter-suggestions were used, since these procedures were found to be difficult in cross-cultural research (Dasen, 1975).

Route Memory. This task was inspired by the previous work of Gauvain and Rogoff (1989) and Cottereau-Reiss (1999, 2001). A pathway is laid out on the ground consisting of several segments (six for children up to age 9, eight for older children) with right angle turns, set out along the main cardinal directions, one diagonal and one circular turn (see Figure 1). A number of objects (six for children up to age 9, nine for older children) are placed at different points of the route. The child moves along the route and names each object as it is encountered. On reaching the end point, located in another room, the child is turned 180°, and then asked to tell how to go back to the starting point. The child is then asked to recall the objects that were placed along the route, and, based on what they remember, to arrange the models of those objects at appropriate locations along a miniature display of the route. The task is scored on the accuracy of the return path description, the proportion of objects correctly recalled, and the proportion of objects correctly placed.

Rotation of Landscapes. This task was devised by Piaget and Inhelder (1948/1956) and standardized by Laurendeau and Pinard (1968/1970); we used a simplified version of the latter (only 5 items), as in previous research by Dasen (1975). The task proceeds in three phases, the first two being used for training. In the first phase, two similar landscapes are displayed side by side on a table in front of the child. Attention is drawn to different features in the landscape (e.g., house, river, bridge, hill, etc.) and their locations. The experimenter (E) puts a doll on one of the landscapes, and the child is asked to set another doll in the same place and position on the other landscape. In the second phase, one of the landscapes is rotated by 180° in full view of the child, who does the same exercise as in the first phase (placing and positioning the doll). In the third phase, used for scoring, a screen is placed between the landscapes. The child looks at the E's landscape and, based on what they remember, puts the doll exactly at the same place and position in the other landscape. Five such

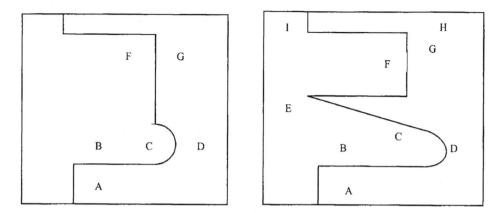

Figure 1: Reverse Route Memory Task (simple and complex). Note: Objects used: A: kettle; B: lamp; C: water jar; D: food carrier; E: pitcher; F: wok; G: bucket; H: chair; I: stool.

trials are given. The task is scored into five sub-stages, the early stages reflecting the use of topological space only, the middle stages projective space, and the last stage Euclidean space.

Horizontality. This task was also devised by Piaget and Inhelder (1948/1956), and used among others by Dasen (1975). A bottle half-filled with colored water is presented on a table. The child's attention is drawn to the level of water in the bottle. Then the bottle is hidden in a cloth bag and the child is asked to draw the level of water in the outline of the bottle presented on the record sheet. The hidden bottle is presented in five different positions: (1) right side up, (2) upside-down, (3) on the side, (4) tilted at 45° to the right, (5) tilted upside-down at 45°. Each time the child draws the level of water in the outline of the bottle.

The task is scored in 5 stages: (1) all positions wrong except position 1, (2) all positions wrong except positions 1 and 2, (3) positions 2 and/or 3 correct and/or some movement of the water drawn for one position among 4 and 5, (4) movement of water in positions 4 and 5, but not horizontal, (5) correct for positions 4 and/or 5.

Perspectives task. This task was also inspired by the original work of Piaget and Inhelder (1948/1956), and its standardization by Laurendeau and Pinard (1968/1970). Three familiar non-fronted objects (a square yellow cube, a big round red box, and a small round green box) are set on the table in a triangle. The child is asked to describe the display from three different positions, and to choose among three pictures the one that represents what she/he sees. The child is then asked to stay at one position and describe the display from the point of view of the experimenter (E). As E moves to different positions – being either opposite to the child, to the right of the child, or at a diagonally opposite corner –, the child has to choose from a set of three pictures the one that matches with E's view of the display. In the last phase, the child is presented with a picture (the display seen from the left of the child) and is asked to tell where E should go to see the display as depicted in the picture.

The task is scored as the number of correct descriptions on the four items, and the number of correct choices of pictures.

Language tasks
The following procedures were used at the beginning or at the end of some of the above tasks for eliciting spatial terms used by children.

Route Description. In this task the child is asked to guide one of the experimenters, who is blindfolded, along a pathway laid out on the ground, consisting of several segments (6 for children up to age 9, eight for older children) with right angle turns, set out along the main cardinal directions, one diagonal and one circular turn. All verbalizations of the child are tape recorded for later transcription. The path is the same one used for the Reverse route memory task, but without objects placed along the path. The route description is carried out before the cognitive part of the task.

Description of tabletop display. Three familiar non-fronted objects are set on the table in a triangle. The child is asked to describe the locations of these objects three times while moving to different positions around the display (opposite to first position, and at 90° to the right). These descriptions are recorded. The display is the same as the one used for the Perspectives task, and the description is performed before the cognitive part of the task.

Language on spatial encoding tasks. These include the "Animals in a Row," "Chips," and "Steve's Maze," described above. On items 4 and 5 of each task, the child is asked to explain his or her choice, i.e., what she/he did to remember the display. The language used is recorded. This is a departure from the standardized form of these tasks (Danziger, 1993), in which no explanation is asked. This format, however, was also used by Wassmann and Dasen (1998) in Bali; only asking for an explanation in regard to the last two items of each task was thought to minimally interfere with the non-verbal aspect of the tasks.

Language coding scheme
The language produced on all three of these tasks was coded using a scheme adapted from Pederson (1993). This is shown in Table 4.

The terms are grouped into the three broad categories of egocentric, projective, and geocentric language. Egocentric references are often called relative because they depend on the speaker's position. The reference to landmarks implies a direction

Table 4
Language Coding Scheme

E	**Egocentric**	
R	Relative	Right, left, in front, in back in relation to speaker
P	**Projective**	
SL	Situation-specific Landmarks	Towards the window, the door (landmarks within the room)
CL	Conventional Landmarks	Towards the temple, the hospital, a locality (landmarks outside the room)
G	**Geocentric**	
N	NSEW	Cardinal directions, north, south, east, west
O	**Other**	
I	Intrinsic	One object related to another, e.g., next to, near, before, etc.
D	Deictic	"This way, that way" (usually accompanied with the gesture of a finger or the whole hand)

away from the display and from the viewer, and hence projective properties; it can be considered intermediate between egocentric and geocentric language, because it implies a distancing from the display, but not the application of a right-angle (Euclidean) geocentric grid. Within this category, there is also a progressive distancing between situation specific landmarks, that are nearby and inside of the room, and conventional landmarks that are further and even quite far if they are localities outside of view.

The geocentric category is represented by the use of cardinal directions. Categorized separately, are the intrinsic (I) and deictic (D) references. The accompanying gestures of the deictic category are ambiguous in terms of encoding: Since a body movement is involved, it could be body-related, and could mean "to the right/left"; however the pointing could also be projective (towards a landmark) or even to a direction independently of the body. As will be seen in the next section, mainly very young children, from whom it is difficult to receive more precise verbal explanations, use D. The interpretation of D is therefore left for further research.

The frequency of spatial words used by children on each language elicitation task was counted and converted to proportions of the total words recorded; for each child, these proportions were averaged over the three tasks.

Results

Spatial language
Table 5 presents the change with age of the language used on the three language elicitation tasks, namely Route description, Perspectives and Items 4 and 5 of the Nijmegen tasks (2 tasks for 4- to 5-year-olds, 3 tasks for 6- to 14-year-olds). The developmental trends are highlighted in bold.

Table 5
Proportions of Modal Language Use on Combined Tasks, by Age Group

Age	Village							City					
	R	SL	CL	N	I	D	O	R	SL	CL	N	I	D
4- 5	0	27	0	0	0	70	3	01	14	0	0	3	82
6- 8	3	39	0	37	11	12	0	18	29	0	25	14	14
9-11	1	12	0	73	8	3	3	28	16	0	40	10	6
12-14	8	6	0	76	8	2	0	55	4	0	30	6	5

Note. R: Relative; SL: Situation-specific Landmarks; CL: Conventional Landmarks; N: Geocentric; I: Intrinsic; D: Deictic; O: Other.

In both samples, it is noticeable that the youngest children (4 to 5 years) predominantly use "this way" and "that way," usually accompanied by a gesture of a finger or the whole hand. The status of this category is inherently ambiguous in terms of absolute/relative encoding: it could be body related since a body movement is involved, and mean "to the right/left," but the movement may also point to a direction that is outside of the display. The latter interpretation is reinforced by the fact that in both samples in India, the very young children also use SL references (i.e., outside of the display, but within the room), a category that is still quite strong at age 6 to 8 years but then diminishes with age. Conventional landmarks (CL) were not used by any children[3].

The main difference in language use between the samples is that the city sample is the only one where a significant number of children use the Relative (R) references of right and left, and this increasingly with age. Geocentric language (N) use increases over age in both samples, and is the major category used in the village after the age of 9.

This distinctive pattern of language use makes sense in terms of the different ecologies. In the village situated in the Ganges plain, the terrain is completely flat, there are no major features such as mountains or hills, in fact, there are hardly any landmarks at all, except different fields or the occasional house or tree. In such ecological conditions, the use of NSEW based on the daily path of the sun (and reinforced by cultural and religious practices) is quite obviously adaptive.

What we find in the city of Varanasi is a mixed pattern: right/left being increasingly used with age as an alternative to geocentric references. The use of relative terms is no doubt linked to the topographical features of the city; it certainly makes more sense to turn left and right in a city, whether driving or walking, than in open

---

[3] The two groups of 32 4- to 5-year-old children were tested for language use on the Perspectives layout both inside a room and on the flat roof of a house. In each sample, 14 children used at least some SL when tested inside but no CL outside; 21 children in the city and 25 in the village used CL consistently. This contextual effect was statistically significant beyond the .01 level (chi-squared).

countryside. The reference to geocentric cues such as the sun is more likely to be obscured in narrow lanes, which, in Varanasi, are generally not organized in a grid pattern.

Spatial encoding ("Nijmegen") tasks
Table 6 shows the R-A gradients (proportion of "absolute," i.e., geocentric, encoding in 5 trials) over age in the two Indian samples and in the previous study in Bali. With the youngest children Steve's Maze was not used, and the Animals task was performed with two animals only. In Bali, the oldest age group consisted of two children in the age group of 12 to 14 years, and 12 adults.

It is immediately obvious that the three tasks differ consistently in absolute values, but reflect a similar developmental pattern in both Indian samples. On the Animals task most of the encoding is absolute (A), even among the youngest children, this proportion further increasing over age. On the Chips task a similar increase of A encoding with age is noticeable, but at a slightly lower level. If we had only used these two tasks, we might have concluded that there is an overall preference for Absolute encoding, with an age trend from more relative to more absolute. On Steve's Maze, however, there is almost no age trend, and, in fact, there is a slight predominance of Relative encoding.

In Bali, Wassmann and Dasen (1998) similarily found a marked difference between the two Nijmegen tasks used, with almost systematic Absolute encoding on Animals, and somewhat more Relative encoding on Steve's Maze. However, in Bali there seemed to be a trend from complete absolute encoding towards more relative encoding with increasing age and/or schooling; a trend that contradicts mainstream (western) theories of cognitive development. In the present study, this trend was not confirmed; both samples showed a trend opposite to that found in Bali, i.e., slightly more relative encoding in young children and then increasing absolute encoding. This trend however is not reflected in the modal language use, where relative language almost never occurs, except in the city of Varanasi (where it increases with age, while relative encoding decreases with age, in contradiction to the hypothesis of linguistic relativism).

Table 6
R-A Gradients on Spatial Encoding Tasks by Age Group

Age	India, village			India, city			Bali	
	Animals	Chips	Steve's Maze	Animals	Chips	Steve's Maze	Animals	Steve's Maze
4- 5	.73	.50	–	.55	.40	–	.96	–
6- 8	.80	.65	.41	.68	.46	.39	.80	.58
9-11	.90	.70	.51	.79	.51	.42	.73	.58
12-14	.94	.76	.47	.75	.53	.40	.86	.49

We are thus left with the question of whether the results in Bali could be replicated in Bali itself using a larger sample and more tasks, or in other island locations using a similar orientation system. Further developmental research of this kind is also needed in populations where LRFB are not used at all, as well as in those where it is the main reference system. Curiously, except for some small studies with French children (Cottereau-Reiss, personal communication; Troadec & Martinot, 2001), there has been little research carried out with children who speak a European language.

The fact that the instructions can influence the type of encoding was used by Wassmann and Dasen (1998) in Bali to assess the flexibility with which subjects could change from their spontaneous preferred mode to the other. They repeated the Animals and Steve's Maze tasks by changing the instructions, in particular explicitly using relative language for those who had first used geocentric encoding, and placing the table at 30° of the main orientation axis. They found that young children (7 to 9 years) would not change their mode despite prompting, while approximately 50% of the older children and adults would do so easily. In the present study, only 6% of the children in the village and 21% in Varanasi changed their encoding; there was no significant age trend, except that in both samples, among those children who did change, the younger ones (6 to 8 years) changed from relative to geocentric, and the older ones in the reverse direction.

How does the language predominantly used by each child correlate with encoding? In previous research by the CARG group, the correspondence between these two variables was only assessed at the group level, i.e., correlations based on the individual measures of the two variables were not used. In our study, such correlational data is available. Since both language and spatial encoding change with age and with schooling, these two variables were partialled out (see Table 7).

Table 7

Partial Correlations between Language and Encoding (R-A Gradients on Three Tasks) Controlling for Age and Schooling

	Relative (R)	Situation-specific Landmarks (SL)	Geocentric (N)	Intrinsic (I)	Deictic (D)
City (n = 142)					
Animals	-.18*				
Chips	-.23**				-.20*
Steve's Maze	-.18*	.17*		.17*	
Village (n = 154)					
Animals		-.25**	.23**		
Chips		-.24**	.25**	-.19*	
Steve's Maze					

Note. Only statistically significant coefficients are reported: *p < .05, **p < .01 two-tailed.

The pattern of results is quite different in the two locations. In the city, children who use relative language consistently also use more relative encoding (negative correlations with R-A gradients on all three tasks). On the other hand, the expected positive correlations with geocentric language do not occur, while they do so in the village, at least in two tasks out of the three. Since relative language is almost never used in the village, the absence of significant correlations is not surprising. The use of situation-specific landmarks (SL) is negatively correlated with geocentric encoding on two tasks in the village, suggesting that the projective nature of SL is closer to egocentric rather than geocentric space, but this is speculative since it is not replicated in the city. Generally speaking, we can conclude that the correlation between the two variables is weak, much weaker than a strong hypothesis of linguistic relativity would have predicted.

Cognitive tasks
Is there a relationship between modal language use and cognitive performance? The results of correlations between these two domains are presented in Table 8. Since the cognitive developmental tasks evinced, in analyses reported elsewhere (Dasen, Mishra, & Niraula, 2003), significant correlations with age and schooling but not with gender, partial correlations are used, controlling for age and schooling.

The use of cardinal directions (N) is positively correlated to performance on most of the cognitive tasks, and is statistically significant with the simple path in both locations as well as the complex path in the village. The use of relative

Table 8
Partial Correlations, Controlling for Age and Schooling, between the Proportions of the Different Language Categories and Cognitive Tasks

	Horizontality	Perspectives	Rotation	Simple path	Complex path
City (n = 142)				n = 73	n = 113
R	.05	.19*	.08	.01	-.05
SL	-.17*	-.02	-.15	-.21	-.07
N	.13	-.15	.12	.25*	.14
I	-.09	.05	-.22**	-.17	-.11
D	-.19*	-.07	-.18*	-.04	-.16
Village (n = 154)				n = 84	n = 102
R	.11	.04	.13	-.01	-.10
SL	-.21**	-.10	-.19*	-.26*	-.20*
N	.13	.10	.13	.28**	.18*
I	.04	-.12	.00	-.24*	-.05
D	-.14	-.06	-.13	-.28**	-.31**

Note. R: Relative; SL: Situation-specific Landmarks; N: Geocentric; I: Intrinsic; D: Deictic.
*p < .05. **p < .01.

language (R) is not linked to cognitive performance, even in the city (with the exception of Perspectives. But this correlation is most likely spurious, as this task does not correlate with anything else). D, SL, and I tend to be negatively correlated with cognitive performance, particularly in the village sample. These language categories are, as we have seen, typical of younger children. However, in this case, since age was controlled, this finding suggests a developmental pattern in which children who are less advanced in spatial cognitive development (at any given age) also tend to use language typical of children younger than their age. On the other hand, there are no relationships between the encoding on the Nijmegen tasks and performance on cognitive tasks.

Discussion

In relation to the eco-cultural theoretical framework, we have found that the spatial orientation system, and the language that accompanies it, is adapted to the respective ecological conditions. In the flat plains of the Ganges, in rural areas where there is barely a hill and few obvious landmarks, using cardinal directions is the norm. The ecology of the city is more varied, and the processes involved will no doubt warrant a more detailed study; city-dwellers use either relative ("left/right") spatial references or geocentric ones, or a combination of both.

We do not claim that the physical environment is the single determinant for these orientation systems and the accompanying language; ethnology is quick to demonstrate cultural and linguistic diversity within the same ecological conditions. But we argue that it is not possible to distinguish language as a causal factor in relation to cognition, since it does not occur out of a more general cultural context that is itself adaptive to the ecological context. An orientation system based on cardinal directions, such as it occurs in rural India, is completely congruent with Hinduism, and the attached symbolism, as well as with daily routines and practices. The same, of course, is true in Bali (Wassmann & Dasen, 1998). In other words, language comes as a package with other cultural features. Determining which, of language, culture, and cognition, comes first is a chicken and egg problem that does not make much sense in solving.

Children learn the normative adult system and language progressively, and become competent in it by about the age of 9. Before that (in the age group of 6 to 8 years), they may attempt to use the adult system without being able to do so correctly (particularly in the case where cardinal directions have to be learned). They may also use situation based local landmarks (outside of the display, but inside the room) or, when testing is done outside, conventional landmarks. Even younger children (4 to 5 years) tend to say "this way/that way" (D), a fairly restricted linguistic code accompanied by gestures, and one that needs more detailed research, as it may obscure markedly different processes (egocentric and/or geocentric). Whatever the interpretation of D may be, the developmental path seems to be a gradual progression from projective references to immediate surroundings (SL) to an often incorrect use of the geocentric system, until the latter is fully mastered by about the age of 9. This occurs, however, without the use of relative language (R). The latter occurs only in the city, and only with older children.

When a simple spatial array has to be encoded (as in the spatial encoding tasks we used), most of the children do so in an "absolute" rather than a "relative" frame. This is congruent with the geocentric orientation system that is prevalent in both locations. While this finding seems to fit a hypothesis of linguistic relativism at the group level, there are limitations that argue against any strong form of such a hypothesis; e.g., the fact that the choice of spatial frame is partly task-specific.

Task specificity
Indeed, the results show more absolute encoding on Animals, also absolute but to a somewhat less degree on Chips, and more relative encoding on Steve's Maze. This shows that there is no overall linguistic determinant of a frame, but rather that the two frames coexist in every individual, with situational determinants as to which frame is preferentially used.

The fact that spatial tasks are very sensitive to small changes in the display or the instructions has been found repeatedly both in infancy (Acredolo, 1990) and at later ages. Cottereau-Reiss (1999) cites Hatwell (1990) in this respect: "Seemingly minor variations in the content or procedures that do not change the formal structure of the problem sometimes have important effects on behavior, and significantly change the proportion of responses classified as egocentric or exocentric at a given age" (p. 56, our translation). More specifically, the fact that the Animals task results in more absolute and Steve's Maze more relative encoding has been found repeatedly, in Bali (Wassmann & Dasen, 1998), in New Caledonia (Cottereau-Reiss, 1999, 2001), in Nepal (Niraula et al., in press), and in this study in India[4].

One feature explaining this systematic difference could be the ease linguistic encoding, of how many words or sentences are needed to describe the display in order to remember it verbally or iconic encoding can be applied given the subject material. On the Animals task, the display consists of three discrete objects, each of which is oriented, so the overall pattern is easy to encode in linguistic terms (e.g., "they all look East/to the right"). On the Chips task, although the objects are also discrete, they are not oriented; it is the spatial relationship between the two shapes that defines the orientation, and although a linguistic encoding is quite likely (e.g., "The small blue square is North, the big red one is South"), when confronted with a selection of four such cards set out in a pattern (cross), the visual image is likely to predominate. This may explain why relative encoding is more frequent here than with Animals. The visual pattern is of course even more striking on Steve's Maze, where encoding the path linguistically would entail a rather complex route description.

---

[4] But in the Trobriand Islands, Senft (2000) predominantly found geocentric encoding on four tasks, including Animals, Chips and Steve's Maze, while he found more relative encoding on a task we have not used, the Motion maze task.

Therefore, remembering a shape (or a pattern of movement, as shown by some children who actually move their finger or hand) is more likely and hence more prone to be related to the body.

It has been found repeatedly that the same task can produce quite different results depending on the details of the procedure. Cottereau-Reiss (1999), for example, had the Kanak children in New-Caledonia carry the animals themselves from the first to the second table; this form of the task produced much more relative encoding than the standard format. A recent controversy between Li and Gleitman (2002) and Levinson, Kita, Haun, and Rasch (2002) also illustrates this point. Li and Gleitman (2002) found markedly different results on the Animals task with American students depending on the availability of landmarks in the experimental setting, i.e., when the task was set inside a room with shutters closed, shutters open or outside on the campus, or when a reference object was placed on the table. Levinson et al. (2002) remark that an allocentric encoding is inherently ambiguous as to the frame of reference actually used, which can be either intrinsic or geocentric[5]. Levinson et al. (2002) also remark that a small change in the procedure, such as giving the subject only the three animals on the second table, or four animals out of which to choose the three relevant ones, can change the results considerably. Presumably this results from changing the memory load of the task, and/or attracting attention to the order of the animals rather than only their direction. Levinson et al. (2002) therefore advocate the use of several more complex encoding tasks, such as the Motion-maze task and the Transitivity task (cf. Danziger, 1993).

In a study in Tahiti and in France, in addition to using either the Animals or the Chips tasks, Troadec (Troadec & Martinot, 2001; Troadec, Martinot, & Cottereau-Reiss, 2002) also used different types of verbal induction, and found various effects of eco-cultural setting, age, gender, and task content. In Papeete, Tahiti, older children (10 to 11 years) were more prone to follow either a relative or an absolute induction from the instructions than were younger children (5 to 6 years). Wassmann and Dasen (1998) found a similar age effect in Bali, but this was not repeated in the study in India. In conclusion, the task specificity can be used for a finer analysis of the processes that are involved. Varying the tasks and the task instructions should be done systematically instead of relying on single measures.

Linguistic relativism
Looking at the data at the individual rather than at the group level, one finds that the relationship between language use and frame of encoding is certainly less than perfect; it was found that children may encode a situation with a relative frame, but when asked to explain how they did it, used absolute language, this being easily understood in terms of the dominant geocentric adult norm. However, the reverse was also found: i.e., they used absolute modes of encoding and explained it with

---

[5] Additional situations would have to be used to distinguish between the two, for example a 90° rotation, or using a two-dimensional array by placing a fourth animal at a right angle with the row of three animals.

relative language, a more puzzling (and also less frequent) combination. That individuals say one thing and yet do another is of course a common problem in psychology when dealing with attitudes and values, but it also holds true in the cognitive domain.

Previous research (such as Wassmann & Dasen, 1998, and by the CARG group) examined the relationship between language and spatial encoding only at the group level: A linguistic analysis shows that in many of the societies that have been studied, if an absolute orientation system exists in the culture it is accompanied by a predominance of absolute language and goes along with a strong trend towards absolute encoding. Hence, there is seemingly a strong confirmation of linguistic relativism. In this study, we have been able to record the language used by each individual, and to relate the dominant language use for each individual to his or her encoding, measured task by task. With such an analysis at the individual level, it can be observed that the correspondence between language and encoding, while not completely absent, is much less impressive.

Another important question was whether the use of geocentric orientation systems and absolute language would only have an impact on spatial encoding in situations (tasks) specifically geared to be sensitive to this feature, such as the tasks developed by the CARG group, or whether it would have an impact on spatial cognitive development at a more general level. Using a series of Piagetian tasks in the area of spatial concept development, we found no relationship between absolute or relative spatial encoding (on the Nijmegen tasks) and broader aspects of cognitive development. On the other hand, the data showed some correlations between modal language use and some of the cognitive development tasks, even when age and schooling are controlled; this is in line with previous research in Nepal by Niraula (Niraula, 1998; Niraula & Mishra, 2001).

Summary

To close, let us come back to our research questions and summarize the findings: The spatial language used by children changes with age in both rural and urban settings from more proximal (deictic and projective) to more distal (geocentric) reference usage, and the latter represents the normative language after age 9 in the village. While egocentric (relative) language is not at all used in the village, in the city its use increases with age.

Despite this increase in egocentric language in the city, the developmental trends in spatial encoding are similar in both locations, with an increase over age of the use of a geocentric frame of reference. Hence, the possible reversal found in previous research in Bali is not confirmed in these two locations in India, despite the existence of a strong geocentric orientation system. Only weak relationships were found between spatial language use and spatial encoding.

There are some significant relationships (controlling for age and schooling) between spatial language use and spatial concept development, but not between the latter and spatial encoding. However, these relationships are not sufficiently strong and systematic enough to conclude with certainty that using more geocentric language promotes spatial conceptual development in general, and Euclidean spatial concepts in particular.

We expect to continue our research by taking advantage of the ecological, cultural, and linguistic diversity in India and elsewhere in order to add more samples – always basing the selection on theoretical considerations – to this comparative research. We also need more data on language acquisition and comprehension at earlier ages, on possible links between the choice of different frames of spatial reference and cognitive style, as well as information as to neuropsychological bases in hemispheric dominance. As Trommsdorff's research has demonstrated throughout her career, in order to be fruitful, the cross-cultural study of human development needs a long-term commitment if we hope to capture the complexity of the interactions between eco-cultural, linguistic and other significant variables.

References

Acredolo, L. (1990). Individual differences in infant spatial cognition. In J. Colombo & Fagen, J. W. (Eds.), *Individual differences in infancy: Reliability, stability, prediction* (pp. 321-340). Hillsdale, NJ: Erlbaum.

Barnes, R. H. (1993). Everyday space: Some considerations on the representation and use of space in Indonesia. In J. Wassmann & P. R. Dasen (Eds.), *Alltagswissen/Les savoirs quotidiens/Everyday cognition* (pp. 159-180). Fribourg, Switzerland: Presses de l'Université de Fribourg.

Berry, J. W., Dasen, P. R., & Saraswathi, T. S. (Eds.). (1997). *Handbook of cross-cultural psychology: Vol. 2. Basic processes and human development* (2nd ed.). Boston: Allyn & Bacon.

Berry, J. W., Poortinga, Y. H., Segall, M. H., & Dasen, P. R. (2002). *Cross-cultural psychology: Research and applications* (2nd rev. ed.). Cambridge, UK: Cambridge University Press.

Bickel, B. (1997). Spatial operations in deixis, cognition, and culture: Where to orient oneself in Belhare. In J. Nuyts & E. Pederson (Eds.), *Language and conceptualization* (pp. 46-83). Cambridge, UK: Cambridge University Press.

Brown, P., & Levinson, S. C. (1993). 'Uphill' and 'downhill' in Tzeltal. *Journal of Linguistic Anthropology, 3*, 46-74.

Brown, P., & Levinson, S. C. (2000). Frames of spatial reference and their acquisition in Tenejapan Tzeltal. In L. Nucci, G. Saxe, & E. Turiel (Eds.), *Culture, thought, and development* (pp. 167-197). Mahwah, NJ: Erlbaum.

Clark, H. (1973). Space, time, semantics, and the child. In T. E. Moore (Ed.), *Cognitive development and the acquisition of language* (pp. 27-63). New York: Academic Press.

Cottereau-Reiss, P. (1999). L'espace kanak, ou comment ne pas perdre son latin! [Kanak space or how not to get lost]. *Annales Fyssen, 14*, 34-45.

Cottereau-Reiss, P. (2001). Langages d'espace: L'exemple kanak [Spatial languages: The example of Kanak]. In C. Sabatier & P. R. Dasen (Eds.), *Cultures, développement et éducation. Autres enfants, autres écoles* [Cultures, human development, and education. Different children, different schools] (pp. 159-168). Paris: L'Harmattan.

Danziger, E. (Ed.). (1993). *Cognition and space kit, version 1.0.* Nijmegen, The Netherlands: Cognitive Anthropology Research Group, Max Planck Institute for Psycholinguistics.

Dasen, P. R. (1975). Concrete operational development in three cultures. *Journal of Cross-Cultural Psychology, 6*, 156-172.

Dasen, P. R. (1993). Schlusswort. Les sciences cognitives: Do they shake hands in the middle? In J. Wassmann & P. R. Dasen (Eds.), *Alltagswissen/Les savoirs quotidiens/Everyday cognition* (pp. 331-349). Fribourg, Switzerland: Presses de l'Université de Fribourg.

Dasen, P. R. (1998a). Cadres théoriques en psychologie interculturelle [Theoretical frameworks in cross-cultural psychology]. In J. G. Adair, D. Bélanger, & K. L. Dion (Eds.), *Advances in psychological science/Récents développements en psychologie scientifique: Vol. 1. Social, personal and cultural aspects/Aspects sociaux, personnels et culturels* (pp. 205-227). London: Psychology Press.

Dasen, P. R. (1998b). Piaget, entre relativisme et universalité [Piaget between relativism and universality]. In C. Meljac, R. Voyazopoulos, & Y. Hatwell (Eds.), *Piaget après Piaget: Evolution des modèles, richesse des* pratiques [Piaget after Piaget: Evolution of models, abundance of practices] (pp. 135-153). Grenoble, France: La Pensée Sauvage.

Dasen, P. R., & Heron, A. (1981). Cross-cultural tests of Piaget's theory. In H. C. Triandis & A. Heron (Eds.), *Handbook of cross-cultural psychology: Vol. 4. Developmental psychology,* (pp. 295-342). Boston: Allyn and Bacon.

Dasen, P. R., Mishra, R. C., & Niraula, S. (2003). Ecology, language, and performance on spatial cognitive tasks. *International Journal of Psychology, 38*, 366-383.

Gauvain, M., & Rogoff, B. (1989). Ways of speaking about space: The development of children's skill in communicating spatial knowledge. *Cognitive Development, 4*, 295-307.

Gladwin, T. (1970). *East is a big bird. Navigation and logic on Puluwat Atoll.* Cambridge, MA: Harvard University Press.

Gumperz, J. J., & Levinson, S. C. (Eds.). (1996). *Rethinking linguistic relativity.* Cambridge, UK: Cambridge University Press.

Hatwell, Y. (1990). Le développement des concepts spatiaux: De la théorie de Piaget aux théories du traitement de l'information [The development of spatial concepts from Piaget to information processing theories]. In G. Netchine-Grynberg (Ed.), *Développement et fonctionnement cognitifs chez l'enfant* [Cognitive development and functioning in children] (pp. 53-69). Paris: PUF.

Holenstein, E. (1993). Moderne vs. klassische Universalienthesen [Modern vs. classical affirmations about universals]. In J. Wassmann & P. R. Dasen (Eds.), *Alltagswissen/Les savoirs quotidiens/Everyday cognition,* (pp. 305-308). Fribourg, Switzerland: Universitätsverlag.

Hutchins, E. (1983). Understanding Micronesian navigation. In D. Gentner & A. Stevens (Eds.), *Mental models* (pp. 191-225). Hillsdale, NJ: Erlbaum.

Kagitçibasi, Ç. (1997). Individualism and collectivism. In J. W. Berry, M. H. Segall, & Ç. Kagitçibasi (Eds.), *Handbook of cross-cultural psychology: Vol. 3. Social psychology* (2nd ed., pp. 1-50). Boston: Allyn and Bacon.

Laurendeau, M., & Pinard, A. (1970). *The development of the concept of space in the child.* New York: International Universities Press (First published 1968, *Les premières notions spatiales de l'enfant.* Neuchâtel, Switzerland: Delachaux & Niestlé).

León, L. de (1994). Exploration in the acquisition of geocentric location by Tzotzil children. *Linguistics, 32*, 857-884.

León, L. de (1995). *The development of geocentric location in young speakers of Guugu Yimithirr.* Nijmegen, The Netherlands: CARG working paper no. 32.

Levinson, S. C. (1991). Primer for the field investigation of spatial description and conception. *Pragmatics, 2*, 5-47.

Levinson, S. C. (1996). Frames of reference and Molyneux's question: Cross-linguistic evidence. In P. Bloom, M. Peterson, L. Nadel, & M. Garrett (Eds.), *Language and space* (pp. 109-169). Cambridge, MA: MIT Press.

Levinson, S. C. (1997). From outer to inner space: Linguistic categories and non-linguistic thinking. In E. Pederson & J. Nuyts (Eds.), *With language in mind: The relationship between linguistic and conceptual representation* (pp. 13-45). Cambridge, UK: Cambridge University Press.

Levinson, S. C. (2003). *Space in language and cognition.* Cambridge, UK: Cambridge University Press.

Levinson, S. C., & Nagy, L. K. (1998). *Look at your Southern leg: A statistical approach to cross-cultural field studies of language and spatial orientation.* Unpublished manuscript.

Levinson, S. C., Kita, S., Haun, D., & Rasch, B. (2002). Returning the tables: Language affects spatial reasoning. *Cognition, 84*, 155-188..

Lewis, S. (1980). *We, the navigators; the ancient art of landfinding in the Pacific.* Canberra: Australian National University Press.

Li, P., & Gleitman, L. (2002). Turning the tables: Language and spatial reasoning. *Cognition, 83*, 265-294.

Lucy, J. (1992). *Grammatical categories and cognition: A case study of the linguistic relativity hypothesis*. Cambridge, UK: Cambridge University Press.

Miller, G., & Johnson-Laird, P. (1976). *Language and perception*. Cambridge, UK: Cambridge University Press.

Mishra, R. C. (1997). Cognition and cognitive development. In J. W. Berry, P. R. Dasen, & T. S. Saraswathi (Eds.), *Handbook of cross-cultural psychology: Vol. 2. Basic processes and human development* (2nd ed., pp. 143-176). Boston: Allyn and Bacon.

Mishra, R. C. (2001). Cognition across cultures. In D. Matsumoto (Ed.), *The handbook of culture and cognition* (pp. 119-135). New York: Oxford University Press.

Mishra, R. C., & Dasen, P. R. (2004). The influence of schooling on cognitive development: A review of research in India. In B. N. Setiadi, A. Supratiknya, W. J. Lonner & Y. H. Poortinga (Eds.), *Ongoing themes in pychology and culture. Selected papers from the XVI. International Conference of the International Association of Cross-Cultural Psychology* (pp. 207-222). Yogyakarta, Indonesia: Kanisius.

Mishra, R. C., Sinha, D., & Berry, J. W. (1996). *Ecology, acculturation, and psychological adaptation: A study of Adivasi in Bihar*. New Delhi, India: Sage.

Mohanty, A. K., & Perregaux, C. (1997). Language acquisition and bilingualism. In J. W. Berry, P. R. Dasen, & T. S. Saraswathi (Eds.), *Handbook of cross-cultural psychology: Vol. 2. Basic processes and human development* (2nd ed., pp. 217-254). Boston: Allyn and Bacon.

Niraula, S. (1998). *Development of spatial cognition in rural and urban Nepalese children*. Unpublished doctoral thesis, Banaras Hindu University, Varanasi, India.

Niraula, S., & Mishra, R. C. (2001). Spatial orientation of the Newar children in Nepal. *Social Science International, 17*, 36-48.

Niraula, S., Mishra, R. C., & Dasen, P. R. (in press). Linguistic relativism and spatial concept development in Nepal. *Psychology and Developing Societies*.

Ozanne-Rivierre, F. (1987). L'expression linguistique de l'orientation dans l'espace: Quelques exemples océaniens [The linguistic expression of spatial orientation: Some examples from Oceania.]. *Cahiers du LACITO, 2*, 129-155.

Pederson, E. (1993). Geographic and manipulable space in two Tamil linguistic systems. In A. U. Frank & I. Campari (Eds.), *Spatial information theory* (pp. 294-311). Berlin, Germany: Springer Verlag.

Pederson, E., Danziger, E., Levinson, S., Kita, S., Senft, G., & Wilkins, D. (1998). Semantic typology and spatial conceptualization. *Language, 74*, 557-589.

Piaget, J., & Inhelder, B. (1956). *The child's conception of space*. London: Routledge and Kegan Paul. (First published 1948. *La représentation de l'espace chez l'enfant*. Paris: PUF.)

Ruiter, J. P. de, & Wilkins, D. (Eds.). (1997). *Annual report 1996*. Nijmegen, The Netherlands: Max-Planck-Institut für Psycholinguistik.

Segall, M. H., Dasen, P. R., Berry, J. W., & Poortinga, Y. H. (1999). *Human behavior in global perspective: An introduction to cross-cultural psychology* (2nd ed.). Boston: Allyn and Bacon.

Senft, G. (Ed.). (1997). *Referring to space*. Oxford, UK: Oxford University Press.

Senft, G. (2001). Frames of spatial reference in Kilivila. *Studies in Language, 25*, 521-555.

Taylor, H. A., & Tversky, B. (1996). Perspective in spatial descriptions. *Journal of Memory and Language, 35*, 371-391.

Trommsdorff, G. (1993). Entwicklung im Kulturvergleich [Cross-cultural human development]. In A. Thomas (Ed.), *Kulturvergleichende Psychologie* (pp. 103-144). Göttingen, Germany: Hogrefe.

Trommsdorff, G. (Ed.). (1995). *Kindheit und Jugend in verschiedenen Kulturen.* [Childhood and youth in different cultures]. Weinheim, Germany: Juventa.

Troadec, B., & Martinot, C. (2001, September). *De la variabilité interindividuelle à la variabilité interculturelle: L'exemple du développement de la représentation de l'espace chez l'enfant de Tahiti (Océanie)* [From interindividual variability to cross-cultural variability: The example of the development of spatial representation in Tahitian children]. Paper presented at the 8ème congrès international de l'ARIC, Genève, Switzerland. Retrieved from *http://www.unige.ch/fapse/SSE/groups/aric*

Troadec, B., Martinot, C., & Cottereau-Reiss, P. (2002). A cross-cultural study of diversity in cognitive development: Categorization and space. In P. Boski, F. J. R. van de Vijver, & M. Chodynicka (Eds.), *New directions of cross-cultural psychology* (pp. 243-258). Warsaw, Poland: Polish Academy of Sciences.

Wassmann, J. (1994). The Yupno as post-Newtonian scientists. The question of what is "natural" in spatial description. *Man, 29*, 1-24.

Wassmann, J. (1997). Finding the right path. The route knowledge of the Yupno of Papua New Guinea. In G. Senft (Ed.), *Referring to space* (pp. 143-174). Oxford, UK: Oxford University Press.

Wassmann, J., & Dasen, P. R. (1994a). "Hot" and "cold": Classification and sorting among the Yupno of Papua New Guinea. *International Journal of Psychology, 29*, 19-38.

Wassmann, J., & Dasen, P. R. (1994b). Yupno number system and counting. *Journal of Cross-Cultural Psychology, 25*, 78-94

Wassmann, J., & Dasen, P. R. (1996). Comment ne pas perdre le Nord à Bali. Processus cognitifs - Une combinaison de méthodes ethnographiques et psychologiques [How not to loose the North in Bali. Cognitive processes - a combination of ethnographic and psychological methods]. *Bulletin de l'Académie suisse des sciences humaines et sociales (SAGW/ASSH)(1)*, 17-26, (2),13-16.

Wassmann, J., & Dasen, P. R. (1998). Balinese spatial orientation: Some empirical evidence for moderate linguistic relativity. *The Journal of the Royal Anthropological Institute,Iincorporating Man (N.S.), 4*, 689-711.

Part III

Intergenerational Relationships

8

Changing Value of Children: An Action Theory of Fertility Behavior and Intergenerational Relationships in Cross-Cultural Comparison[*]

Bernhard Nauck

The Starting Point of the "Value-of-Children Studies"

The "Value of Children" (VOC) concept is based on work carried out by Hoffman and Hoffman (1973). They provided the first – and up to now only – approach for international comparison of variations in fertility decision-making by explicitly taking cultural factors into account. Moreover, they developed an approach that took into consideration "objective" economic and normative factors as well as psychological effects influencing fertility behavior. These psychological aspects were seen as crucial determinants for the births of children. "Value of Children" was considered to be the central mediator variable at the individual level. However, this variable is subject to variation due to changes in society and its respective culture. VOC

[*] This paper is related to the research project "Value of Children in Six Cultures. A Replication and Extension of the 'Values-of-Children Studies' with regard to Generative Behaviour and Parents-Child Relationships" which is supported by the *Deutsche Forschungsgesellschaft* (principal investigators: Bernhard Nauck, Chemnitz and Gisela Trommsdorff, Konstanz) and conducted in China, Korea, Indonesia, Israel/Palestine, Turkey, and Germany. I thank Paul B. Hill, Johannes Huinink, Thomas Klein, Annette Kohlmann, Johannes Kopp, Wolfgang Lauterbach, and Gisela Trommsdorff for critical comments on earlier versions of this paper.

itself influences fertility and the behavior towards children: "Value of children refers to the functions they serve or the needs they fulfill for parents" (Hoffman & Hoffman, 1973, p. 20). Obviously therefore, this approach focuses on the value of children for their parents. This starting point takes the basic asymmetry of the parent-child relations into account. This asymmetry is established by the fact that only parents can choose whether or not to enter into such a relationship (whether to have children or not). It is thus an unconditional decision, whereas the ensuing decisions become increasingly conditional (based on mutual influence).

To establish an inventory of the several components of the value children have for their parents, Hoffman and Hoffman (1973) categorize various sources of inductively collected empirical findings and arrive at the following categorization:

1.   Adult status and social identity.
2.   Expansion of the self, tie to a larger entity, and "immortality."
3.   Morality: religion, altruism, good for the group, norms regarding sexuality, action on impulse, and virtue.
4.   Primary group ties and affection.
5.   Stimulation, novelty, and fun.
6.   Achievement, competence, and creativity.
7.   Power, influence, and effectiveness.
8.   Social comparison and competition.
9.   Economic utility.

The nine categories of the *value of children* are an integral part of a model that also takes several other influential factors into account: alternative sources of the value of children, costs of children, barriers and incentives. The central assumption is that the value of children varies according to the type of existing society, and has various far-reaching consequences for generative decisions and the type of parent-child relations. Hoffman and Hoffman's (1973) initial model already comprises *alternative sources* of value in people and institutions that produce the same result for the (potential) parents. For example, public social-security systems may make up for the children's economic value. *Costs* emerge for parents *directly* (financial and time costs) and *indirectly* as opportunity costs, when abstaining from other goods and activities in favor of the children. *Barriers* are defined as factors that make it more difficult to attain the desired value of children, as for example family poverty, less-than-ideal housing conditions, or maternal illness. The model also comprises *incentives* as factors that make it easier to reach the desired value of children: wealth, adequate housing conditions, family support, and generally positive attitudes towards children in the social context.

The VOC approach has been conceptualized to develop an instrument for cross-cultural comparisons of the decisive influences on parent's fertility decisions. Different phenomena in several countries are thus been explained in terms of the variations of the *same* determinants. This is to be seen as an attempt to establish an economic model of complex relationships. Assuming differing costs, barriers and incentives, but also values of children – all of which vary according to conditions in the respective cultures – permits cross-cultural comparisons of fertility levels. The model integrates aspects of explanations of generative behavior from different scientific disciplines (Fawcett, 1976) and, surprisingly, anticipates essential elements of explanatory models in modern social science (Coleman, 1990). In particular, it provides all the necessary elements for an *action-based theoretical model of generative behavior*. Thus, the VOC approach, rather than being a competing explanation, offers an interdisciplinary, integrative explanatory concept that combines essential components of approaches from various disciplines. It also offers a conceptual frame to enable the development of a coherent, methodologically complete explanation of intercultural differences in generative behavior. The strength of this approach is not only its integrative potential but also its combination of individual actor-based components with structure-based perspectives on fertility behavior.

An integrated explanation requires resolving a number of conceptual, object-theoretical, measurement-theoretical, and methodological-technical problems that have remained unresolved until now. For example, the VOC studies used the language developed in the tradition of cross-cultural motivation psychology to define their theoretical constructs and are also closely linked to empirical inductivism. These terms need to be translated into the language of social action theory. The VOC list "emerged" inductively from existing empirical research and was not deductively derived from theory (Friedman, Hechter, & Kanazawa, 1994). The value of children therefore remains exogenous and thus unexplained. Its theoretical status is unclear, especially because it is also uncertain whether this list is a complete value system (in the sense of theoretical model building) or whether it may be expanded. Attempts to validate the indicators have been successful, but only to a minor degree and only in intra-cultural studies (especially by Kagitçibasi & Esmer, 1980; Kagitçibasi, 1982). In particular, the distinction between the following dimensions proved to be empirically significant:

- economical-utilitarian VOC value (i.e., contributions to the family economy from child labor, household help and additional income; old-age insurance),
- psychological-emotional VOC (i.e., strengthening emotional group ties; expressive stimulation through interaction with children).

Both of these empirical VOC dimensions perfectly match the distinction between the instrumental value of children (as producers of commodities in the family household) and the immanent value of children (as consumer goods) in economic theories of generative behavior. Finally, the various studies never managed to systematically relate the VOC to the respective opportunity structures and action barriers within the respective social contexts. What are still widely missing are the necessary *bridging hypotheses* connecting the levels of social context to the level of individual action.

Children as Intermediate Goods in the Social Production Function

A promising path for the action-theoretical reconceptualization of the VOC approach is to integrate it into the general *theory of social production functions*. In the theoretical tradition of Adam Smith, it is assumed that human actors "seek to maximize at least two things: social esteem and physical well being" (Lindenberg, 1990, p. 271).

Social esteem is the extent to which an actor receives positive social reinforcement by his social context. According to Lindenberg (1991), social esteem can be differentiated into status, affect and approval. *Status* refers to the relative rank of the position attained in the respective society, whereas rank is defined by control over scarce, highly valued resources. The more control there is over intermediate goods in the social production function, the higher the social status will be. *Affect* refers to the exchange of positive feelings in emotional relationships. *Social approval* refers to the positive reinforcement by "significant actors." *The greater the expected social esteem for any particular action alternative chosen, the more likely it is that this alternative will be chosen.*

Physical well being is the extent to which an actor is able to secure his (physical) survival and improve his well being. This can be achieved through productive labor, competition for scarce goods on the market, and effective organization and cooperation. *The more physical well being expected from any particular action alternative, the more likely it is that this alternative will be chosen.*

The actor cannot satisfy both of these basic needs directly. Rather, they need to be satisfied through various production factors that have to be provided. Contrary to the two basic needs, these production factors are not universal but context-specific: *the greater the efficiency of a production factor in satisfying basic needs within a respective context, the higher the likelihood that it will be chosen.* The more persistent the efficiency of a respective production factor in any respective context, the higher the probability of its intergenerative transmission and of its institutionalization as a cultural routine solution.

The explanatory program for the VOC approach is then to develop a special theory of how and under which conditions children become intermediate goods in their (potential) parents' social production function by optimizing their social esteem and their physical well being. The explanatory program thus provides an indigenous, substantial specification of the value of children, which is lacking in economic fertility theories. Fertility decisions and the shaping of lifelong parent-child relations are analyzed and explained as an aspect of maximizing subjective utility. This maximization comes about as a result of specific perceived conditions. The respective situation of action and sociocultural "frames" determine the action alternatives available in achieving the actor's goals. They also determine, whether and to what extent parenthood is an efficient strategy within these alternatives. This means that children are important intermediate goods, for whom it is worthwhile to bear them, bring them up, nurture them, and invest into them every possible way.

Significant short-term and long-term aspects of the social production function, including intergenerational relationships over the entire life span, can be distinguished:

Children help to improve their parents' material well being if they actively contribute to increasing household production and thus function as productive and not just as consumption goods. This can be achieved through their own contributions to welfare production within the parental household as well as by contributing their own income value earned on the labor market. It can also be related to the short-term effect of early assistance in the family household as well as to the long-term effect of contributions to parental insurance against life risks. Striking examples for the inclusion of children into the welfare production of the family household are child labor in subsistence agricultural economies, children's assistance in family business (i.e., small trade or service shops), and the help (of girls) with the housework and child care. Typically, this utility of children is especially salient if the investments in education and human capital are relatively small and child labor can therefore start relatively early, i.e., this utility is mainly based on a short-term perspective. Regarding insurance against life risks, be they illness, catastrophes, unemployment, or old age, many societies do not offer institutionalized alternatives to family or kin. Mutual intergenerative insurance against life risks is obviously based on a perspective covering the entire life span. This perspective will necessarily imply ideas of intergenerational justice and respective expectations of reciprocity. Therefore, children's general utility for optimizing physical well being of their parents lies in their potential for *income utility* valueand *insurance utility*.

Children can both directly and indirectly optimize their parents' social esteem. They contribute indirectly to the social esteem of their parents when creating (additional) relations to others or when intensifying existing relations and improving their quality. For example, children may establish contacts to other parents; the commonalities of the parental role may lead to social integration, especially of mothers. Additionally, parenthood changes the quality of the spousal relationship and the relationship with one's parents and parents-in-law. Finally, children themselves can be a status symbol and, in a specific social context, serve as a positional good that may "produce" social recognition in a very direct way. This status gain can work like a threshold (with the birth of the first child or the birth of a child of a distinct sex) or it can steadily increase with the number of children born. Typically, this utility of children already appears in a short-term perspective. Moreover, children contribute quite genuinely to a direct optimization of social recognition. Parenthood creates a "native," close, intimate, emotional, lifelong, bonded, and committed social relationship that contributes very directly to self-validation and personal identity formation and gives meaning and relevance to personality. Intergenerational relationships are constituted and largely characterized by dialogical interactions (Huinink, 1995). As social approval from significant others becomes more and more specific in functionally differentiated societies, "authentic" intergenerational relationships with their "unlimited time" perspective may increase in importance. It is typical for this utility of children that it is related to a long-term perspective (even though a number of aspects emerge immediately upon establishing the relationship). Therefore, children's general utility for optimizing social recognition of their parents is their potential for *social utility through status attainment* and for *emotional utility* in the quality of the very parent-child relationship.

There is a striking correspondence between these action-theoretical considerations and the empirical arguments developed in VOC studies, solving the initially serious explanation problems of the VOC approach (see Table 1). The conceptual equivalence provides utmost theoretical consistency, because the model comprises the two different values of children from empirical research and at the same time the basic distinction between production and consumption within economic theory. Thus, the theoretical content is extended in a way that also allows explaining generative behavior in non-affluent societies. This reconceptualization of the VOC approach comes relatively close to Leibenstein's (1957, 1974) economic fertility model with its basic distinction between "consumption utility," "utility as a source of security," and "utility as a productive agent" of children. The latter utilities are the most important empirical differentiations of the economical-utilitarian VOC. They correspond to the labor utility and the insurance utility of children for increasing physical well being in the social production function. What the reconceptualized VOC approach and Leibenstein's approach have in common is that they operate on a basis of multi-dimensional utility functions that are economically modeled and theoretically well grounded.

Table 1
Value of Children in the Social Production Function

	Physical well being	Social recognition
Short-term	(a)	(c)
	Labor utility	Status-attainment utility
Long-term	(b)	(d)
	Insurance utility	Emotional utility

Modeling Cultural Differences of VOC in the Framework of Action Theory

In the following, some action-theoretical hypotheses concerning value of children are to be developed. They will demonstrate the theoretical potential of the VOC approach when embedded in the framework of the theory of social production functions and for explaining context-dependent generative behavior in cross-cultural comparison. The modeling attempt refers to a few constitutive dimensions of the family action system. Accordingly, families are understood as purposively long-lasting social groups, being constituted by clear criteria of membership based on gender and generational relationships, producing collective goods exclusively for their members. Thus, the model refers to the *size* of the family determined by the number of children, its purposive *permanence* (longevity), the interdependence of the household production with the extra-familial context and its *opportunities* and *restrictions*, the scarce *individual resources* of parents for the household production, the institutionalization of *intergenerational relationships* and *gender relationships* in the respective sociocultural context, and finally, the extent of *exclusivity* of the family group in its social context (Nauck, 2001). Because of space limitations, the more "structural" dimensions, like "context opportunities and restrictions" and "individual resources," which play an important role in sociological explanations, are omitted in favor of the "cultural" dimensions.

Size of the family group

If the special case of polygamy is disregarded, the family size is only to be influenced by generative behavior. Depending on whether the generative behavior is primarily optimized with regard to work and insurance utility, or with regard to emotional and social utility, this has implications for the number of children with which these utilities can be achieved efficiently (Kagitçibasi, 1982; Nauck, 1989, 1997).

a.   If the work utility of children is highly evaluated then it is an efficient strategy to be "rich in children," as each additional child will linearly increase the work utility. It is an additional source for the family income value because of its (early) work contribution or as it distributes the existing workload on more shoulders. The strategy is restricted by the initial investment costs in children and the available opportunity structures for (early) unqualified labor, largely varying from one socio-ecological context to the other. As the unit costs of children decrease with their number, the ratio becomes increasingly favorable with increasing dependents.

b.   If the insurance utility of children is highly evaluated, then many children are also an efficient strategy, as it distributes the burden of the supply for the parents on more shoulders and thus reduces the duty for each child. Accordingly, if an institutional regime of old age security is not based on an indirect "cohort" contract but on a direct "generation"-contract, it will increase the interest not only of (potential) parents in many descendants, as it makes old age support more *certain*, but it will also increase the interest of the descendants in many siblings, as it *reduces* the individual burden.

c.   If the creation of additional social relationships is highly evaluated, then it is not an efficient strategy to have as many children as possible, because the number of additional social relationships will not increase linearly with the number of children. Moreover, the number of additional relationships will reach its saturation point quite early. Accordingly, the ratio is favorable for small numbers of children, but unfavorable for childlessness and high parity. It may be assumed additionally that the stabilization of existing social relationships (especially with the spouse and to the families of origin) will not increase linear-additively, so that even with regard to this aspect no additional gain of efficiency is to be expected. No definite solution exists for the increase of social status attainment utility of children, as this depends directly on the social norms shared in the respective context. Accordingly, conforming behavior can consist of childlessness or of single or multiple parenthood. It is to be assumed, however, that such norms are strongly related to the opportunity structures in the respective context. It is then probable that social esteem may be increased with many descendants in those contexts, where these are an efficient strategy for the increase of physical well being anyway. In the same way, social esteem may be increased with childlessness in those social contexts in which childless people are at an advantage in the competition for scarce, highly valued goods. Consequently, such norms are primarily an expression of the tradition of efficient routine solutions in the respective social context in the past, and following them is efficient as long as no salient changes in the opportunity structure occur.

d.   If the emotional utility of having children is highly evaluated, then it is also not an efficient strategy to have many children, as emotional benefits cannot be accumulated in the same way as labor or insurance utility. One or two children can provide as much psychological satisfaction as four or more children. At the same time, the absolute (economic and probably even psychological) costs increase, so that the ratio is favorable for few descendants, but unfavorable for childlessness and high parity. In this respect, a self-enforcing process of fertility reduction may be caused by the fact that children compete in the emotional relationship with their parents. As a result, their interest in (additional) siblings is the lower the more they resemble them with regard to their characteristics (such as age and sex). As this will not be without feedback to the emotional quality of the parent-child relationship, incentives decrease for the parents to optimize emotional benefits through additional children.

Purposive longevity

Parenthood, more than any other social relationship, is purposively permanent. This implies self-binding which practically covers the rest of one's entire life course. This long-term life course perspective has decisive consequences for parental investment strategies and for their control rights, for the bonding of parents and their offspring, for the development of "naïve" educational theories, and for conceptions of equity in intergenerational relationships (Trommsdorff, 1993; Voland & Engel, 2000).

a.   If the income value and work utilities of children are highly valued, then the efficiency of parental control will focus on those descendants who productively contribute to the household economy. Accordingly, parental control is relatively low as long as the children make no contribution, and it vanishes as soon as the children leave the family household. This corresponds to the fact that early child care practices are characterized by a "laissez-faire" style and that child care and educational tasks are frequently delegated as long as these children are not a productive part of the family economy. Education duties being performed by older siblings, by available kinship members, by nurses, or in foster homes are especially frequent under these conditions. At least until children leave the parental household, autonomy, and self-reliance in decision-making and action are not highly evaluated educational goals. Much more important is the early and independent performance of tasks in the household economy, as well as obedience (Kornadt & Trommsdorff, 1984; Trommsdorff, 2001; Whiting & Whiting, 1975). With regard to income value and work utility, the cost of child loss is highest when the initial investments into the child have already been concluded but no return has yet occurred. The loss is relatively small in comparison for newborn children and for children who have left the household economy. Accordingly, rituals of grieving for children vary with their age and household status in societies with predominant work related VOC. Similarly, the "demand" for children (for adoption) is under these conditions highest for children at the beginning of their productive phase, and it is lower for newly born children or those entering adulthood (Zelizer, 1994). Restrictions for material investments in children (e.g., in case of illness) result from their expected or realized contributions to the family economy, i.e., they are lower for smaller children than for grown-up children. Prevalent income value and work utility of children result in insecure attachment between parents and children, especially under the "typical" conditions of poverty economy, high birth rates, and high infant mortality (deMause, 1992).

b.   If the insurance utility of children is highly valued, then the efficiency of parental control will focus on the lifelong loyalty of these descendants to their parents, for whom the insurance utility is expected. Accordingly, parental control will remain on a high level even in the adulthood of the offspring. The more the insurance utility of children can be increased through investments in their human capital, the earlier the parents raise their achievement expectations and the earlier achievement-related "pedagogical" interactions start. This is true not only for parents' side but also for specific "achievement increasing" educational institutions as well. Decision making autonomy and self-reliance remain less highly valued educational goals throughout the life course of the child, while an enduring, dutiful, and "harmonic" fit into the social order, obedience, and loyalty according to the principle of ancient are positively valued. It is to be expected that the loss of a child be more intensively felt the older the child (and the parent) is, to the extent that the child is a target of insurance related expectations. Variance is introduced because (1) the insurance utility does not function on a curvilinear basis throughout the life course, as does the work and income utility value, but rather increases steadily and (2) as the insurance utility must not apply to every descendant to the same extent. The input of material investments should follow the same pattern of variance, which accordingly should result, for example, in varying mortality risks of children according to age, parity, and sex. The attachment between parents and children should be more secure the higher the expected insurance utility is (frequently sons of highest parity). This attachment is less secure when the insurance utility is less probable (frequently daughters).

c.   The status-attainment utility of children needs no increased efficiency through parental investments if it is provided by parenthood in itself or by the sheer number of descendants. Parenthood that is primarily rooted in status-attainment utility will result in insecure attachment between the (many) children and their parents, with no varying results for attachment, demand for a child, or the severity of felt loss for a child. However, if the social recognition results from the future status of the child, then the parental control and investment will be targeted towards the achievement of the specific status goals and the necessary intermediate goods (e.g., educational certificates). Attachment will be related to the expected or achieved status of the child and the felt loss of a child is all the more severe the higher the status already is. This means that felt loss typically increases with the age of the child. If the social recognition results from newly established social relationships through parenthood, then this will be efficiently achieved through the child's continuously increasing decision-making autonomy and self-reliance, as these qualities are more likely to provide new, non-redundant social circles. Variation in attachment, demand, or loss is not related.

d.   If the emotional utility of children is highly valued, then an efficient strategy for increasing this utility is to grant the highest possible decision-making autonomy and self-reliance to the child at the earliest possible stage, as the value of emotional gratification increases with the autonomy of child's personality. Accordingly, "autonomy" and "creativity" are positively evaluated educational goals throughout childhood, while "obedience" and "early performance of delegated tasks" are not. Parental investments will target those activities and institutional supports that are supposed to encourage an early unfolding of an autonomous personality (Friedlmeier, 1995; Trommsdorff, 1995). High emotional utility expectations imply that in case of illness all possible efforts have to be made for the medical care of the child – up to the total financial ruin of the family, regardless of the child's age and sex, i.e., parental investments are equally distributed among all descendants and are not specifically restricted. As the emotional benefit is higher when it lasts long and is exclusive, the demand for adopted children decreases with the child's age. Similarly, the felt loss of a newborn child is extremely severe. The attachment between parents and children increases according to the emotional benefit the parents expect to get out of the relationship.

Institutional regulation of intergenerational relationships

The way children can be used as intermediate goods for optimizing physical well being and social esteem is strongly related to the institutional rules that structure and shape intergenerational relationships. Such rules are easy to perceive within the predominant marriage and inheritance rules (Zelditch, 1964). Societies differ enormously in whether affinal or descent kinship regimes dominate institutional rules. The affinal regime is typically characterized by independent, "autonomous" choice of spouse, which is most frequently legitimated as "romantic love," and by a priority set on the solidarity between spouses (as against intergenerational solidarity). This commonly results in a strong separation between the family of procreation and the family of origin. Inheritance rules accordingly favor the remaining spouse first; in case of conflict the prime solidarity belongs to the members of the conjugal family.

The descent regime is primarily based on the intergenerational solidarity in the community of descent; accordingly, parents (and the broader community of descent) are highly influential in the choice of the marriage partner, and the inheritance rules favor primarily the children. In case of conflict, the primary solidarity belongs to the community of descent. In societies where the solidarity of descent predominates, children are more important intermediate goods in the social production function than in societies where affinal solidarity predominates. The primacy of descent is institutionalized as either matrilinearity or patrilinearity.

a.   Whether a society is organized according to the descent or the affinal regime has an influence on the work utility, because the work utility depends not only on the age and the sex of the child but also on the child's position in relation to her parents. In societies with a descent regime *no* differences are made between biological and in-married children - both types of children typically have to perform the same age- and sex-specific tasks. This is typically not the case in societies with the affinal regime. It makes a difference with regard to the work utility whether the work is to be performed by the biological daughter, or the daughter-in-law, for example. Some tasks are considered to be reasonable demands for the former but unreasonable for the latter. The potential work utility of biological children is always higher than of in-married children in societies with an affinal regime.

b.   Intergenerational solidarity is institutionally more secured in societies with a descent regime, which makes the insurance utility more "certain" than in affinal societies. This institutional safeguard refers, however, only to those children of the sex on which the system of descent is based. Accordingly, the possibility of optimizing the insurance utility through long-term educational investments in their human capital exists only for children of the right sex, whereas for future members of the opposite sex optimization only exists in the form of control of the partner selection. In societies with a descent regime, the interest in the optimization of work and insurance utility of in-married children is thus a further incentive for parental control of the marriage process of their descendants. This in turn serves to stabilize these institutional regulations.

c.   The work utility is institutionally more secured also in societies with a descent regime in which the "possession" of children increases the social esteem of the parents within the community of descent itself (at least). In this case, children are the visible sign of the successful continuation of the lineage. This is especially true for those children of the sex on which the system of descent is based. The higher the number of male descendants in patrilineal societies, or the higher the number of female descendants in matrilineal societies, the more the relative social status of the parents increases in the community of descent. This status gain also refers to parents of opposite sex who marry into the lineage.

d.   Strong incentives exist in societies with a descent regime to separate emotional relationships within the lineage from those, which might exist towards members of the affinal kinship system – including the spouse. In societies with an affinal regime, however, a competition in the emotional relationship between the spouses on the one hand, and within the parent-child relationship on the other hand is institutionalized. As the (weaker) relationships to the families of origin are organized typically in bi-linear fashion, this weakens further the influence of the communities of origin on the conjugal family and lets it become an intimate group with especially strong boundaries. Accordingly, children are a non-transferable, "marriage specific" capital (in the sense of micro-economic theories) only in societies with an affinal regime. In societies with a descent regime, strong incentives exist to give priority to close emotional ties with the descendants as compared to a close relationship with the spouse. Conflicts with regard to the control rights over the children in case of a separation or divorce do not exist, as these always stay with the lineage of descent.

Institutional regulations of gender relations

The more institutional regulations that give priority to relationships based on descent kinship as compared to relationships based on affinal kinship predominate in a society, the stronger is the status differentiation between genders. The stronger the status differentiation between genders, the stronger different loyalty expectations towards male and female descendants, and the more gender-specific are parental investment strategies. The inherent mechanisms are described for the prevalent type of patrilineal systems of descent.

a.   Strong gender differences and a sex preference towards sons are combined in patrilineal societies with a status-differentiated sex-specific division of labor. This has a strong effect on the labor utility of male and female descendants. With regard to work utility in patrilineal societies, a one-sided concentration on male descendants would thus in no way be an optimal strategy. Male descendants cannot easily be assigned to do "female" work, i.e., lower-status members are more "flexible" to be used for a variety of tasks (Schiffauer, 1987). Accordingly, the efficiency of the household economy increases the incentive to substitute existing female household members in case of marriage immediately with daughters-in-law. This, in turn, contributes to an early, standardized marriage process in patrilineal societies. Parents in patrilineal societies, who (have to) optimize labor utility of children, are thus always interested in the marriage of their sons, as this inserts another welcomed worker into the family economy. The marriage of a daughter is, however, under specific conditions not welcomed at all (and sometimes blocked), namely, if she is the only child or the last in a line of female descendants. Under the precondition that marriage is seen as a favorable prospect as compared to staying permanently in the family of origin, then it may be concluded, that even female descendants have strong incentives to prefer brothers as siblings. Relative to the work utility, sex preferences are more pronounced in the case of the income utility value of children. The income utility of male descendants is not only more "certain" and lasts longer, but it is also normally higher because of the combination of human capital investments and length of stay on the labor market. All this will *increase* the male sex preference in patrilineal societies, when shifting from subsistence economy to functionally differentiated market economy. No special incentives for a gender-specific differentiation of the work and income utility of children, or for a gender-specific differentiation of control interests of parents are to be expected for societies with an affinal regime. But as the loyalty of children is predominantly based on intergenerational emotional bonds, the work utility of female descendants may be more "certain," and – because of the sex-specific inequality in the survival probability – the control interests of mothers may be more intensive than those of fathers.

b.   Different lengths of stay of descendants with different sexes result in gender-specific optimization strategies for the insurance utility of children. In patrilineal societies, male descendants belong to the community of descent for their entire life. At the same time, descendants of the opposite sex will not in the long run contribute to the parents' insurance against life risks because they typically leave the community of descent with their marriage. They thus potentially increase work and income utilities value only until their marriage into another lineage. The insurance utility provides no incentive to invest in their human capital. This differential investment, in turn, contributes to the adjustment of gender-specific status differentiation. If the insurance utility is highly evaluated in patrilineal societies, this will lead to strong preferences for male descendants. As the marriage process of female descendants in patrilineal societies starts relatively early and also comes to an end early, this favors marked age differences between spouses. Together with higher female life expectancy, wives have a much more pronounced survival probability. Accordingly, the interest in the insurance utility of (male) descendants is more probable in (patrilineal) societies with a descent regime as compared to affinal societies, and the interest is stronger in mothers than in fathers.

c.   Social esteem is derived from the control over important intermediate goods. In societies with a descent regime the status-attainment utility of children is optimized directly through the number of descendants of the sex on which descent is based and which are thus under the permanent control of their parents. Accordingly, social esteem increases in patrilineal societies linearly with each additional birth of a son. This utility of male descendants exists for fathers and mothers in the same way. A multiplicative relationship exists between the social status of the parents and the social esteem derived from male descendants; it is highest in high status families and low in low status families. In societies with an affinal regime, the status-attainment benefit of children is only optimized through the (additionally) generated, "weak" social relationships. For this, the sex of the child is of no importance, as male and female descendants generate social contacts with the same probability and quality.

d.   In general, girls and boys are – for both parents – a source of emotional satisfaction to the same extent, but societies with an affinal or a descent regime differ in their opportunity structures. The stronger the sex segregation is in a society, the less emotional satisfaction can derive from children of both sexes. In societies with a descent regime, the preferences of parents are directed towards the descendants of the same sex because of the gender-related status differentiation and sex segregation. Accordingly, fathers will prefer sons and mothers will prefer daughters as a source of emotional satisfaction. The "certainty" of this utility is, however, gender-differentiated. While for fathers the lifelong relationship to their son is probable, the change of a daughter to another lineage is an important factor of uncertainty. In societies with an affinal regime with its bi-linear organization of descent, strong incentives for parents exist for a "complete" reproduction. On the base of these utility expectations, the "ideal" family will comprise a "complete" role-set of mother, father, daughter, and son. It is, however, possible that it is combined with a slight preference for daughters, as these maintain family relationships and thus are in the long run a more certain source of emotional utility for fathers and mothers.

Exclusivity of the family group
The extent to which the family in a society is institutionalized as an exclusive, self-regulated social group, specialized on affective relationships, with distinct borders in regard to membership, and legitimized validity of action norms, has consequences for the efficiency of children as intermediate goods in the social production function. The more specialized and the more exclusive the family in a society, the higher the restrictions for parents to optimize their value income-, insurance-, and status-attainment utilities with children. However, the emotional utility is not affected by this specialization and correspondingly becomes more "salient." The less exclusive the family group in the respective society is, the less the utility of children is solely family-specific and the more it is related to potential utility of descendants in exchange processes with the social context related to the family's welfare production.

a.   The lower the exclusivity of the family group, the more internal and external resources of the family are pooled and used reciprocally. This creates incentives in the employment sector to rely preferably on members of the kinship system. Thus, kinship related and occupational control rights coincide, which at least increases the efficiency of employment, as long as work effectiveness is primarily increased by loyalty and not by specialized knowledge and skills. Low exclusivity of the family group accordingly creates good conditions for the effective use of child labor (and nepotism, patronage, and clientelism). A low exclusivity of the family group also creates incentives for establishing efficient exchange systems between communities of descent. This ensures an evolutionarily stable, balanced system of interchange of descendants' gender-specific work utility (Levi-Strauss, 1984). Bride payments for the costs and the forgone labor utility of daughters as well as the direct or generalized exchange of descendants between communities of descent are important parts of this system. Parental control interests in the communities of descent favor high marriage rates. The level of the marriage rate simultaneously influences directly the length of the achievable labor and income utility value of children. The higher the marriage rate in a society, the stronger is the incentive for an early marriage, as any extension of the seeking process will drastically reduce the supply on the marriage market. The result is an early, highly standardized marriage process, which is even more reinforced if it is not the partners themselves, but the communities of descent instead who decide on the partner selection and contractually "secure" a later marriage. As a result, female members leave the community of descent as early as calculable.

b.   The higher the children's insurance utility is valued in patrilineal societies, the stronger is the preference for male descendants and the stronger is gender-specific status differentiation. Sex preferences for one's own descendants are made more pronounced by the restrictions of the opposite sex supply on the marriage market and by a high marriage rate. Accordingly, opposite sex partners are a scarce, highly valued good on a very "inelastic" marriage market. The lower the exclusiveness of the family group in the society, the more intense are the incentives to react to this supply structure with compensatory bargains, i.e., to combine intermarriage with material transfers between the communities of descent. Material transfers thus regulate the market balance between the social status of the communities of descent and the supply of human capital. At the same time, a marriage market of this structure always offers the chance of hypergamy for women due either to special offers in human capital or to transfer payments. Hypergamy forcefully stabilizes the existing gender-specific status differentiation, but at the same time opens opportunities for upward mobility of lower status women. These mechanisms of the marriage market also explain why under these conditions the preference for boys decreases with the social status of the community of descent. Only low-status female descendants have the chance of hypergamy in patrilineal societies. They create at the same time the structural conditions for higher rates of never-married women from higher status groups and possibly also the institutionalization of dowry. Societies with an affinal regime typically do not offer these chances of hypergamy but rather create strong incentives for status-homogeneous marriages and thus decrease status mobility through marriage.

c.   The higher the exclusivity of the family group in a society, the more social recognition is optimized mainly through primary relationships and not through appraisal of members with high status in the community (of descent). As a result, no incentives exist for parents to increase their social recognition through the "public" visibility of children. The lower the exclusivity of the family group, the more the parents' social recognition is increased through investments in children, i.e., the occupational or marriage mobility of their children directly increases the parents' social esteem.

d.   The higher the exclusivity of the family group in a society, the greater the specialization on the children's emotional utility and the greater the personalization of the relationship between parents and children. Accordingly, this utility increases in importance with the strength of the structural differences between the family group and the parents' other fields of action. When these structural differences are small, children compete with other personalized relationships, lowering their specific utility and increasing the opportunity costs of parenthood. Therefore, it is to be expected that the incentive for parenthood is smaller for "social" professions with complex interpersonal relationships than for professions with specific, formalized tasks. The fewer the alternatives to parenthood for strong, personalized relationships are in a society, the stronger are the incentives to draw emotional utility from parenthood.

Discussion

The attempt of a systematic elaboration of a special action theory of generative behavior and of intergenerational relationships on the basis of the VOC approach makes it easy to classify societies according to their constellations of marginal conditions and to explain the resulting differences. It thus considerably contributes to the theoretical integration of "cultural" factors within the general explanation model.

The special action theory provides insight into patterns of childhood that are sustained by great cultural legitimacy and are lived in great structural homogeneity in many corporate welfare societies. From a worldwide cross-cultural perspective, they seem to be rather outlying patterns: the widely accepted dominance of an affinal kinship system, bi-lateral descent, the high exclusivity of the family group, an extremely high trust in a state-run insurance system against life risks, and a high general welfare level with the resulting high resources for (potential) parents. The action theory also explains, how these conditions are related to specific utility expectations of (potential) parents towards children and towards intergenerational relationships, how these utility expectations are pursued with efficient action alternatives, and which role children have therein. It is obvious for corporate welfare societies, that one's *own* children are not efficient intermediate goods in the social production function, as far as the increase or the maintenance of the parent's physical well being is concerned. Children contribute to the parental household neither through work nor through income value in any substantial way. Insuring oneself against life risks through one's own children corresponds with a reversed subsidiary system. It comes into force after all other insurance systems have failed.

A more differentiated picture results when children are understood as intermediate goods for the increase of social recognition. On the one hand, it is to be assumed that the status-attainment utility of children is extraordinarily low because of the high exclusivity of the family group, and that the number of social contexts rewarding childlessness increases. Accordingly, the proportion of people who gain new social contacts through their children will decrease as compared to the proportion of people for whom children prevent new social contacts. On the other hand, the efficiency of intergenerational relationships for optimizing emotional utility is extraordinary high, especially since they are without alternative for people whose professional lives are characterized by highly specialized and formalized tasks. It is therefore not surprising that children's emotional utility dominates the frame of generational behavior and of intergenerational relationships to an extraordinary extent. However, the number of people having increased their alternatives for the optimization of emotional utility increases with the tertiarization of the economy. This will lead to a further polarization of the society into a family sector, which oscillates around the optimum of two children for emotional utility, and a non-family sector, i.e., increasing childlessness.

The special action theory also makes understandable why high parity is probable in societies of poverty. It is surely the special merit of the VOC studies in the 1970s that they developed a value-neutral context of explanation for why high numbers of children are neither the result of "blind" clinging to primordial "cultural" traditions, nor the result of lacking knowledge in regard to effective methods of birth control. Rather, the empirical findings have impressively clarified that (potential) parents must have a strong "rational" interest in having many descendants under these constellations of context opportunities and individual resources. Accordingly, concern over not having enough descendants or their not surviving during the first years of their lives is possibly much more widespread than the wish to prevent unwanted pregnancies or additional births (Darroch, Meyer, & Singarimbun, 1981). This theory has named the conditions lying behind this type of intergenerational relationship and generative behavior: A low welfare level and high life risks in connection with an absence of a non-family-based insurance system.

Thus, there are practically no realistic alternatives to kinship-based communities of solidarity. The action theory has also explains how these conditions are related to specific utility expectations of (potential) parents towards children and intergenerational relationships, how these utility expectations are pursued through efficient action alternatives, and which importance children have not only for the welfare production of the family of origin, but also for the balance of control interests between communities of descent. It is thus obvious that *one's own* children are very efficient, non-substitutable intermediate goods in the social production function for the maintenance, and increase of physical well being. The short-term planning horizon then gives priority to the work utility of children as compared to the future insurance utility. It is more than understandable that under these conditions the visible sign of having control over such an important intermediate good, namely the "possession" of children, simultaneously increases social status. It is then also not surprising that, when coping with such problems of scarcity, the cultivation of intimate personal relationships will lag behind. This is all the more true as higher life risks also result in a situation where "indefinite duration of the length of the relationship" has not the connotation of "longevity" or "lifelong," but the connotation of "it may end quite soon." In sum, the special action theory also makes a valuable contribution to an in-depth understanding of intergenerational relationships and generative behavior in impoverished societies (Nauck, 2002). The ability of this special action theory, to explain intergenerational relationships and fertility behavior in modern, corporate, and affluent societies as well as in segmented impoverished societies demonstrates its great range of application and explanatory power.

References

Coleman, J. S. (1990). *Foundations of social theory.* Cambridge, MA: Harvard University Press.

Darroch, R. K., Meyer, P. A., & Singarimbun, M. (1981). *Two are not enough: The value of children to Javanese and Sundanese parents.* Honolulu, HI: East-West Center.

deMause, L. (1992). Evolution der Kindheit [Evolution of the childhood]. In L. deMause (Ed.), *Hört ihr die Kinder weinen. Eine psychogenetische Geschichte der Kindheit* (7th ed.). Frankfurt/M., Germany: Suhrkamp.

Fawcett, J. T. (1976). The value and cost of children: Converging theory and research. In L. T. Ruzicka (Ed.), *The economic and social supports for high fertility* (Vol. 2, pp. 91-114). Canberra, Australia: Australian National University.

Friedlmeier, W. (1995). Subjektive Erziehungstheorien im Kulturvergleich [Subjective child-rearing theories in cross-cultural comparison]. In G. Trommsdorff (Ed.), *Kindheit und Jugend in verschiedenen Kulturen. Entwicklung und Sozialisation in kulturvergleichender Sicht* (pp. 43-64). Weinheim, Germany: Juventa.

Friedman, D., Hechter, M., & Kanazawa, S. (1994). A theory of the value of children. *Demography, 31,* 375-401.

Hoffman, L. W., & Hoffman, M. L. (1973). The value of children to parents. In J. T. Fawcett (Ed.), *Psychological perspectives on population* (pp. 19-76). New York: Basic Books.

Huinink, J. (1995). *Warum noch Familie? Zur Attraktivität von Partnerschaft und Elternschaft in unserer Gesellschaft* [Why family? On the attractiveness of partnership and parenthood in our society]. Frankfurt/M., Germany: Campus.

Kagitçibasi, C. (1982). *The changing value of children in Turkey.* Honolulu, HI: East-West Center.

Kagitçibasi, C., & Esmer, Y. (1980). *Development, value of children, and fertility: A multiple indicator approach.* Istanbul, Turkey: Bogazici University.

Kornadt, H.-J., & Trommsdorff, G. (1984). Erziehungsziele im Kulturvergleich [Child-rearing goals in cross-cultural comparison]. In G. Trommsdorff (Ed.), *Erziehungsziele. Jahrbuch für empirische Erziehungswissenschaft* (pp. 191-212). Düsseldorf, Germany: Schwann.

Leibenstein, H. (1957). *Economic backwardness and economic growth. Studies in the theory of economic development.* New York: Wiley.

Leibenstein, H. (1974). An interpretation of the economic theory of fertility: Promising path or blind alley? *Journal of Economic Literature, 12,* 457-479.

Levi-Strauss, C. (1984). *Die elementaren Strukturen der Verwandtschaft [The basic structures of kinship].* Frankfurt/M., Germany: Suhrkamp.

Lindenberg, S. (1990). Rationalität und Kultur. Die verhaltenstheoretische Basis des Einflusses von Kultur auf Transaktionen *[Rationality and culture: The behavior theoretical basis of culture's effects on transactions]*. In H. Haferkamp (Ed.), *Sozialstruktur und Kultur* (pp. 249-287). Frankfurt/M., Germany: Suhrkamp.

Lindenberg, S. (1991). Social approval, fertility, and female labour market. In J. J. Siegers, J. de Jong-Gierveld, & E. Imhoff (Eds.), *Female labour market behavior and fertility* (pp. 32-58). Berlin; Germany: Springer.

Nauck, B. (1989). Intergenerational relationships in families from Turkey and Germany. An extension of the 'Value of Children' approach to educational attitudes and socialization practices. *European Sociological Review, 5*, 251-274.

Nauck, B. (1997). Sozialer Wandel, Migration und Familienbildung bei türkischen Frauen [Social change, migration, and family formation in Turkish women]. In B. Nauck & U. Schönpflug (Eds.), *Familien in verschiedenen Kulturen* (pp. 162-199). Stuttgart, Germany: Enke.

Nauck, B. (2001). Der Wert von Kindern für ihre Eltern. 'Value of Children' als spezielle Handlungstheorie des generativen Verhaltens und von Generationenbeziehungen im interkulturellen Vergleich [Value of children for their parents. The 'Value of Children' approach as a specific action theory of generative behavior and of intergenerational relationships in an intercultural comparison]. *Kölner Zeitschrift für Soziologie und Sozialpsychologie, 53*, 407-435.

Nauck, B. (2002). Families in Turkey. In R. Nave-Herz (Ed.), *Family change and intergenerational relations in different cultures* (pp. 11-48). Würzburg, Germany: Ergon.

Schiffauer, W. (1987). *Die Bauern von Subay. Das Leben in einem türkischen Dorf [The farmers of Subay. Life in a Turkish village]*. Stuttgart, Germany: Klett-Cotta.

Trommsdorff, G. (1993). Geschlechtsdifferenz von Generationenbeziehungen im interkulturellen Vergleich. Eine sozial- und entwicklungspsychologische Analyse [Gender differences in intergenerational relations in cross-cultural comparison. A social and developmental psychological analysis]. In K. Lüscher & F. Schultheis (Eds.), *Generationenbeziehungen in "postmodernen" Gesellschaften* (pp. 265-285). Konstanz, Germany: Universitätsverlag.

Trommsdorff, G. (1995). Parent-adolescent relations in changing societies: A cross-cultural study. In P. Noack, M. Hofer, & J. Youniss (Eds.), *Psychological responses to social change. Human development in changing environments* (pp. 189-218). Berlin: W. de Gruyter.

Trommsdorff, G. (2001). Eltern-Kind-Beziehungen aus kulturvergleichender Sicht [Parent-child relations in cross-cultural perspective]. In R. Pekrun & S. Walper (Eds.), *Familie und Entwicklung: Perspektiven der Familienpsychologie* (pp. 23-50). Göttingen, Germany: Hogrefe.

Voland, E., & Engel, C. (2000). Menschliche Reproduktion aus verhaltensökologischer Perspektive [Human reproduction from a behavioral-ecological perspective]. In U. Mueller, B. Nauck, & A. Diekmann (Eds.),

Handbuch der Demographie: Bd. 1. Modelle und Methoden (pp. 387-437). Berlin, Germany: Springer.

Whiting, B. B., & Whiting, J. W. M. (1975). *Children of six cultures. A psychocultural analysis.* Cambridge, MA: Harvard University Press.

Zelditch, M. (1964). Cross-cultural analyses of family structure. In H. T. Christensen (Ed.), *Handbook of marriage and the family* (pp. 462-500). Chicago: Rand McNally.

Zelizer, V. A. (1994). *Pricing the priceless child. The changing social value of children* (2nd ed.). Princeton, NJ: Princeton University Press.

9

Relations between Value Orientation, Child-Rearing Goals, and Parenting: A Comparison of German and South Korean Mothers[1]

Beate Schwarz, Esther Schäfermeier and Gisela Trommsdorff

Introduction

A major goal of parenting is to socialize, i.e., to support the child in successfully adapting to the conditions of its society and culture, in order for the child to become a functioning member of the society (LeVine, 1977; Trommsdorff & Kornadt, 2003). Parenting is influenced by the cultural norms and values, which are partly reflected in the child-rearing goals of the parents and their views of the development of their children. In the following chapter, two cross-cultural studies on the relations between cultural values, parental beliefs, and parenting are presented, focusing on a comparison between South Korean and German mothers.

[1] This research was supported by two grants from the Deutsche Forschungsgemeinschaft awarded to the third author: (1) "Value of Children and Intergenerational Relations" (TR 169/9-1, 2; principal investigators: G. Trommsdorff and B. Nauck), (2) "Subjective developmental and child-rearing theories in cultural perspective" (SFB511/TP15; principal investigators: G. Trommsdorff and W. Friedlmeier). The data in the Republic of Korea for the first study was collected by Uichol Kim, Chung-Ang University, Seoul and for the second study by Hye-On Kim and Jin-Kyung Kim-Lee, Mokpo University, Mokpo.

First, we discuss the concept of child-rearing goals within the theoretical framework of the developmental niche, the concept of individualism and collectivism, and the interplay of cultural values and norms, child-rearing goals and parenting behavior. Next, several relevant sociocultural conditions of the two selected cultures, the Republic of Korea and Germany, are presented. Based on this review of research we develop our hypotheses. Two studies from the research group of Gisela Trommsdorff were used to test the hypotheses. At the end, the results are discussed in light of the theoretical background and the culture specificities.

Child-Rearing Goals as Part of the Developmental Niche

Parents build up expectations for the development of their child as well as ideas and beliefs about appropriate parenting behavior instrumental to achieve the desired developmental outcomes. These expectations, ideas, and beliefs constitute subjective theories of parenting and child development, which play an important role in guiding their behavior (Goodnow, 1984; Kornadt & Trommsdorff, 1990). Child-rearing goals are part of these subjective theories. The child-rearing goals define preferences which characteristics the child should acquire (Goodnow & Collins, 1990). Parental goals vary among cultures (Trommsdorff & Kornadt, 2003). The subjective theory of parenting is constructed in the process of interactions with the sociocultural environment, and therefore it is influenced by norms and values of the respective culture, other persons, social groups and social institutions, including the media (Friedlmeier, 1995; Friedlmeier, Trommsdorff, Vasconcellos & Schäfermeier, 2004; Goodnow, 1988; Trommsdorff & Friedlmeier, 2004).

The concept of the developmental niche (Super & Harkness, 1997) helps to understand the interrelation between norms, values, parental theories, and child-rearing goals. The developmental niche consists of three interdependent subsystems: First, the physical and social environment (e.g., climate, people in the setting); second, the culturally regulated customs of child care and child rearing (e.g., time of weaning), and third, the caretaker's psychology (e.g., affective orientation of the caregiver). This latter component includes values and attitudes as well as the child-rearing goals. These goals as part of the caretaker's psychology are influenced by the physical and social environment, as well as the cultural customs. The entire developmental niche is embedded in the larger sociocultural context and mediates the cultural influences onto the child. Thus, in order to understand child-rearing goals and parenting within a cultural context, one has to take into account relevant cultural characteristics. One of these characteristics can be seen in the dominant cultural values such as individualism/collectivism.

Individualism/Collectivism

Hofstede's seminal work (Hofstede, 1980, 2001) has suggested four dimensions to classify cultures: Power distance, uncertainty avoidance, masculinity/femininity, and individualism/collectivism. The most prominent dimension, which has been widely used in cross-cultural studies, is the dimension of individualism/collectivism. Individualistic cultures (unlike collectivistic cultures) are characterized by their emphasis on individual autonomy (instead of group unity and harmony), pursuit of personal goals (instead of subordination to the group's goals), uniqueness and independence (instead of conformity and interdependence), equity and competition (over equality and cooperation), and a nuclear family system (instead of extended families).

According to Hofstede's study on 50 countries in the 1970s (Hofstede, 1980), Anglo-American countries (USA, Australia, Great Britain, Canada) ranked highest in individualism, followed by the Western and Northern European countries (e.g., West Germany); lowest in individualism were countries from South America and Asia (e.g., Guatemala, Ecuador, Indonesia, Pakistan, Republic of Korea). The first publication of Hofstede's work has stimulated an enormously rich initiative of research, including criticism of the concept. For example, it has been noted that individualism/collectivism is not a unidimensional but a bidimensional construct (Triandis, 1995), i.e., individualistic and collectivistic values can prevail simultaneously within one culture.

Although individualism-collectivism has proved to be a useful dimension for cultural comparisons, it may disregard cultural complexity, as cultures usually are heterogeneous (e.g., Killen & Wainryb, 2000; Oyserman, Coon, & Kemmelmeier, 2002). Also, cultural values refer to abstract notions of general cultural beliefs; therefore, individual value orientations have to be differentiated conceptually from cultural values. Therefore, individualistic and collectivistic orientations have to be assessed on the individual level. Accordingly, Triandis (1995) introduced the concept of idiocentrism vs. allocentrism (in correspondence to the concepts of individualism vs. collectivism on the general cultural level).

Relations between Individualism and Child-Rearing Goals and Parenting

A large body of research has shown that individualistic and collectivistic cultures differ in their child-rearing goals and parenting behavior (Greenfield, 1994; Triandis, 1995, Trommsdorff, 1999, Trommsdorff & Kornadt, 2003) because collectivistic cultures emphasize integration into the social group and their hierarchy, while in individualistic cultures a person should be rather self-responsible and pursue his/her own goals. Kornadt and Trommsdorff (1990) reported that for Japanese mothers, who serve as an example of parents from a collectivistic culture, child-rearing goals such as cooperation, indulgence, thoughtfulness, and empathy were more important than for German mothers, who belong to a more individualistic culture. Chinese-American mothers, as representatives of a collectivistic culture, reported on goals such as obedience, respect of the child and sustaining a good relationship with the child, while European-American mothers emphasized the self-maximization of the child and stated their intention of facilitating the child's exploration (Chao, 1995). Some studies found that child-rearing goals such as good manners and politeness are more important in collectivistic cultures (Harwood, Schölmerich, Ventura-Cook, Schulze & Wilson, 1996; Rosenthal & Bornholt, 1988), while a very recent study showed that these results vary with the methodology (Wang & Tamis-LeMonda, 2003). Another topic for child-rearing goals is school achievement or achievement-related competences, e.g., Vietnamese-Australian mothers rated intelligence as more important for their children than Anglo-Australian mothers (Rosenthal & Gold, 1989).

Taken together, these empirical findings support our expectation that in individualistic cultures individual-oriented child-rearing goals (e.g., "is independent and self-reliant," "self-realization") are emphasized, while in collectivistic cultures group-oriented child-rearing goals (e.g., "mind his/her parents," "cooperation") and proper demeanor (e.g., "be a good person") are of greater importance. In addition, achievement- or task-oriented goals (e.g., "ability to concentrate," "to do well in school") seem to be another dimension of child-rearing goals, which cannot simply be assigned to individualism or collectivism. Nevertheless, the findings suggest that Asian parents emphasize achievement as a child-rearing goal to a greater extent than parents from western cultures.

With respect to parenting, Maccoby and Martin (1983) suggested control/demandingness and acceptance/responsiveness as two comprehensive dimensions for parenting behavior. In East Asian cultures, the parent-child relation is described as warm and supportive (Chao, 2001; Stevenson & Zusho, 2002), the parenting as more controlling and authoritarian (Chao, 2001; Dornbusch, Ritter, Leiderman, Roberts, & Fraleigh, 1987). Beyond this cross-cultural mean difference, differences with respect to the relation of both parenting dimensions are striking. Contrary to western cultures like the USA or Germany, in East-Asian cultures parental control and warmth are positively related (Rohner & Pettengill, 1985; Trommsdorff, 1985; Trommsdorff & Friedlmeier, 1993).

Nevertheless, a number of studies about cultural differences in child rearing has criticized that conceptualizing cultures on a general level as individualistic or collectivistic can be misleading. Harkness, Super and van Tjen (2000) pointed to the problem of classifying cultures only on a general level of individualism and collectivism while neglecting the individual representations of the cultural norms and values. Comparing parents from two "individualistic" cultures, the USA and the Netherlands, these authors demonstrated substantial differences in the parents' child-rearing theories, e.g., in the understanding of independence and dependence.

Therefore, individual representations of values should be considered when comparing cultures, which have been classified as individualistic or collectivistic, in order to take into account intracultural differences in values and child-rearing theories. Another problem is that the concepts of "subjective theories," "parental beliefs and goals," "individual representations," etc. are not well elaborated in the literature. Careful theoretical analyses of these concepts and their relations are needed. Furthermore, one should explain individual differences on the basis of theoretical assumptions. One assumption is that certain general value orientations predict specific parental goals on the individual level (Trommsdorff & Friedlmeier, in press; Trommsdorff, Mayer, & Albert, 2004).

Effects of self-concept as well as perception and evaluation of cultural norms on preferences for certain child-rearing goals were studied with Brazilian and German mothers and kindergarten teachers (Friedlmeier, Schäfermeier, Trommsdorff, & Vasconcellos, 2004). While the self-concept of the caregivers had no relation, their perception of cultural norms was significantly related to their preference of certain child-rearing goals. Interestingly, the caregivers oriented their child-rearing goals more into the direction of the perceived cultural norms than of their personal evaluation of these norms.

Based on this literature, the aim of our study was to compare child-rearing goals and parenting of mothers from a more collectivistic culture (Korea) and a more individualistic culture (Germany). Furthermore, we were interested in the associations between the individualistic and collectivistic values held by the mothers and their child-rearing goals and parenting behavior.

Relations between Child-Rearing Goals and Parenting

Goals include certain expectations and wishes as to how the child should develop. Such goals may motivate the parents to behave in certain ways, which facilitate the development of these characteristics in the child. The normative function of child-rearing goals for generating certain parenting behaviors has been described e.g., by Goodnow and Collins (1990). Thus, parenting behavior is a means to achieve child-rearing goals.

While several studies have theoretically discussed the possible function of child-rearing theories for parenting behavior, only a few studies have empirically tested this question. The lack of empirical studies may be related to the complexity of the topic as well as to methodological difficulties in providing measures for different levels of parenting (beliefs, goals, behavior). When empirical work was carried out, generally only weak relations were found between child-rearing goals and behavior. These weak relations might be due to the fact that interplay of several factors is involved in the process of parenting. The capturing of this interplay is often difficult to elicit in empirical work (for discussion see Sigel, 1992).

The previous section has shown that parents from different cultures differ in their child-rearing goals and parenting behavior. This study focuses on the question, whether the relation between certain child-rearing goals and parenting behaviors also differs between cultures. This research question is based on two arguments. First, as described before, the meaning of parenting behavior (here: control) depends on the cultural context and differs in western and eastern cultures. In contexts where controlling parenting has a positive meaning, it is assumed that other child-rearing goals will be achieved through this parenting behavior, than those arising in contexts where control has a negative meaning. Thus, different directions of the relations between child-rearing goals and parenting behavior in the Korean and German samples are expected.

Second, cross-cultural studies have shown that parents differ in the way they personally feel responsible for or powerful enough to influence the development of their child. In some cultures, parents rather designate a greater role to metaphysical conditions or fate (e.g., *karma*) (Chakkarath, in press, in this volume), in other cultures they believe in internal natural processes of development (Trommsdorff & Friedlmeier, 2003). Thus, the strength of the relation between child-rearing goals and parenting behavior can be different in the Korean and German samples.

Values, Child-Rearing Goals, and Parenting in Korea and Germany

According to Hofstede (1980), the value orientations in these two cultures differed: The Republic of Korea had lower scores in individualism (rank: 43, index value: 18) as compared to (West) Germany (rank: 15, index value: 67). In spite of considerable social and economic changes in the Republic of Korea and in Germany since the 1970s (Gwartney, Lawson, & Block, 1996, see also Schwarz, Chakkarath, & Trommsdorff, 2002), a more recent study (with pilots as respondents) reports similar results for Koreans and Germans as in the Hofstede study (Merritt, 2000). Studies using other instruments to measure individualism and collectivism also confirmed the classification of Germany as an individualistic culture (Fernandez, Carlson, Stepine, & Nicholson, 1997; Triandis, Chen, & Chan, 1998) and of Korea as a collectivistic culture (Kim & Choi, 1994).

However, other studies suggested a more differentiated view on the effects of social change within the Korean culture. Urban and well-educated Koreans were lower in collectivism than rural and low educated Koreans (Cha, 1994). In particular, young, well-educated, female Koreans were less likely to agree with traditional values (Hyun, 2001). Nevertheless, Cha (1994) concluded, that even young Koreans are still comparatively collectivistic.

The child-rearing goals of parents also differ between the two cultures. In the original Value-of-Children Study (Arnold et al., 1975) parents were asked to choose their most important child-rearing goal out of five. The largest proportion of South Korean parents chose the goal "to be independent and self-reliant," while only a minority chose "to mind the parents." This was true for men and women (Kagitçibasi, 1984), for rural and urban women, and across almost all occupational levels, except for farmers (Hoffman, 1988).

This is a surprising result because in a culture influenced by Confucianism like Korea, obeying and respecting the older generation is a very important value as emphasized even in recent publications (e.g., Kim & Choi, 1994). One possible explanation is that the interviewed parents were a highly selected group: representing young parents with young children (Lee & Kim, 1979). Particularly, in the first years of a child's life, one of Korean parents' norms for their behavior describes the virtue of patience ("In-nae"), meaning that they do not enforce obedience (Kim, 2003). However, in samples of mothers with older children (as investigated in the new Value-of-Children Study) obedience is presumably a more important child-rearing goal in Korea than in Germany.

This is supported by a recent survey by Inglehart, Basanez, and Moreno (1998), where independence as a child-rearing goal was more important in Germany than in Korea, and respect for parents was more important in Korea than in Germany (94% very important in Korea, 76% in East Germany, and 63% in West Germany). Korean mothers and grandmothers expected independent behavior of their (grand-)children at a later age than German mothers and grandmothers (Schwarz et al, 2002). This can be taken as further evidence, that independence is less valued in Korea than in Germany.

Another study showed that Korean mothers of school-aged children most strongly expected intellectual ability and emotional competence, and least physical and artistic abilities (e.g., Park, 2003). In this study, also relations between parents' expectations and their parenting behavior were reported. The more the parents valued intellectual and emotional competence, the more likely they showed warmth and acceptance towards their children.

With respect to parenting behavior, no Korea-Germany comparisons have been done, as far as we know. Hoppe-Graff, Kim, Latzko and Lee (2003) investigated the adolescent-parent relationship and reported that the Korean adolescents experienced more emotional strain in the relationship but also more mutual appreciation than the German adolescents. Based on results from other studies with East Asian samples, we expect that Korean mothers do not differ from German mothers with respect to maternal acceptance and warmth, but that they are more controlling. Following Rohner and colleagues (Khaleque & Rohner, 2002) who emphasized that acceptance is universally positively correlated with personality development of children; we extend the argument to the relation between child-rearing goals and parenting. We do not expect different patterns of relations between child-rearing goals and acceptance for the Korean and German mothers.

However, the control dimension of parenting has a different meaning for Koreans as compared to western parents and children. For Korean adolescents, parental acceptance and control were positively (and not negatively) related (Rohner & Pettengill, 1985). This result complements other findings that the influence of control and authoritarian parenting on children's development differs with culture. Among Asian Americans, authoritarian as compared to authoritativeness parenting inhibited school performance less than for Anglo-Americans (Chao, 2001; Dornbusch et al., 1987; Steinberg, Lamborn, Darling, Mounts, & Dornbusch, 1994). Although, these studies did not investigate culture-specific patterns of relations between child-rearing goals and parenting, we expect that achievement-oriented goals are positively related to parental control in the Korean but negatively related in the German sample. In the following, the hypotheses and questions underlying our empirical studies are summarized.

Hypotheses

It was expected, that Korean mothers are less individualistic and more collectivistic in their value orientation as compared to German mothers. We also assumed that Korean mothers favor group-oriented and achievement- or task-oriented child-rearing goals as well as proper demeanor more, and individual-oriented goals less than the German mothers. Moreover, we hypothesized that the Korean and German mothers do not differ in acceptance of their child but the Korean mothers' parenting is more controlling and strict than the German mothers'.

We also expected that mothers' individualistic orientation is positively related with individual-oriented child-rearing goals, and collectivistic orientation is positively related with group-oriented child-rearing goals, while no specific relations are expected between values and achievement-oriented goals. We further investigated a mediator effect: Can the cultural differences in child-rearing goals be explained by the cultural differences in values? Since it is an open question whether values and child-rearing goals are related in culture-specific ways, we also analyzed the moderator function of culture for the relation between values and child-rearing goals, but this question was investigated explorative.

Furthermore, we expected that all child-rearing goals be positively related with parental acceptance, independent of culture. The group-oriented as well as the achievement-oriented goals are expected not only to be related to parental control but also to show culture-specific patterns. More specifically, we expect that particularly the achievement-oriented goals are positively related with control and strictness for Korean mothers and negatively related for German mothers. Thus, with respect to the relation between child-rearing goals and parenting behavior, we focus on the moderator role of culture.

Two Studies on the Importance of Values, Child-Rearing Goals, and Parenting

Questions of cultural values, child-rearing goals, and parenting have been dealt with in two larger cross-cultural studies at the University of Konstanz, each starting from different methodological approaches. Both studies investigated mothers with children of different age groups, thus covering different phases of family development.

The Value-of-Children-and-Intergenerational-Relationship Study was conducted as a replication and extension of the original Value-of-Children Study (Arnold et al., 1975). Samples from the following cultures are included: People's Republic of China, Germany, Indonesia, Israel, Republic of Korea, and Turkey (total $N = 6000$). The Child-Rearing-Theory Study was part of an interdisciplinary research centre. Brazilian, South Korean, and German mothers and children as well as kindergarten teachers were interviewed ($N = 400$).

Here, the data of the Korean and German mothers was selected for further analyses. Therefore, we will primarily focus on data from the Value-of-Children-and-Intergenerational-Relationship Study [VOC study] for testing the hypotheses due to the larger sample size. Results from the Child-Rearing-Theory Study [CRT study], will be used to complement the results of the VOC study.

The Value-of-Children-and-Intergenerational-Relationship Study

Participants
On the basis of a standardized questionnaire $n = 398$ Korean and $n = 313$ German mothers with an adolescent as the target child were interviewed. Table 1 summarizes some characteristics of the two samples and the differences in these characteristics between the Korean and German mothers. Compared to the German mothers, the Korean mothers were significantly younger, less engaged in paid employment, and had a smaller number of children. The mean age of the target children in the Korean

sample was significantly higher than in the German sample and more girls participated in Korea as compared to Germany. With respect to the religions and beliefs
the mothers held, in the Korean sample 24% held no religion at all, 31% were Protestants, 23% Buddhists, and 16% Catholics. In the German sample 33% held no
religion, 33% were Catholics, and 29% were Protestants.

Table 1
Characteristics of the Mothers From the Republic of Korea and Germany in the VOC Study

	Korea (n = 311)	Germany (n = 348)
Mother's age: *M (SD)*	42.29 (3.16)	44.04 (4.90)
Employed mothers: Percent	61.00	79.00
Number of children: *M (SD)*	2.15 (.65)	2.29 (.91)
Age of target child: *M (SD)*	16.64 (1.50)	16.17 (1.03)
Daughters: Percent	63.00	55.00

Note. All comparisons between the Korean and German samples were significant at least at *p*
< .05.

Measures

In order to assess the *individualistic/collectivistic value orientation*, a short version
of the Schwartz instrument (Schwartz & Bilsky, 1990), developed as part of the
Colindex (Chan, 1994), was used. Seven items referring to Individualism and six
items referring to Collectivism were rated by the mothers on a five-point Likert-type
scale. Separate scales for individualism and collectivism were constructed in the
VOC study. Cronbach's αs in the Korean sample were .73 for Individualism and .79
for Collectivism, the respective internal consistencies in the German sample were α
= .68 and α = .74.

Child-rearing goals were assessed with an instrument from the original Value-
of-Children Study (Hoffman, 1988). Instead of selecting one of the child-rearing
goals, as the most preferred one, the participants in the new VOC study had to rate
the importance of each of the five items on a five-point Likert-type scale. Since the
four items referred to heterogeneous goals they were used as single-item indicators.
The goal "minds his/her parents" can be assigned to group-oriented goals, the goal
"is independent and self-reliant" to individual-oriented goals, and "does well in
school" to achievement-oriented goals. The child-rearing goal "is a good person"
can be labeled as "proper demeanor" (Harwood, 1992).

Parenting behavior was assessed by the Parental Acceptance-Rejection Questionnaire and the Control-Supplement, both of which have often been used in cross-cultural studies (e.g., Rohner, Rohner, & Roll, 1980; Rohner & Cournoyer, 1994). Mothers answered the 14 questions concerning acceptance and control on a four-point Likert-type scale. Based on the factor and item analyses of a short version of the Acceptance scale (Sherman & Donovan, 1991), the scale used in the VOC study was shortened further, now comprising 10 items. The original Control scale was also reduced to restrict the length of the multi-thematic questionnaire. The internal consistency of Acceptance was satisfying (Korea: α = .83, Germany: α = .61). The Control scale for the German mothers comprised four items with a Cronbach's α = .56. In the Korean sample the best solution was a three-item scale with an α = .57. We decided to use the control scale despite the low internal consistency because of the importance of this parenting dimension (Maccoby & Martin, 1983). Though the structure of the indicators in Germany and Korea were not totally equal, the overlap of 75% seemed to be large enough to suppose construct equivalence, which, moreover, does not necessarily need equal operationalization (Trommsdorff, 2003; van de Vijver & Leung, 1997).

The Child-Rearing-Theory Study

Participants
In this study, n = 43 German and n = 52 Korean mothers with one of their children participated in the study. The target children of the interviewed mothers were approximately five years old. Table 2 summarizes some characteristics of the two samples.

Table 2
Characteristics of the Mothers from the Republic of Korea and Germany in the CRT Study

	Korea (n = 50)	Germany (n = 50)
Mother's age[a]: *M (SD)*	33.73 (2.92)	36.16 (4.56)
Employed mothers[a]: Percent	58.00	27.00
Number of children: *M (SD)*	1.05 (0.57)	0.93 (0.73)
Age of target child[a]: *M (SD)*	76.38 (4.47)	68.77 (9.17)
Daughters: Percent	42.31	41.86

Note. [a] The comparison between the Korean and German samples was significant at least at p < .01.

Compared to the German mothers, the Korean mothers were younger and fewer of them were engaged in a paid employment. The mean age of the Korean target children was significantly higher than the mean age of the German target children. The German and Korean sample did neither differ in the number of girls and boys in each sample, the total number of children of the mother nor in the percentage of mothers with a university degree.

Measures

The instrument used to measure *allocentrism* was the Colindex, which is a synthesis of a number of well-known instruments (Chan, 1994). It consists of three parts: First, 13 attitude items similar to Triandis' attitude items (Triandis, Leung, Villareal, & Clark, 1985); second, 13 of Schwartz's value items (Schwartz & Bilsky, 1990) (this part was also used in the VOC study); third, the social content of the self in an adaptation of the Kuhn and McPartland method (1954). As the internal consistency of the attitude items was unsatisfactory these items were not considered in the further analyses. To form the so-called Colindex the value items and the self-content were summed up. The Colindex stands for the degree of allocentrism of each individual. The score ranged from 3 ("low allocentrism") to 9 ("high allocentrism").

In order to measure the preference of *child-rearing goals*, mothers were asked to rank 12 child-rearing goals. These goals were selected on the basis of results in former studies on child-rearing goals; accordingly they represent highly important parental goals for various cultures. These 12 goals can be categorized into three main sets: individual-oriented child-rearing goals (e.g., independence and self-realization), group-oriented child-rearing goals (e.g., cooperation and responsibility) and task-oriented child-rearing goals (e.g., the ability to concentrate). The task-oriented goals covered a broader range of goals than the achievement-oriented goals in the VOC study. The goals were written on paperboards and shown to the caregiver. The mother was asked to choose five goals out of the 12, which she felt, were the most important for her and to rank them according to their importance.

To determine the preferences for the developmental goals with regard to the three designated categories (individual-, group-, and task-oriented goals), the rankings within each category (1 = "least important" to 5 = "most important") were derived. Since each category was represented by four goals, the respondent could not choose five goals from the same category, but had to select at least one goal from another category. In order to avoid a "forced choice" of another category, the indicator "preference for developmental goals" was based on the selection of the four most important goals. The maximum value for one category thus adds up to 14 points.

To assess *self-reported parenting behavior* the mothers were asked to rate three single items on a 7-point scale. They reported in how far they would describe their parenting as accepting (egalitarian, loving) and controlling (strict). The higher the value on the scales, the more the mothers prefer this particular parenting style.

Mothers' acceptance perceived by the child was measured with the subscale for mothers' acceptance from the "Pictorial scale of perceived competence and social acceptance scale for young children" (Harter & Pike, 1984) consisting of 6 items. Here the child was asked, in how far she or he felt accepted by the mother. The scale ranged from 1 to 4. The higher the value the more the child feels accepted by the mother. In order to achieve a better internal consistency one item had to be dropped from the scale (Korea: $\alpha = .61$; Germany: $\alpha = .62$).

Results

Differences between Korean and German mothers with respect to their values, child-rearing goals, and parenting
In both studies significant differences between Korean and German mothers were found with respect to *individualistic and collectivistic value orientations*. In the VOC study no differences in the subscale of collectivistic values but in the subscale of individualistic values were found. The Korean mothers were less individualistic as compared to the German mothers.[2] According to the data from the CRT study on the basis of the overall Colindex, the Korean mothers were more allocentric than the German mothers. The means and standard deviations of these and the following comparisons are depicted in Table 3.

With respect to the *child-rearing goals*, differences in the expected direction were found. In the VOC study, Korean mothers were stronger in their support of the group-oriented goal (minds the parents) and the achievement-oriented goal (doing well in school) as compared to the German mothers, but they supported the individual-oriented goal (to be independent and self-reliant) less. Contrary, to our expectation they valued also proper demeanor (be a good person) less.

In the CRT study a very similar picture was found: the Korean mothers preferred group- and task-oriented goals significantly more than the German mothers. Also, in line with the hypotheses they preferred the individual-oriented goals less than the German mothers.

Parenting behavior was assessed in terms of the concepts of acceptance and control. In the VOC study mothers from both cultures did not differ in acceptance. The results in the CRT study corresponded with this finding, since it did not reveal cultural differences in mothers' acceptance perceived by the child, nor in mothers' self-report on egalitarian and loving parenting.

---

[2] This result as well as the following results did not change after control for age of mother and age and sex of target child.

Table 3
Comparisons between Values, Child-Rearing Goals, and Parenting of the Korean and German Mothers

	Korea		Germany		t-Values
	M	SD	M	SD	
General cultural values					
Individualism (VOC)	3.52	.58	3.81	.47	6.90 ***
Collectivism (VOC)	4.11	.58	4.14	.50	.31
Allocentrism (CRT)	7.11	.87	5.63	1.19	-6.78 ***
Preference of child-rearing goals					
Group-oriented goals (VOC)	3.71	.75	3.57	.73	-2.43*
Group-oriented goals (CRT)	6.90	2.31	4.81	2.78	-3.99***
Individual-oriented goal (VOC)	3.95	.70	4.44	.58	9.26***
Individual-oriented goals (CRT)	3.31	2.26	7.05	3.11	6.58***
Achievement-oriented goal (VOC)	4.04	.74	3.91	.69	-2.37*
Task-oriented goals (CRT)	3.63	2.40	1.91	1.96	-3.78***
Proper demeanor (VOC)	4.46	.71	4.62	.53	3.44***
Parenting behavior					
Acceptance (VOC)	3.37	.37	3.35	.23	-.63
Acceptance (CRT)	2.86	.70	2.88	.69	.15
Control (VOC)	3.37	.51	2.79	.53	-14.56***
Strictness (CRT)	5.08	1.36	4.21	1.06	-3.47***
Egalitarian (CRT)	5.55	1.20	5.32	0.99	-.97
Loving (CRT)	6.01	0.90	6.09	0.75	.42

Note. VOC = Value-of-Children Study; CRT = Child-Rearing-Theory Study.
* $p < .05$, *** $p < .001$.

With respect to control, the Korean mothers in the VOC study reported more control of the children than the German mothers, and the Korean mothers in the CRT study a higher degree of strictness than German mothers.

Associations between mothers' values and child-rearing goals
We hypothesized that an individualistic value orientation is positively related to individual-oriented goals, and collectivism to group-oriented goals, while we did not expect specific correlations between values and achievement-oriented child-rearing goals and proper demeanor. Given the cultural differences described in the last section, we also wanted to investigate how much of the variance of cultural differences in child-rearing goals could be explained by mothers' value orientation. A third aim of our study was to explore culture-specific patterns of relations. Thus, the moderat-

ing effect of culture on the relations between values and child-rearing goals was investigated.

For the VOC study, we chose a strategy for analysis, which allowed the investigation of all three questions in one procedure. We conducted hierarchical regressions with each of the child-rearing goals, introducing culture in the first step, individualistic values and collectivistic values in a second step, and the interaction terms of culture and individualistic and collectivistic values, respectively, in the third step. According to Aiken and West (1991), the continuous indicators of individualistic and collectivistic values were centred, before the multiplication with the culture dummy was carried out (see also Cohen & Cohen, 1983). Table 4 summarizes the results of the last steps of the regressions. Changes from step to step are mentioned in the text.

As predicted, the group-oriented goal (to mind the parents) was related to collectivistic values: the higher the collectivism the more important was this goal. As the culture effect remained significant, this relation did not explain the cultural differences ($\beta = .10$ in step 1 and 3). This weak explanation of the culture effect was also found in all further analyses[3]. No interaction was significant, indicating that the association between collectivism and the group-oriented goal was the same in the Korean and German sample.

The analyses also confirmed the hypothesis that the individual-oriented goal (to be independent and self-reliant) was correlated with individualism. Furthermore, a significant interaction of culture and collectivistic values occurred. Inspection of the slopes indicated that there was only a positive correlation in the Korean sample (slopes .378 vs. .080). Thus, while in the German sample the child-rearing goal of independence was only associated with individualistic values, in the Korean sample this goal was positively associated with individualistic as well as collectivistic values.

With respect to the achievement-oriented child-rearing goal (to do well in school), we had no specific expectations with regard to a relation to the two kinds of values. The regression analysis indicated that, irrespective of culture, collectivistic values were positively related with this goal. The interaction between culture and individualism was significant. As indicated in Figure 1, the relations in the two cultures were in opposite directions and only significant in the Korean sample. For Korean mothers, the higher their individualism, the more important was their child's high achievement in school.

---

[3] For the individual-oriented goal, β of culture changed from -.34 to -.30, for the achievement-oriented goal from .08 to .09, and for good demeanor from -.14 to -.11.

Table 4

Mothers' Child-Rearing Goals Predicted by Culture, Mothers' Value Orientations, and the Interactions between Culture and Values; Last Step of Hierarchical Regressions, Standardized Regression Coefficients (N = 613-614)

	Group-oriented goal	Individual-oriented goal	Achievement-oriented goal	Proper demeanor
Culture[a] (C)	.10*	-.30***	.09*	-.11**
Individualism (IN)	-.02	.14*	-.11	.03
Collectivism (CO)	.42***	.06	.28***	.11
C x IN	-.01	.01	.24***	.10
C x CO	-.08	.17**	-.08	.14*
R^2	.14	.20	.09	.11

Note. Analyses were based on the VOC study. [a] 0 = German, 1 = Korean. $p < .05$, ** $p < .01$, *** $p < .001$.

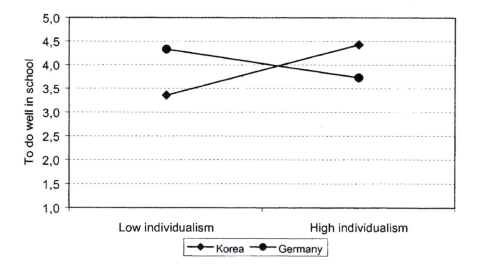

Figure 1. Significant Interaction between Culture and Mothers' Individualism on the Achievement-Oriented Child-Rearing Goal

The child-rearing goal of proper demeanor (to be a good person) was not related with value orientations. Only culture and the interaction between culture and collectivism were significant. The slopes for the Korean ($\beta = .338$) and German samples ($\beta = .125$) indicated that the positive correlation between collectivism and proper demeanor was stronger in the Korean sample.

In the CRT study, separate analyses for the two cultures revealed no significant correlations between mothers' allocentrism and the importance of group-oriented, individual-oriented, or task-oriented child-rearing goals. Here, the small sample size should be taken into account.

Associations between mothers' child-rearing goals and parenting
The analyses of the VOC data with respect to the relationship between child-rearing goals and parenting aimed at the moderator effect of culture on the relation between child-rearing goals and parenting (particularly control). Thus, a parallel procedure as described in the former section was used, also allowing for investigating the mediating role of child-rearing goals for cultural differences in parenting. The results of the last step of hierarchical regressions are documented in Table 5.

As shown in Table 5, only the group-oriented child-rearing goal (to mind the parents) was associated with acceptance. The more important this goal, the higher was the mothers' acceptance. As expected this was true for both cultures, as indi-

Table 5

Mothers' Parenting Behavior Predicted by Culture, Mothers' Child-Rearing Goals, and the Interactions between Culture and Child-Rearing Goals; Last Step of Hierarchical Regressions, Standardized Regression Coefficients ($N = 637$)

	Acceptance	Control
Culture[a] (C)	.01	.46***
Group-oriented goal (G)	.19**	.33***
Individual-oriented goal (I)	-.04	-.14*
Achievement-oriented goal (A)	.11+	.13**
Proper demeanor (P)	.06	.08
C x G	.03	-.12*
C x I	.08	.14*
C x A	-.02	-.05
C x P	.13+	.02
R^2	.14	.36

Note. Analyses were based on the VOC study. [a]0 = German, 1 = Korean. $+ p < .10$, $* p < .05$, $** p < .01$, $*** p < .001$.

cated by a non-significant interaction term. The interaction effects in all other analyses were also not significant. In the regressions without controlling for the interactions, all child-rearing goals, except for independence, were significantly and positively related to acceptance. The highest relation was observed between acceptance and the group-oriented goal (to mind the parents), $\beta = .21$, $p < .001$, followed by proper demeanor (to be a good person), $\beta = .16$, $p < .001$, and the achievement-oriented goal (to do well in school), $\beta = .12$, $p < .01$. Thus, our expectation that acceptance is positively related to all child-rearing goals independent of culture was largely confirmed.

With respect to mothers' control, the group-oriented goal (to mind the parents) and the achievement-oriented goal (to do well in school) were positively, and the individual-oriented-rearing goal (to be independent and self-reliant) negatively associated with control. The latter association only appeared after controlling for the interactions. The interaction between culture and the group-oriented goal is depicted in Figure 2. The slopes indicated that the positive association between the group-oriented goal (to mind the parents) and controlling parenting was more pronounced in the German sample.

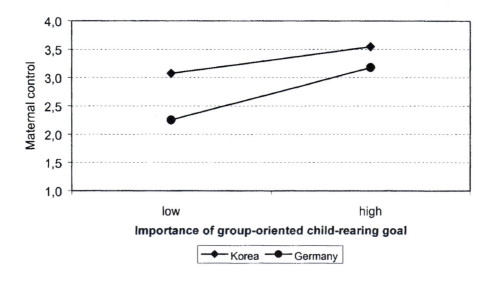

Figure 2. Significant Interaction between Culture and Importance of the Group-Oriented Child-Rearing Goal on Mothers' Control

The slopes of the interaction between culture and the individual-oriented child-rearing goal (to be independent and self-reliant) showed a similar result: the relation in the German sample was stronger than in the Korean sample, where the relation was close to zero. Furthermore, here the relation was negative in the German sample and positive in the Korean sample (-.119 vs. .021). Our expectation that control was only positively associated with achievement-oriented goals in the Korean sample was not supported. In fact, we found a positive association in both the Korean and German samples.

In the CRT study, correlations between child-rearing goals and parenting behavior were conducted separately for the two cultures. Only one nearly significant correlation was observed between egalitarian parenting and the preference for individual-oriented child-rearing goals in Germany ($r = .27, p = .07$).

Discussion

Based on the theoretical framework of the developmental niche, we investigated the associations between value orientations and child-rearing goals, and the association between child-rearing goals and parenting in a comparison of Korean and German mothers. We aimed at specifying possible universal as well as culture-specific patterns. Furthermore, we investigated the mediating role of values for cultural differences in child-rearing goals, and the moderator role of culture for the relation between child-rearing goals and parenting behavior. The analyses of two different data sets partly confirmed our expectations of cultural differences in value orientations, child-rearing goals, and parenting, as well as the hypothesized association between the three aspects, in some cases with culture-specific patterns. However, our results did not confirm the expectation that individualistic/collectivistic values are powerful mediators of cultural differences in child-rearing goals.

Differences between Korean and German mothers
The Korean mothers were less individualistic (in the VOC study) and showed more allocentrism (in the CRT study) than German mothers. Compared to the German mothers, in both studies, Korean mothers preferred group-oriented and achievement- (or task-) oriented child-rearing goals, while individual-oriented goals and proper demeanor were less important. The mothers from the two cultures did not differ in loving and accepting their children, but Korean mothers were more controlling and strict with their children.

The results were in line with our hypothesis, indicating that the Koreans have preserved their more traditional orientation towards values and child rearing despite the experience of rapid social change towards modernization and industrialization in the last few decades (Gwartney et al., 1996). Nevertheless, in the VOC study, Korean and German mothers were similar in their collectivistic orientation. Thus, it seems that German and Koreans share similar collectivistic values when they are asked about these values on a more abstract level referring more to societal than individual concerns.

Association between values and child-rearing goals
The analyses of the VOC data showed that independent of culture individualistic orientations were positively associated with the goal of child's independence, while collectivistic orientations were related to the child-rearing goals that the child should mind the parents and to do well in school. Thus, our hypotheses were confirmed. However, culture-specific patterns occurred. For Korean mothers, individualistic orientations were associated with achievement-oriented goals and collectivistic orientations with individual-oriented goals (to be independent and self-reliant); these relations did not occur in the German sample.

Taking into account the Confucian value orientation of learning and achievement (e.g., Chen & Stevenson, 1995), it seems plausible that the Korean mothers perceive school achievement much more as a chance to enhance personal success than the German mothers do. The association between collectivistic orientation and the individual-oriented child-rearing goal seems surprising at first sight. This item focused on independence *and* self-reliance. Independence and self-reliance may have a different meaning depending on the cultural context and the general value orientation as several studies have pointed out (Kagitçibasi, 1996; Rothbaum & Trommsdorff, in press; Trommsdorff, 1999; Trommsdorff & Friedlmeier, in press). Independence may have the meaning of autonomy, self-fulfillment, and strong will. In an individualistic context the focus will be more on this side of the item. In a more collectivistic context self-reliance, which refers to responsibilities in and help for the family is also of great importance. Here, social obligations have to be fulfilled by the children already at an early developmental age. As a study on developmental timetables showed, the more collectivistic Greek-Australians expected responsibilities in the household at an earlier age than the more individualistic Anglo-Australians (Rosenthal & Bornholt, 1988).

In the CRT study no associations between allocentrism and child-rearing goals were found. This may be due to the small sample size. However, other analyses with this sample pointed out that the caregivers' perceptions of the cultural norms are more influential than their individual norms for child-rearing goals (Friedlmeier et al., 2004).

Even though we found cultural differences in value orientations, and associations between value orientations and child-rearing goals, the mediating role of value orientations for the cultural differences in child-rearing goals was only weak. Beyond this, other factors may affect the differences in importance of the child-rearing goals for Korean and German mothers. Future research should analyze whether sociostructural and specific socialization conditions have an impact on the cultural differences in child-rearing goals in Korean and German mothers.

Associations between child-rearing goals and parenting

Independent of culture all child-rearing goals were positively associated with the mothers' acceptance of their children. This result extends Rohner's hypothesis that acceptance is universally associated with various aspects of child's development; this parenting style seems to be universally (here, in Korea and Germany) associated with certain child-rearing goals. Furthermore, we found associations between child-rearing goals and control of children that were significant even when culture and the interaction terms were controlled. This points out to universally relevant relations between certain child-rearing goals and controlling parenting: The group- and achievement-oriented goals are positively, and the goal of independence is negatively associated with control.

Furthermore, in our German sample the positive relations between the group-oriented child-rearing goal ("to mind the parents") and control as well as the negative relation between the individual-oriented goal ("being independent and self-reliant") and control were more pronounced than in the Korean sample. Assuming that obedience has a more negative connotation, and independence a more positive connotation in Germany than in Korea, these results are in line with other studies, which also assume a more negative meaning of control in western cultures as compared to eastern cultures (Chao, 2001; Dornbusch et al., 1987; Steinberg et al., 1994; Trommsdorff & Kornadt, 2003).

Another (more speculative) explanation is also possible. As further analyses of the CRT study revealed, the Korean and German mothers differed in their subjective theories with respect to their influences on children's development. The Korean as compared to the German mothers rather emphasized that the inborn characteristics and the activity of the child contribute to the developmental outcomes of the child (Trommsdorff & Friedlmeier, in press). Thus, the association between mothers' child-rearing goals and their parenting behavior might be weakened in the Korean sample because the Korean mothers may be less trusting in the power of parenting.

Caveats and open questions

The sample of the CRT study was small, so the generalization of these results is difficult. However, the concordance of the results from the CRT and the much larger VOC study increases the validity of the results. The data from the VOC study was only based on reports of the mothers. This increases the risk of confounded reports on the different aspects of values, child-rearing goals and parenting in the analyses.

However, with respect to cultural comparisons of parenting, the CRT study added results based on reports of the child, which were in line with the VOC data obtained from mothers.

Nevertheless, further analyses of the VOC study will include reports on different sources, like mothers and adolescents. The VOC study allows of extending the analyses of the interplay between culture, values, child-rearing goals, and parenting to other cultures, including comparisons with other Asian cultures such as China or Indonesia that differ from Korea with respect to their extent of modernization, their political organization, and their religious background.

One important question, which remains open, is how cultures influence child-rearing goals and practices. This question will be dealt with in further studies, basing on the data from the VOC study, by taking into account the possible transmission links between culture and individual values and beliefs (cf. Trommsdorff & Friedl-meier, in press; Trommsdorff, Albert, & Mayer, 2004). Furthermore, it will be tested whether less abstract values than the Schwartz-Items, like interdependence, inde-pendence, and family-oriented values, offer more information on the relations be-tween the cultural context and individual values and beliefs. As indicated by the additional analyses of the CRT study, the association between child-rearing goals and parenting may be moderated by the mothers' subjective theories on their influ-ence on children's development.

Conclusions

Despite the above mentioned caveats and the need for further research, one strength of the reported results from the two studies is that they not only refer to the individ-ual representation of values held by mothers from different cultural contexts, but also yielded several meaningful associations between such values and child-rearing goals which are partly similar and partly different in these cultures. Furthermore, the results have shown that child-rearing goals are related to parenting behavior. This is in line with some of the assumptions of the developmental niche (Super & Harkness, 1997). The results on universal associations and culture-specific patterns may be a good starting point for further more specific cross-cultural studies.

References

Aiken, L. S., & West, S. G. (1991). *Multiple regression: Testing and interpreting interactions.* Newbury Park, CA: Sage.

Arnold, F., Bulatao, R. A., Buripakdi, C., Chung, B. J., Fawcett, J. T., Iritani, T., Lee, S. J., & Wu, T.-S. (1975). *The value of children. A cross-national study* (Vol. 1). Honolulu, HI: East-West Population Institute.

Cha, J.-H. (1994). Aspects of individualism and collectivism in Korea. In U. Kim, H. C. Triandis, C. Kagitçibasi, S.-C. Choi, & G. Yoon (Eds.), *Individualism and collectivism. Theory, methods, and applications* (pp. 157-174). Thousand Oaks, CA: Sage.

Chan, D. K.-S. (1994). Colindex: A refinement of three collectivsm measures. In U. Kim, H. C. Triandis, C. Kagitçibasi, S.-C. Choi, & G. Yoon (Eds.), *Individualism and collectivism: Theory, method, and applications* (pp. 200-210). Thousand Oaks, CA: Sage.

Chakkarath, P. (in press). Religionen und Weltanschauungen [Religions and worldviews]. In G. Trommsdorff & H.-J. Kornadt (Eds.), *Kulturvergleichende Psychologie. Vol. 1: Theorien und Methoden in der kulturvergleichenden und kulturpsychologischen Forschung* (Enzyklopädie der Psychologie: Themenbereich C Theorie und Forschung, Serie VII). Göttingen, Germany: Hogrefe.

Chao, R. K. (1995). Chinese and European American cultural models of the self reflected in mothers' childrearing beliefs. *Ethos, 23*, 328-354.

Chao, R. K. (2001). Extending research on the consequences of parenting style for Chinese Americans and European Americans. *Child Development, 72*, 1832-1843.

Chen, C., & Stevenson, H. W. (1995). Motivation and mathematics achievement: A comparative study of Asian-American, Caucasian-American, and East Asian high school students. *Child Development, 66*, 1215-1234.

Cohen, J., & Cohen, P. (1983). *Applied multiple regression/correlation analysis for the behavioral sciences* (2nd ed.). Hillsdale, NJ: Erlbaum.

Dornbusch, S. M., Ritter, P. L., Leiderman, H., Roberts, D. F., & Fraleigh, M. J. (1987). The relation of parenting style to adolescent school performance. *Child Development, 58*, 1244-1257.

Fernandez, D. R., Carlson, D. S., Stepina, L. P., & Nicholson, J. D. (1997). Hofstede's country classification 25 years later. *Journal of Social Psychology, 137*, 43-54.

Friedlmeier, W. (1995). Subjektive Erziehungstheorien im Kulturvergleich [Subjective parenting theories in a cross-cultural perspective]. In G. Trommsdorff (Ed.), *Kindheit und Jugend in verschiedenen Kulturen* (pp. 43-64). Weinheim, Germany: Juventa.

Friedlmeier, W., Schäfermeier, E., Trommsdorff, G., & Vasconcellos, V. (2004). *Self-construal and cultural orientation as predictors for developmental goals: A comparison between Brazilian and German caregivers*. Manuscript submitted for publication.

Friedlmeier, W., Trommsdorff, G., Vasconcellos, V., & Schäfermeier, E. (2004). *Allocentrism and developmental goals: A cross-cultural comparison between Brazilian, Korean, and German caregivers*. Manuscript submitted for publication.

Goodnow, J. J. (1984). Parents' ideas about parenting and development: A review of issues and recent work. In M. E. Lamb, A. Brown, & B. Rogoff (Eds.), *Advances in developmental and social psychology* (Vol. 3, pp. 193-242). Hillsdale, NJ: Erlbaum.

Goodnow, J. J., & Collins, W. A. (1990). *Development according to parents: The nature, sources, and consequences of parents' ideas*. Hillsdale, NJ: Erlbaum.

Greenfield, P. M. (1994). Independence and interdependence as a developmental script: Implications for theory, research, and practice. In P. M. Greenfield & P. R. Cocking (Eds.), *Cross-cultural roots of minority child development* (pp. 1-37). Hillsdale, NJ: Erlbaum.

Gwartney, J., Lawson, R., & Block, W. (1996). *Economic freedom of the world 1975-1995*. Vancouver, Canada: Fraser Institute.

Harkness, S., Super, C. M., & van Tijen, N. (2000). Individualism and the "Western mind" reconsidered: American and Dutch parents' ethnotheories of the child. In W. Damon (Series Ed.), S. Harkness, C. Raeff, & C. M. Super (Vol. Eds.), *New directions for child and adolescent development, 87. Variability in the social construction of the child* (pp. 23-39). San Francisco, CA: Jossey Bass.

Harter, S., & Pike, R. (1984). The pictorial scale of Perceived Competence and Social Acceptance for Young Children. *Child Development, 55*, 1969-1982.

Harwood, R. L. (1992). The influence of culturally derived values on Anglo and Puerto Rican mothers' perceptions of attachment behavior. *Child Development, 67*, 2446-2461.

Harwood, R. L., Schölmerich, A., Ventura-Cook, E., Schulze, P. A., & Wilson, S. P. (1996). Culture and class influences on Anglo and Puerto Rican mothers' be-liefs regarding long-term socialization goals and child behavior. *Child Develop-ment, 67*, 2446-2461.

Hoffman, L. W. (1988). Cross-cultural differences in childrearing goals. In R. A. LeVine, P. M. West, & M. M. West (Eds.), *Parental behavior in diverse societies* (New Directions for Child Development, Vol. 40, pp. 99-122). San Francisco: Jossey Bass.

Hofstede, G. (1980). *Culture's consequences: International differences in work-related values*. Beverly Hills, CA: Sage.

Hofstede, G. (2001). *Culture's consequences: Comparing values, behaviors, institutions, and organizations across nations* (2nd ed.). Thousand Oaks, CA: Sage.

Hoppe-Graff, S., Kim, H.-O., Latzko, B., & Lee, S.-I. (2003). *Independence, autonomy, and detachment in German and Korean adolescents: A questionnaire study*.

Paper presented at the IACCP Regional Congress 2003 "Cultures in inter-action," Budapest, Hungary.

Hyun, K. J. (2001). Sociocultural change and traditional values: Confucian values among Koreans and Korean Americans. *International Journal of Intercultural Relations, 25*, 203-229.

Inglehart, R., Basanez, M., & Moreno, A. (1998). *Human values and beliefs. A cross-cultural sourcebook: Political, religious, sexual, and economic norms in 43 societies.* Ann Arbor, MI: University of Michigan Press.

Kagitçibasi, Ç. (1984). Socialization in traditional society: A challenge to psychology. *International Journal of Psychology, 19*, 145-157.

Kagitçibasi, Ç. (1996). The autonomous-relational self: A new synthesis. *European Psychologist, 1*, 180-186.

Khaleque, A., & Rohner, R. P. (2002). Perceived parental acceptance-rejection and psychological adjustment: A meta-analysis of cross-cultural and intracultural studies. *Journal of Marriage and the Family, 64*, 54-64.

Killen, M., & Wainryb, C. (2000). Independence and interdependence in diverse cultural contexts. In S. Harkness & C. Raeff (Eds), *Variability in the social construction of the child* (pp. 5-21). San Francisco: Jossey-Bass.

Kim, K. W. (2003, June). *"Hyo" and parenting in Korea.* Paper presented at the ISSBD Asian regional workshop "Parental beliefs, parenting, and child development in cross-cultural perspectives," Seoul, Korea.

Kim, U., & Choi, S.-H. (1994). Individualism, collectivism, and child development: A Korean perspective. In P. M. Greenfield & R. Cocking (Eds.), *Cross-cultural roots of minority child development* (pp. 227-257). Hillsdale, NJ: Erlbaum.

Kornadt, H.-J., & Trommsdorff, G. (1990). Naive Erziehungstheorien japanischer Mütter - deutsch-japanischer Kulturvergleich. [Naive parenting theories of Japanese mothers - a Japanese-German comparison] *Zeitschrift für Sozialisationsforschung und Erziehungssoziologie, 10*, 357-376.

Kuhn, M. H., & McPartland, T. S. (1954). An empirical investigation of self-attitudes. *American Sociological Review, 19*, 68-76.

Lee, S. J., & Kim, J.-O. (1979). *The value of children. A cross-national study: Korea* (Vol. 7). Honolulu, HI: East-West Population Institute.

LeVine, R. A. (1977). Child-rearing and cultural adaption. In P. H. Leiderman, S. R. Tulkin, & A. Rosenfeld (Eds.), *Culture and infancy: Variations in the human experience* (pp. 15-28). New York: Academic Press.

Maccoby, E. E., & Martin, J. A. (1983). Socialization in the context of the family: Parent-child interaction. In P. Mussen & E. M. Hetherington (Eds.), *Handbook of child psychology. Socialization, personality and social development* (pp. 1-101). New York: Wiley.

Merritt, A. (2000). Culture in the cockpit. Do Hofstede's dimensions replicate? *Journal of Cross-Cultural Psychology, 31*, 283-301.

Oyserman, D., Coon, H. M., & Kemmelmeier, M. (2002). Rethinking individualism and collectivism: Evaluation of theoretical assumptions and meta-analyses. *Psychological Bulletin, 128*, 3-72.

Park, Y. Y. (2003, June). *Parental beliefs, parenting, and children's self-esteem in Korea.* Paper presented at the KACS International Conference "Parental beliefs, parenting, and child development in cross-cultural perspectives," Seoul, Korea.

Rohner, R. P., & Cournoyer, D. E. (1994). Universals in youths' perceptions of parental acceptance and rejection: Evidence from factor analyses within eight sociocultural groups worldwide. *Cross-Cultural Research, 28*, 371-383.

Rohner, R. P., & Pettengill, S. M. (1985). Perceived parental acceptance-rejection and parental control among Korean adolescents. *Child Development, 56*, 524-528.

Rohner, E. C., Rohner, R. P., & Roll, S. (1980). Perceived parental acceptance-rejection and children's reported behavioral dispositions. A comparative and intracultural study of American and Mexican children. *Journal of Cross-Cultural Psychology, 11*, 213-231.

Rosenthal, D. A., & Bornholt, L. (1988). Expectations about development in Greek- and Anglo-Australian families. *Journal of Cross-Cultural Psychology, 19*, 19-34.

Rosenthal, D. A., & Gold, R. (1989). A comparison of Vietnamese-Australian and Anglo-Australian mothers' beliefs about intellectual development. *International Journal of Psychology, 24*, 179-193.

Rothbaum, F. & Trommsdorff, G. (in press). Cultural perspectives on relationships and autonomy-control. In J. E. Grusec & P. Hastings (Eds.), *Handbook of socialization.* New York: The Guilford Press.

Schwartz, S. H., & Bilsky, W. (1990). Toward a theory of the universal content and structure of values: Extensions and cross-cultural replications. *Journal of Personality and Social Psychology, 58*, 878-891.

Schwarz, B., Chakkarath, P., & Trommsdorff, G. (2002). Generationenbeziehungen in Indonesien, der Republik Korea und Deutschland [Intergenerational relationships in Indonesia, the Republic of Korea, and Germany]. *Zeitschrift für Soziologie der Erziehung und Sozialisation, 22*, 393-407.

Sherman, B. R., & Donovan, B. R. (1991). Relationship of perceived maternal acceptance-rejection in childhood and social support networks of pregnant adolescents. *American Journal of Orthopsychiatry, 61*, 103-113.

Sigel, I. E. (1992). The belief-behavior connection: A resolvable dilemma? In I. E. Sigel, A. V. McGillicuddy-DeLisi, & Goodnow, J. (Eds.), *Parental belief systems: The psychological consequences for children* (2nd ed., pp. 433-456). Hillsdale, NJ: Erlbaum.

Steinberg, L., Lamborn, S. D., Darling, N., Mounts, N. S., & Dornbusch, S. M. (1994). Over-time changes in adjustment and competence among adolescents from authoritative, authoritarian, indulgent, and neglectful families. *Child Development, 65*, 754-770.

Stevenson, H. W., & Zusho, A. (2002). Adolescence in China and Japan: Adapting to a changing environment. In B. B. Brown, R. Larson, & T. S. Saraswathi (Eds.), *The world's youth: Adolescence in eight regions of the globe* (pp. 141-170). New York: Cambridge University Press.

Super, C. M., & Harkness, S. (1997). The cultural structuring of child development. In J. W. Berry, P. R. Dasen, & T. S. Saraswathi (Eds.), *Handbook of cross-cultural psychology: Vol. 2. Basic processes and human development* (2nd ed., pp. 1-39). Boston: Allyn and Bacon.

Triandis, H. C. (1995). *Individualism and collectivism*. Boulder, CO: Westview Press.

Triandis, H. C., Chen, X. P., & Chan, D. K.-S. (1998). Scenarios for the measurement of collectivism and individualism. *Journal of Cross-Cultural Psychology, 29*, 275-289.

Triandis, H. C., Leung, K., Villareal, M. V., & Clark, F. L. (1985). Allocentric versus idiocentric tendencies: Convergent and discriminant validation. *Journal of Research in Personality, 19*, 395-415.

Trommsdorff, G. (1985). Some comparative aspects of socialization in Japan and Germany. In I. Reyes Lagunes & Y. H. Poortinga (Eds.), *From a different perspective: Studies of behavior across cultures* (pp. 231-240). Amsterdam: Swets & Zeitlinger.

Trommsdorff, G. (1999). Autonomie und Verbundenheit im kulturellen Vergleich von Sozialisationsbedingungen. [Autonomy and connectedness in cultural comparisons of socialization contexts] In H. R. Leu & L. Krappmann (Eds.), *Zwischen Autonomie und Verbundenheit: Bedingungen und Formen der Behauptung von Subjektivität* (pp. 392-419). Frankfurt/M., Germany: Suhrkamp.

Trommsdorff, G. (2003). Kulturvergleichende Entwicklungspsychologie. [Cross-cultural developmental psychology]. In A. Thomas (Ed.), *Kulturvergleichende Psychologie* (2nd ed., pp. 139-179). Göttingen, Germany: Hogrefe.

Trommsdorff, G., & Friedlmeier, W. (1993). Control and responsiveness in Japanese and German mother-child interactions. *Early Development and Parenting, 2*, 65-78.

Trommsdorff, G., & Friedlmeier, W. (in press). Zum Verhältnis zwischen Kultur und Individuum aus der Perspektive der kulturvergleichenden Psychologie [The relation between culture and individual from the perspective of cross-cultural psychology]. In A. Assmann, U. Gaier, & G. Trommsdorff (Eds.), *Positionen der Kulturanthropologie*. Frankfurt/M., Germany: Suhrkamp.

Trommsdorff, G., & Kornadt, H.-J. (2003). Parent-child relations in cross-cultural perspective. In L. Kuczynski (Ed.), *Handbook of dynamics in parent-child relations* (pp. 271-306). Thousand Oaks, CA: Sage.

Trommsdorff, G., Mayer, B., & Albert, I. (2004). Dimensions of culture in intracultural comparisons: Individualism/Collectivism and family-related values in three generations. In H. Vinken, J. Soeters, & P. Ester (Eds.), *Comparing cultures: Dimensions of culture in a comparitive perspective* (pp. 157-184). Leiden, The Netherlands: Brill Academic Publishers.

van de Vijver, F. J. R., & Leung, K. (1997). *Methods and data analysis for cross-cultural research*. Thousand Oaks, CA: Sage.

Wang, S., & Tamis-LeMonda, C. S. (2003). Do child-rearing values in Taiwan and the United States reflect cultural values of collectivism and individualism? *Journal of Cross-Cultural Psychology, 34*, 629-642.

10

Adolescent Future Orientation: Intergenerational Transmission and Intertwining Tactics in Cultural and Family Settings

Rachel Seginer

Introduction

Future orientation is the image individuals have regarding their future, as consciously represented and self-reported. As such, its construction has elements of both map drawing and autobiographical writing, with one notable difference: in the case of future orientation construction, the prior knowledge underlying both is rather limited. As individuals chart their future, information about the terrain is partial and the life to be written about has not been lived yet. Under these circumstances of uncertainty, and in the midst of being preoccupied with multiple developmental tasks, psychologists (e.g., Douvan & Adelson, 1966; Erikson, 1968) and nonprofessionals alike have expected adolescents to think about the future and construct their prospective life course. For Lewin (1939), the adolescent's task was more specific: to structure the future by reconciling ideal and realistic goals.

However, to date only few studies examined ideal and real future orientations, as well as all questions related to them (e.g., Yowell, 2002). Instead, future orientation research has focused on the *construction* of future orientation, narrowly defined as adolescents' formation of images of the future (the thematic approach), or more broadly as also including the motivational forces underlying images of the future and their behavioral outcomes (the three-component approach). Data collected by Trommsdorff (1983, 1986) and by other researchers (e.g., Nurmi, 1991; Poole & Cooney, 1987; Seginer, 1988a; Seginer & Schlesinger, 1998) showed that across cultures, the majority of adolescents have been able and willing to deal with issues of future orientation and invest in its construction.

The importance of future orientation for adolescent development draws on the two premises initially established by Lewin (1939). Namely, that adolescence is a period of transition in which individuals can actively prepare for the future, and that future orientation provides the grounds for setting goals, planning, exploring options, and making commitments, and thereby consequently *guides the person's developmental course* (Bandura, 2001; Nurmi, 1991; Seginer, 1992; Trommsdorff, 1986). Underlying these premises is a worldview contending that the future is open, rather than fixed, and that it is primarily the responsibility of the individual to launch her- or himself into their adult role (Seginer & Halabi-Kheir, 1998).

Given that the majority of adolescents outside the western world grow up in settings that do not fully share this worldview, the objective of this analysis is to examine cultural and family conditions underlying the construction of adolescent future orientation. This analysis is preceded by a brief introduction to future orientation conceptualization and its evolvement from classification (the thematic approach) to the three-component construct. The second and third parts each focus on the cultural and the familial settings, particularly examining the intergenerational transmission of future orientations. The fourth part offers a preliminary analysis regarding the intertwining tactics developed by adolescent girls growing up in cultural and familial settings that do not endorse adolescents' responsibility for their future. The chapter concludes with directions for future research.

Future Orientation

Early research (Frank, 1939; Israeli, 1930, 1932; Lewin, 1939) described future orientation in two ways. One was a-thematic; it focused on how far into the future individuals could think and described as extension of future time perspective (e.g., Wallace, 1956). The second approach was thematic and conceptualized future orientation in terms of multiple thematic representations of the future comprising both positive or approach (i.e., hopes) aspects, and negative or avoidance (i.e., fears) aspects (e.g., Gillespie & Allport, 1955; Monks, 1968) as reflected in "goals, aspirations, and fears" (Nuttin & Lens, 1985, p. 38). This early research laid grounds for the *thematic approach* to future orientation and its assessment in terms of hopes and fears, classified into content categories (Cantril, 1965), or future life domains.

The thematic approach: Future life domains
Data collected from school-attending adolescents across different social and cultural settings showed their future orientation consisted of both a common core and cultur-

ally specific domains. The common core encompassed the quintessence of the normative roles of transition-to-adulthood (education) and adulthood (work and career, marriage and family), as well as concerns about the self (Cross & Markus, 1991; Seginer, 1988a; Trommsdorff, 1982).

The culturally specific domains represented issues that were relevant and unique to the cultural setting. To illustrate, Finnish adolescents listed property and leisure activities (Nurmi & Pulkkinen, 1991), Australians listed leisure (Poole & Cooney, 1987), Israeli Jews and Druze boys listed military service (Seginer, 2001), and Germans listed material comfort (Trommsdorff, 1982). Israeli Arab and Druze adolescents, growing up in societies that endorse familistic and collectivist values, listed others (i.e., family members) and the collective (i.e., my village, country, nation) (Seginer & Halabi-Kheir, 1998). To describe adolescents' future life space, the density of each future life domain was computed as the ratio between the number of domain-specific and total number of hope and fears narratives, respectively.This analysis showed that adolescents -- at both the individual and the aggregate levels -- differed in the extent to which each life domain was represented in their future orientation, as expressed in terms of the density scores.

Analyses further indicated that future life domains were subsumed under *two overarching categories*: prospective life course and existence domains (Seginer & Halabi-Kheir, 1998). The first consisted of developmental task-oriented domains such as education, work and career, and marriage and family, and the second involved emotional and relational themes pertaining to self-concerns (e.g., "To have good life," "That all my hopes will be fulfilled"), others ("That my sister will get married soon"), and the collective ("That nations will stop fighting").

Analyses of the relationships between psychological health indicators (Grotevant, 1998) and density of prospective life course and existence domains, respectively, showed that from pre-adolescence to young adulthood, the prospective life course domains were positively related and the existence domains were negatively related to self-esteem, self-concept, academic optimism, low loneliness, and intimacy (see Table 1). These findings suggested that the existence domains, and particularly the self-concerns domain, earlier interpreted as lacking self-guidance properties, were associated with cultural conditions (e.g., Seginer, 1988a) as well as with intrapersonal characteristics.

In sum, the thematic approach to future orientation identified a core of adolescent future life domains. It showed that individuals and groups construct their future orientation by assigning these domains different weights, and also indicated that the distinction between the two overarching categories of prospective life course and existence domains was relevant to cultural differences, and correlated with intrapersonal characteristics. Finally, it contended that the prospective life course domains facilitate development more than do the existence domains. Analyses of goal attributes (Bandura, 2001) and possible selves (Cross & Markus, 1991) reached similar conclusions. Bandura's contention that "general goals are too indefinite and non-

Table 1

Correlation Coefficients (*r*) between Psychological Health Indicators and Prospective Life
Course (PLC) and Existence (EXIS) Domains

Characteristic	School grade	Gender	N	PLC (hopes)	EXIS (hopes)
Self Esteem (Coopersmith, 1967)[a]	4th grade	B, G	104	.24*	-.21*
(Gelberg,1996)[a]	6th grade	B, G	83	.33**	-.22
Self image (Rosenberg, 1965) (Gur-Lev, 2000)[a]	11th grade	B, G	113	.20*	-.35***
Loneliness (UCLA) (Russell et al., 1980) (Lilach, 1996)[a]	11th grade	B	84	.03	.04
	11th grade	G	62	-.24*	.32**
Academic Defensive Pessimism (Norem & Cantor, 1986) (Snir, 1994)[a]	11th grade	B, G	135	-.25**	
Academic Optimism (Norem & Cantor, 1986) (Snir, 1994)[a]	11th grade	B, G	135	.22**	
Intimacy (Rosenthal et al., 1981) (Noyman, 1998)[a]	Young adults		139	.29***	-.23**
		Men	47	.14	-.10
		Women	92	.45***	-.36***

Note. PLC-Prospective Life Course Domains; EXIS-Existence Domains; B-boys; G-girls;
[a] Research in which these results were reported.
* $p \leq 05$ ** $p \leq .01$ *** $p \leq .001$.

committing to serve as guides and incentives" (Bandura, 2001, p. 8) is applicable to
future orientation and particularly to its self-concerns aspect. Specifically, by focusing on emotional states rather than on specific tasks, self-concerns are less effective
guides of complex behavior.

The three-component model
Prompted by the narrowness of an approach consisting only of the cognitive repre-
sentation of the future, the three-component model (Seginer, 2000; Seginer, 2002;
Seginer, Nurmi, & Poole, 1991) drew on several earlier conceptualizations viewing
future orientation as a complex cognitive-motivational construct (Trommsdorff,
Burger, & Fuchsle, 1982). These conceptualizations included analyses of value
(Raynor & Entin, 1983) and expectations related to these values (Nuttin & Lens,
1985; Trommsdorff, 1983, 1986), positive and negative emotional tone (Nuttin &
Lens, 1985), optimism (Trommsdorff et al., 1982), and control beliefs (Nurmi, 1991;
Seginer, 1988b; Trommsdorff, 1986). Trommsdorff submitted her theoretical analy-
ses to empirical testing and reported positive relationships between optimism and
control beliefs and future orientation (e.g., Trommsdorff et al., 1982; Trommsdorff
& Lamm, 1980).

The three components included in the model pertain to the motivational, cognitive representation, and behavioral aspects of future orientation. The model is *generic* in the sense that it can be applied to different life domains (e.g., Seginer, 2000) and *hierarchical*. Its hierarchical nature is explained below.

The motivational component

Expectations for the future are based on present needs and past experiences regarding the fulfillment of needs in general as well as more specific needs, particularly those resembling the present ones. Thus, they lend value to expected behavior outcomes. They also serve as grounds for the appraisal of internal (ability and effort) and external (environmental) conditions for satisfying needs, and for the subjective estimation of the probability that hopes, plans and goals can be attained.

Drawing on these considerations and their formulation in value (Raynor & Entin, 1983) and expectancy x value models (e.g., Eccles & Wigfield, 2002; Heckhausen, 1977), three motivational variables have been delineated. They are: the *value* of a prospective life domain, *expectance* (i.e., subjective probability) of the materialization of hopes, and attainment of plans and goals along with general positive feelings (Carver & Scheier, 2001) about a prospective life domain and related plans, and a sense of internal (ability and effort) *control* over the materialization of plans and goals.

The pivotal role of the motivational component and the hierarchical nature of the model are depicted in the proposition that the motivational forces incite the cognitive representation of the prospective self as well as behavioral engagement in the future. These components are described below.

The cognitive representational component

This component pertains to the representation of each future orientation domain in terms of hopes, fears and other images and thoughts regarding this domain. It draws from a basic premise of future orientation research that the frequency with which individuals think about a domain reflects its salience and centrality in the life space representing the future. In the three-component model it links the motivational and the behavioral components.

The behavioral component

This component consists of the *exploration* of future options (i.e., seeking information and advice, and probing their suitability) and *commitment* to one specific option (i.e., decision). Because the behavioral component comprises the 'building blocks' of the identity formation conceptualization (Marcia, 1993), it is important to underline the differences between them. In the theoretical framework of ego identity, exploration and commitment are considered as the observable indicators of intrapsychic processes of identity formation whose *combined* presence or absence defines the identity statuses (Marcia, 1993). In the future orientation conceptual framework, each behavior is treated separately, and active engagement therein is assumed to lead to the materialization of prospective hopes, wishes, and plans, as well as affect de-velopmental (Seginer & Noyman, in press) outcomes.

The assessment of future orientation
Assessment of the three components has been carried out using two major instru-ments. The motivational and the behavioral components are gauged by Likert-type scales (Seginer, Nurmi, & Poole, 1994), and the cognitive component by a hopes and fears questionnaire (Seginer, 1988b; Trommsdorff & Lamm, 1975). The latter is an open-ended protocol in which respondents list their hopes and fears for the future. Its two main advantages are that the instrument is relatively free of cultural bias, and it provides a wealth of information on adolescents' aspirations, plans, and concerns, particularly important at the initial stages of research. However, the quantification of the hopes and fears narratives results in a great deal of missing data.

To overcome this loss we recently created a Likert-type scale (e.g., Seginer & Mahajna, 2004), with which adolescents report how often they think about each life domain (e.g., "how often do you think about your future education"). The gain is a more normal distribution of scores, though at the cost of having to sacrifice the spontaneous information and the distinction between approach (hopes) and avoid-ance (fears) responses. To surmount this, both the open-ended and the Likert-type questionnaires should be employed. In addition, a version that is to include both hope and fear items (e.g., "how often do you worry about your future education") is currently being developed.

Future Orientation in Sociocultural Settings

Analyses of the cross-cultural context of future orientation draw on two basic as-sumptions. The first is that governed by different physical conditions and cultural patterns, settings of every kind (e.g., sociocultural, family, peers, school) afford their members different developmental opportunities and models of adulthood. Research findings have shown that despite a push for greater similarities across cultures, the future orientation of adolescents growing up in various cultural groups differs in three respects: the relative representation of the core prospective domains, the inclu-sion of culturally unique domains, and the motivational and behavioral components of future orientation (Seginer, 2001).

Cultural differences in the representation of the core domains were found in sev-eral studies. To illustrate, Poole and Cooney (1987) reported differences between the future orientation of Australian and Singapore adolescents, and Seginer and Halabi-Kheir (1998) showed ethnicity and ethnic-related gender differences in the future orientation of Israeli Druze and Jewish (as a case of western society) adolescents. Lamm, Schmidt, and Trommsdorff (1976) showed that differences were not limited to between-nation comparisons. Instead, they were also found between adolescents growing up in lower and middle class settings, and those attending academic versus occupational schools.

Culturally unique domains can be illustrated by data from Israeli Druze and Arabs, as two instances of transition-to-modernity societies that include in their future orientation collective issues (i.e., hopes and fears regarding their village, nation or ethnic community, country, and the world). Research on cultural differences concerning motivational and behavioral components is only recent and scarce. Existing studies focused mainly on differences between Israeli Arab, Druze, and Jewish adolescents (Seginer, 2001). Specifically, research showed that Arab, Druze, and Jewish adolescents differed in internal and external control: Arabs and Druze scoring higher than Jews on external control, and lower than Jews on internal control, in respect to both education and family domains. In addition, Arabs and Druze scored higher on exploration of higher education, and Druze scored higher than Jews on exploration and commitment to prospective family.

Of particular significance have been findings on the future orientation regarding education as expressed by Arab and Druze girls. These findings differed from western data and showed the cultural specificity of gender differences. Specifically, western gender differences tended to be sex-typed and hence conservative. Girls in the United States (e.g., Douvan & Adelson, 1966), Germany (e.g., Lamm, Schmidt, & Trommsdorff, 1976), Finland (e.g., Nurmi & Pulkkinen, 1991; Pulkkinen, 1990) and the Israeli Jewish society (e.g., Seginer, 1988a) invested more in relational domains, and boys invested more in instrumental domains.

This pattern has one known exception. Arab girls have been constructing future orientation in partial disagreement with adult models. Findings showed that Arab girls endorsed more strongly motivational and behavioral indicators of future orientation regarding education (Seginer, 2001), and scored higher in the higher education domain than did Arab boys, or Jewish girls and boys (e.g., Seginer, 1988a, 2001). This was so despite the fact that their prospective life course score (summarizing high school and matriculation, higher education, work and career, and marriage and family) was lower than that of Jewish girls and boys. A complementary finding related to marriage and family, in which Arab girls and boys scored *lower* than Jewish girls and boys (see Figures 1 and 2). This is explained in a subsequent section (p. 10) by applying Heckhausen's (1977) principle of least necessary expenditure.

Future Orientation in Family Settings

A decade ago, Pulkkinen (1990) wrote: "Knowledge on (about) the impact of child-rearing on the development of future orientation is scarce" (p. 34). Review of the literature shows that despite a consistent interest in adolescent development in the family context (Steinberg, 2001), only one additional study has been published (for a related issue see Crockett & Raymond, 2000) since Pulkkinen's work (Nurmi & Pulkkinen, 1991) on the relationship between parenting and adolescent future orientation.

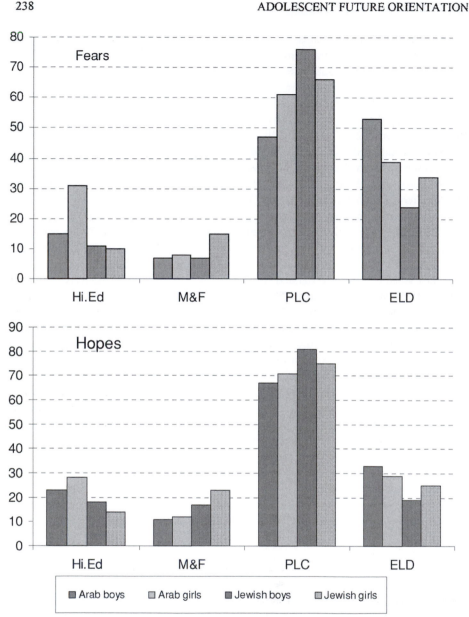

Figure 1. Density Scores for Arab and Jewish Adolescents Hopes and Fears (Seginer, 2001).
The density measure is the ratio between number of domain-specific and total number of hope
resp. fear narratives. HiEd: Higher Education, M&F: Marriage and Family, PLC: Prospective
Life Course, ELD: Existence Life Domains. N for hope narratives: N (Arab boys) = 120; N
(Arab girls) = 150; N (Jewish boys) = 132; N (Jewish girls) = 134; N for fear narratives: N
(Arab boys) = 45; N (Arab girls) = 44; N (Jewish boys) = 86; N (Jewish girls) = 62.

The earliest study on the effect of parent-adolescent relationship on future orientation was carried out by Trommsdorff and her associates. Summarizing work originally published in German, Trommsdorff (1986) wrote:

> We assumed that the experience of parental acceptance would foster a positive, self-assured future orientation in the child. As a matter of fact, we were able to show for adolescents from different age groups that persons who perceived their parents as loving and supporting had a more trusting, hopeful, and positive future orientation, believed more in personal control of their future. (p. 125)

Autonomous-accepting parenting

The question these early findings raise was why do family discussion (Nurmi & Pulkkinen, 1991), positive memories (Pulkkinen, 1990), and parental acceptance (Trommsdorff, 1986) positively affect the development of future orientation? Our explanation draws on the conceptualization of *autonomous-accepting parenting* (Allen, Hauser, Bell, & O'Connor, 1994; Grotevant & Cooper, 1985, 1986), that is conceptually similar to the variables used by the three studies, and partly overlaps with authoritative parenting (Baumrind, 1991; Darling & Steinberg, 1993). The definition of authoritative parenting and its effect on adolescent outcomes have been described as follows:

> Authoritativeness – a constellation of parental attributes that include emotional support, high standards, appropriate autonomy granting, and clear, bi-directional communication – has been shown to help children and adolescents develop an instrumental competence characterized by the balancing of societal and individual needs and responsibilities. (Darling & Steinberg, 1993, p. 487)

Recent empirical analyses, showing that authoritativeness mainly consisted of parental acceptance and autonomy granting (Chao, 2001; Gray & Steinberg, 1999), reconfirmed the relevance of authoritative parenting findings for research about the effects of autonomous-accepting parenting on adolescent outcomes. Thus, the bearing of autonomous-accepting parenting on the development of future orientation rests on two premises. One is that during adolescence, future orientation is an indicator of instrumental competence, and hence facilitated by authoritative as well as by autonomous-accepting parenting. The second is that self-evaluation is one indicator of psychological health (Grotevant, 1998) that is affected by autonomous-accepting (Allen et al., 1994) and authoritative parenting (Gray & Steinberg, 1999), and that in turn affects the construction of future orientation. The propositions drawn from these premises and their empirical testing are described below.

The first proposition is that the development of adolescent future orientation is directly related to autonomous-accepting parenting, this permitting adolescents, if not encouraging them, to pursue their passage into adulthood. Underlying it is the cognitive-motivational principle of *least necessary expenditure*, stating that individuals will not exert maximal effort "[...] on easier tasks or on tasks that overtax one's ability" (Heckhausen, 1977, p. 314). Applied to future orientation it suggests that adolescents will invest in the construction of the future to the extent that they appraise their social setting and their family in particular, as supporting their independent search for a future course. Thus, the proposition is that autonomous-accepting parenting is directly related to future orientation, particularly to its motivational component, and via it to the cognitive and the behavioral components.

The second proposition draws on earlier findings (Allen et al., 1994) regarding self-esteem as an indicator of the evaluative aspect of the self. This proposition predicts that the effect of the autonomous-accepting parenting on the motivational component of future orientation would also be indirect, via its effect on self-evaluation. In sum, this model predicts that autonomous-accepting parenting affects the motivational component of future orientation both directly and indirectly, via self-evaluation, and that the motivational component of future orientation directly affects the cognitive and the behavioral components.

Empirical estimates of this model for the educational prospective domain by means of LISREL (Jöreskog & Sörbom, 1996), carried out on data collected from Israeli Jewish adolescents (N = 458), confirmed the model (see Figure 2 and Table 2). Specifically, they showed that autonomous-accepting parenting was related to the motivational component only indirectly, via self-esteem (Rosenberg, 1979). The empirical estimate of this model resulted in χ^2 (30) = 35.77, p =.22, GFI = .96, $AFGI$ = .93.

The cross-cultural generalizability of these findings indicated by the extent to which autonomous-accepting parenting prompts the construction of future orientation among non-western adolescents still needs to be examined. At present two rival hypotheses can be proposed. In light of the central role of autonomy granting and acceptance for the conceptualization of authoritative parenting, these hypotheses draw on analyses of the effect of authoritative parenting on non-western children's and adolescents' outcomes.

The first hypothesis draws on the contention that autonomy granting is a western characteristic, and on findings showing that autonomous-accepting parenting did not have positive effects for Chinese American adolescents (Chao, 2001), thus predicting that authoritative parenting is facilitative only for western adolescents. Conversely, the second hypothesis draws on the contention that non-western families just like western families vary in their autonomy granting and acceptance, and on findings showing that authoritative parenting was positively related to academic achievement for Chinese children (Chen, Dong, & Zou, 1997). Thus, it predicts that autonomous-accepting parenting will prompt the construction of future orientation among non-western adolescents as well.

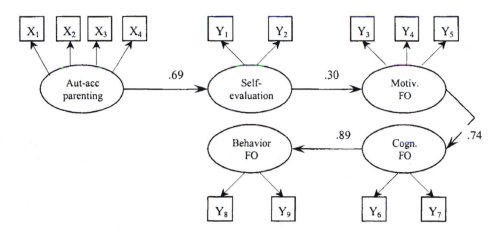

Figure 2. The Education Model: The Effect of Parenting on Future Orientation. Aut-acc parenting: autonomous-accepting parenting, Motiv. FO: Motivational component of future orientation, Cogn. FO: Cognitive component of future orientation, Behavior FO: Behavioral component of future orientation;). $N = 458$; χ^2 (57) = 157.35, $p = .000$, $RMSEA = .062$, $SRMR = .054$, $CFI = .97$, $AGFI = .92$.

Table 2
Factor Loadings (λs) for the Education Model

Manifest variables		Latent variables	λ
Parenting			
X_1	Autonomy father	Autonomous-accepting parenting	.68
X_2	Acceptance father	Autonomous-accepting parenting	.77
X_3	Autonomy mother	Autonomous-accepting parenting	.71
X_4	Acceptance mother	Autonomous-accepting parenting	.80
Self-evaluation			
Y_1	Self-esteem	Self-evaluation	.86
Y_2	Self-agency	Self-evaluation	.72
Future orientation components			
Y_3	Value	Motivational future orientation	.56
Y_4	Expectancy	Motivational future orientation	.54
Y_5	Internal control	Motivational future orientation	.57
Y_6	My future education	Cognitive future orientation	.67
Y_7	Thinking about education	Cognitive future orientation	.80
Y_8	Exploration	Behavioral future orientation	.83
Y_9	Commitment	Behavioral future orientation	.74

Parental beliefs

The definition of parental beliefs as the ideas, expectations, and subjective knowledge individuals hold about issues relevant to their role as parents (McGillicuddy-DeLisi & Sigel, 1995) suggests their influence on a wide range of children's and adolescents' outcomes. Earlier research examined the effect of two kinds of parental beliefs on future orientation. One focused on parents' beliefs about the importance and viability of each of four prospective domains for the target adolescent (Schlesinger, 2002). The four domains were higher education, military service, work and career, and marriage and family. Importance and viability beliefs were comparable to the motivational component variables. Specifically, they were conceptualized as parents' view of the value each domain has for their child, their confidence about the materialization of their child's hopes and plans (expectance), and their evaluation of their child's ability to control the materialization of hopes and plans (internal control).

Data collected from parents (90 mothers and 74 fathers) and their 11th grade children (128 girls and 133 boys) were analyzed by hierarchical regressions (for each of the prospective life domains, and for mothers and fathers separately). The sequence was parental beliefs, and the motivational and behavioral components of future orientation (the cognitive representation variable was omitted due to low and non-significant correlations with the other variables). Analyses indicated three major findings. First, mothers' and fathers' beliefs had a significant effect only on one prospective domain: military service. Given that military service is an experience shared by contemporaries like peers and older siblings, this finding was explained by the special social and developmental significance of military service for Israeli Jewish adolescents, and the fact that the majority of parents were Israeli born and had at their time served in the army.

Second, the *value* mothers and fathers attributed to military service had a stronger effect than any of the other beliefs. Specifically, for mothers value was the only belief directly related to adolescents' future orientation (βs ranging from .32, $p < .01$ to .50, $p < .001$), and for fathers the only belief that affected all the motivational variables (βs ranging from .36, $p < .05$ to .48, $p < .001$). Third, beliefs, like autonomous-accepting parenting, had an effect on the motivational component of future orientation and via it on the behavioral component. However, mothers' value of military service had a direct effect on adolescents' commitment as well ($\beta = .50$, $p < .001$). These analyses explained 25% to 27% of the variance of exploration and commitment for mothers and fathers, respectively.

The second study was conducted among Israeli Arab girls (Mahajna, 2000; Seginer & Mahajna, 2003). It focused on perceived fathers' beliefs regarding girls' early marriage and higher education, and their effect on two future orientation domains (marriage and family, and higher education) and on academic achievement. In this study each future orientation domain was represented by two variables: expectance as a motivational indicator, and commitment as a behavioral indicator. Two findings should be specifically noted. One is that perceived fathers' beliefs had a direct effect only on future orientation regarding marriage and family (expectance and commitment), and via it on future orientation regarding higher education (expectance) and academic achievement.

The second finding was that perceived fathers' beliefs prompted two trajectories: the traditional and the progressive. Both were positively linked to perceived fathers' beliefs about early marriage and higher education, and differed in the links between the marriage and family variables and higher education expectance. Specifically, in the *traditional* trajectory, marriage and family *commitment* were negatively linked to higher education expectance, in turn positively linked to academic achievement. Thus, girls opting for high commitment to marriage and family renounced their aspirations for high academic achievement. In the *progressive* trajectory, marriage and family *expectance* (i.e., the confidence in materializing their hopes and plans) was positively related to higher education expectance and to academic achievement. Thus, confidence in the materialization of plans (expectance) for marriage promoted academic achievement directly as well as indirectly via a link to higher education expectance. This has led Seginer and Mahajna (2003) to conclude that the complexity of the future orientation of Israeli Arab adolescent girls, whose prospective education and prospective family are interdependent, reflects the intricacy of these girls' process of transition to adulthood.

In sum, although differing in several respects, both studies showed that parental beliefs have an effect on future orientation, albeit limited. Specifically, in the Israeli Jewish adolescents study, parental beliefs affected only one of the four future life domains, and, in the Israeli Arab girls study, they directly affected only one of the two future orientation domains. They also reiterated earlier findings (Nurmi & Pulkkinen, 1991; Pulkkinen, 1990; Trommsdorff, 1986) that reported adolescent future orientation as related to several aspects of parenting, and that parents' influence on adolescents' future orientation is to be seen as a cross-cultural phenomenon.

Intergenerational transmission of future orientation
Do positive relations between parenting and future orientation indicate that future orientation is transmitted across generations? Considering the definition of intergenerational transmission as parent-child congruence and its meaning as the conservation of existing patterns, the answer is context-dependent. Moreover, as contended below, parent-child congruence does not necessarily indicate intergenerational transmission (Seginer & Vermulst, 2001), and parents may inadvertently facilitate the construction of future orientation by creating the conditions necessary for the construction of future orientation. To address these issues, intergenerational transmission will be discussed in relation to three topics: parents as models for their children, the meaning of parent-adolescent congruence, and transmission and facilitation as two processes that can promote adolescents' construction of future orientation.

Parents as models

In this respect, the Arab and Jewish samples discussed here differ considerably. Drawing first on the Arab adolescents, the hopes and fears of the future listed by Arab girls will be considered. These data were collected in a recent study of 11th grade Arab adolescents (Suleiman, 2001). Although not explicitly requested, many respondents referred to a specific future career they were considering. Girls (N = 129) mentioned, spontaneously, the following occupations: teacher, sports teacher, English teacher, social worker, medical doctor, pediatrician, dentist, pharmacist, psychologist, journalist and TV announcer, engineer, travel agent, lawyer. By comparison, boys (N = 75) mentioned: medical doctor, lawyer, engineer, computer engineer, and accountant. Given that of these adolescents less than one third grew up in families where one or both parents had above high school education, and considering the low frequency of these professions in the Arab population in general and among women in particular, it is plausible that the majority did not use their parents as models of career.

Thus, as a group, Arab adolescents, and especially girls, are developing an educational and career future orientation that is different from that of their parents' generation. For them, as for other adolescents in the majority world (Kagitçibasi, 1996), future orientation is not intergenerationally transmitted but rather a task of bridging between different worlds (Cooper, in press).

Based on criteria of parents' education and the percentage of individuals holding jobs in the professions in the Jewish population, the chances that Jewish adolescents participating in our studies would use their parents as models are higher. However, congruence regarding higher education and career choices, and the beliefs about them, does not necessarily indicate intergenerational transmission. This is explained in the next section.

The meaning of parent-child congruence

While intergenerational transmission is defined as parent-child congruence, not all cases of congruence indicate parent-child congruence. Confounding may occur in two ways. One is the direct effect of factors like genetic inheritance and across-cohort value stability (van IJzendoorn, 1992). The second is when family values are in accordance with other societal institutions such as educational and political systems, as is the case in many western middle class families. Super and Harkness' (2002) recent analysis of the developmental niche described it as across-system regularities generated by processes of redundancy, elaboration, and chaining.

While these regularities are important for child development, they may have a confounding effect on the assessment of intergenerational transmission in terms of congruence. To control for such confounding effects when assessing congruence, a statistical procedure was developed (Lanz, Scabini, Vermulst, & Gerris, 2001; Vermulst, Leeuwe, & Lanz, 2004) that compares the mean of the observed congruence score of related dyads (e.g., parent-adolescent) with the mean expected congruence score of unrelated 'artificial dyads' (e.g., parent of one family and adolescent of another family). Analyses showing significant congruence scores for the parent-child cohort would indicate an intergenerational transmission while analyses showing significant congruence scores for the artificial dyads would indicate a cultural phenomenon and should not be interpreted as indicating intergenerational transmission.

Transmission and facilitation

Findings presented earlier showed that for Jewish adolescents (as a case of western adolescents) perceived autonomous-accepting parenting prompted adolescents' future orientation, albeit via the effect of parenting on self-evaluation and of self-evaluation on the motivational component of future orientation. Thus, parents perceived by their children as employing autonomous-accepting parenting *facilitated* the development of future orientation.

Assuming that most parents provide their children with some measure of acceptance and autonomy (varying in meaning and magnitude according to cultural conventions), autonomous-accepting parenting may affect future orientation across cultures. The empirical effect of autonomous-accepting parenting on the future orientation of non-western adolescents awaits examination in future research.

The Individual: Intertwining the Progressive with the Traditional

The importance of the individual in prompting her or his development has been addressed by several researchers in different ways: focus on the "goodness-of-fit" between individual characteristics and environmental demands (Lerner, 1982), the preservation of one's style by selecting environments or social interaction opportunities that reinforce this style (Caspi, Bem, & Elder, 1989), or regarding "myself" as the main source of influence on decision-making (Sebald, 1986). Israeli Arab girls have not been familiar with these analyses, nor do they explicitly express the "myself" orientation. However, they seem to be practicing it. The process of thinking about the future has been described by one of the Arab girl's respondents as follows,

Nowadays I think a lot about my future. That is, what I would like to happen and what is the subject I would like to study at the university. And after thinking for a long time I decided to study teaching at a teachers' college, and want to start immediately after [graduating from] high school and don't want to take a year off and rest at home or get a job. (Suleiman, 2001)

Moreover, they have developed tactics for narrowing the gap between the culturally prescribed and personally desired prospective life courses as means for gaining family approval. To break away from the traditional course of Arab women, these girls have resorted to a special tactics of *intertwining* the progressive path of higher education desired by them with the traditional path of early marriage expected of them by their family and community (Seginer & Mahajna, 2003). These tactics, based on balancing primary and secondary control orientations (Seginer, Trommsdorff, & Essau, 1993) are reflected in hopes such as "Get married and be a college student, both at the same time," "That my [future] husband will be well educated and allow me to attend college during our engagement period," "[I hope to] develop a career that will help me and my community, and be a good mother to a generation of educated children" (Seginer & Mahajna, 2003).

Findings that many girls at the same school voice such hopes suggest two further matters. One is the role of other socialization settings such as peers, adult mentors and the media in the construction of future orientation. The second is the development of intertwining tactics, especially in sociocultural settings that do not endorse higher education and career development for women. The processes underlying this and the personal characteristics of the girls developing these tactics will be examined in future research.

Summary and Future Directions

This chapter focused on four issues. The first was the main research approaches to adolescent future orientation that have been applied in the past, and the major findings each approach has yielded. The second and third issues pertained to the cultural context and family conditions facilitating the construction of future orientation, particularly those addressing issues of intergenerational transmission. The fourth issue concerned the role of the individual, especially pertaining to the tactics used by transition-to-modernity girls seeking to overcome cultural barriers, and construct an emancipated orientation for their future.

This research suggests several directions for future research. One is the continued search for the validity of the three-component model for non-western adolescents. The second is the extent to which family environments, particularly applying to autonomous-accepting parenting, parental beliefs and the support of older siblings, promotes the construction of future orientation regarding the three core prospective tasks of education, career, and family. This issue needs to be studied in both western and non-western cultural settings. The third issue pertains to non-family social settings: how do peers, teachers, other adult mentors and the media affect the construction of future orientation? The fourth issue relates to the intrapersonal factors affecting the construction of future orientation. The last two issues are particularly relevant to adolescents growing up in non-western societies seeking to pursue an emancipated prospective life course.

References

Allen, J. P., Hauser, S. T., Bell, K. L., & O'Connor, T. G. (1994). Longitudinal assessment of autonomy and relatedness in adolescent-family interactions as predictors of adolescent ego development and self-esteem. *Child Development, 65*, 179-194.

Bandura, A. (2001). Social cognitive theory: A genetic perspective. *Annual Review of Psychology, 52*, 1-26.

Baumrind, D. (1991). Parenting styles and adolescent development. In R. M. Lerner, A. C. Petersen, & J. Brooks-Gunn (Eds.), *Encyclopedia of adolescence* (Vol. 2, pp. 746-758). New York: Garland.

Cantril, H. (1965). *The patterns of human concerns*. New Brunswick, NJ: Rutgers University Press.

Carver, C. S., & Scheier, M. F. (2001). Optimism, pessimism, and self-regulation. In E. C. Chang (Ed.), Optimism & pessimism: Implications for theory, research, and practice (pp. 31-51). Washington, DC: American Psychological Association.

Caspi, A., Bem, D. J., & Elder, G. H. (1989). Continuities and consequences of interactional styles across the life course. *Journal of Personality, 57*, 375-406.

Chao, R. K. (2001). Extending research on the consequences of parenting style for Chinese Americans and European Americans. *Child Development, 72*, 1832-1843.

Chen, X., Dong, Q., & Zhou, H. (1997). Authoritative and authoritarian parenting practices and social and school performance in Chinese children. *International Journal of Behavioral Development, 21*, 855-873.

Cooper, C. R. (in press). *The weaving of maturity: Cultural perspectives on adolescent development*. New York: Oxford University Press.

Coopersmith, S. (1967). *The antecedents of self esteem*. New York: W. H. Freeman.

Crockett, L. J., & Raymond, C. (2000). Anticipating adulthood: Expected timing of work and family transitions among rural youth. *Journal of Research on Adolescence, 10*, 151-172.

Cross, S., & Markus, H. R. (1991). Possible selves across the life span. *Human Development, 34*, 225-230.

Darling, N., & Steinberg, L. (1993). Parenting style as context: An integrative model. *Psychological Bulletin, 113*, 487-496.

Douvan, E., & Adelson, J. (1966). *The adolescent experience*. New York: Wiley.

Eccles, J. S., & Wigfield, A. (2002). Motivation, beliefs, and goals. *Annual Review of Psychology, 53*, 109-132.

Erikson, E. H. (1968). *Identity: Youth and crisis*. New York: Norton.

Frank, L. K. (1939). Time perspectives. *Journal of Social Philosophy, 4*, 293-312.

Gelberg, Y. (1996). *The development of future orientation in preadolescence*. Unpublished master's thesis, University of Haifa, Haifa, Israel.

Gillespie, J. M., & Allport, G. W. (1955). *Youth's outlook on the future: A cross-national study*. Garden City, NY: Doubleday & Company.

Gray, M. R., & Steinberg, L. (1999). Unpacking authoritative parenting: Reassessing a multidimensional construct. *Journal of Marriage and the Family, 61*, 574-587.

Grotevant, H. D. (1998). Adolescent development in family contexts. In W. Damon (Series Ed.) & N. Eisenberg (Vol. Ed.), *Handbook of child psychology: Vol. 3. Social, emotional, and personality development* (5th ed., pp. 1097-1149). New York: Wiley.

Grotevant, H. D., & Cooper, C. R. (1985). Patterns of interaction in family relationships and the development of identity exploration in adolescence. *Child Development, 56*, 415-428.

Grotevant, H. D., & Cooper, C. R. (1986). Individuation in family relationships: a perspective on individual differences in the development of identity and role-taking skill in adolescence. *Human Development, 29*, 82-100.

Gur-Lev, S. (2000). *Personality correlates of adolescent future orientation.* Unpublished master's thesis, University of Haifa, Haifa, Israel.

Heckhausen, H. (1977). Achievement motivation and its constructs: A cognitive model. *Motivation and Emotion, 1*, 283-329.

Israeli, N. (1930). Some aspects of social psychology of futurism. *Journal of Abnormal and Social Psychology, 25*, 121-132.

Israeli, N. (1932). The social psychology of time. *Journal of Abnormal and Social Psychology, 27*, 209-213.

Jöreskog, K. G., & Sörbom, D. (1996). *LISREL 8: User's Reference Guide.* Chicago: Scientific Software International Inc.

Kagitçibasi, Ç. (1996). *Family and human development across cultures: A view from the other side.* Mahwah, NJ: Erlbaum.

Lamm, H., Schmidt, R. W., & Trommsdorff, G. (1976). Sex and social class as determinants of future orientation (time perspective) in adolescence. *Journal of Personality and Social Psychology, 34*, 317-326.

Lanz, M., Scabini, E., Vermulst, A. A., & Gerris, J. R. M. (2001). Congruence on child rearing families with early adolescent and middle adolescent children. *International Journal of Behavioral Development, 25*, 133-139-

Lerner, R. M. (1982). Children and adolescents as producers of their own behavior. *Developmental Review, 2*, 342-370.

Lewin, K. (1939). Field theory and experiment in social psychology: Concepts and methods. *The American Journal of Sociology, 44*, 868-897.

Lilach, E. (1996). *The future orientation of lonely adolescents.* Unpublished master's thesis, University of Haifa, Haifa, Israel.

Mahajna, S. (2000). *Future orientation in sociocultural and family context: The case of Arab adolescent girls.* Unpublished master's thesis, University of Haifa, Haifa, Israel.

Marcia, J. E. (1993). The ego identity status approach to ego identity. In J. E. Marcia, A. S. Waterman, D. R. Matteson, S. L. Archer, & J. L. Orlofsky (Eds.), *Ego identity: A handbook for psychological research* (pp. 3-21). New York: Springer.

McGillicuddy-DeLisi, A. V., & Sigel, I. E. (1995). Parental beliefs. In M. H. Bornstein (Ed.), *Handbook of parenting: Vol. 3. Status and social conditions of parenting* (pp. 333-358). Mahwah, NJ: Lawrence Erlbaum Associates.

Monks, F. (1968). Future time perspective in adolescence. *Human Development, 11,* 107-123.

Noyman, M. S. (1998). *Future orientation and identity in early adulthood.* Unpublished master's thesis, University of Haifa, Haifa, Israel.

Nurmi, J. E. (1991). How do adolescents see their future? A review of the development of future orientation and planning. *Developmental Review, 11,* 1-59.

Nurmi, J. E., & Pulkkinen, H. (1991). The changing parent child relationship, self-esteem and intelligence as determinants of orientation to the future during early adolescence. *Journal of Adolescence, 14,* 35-51.

Nuttin, J., & Lens, W. (1985). *Future time perspective and motivation: theory and research method.* Hillsdale, NJ: Erlbaum.

Poole, M. E., Cooney, G. H. (1987). Orientation to the future: A comparison of adolescents in Australia and Singapore. *Journal of Youth and Adolescence, 16,* 129-151.

Pulkkinen, L. (1990). Home atmosphere and adolescent future orientation. *European Journal of Psychology of Education, 1,* 33-43.

Raynor, J. O., & Entin, E. E. (1983). The function of future orientation as a determinant of human behavior in a step-path theory of action. *International Journal of Psychology, 18,* 463-487.

Rosenberg, M. (1979). *Conceiving the self.* New York: Basic Books.

Rosenthal, D., Gurney, R. M., & Moore, S. M. (1981). From trust to intimacy: A new inventory for examining Erikson's stages of psychosocial development. *Journal of Youth and Adolescence, 10,* 525-537.

Schlesinger, R. (2002). *Family correlates of adolescents' future orientation.* Unpublished doctoral dissertation, University of Haifa, Haifa, Israel.

Sebald, H. (1986). Adolescents' shifting orientation toward parents and peers: A curvilinear trend over recent decades. *Journal of Marriage and the Family, 48,* 5-13.

Seginer, R. (1988a). Adolescent orientation toward the future: Sex role differentiation in sociocultural context. *Sex Roles, 18,* 739-757.

Seginer, R. (1988b). Social milieu and future orientation: The case of kibbutz vs. urban adolescents. *International Journal of Behavioral Development, 11,* 247-273.

Seginer, R. (1992). Future orientation: Age related differences among adolescent females. *Journal of Youth and Adolescence, 21,* 421-437.

Seginer, R. (2000). Defensive pessimism and optimism correlates of adolescent future orientation: A domain specific analysis. *Journal of Adolescent Research, 15,* 307-326.

Seginer, R. (2001). Young people chart their path into adulthood: The future orientation of Israeli Druze, Arab and Jewish adolescents. Special Issue: *The child in Israel, Megamot, 41*, 97-112. [Original in Hebrew].

Seginer, R., & Halabi-Kheir, H. (1998). Adolescent passage to adulthood: Future orientation in the context of culture, age, and sex. *International Journal of Intercultural Relations, 22*, 309-328.

Seginer, R., & Mahajna, S. (2003). "Education is a weapon in women's hands": How Israeli Arab girls construe their future. *Zeitschrift für Soziologie der Erziehung und Sozialisation, 23*, 200-214.

Seginer, R., & Mahajna, S. (2004). How the future orientation of traditional Israeli Palestinian girls beliefs about women's roles and academic achievement. *Psychology of Women Quarterly, 28*, 122-135.

Seginer, R., & Noyman, M. S. (in press). Future orientation, identity, and intimacy: Their relationships in emerging adulthood. *European Journal of Developmental Psychology*.

Seginer, R., & Nurmi, J. E., & Poole, M. E. (1991, July). *Adolescent future orientation in cross-cultural perspective: Research prospect*. Paper presented at the 11th meeting of the ISSBD, Minneapolis, MN.

Seginer, R., Nurmi, J. E., & Poole, M. E. (1994). *Future Orientation Questionnaire* (revised). Haifa, Israel: University of Haifa.

Seginer, R., & Schlesinger, R. (1998). Adolescents' future orientation in time and place: The case of the Israeli kibbutz. *International Journal of Behavioral Development, 22*, 151-167.

Seginer, R., Trommsdorff, G., & Essau, C. (1993). Adolescent control beliefs: Cross-cultural variations of primary and secondary control orientations. *International Journal of Behavioral Development, 16*, 243-260.

Seginer, R., & Vermulst, A. A. (2001). The intergenerational transmission of child rearing stress: Congruence, psychological mediators, and ecological moderators. In J. R. M. Gerris (Ed.), *Dynamics of parenting* (pp. 157-178). Leuven, Belgium: Garant.

Snir, N. (1994). *Facing the future: future orientation and cognitive strategies of defensive pessimism and optimism*. Unpublished master's thesis, University of Haifa, Israel.

Steinberg, L. (2001). We know some things: Parent-adolescent relations in retrospect and prospect. *Journal of Research on Adolescence, 11*, 1-19.

Suleiman, M. A. (2001). *Parental style and Arab adolescents' future orientation*. Unpublished master's thesis, University of Haifa, Israel.

Super, C. M., & Harkness, S. (2002). Culture structures the environment for development. *Human Development, 45*, 270-274.

Trommsdorff, G. (1982). Group influences on judgments concerning the future. In M. Irle (with L. B. Katz) (Ed.), *Studies in decision making: Social psychological and socio-economic analyses* (pp. 145-165). Berlin, Germany: Walter de Gruyter.

Trommsdorff, G. (1983). Future orientation and socialization. *International Journal of Psychology, 18*, 381-406.

Trommsdorff, G. (1986). Future time orientation and its relevance for development as action. In R. K. Silbereisen, K. Eyferth, & G. Ruding (Eds.), *Development as action in context* (pp. 121-136). Berlin, Germany: Springer.

Trommsdorff, G., Burger, C., & Fuchsle, T. (1982). Social and psychological aspects of future orientation: In M. Irle (with L. B. Katz) (Ed.) *Studies in decision making: Social psychological and socio-economic analyses* (pp. 167-184). Berlin, Germany: Walter De Gruyter.

Trommsdorff, G., & Lamm, H. (1975). An analysis of future orientation and some of its social determinants. In J. T. Fraser & N. Lawrence (Eds.), *The study of time II* (pp. 343-361). New York: Springer.

Trommsdorff, G., & Lamm, H. (1980). Future orientation of institutionalized and non-institutionalized delinquents. *European Journal of Social Psychology, 10*, 247-287.

van IJzendoorn, M. H. (1992). Intergenerational transmission of parenting: A review of studies in nonclinical populations. *Developmental Review, 12*, 76-99.

Vermulst, A. A., van Leeuwe, J. F. J., & Lanz, M. (2004). *Measuring and testing congruence in dyads*. Manuscript submitted for publication.

Wallace, M. (1956). Future time perspective in schizophrenia. *Journal of Abnormal and Social Psychology, 52*, 240-245.

Yowell, C. M. (2002). Dreams of the future: The pursuit of education and career possible selves among ninth grade Latino youth. *Applied Developmental Science, 6*, 62-72.

Part IV
Social Change

11

Modernization Does Not Mean Westernization: Emergence of a Different Pattern

Çigdem Kagitçibasi

Introduction

Modernization is usually defined in terms of societal level institutional change, involving modifications in economic, political, and sociocultural spheres. In economic terms modernization includes a more profound application of scientific technology to production, greater specialization of labor, larger scale financial markets, and a generally rising level of material well being, among other things. In political terms it refers to the rise of centralized national authority, the emergence of political institutions such as political parties and interest groups, and democratic government among other things. Finally, in sociocultural terms it entails social structural changes such as urbanization, the expansion of public education, secularization, and the intensification of mass communication, among other things (Huntington, 1966; Ward & Rustow, 1964; Yang, 1988).

It is clear from the above that modernization is considered to be a most comprehensive process of societal change. As such, it has been a topic of much study and speculation in the social sciences such as economics, political science and sociology in the 20th century, though historically the precursors of modernization date back to the enlightenment in Europe. It has been considered to be an evolutionary paradigm positing a progressive development over time toward a more advanced state (Caldwell, 1977; Klages, this volume; Mazrui, 1968; Ozdalga, 2002; see Kagitçibasi, 1996a, for a review).

Given the supra-individual and societal level of analysis in this scholarship, the individual was not the focus of study. Nevertheless, afterwards the "modern man syndrome" was put forth as the "personification" of the process of societal modernization, at least tacitly (Inkeles, 1969; Inkeles & Smith, 1974). This perspective has paved the way for the construal of psychological modernization underlying the processes of economic, political, and sociocultural modernization. Psychological perspectives were advanced starting particularly in the 1950s to draw attention to the non-economic aspects of modernization.

Westernization, in turn, has been put forth mainly as a political framework for societal change. The colonial domination of the non-western world by the western powers marked the process of westernization, in most cases being imposed from the outside. Westernization commonly referred to influences from and orientations toward Western Europe, particularly Britain and France, and subsequently the USA. Even in countries that had not been colonized, there was wide scale emulation of the West in the 19th and 20th centuries, at times self-imposed. For example, the emergence of the Turkish Republic after the collapse of the Ottoman Empire was based on the premises of westernization in a concerted effort to sever all the ties with a traditional past and to achieve progress.

The overlap between modernization and westernization is rather obvious. Modernization in all its different manifestations, be it economic, political, or sociocultural, has meant becoming more and more similar to the western pattern. Even in psychological terms, "the modern individual" syndrome characterizes "the western individual." Possibly a reason for the more ready use of the term modernization, rather than westernization, is a hesitation not to sound overly imposing or ethnocentric and to break the ties with the colonial past. What is implied is that the less developed countries modernize from within, not from without as an imposition from the West. Nevertheless, the strong assumption is that the process involves a unidirectional convergence toward the western pattern (e.g., Eisenstadt, 1987). Indeed, the essence of both modernization and westernization is this assumed *convergence* toward the West of diverse human patterns, reflecting a social Darwinist progression model (Kagitçibasi, 1998; Marsella & Choi, 1993; Yang, 1988).

The social evolutionist worldview that considers whatever is different from the western pattern as deficient and therefore bound to change with socioeconomic development, has served as the *raison d'être* of modernization. This view has its precursors in the 19th century social evolutionism of Tylor (1865), Spencer (1876), and Morgan (1877), who reinterpreted Darwin's *Origin of Species* in terms of a linear social/cultural progression from savagery to civilization. "Less developed" populations were seen to be akin to children; the famous analogy "Ontogency recapitulates phylogeny" reflects this misconception. Though later on the inadequacy of a unidimensional single key concept explanation of societal development was recognized (Segall, Dasen, Berry, & Poortinga, 1990), the social evolutionary views lingered on well into the 20th century, as for example seen in the work of well-known developmental psychologists Werner (1948) and Hall (quoted in Muschin-ske, 1977).

Psychological Modernization: Then and Now

It was a short step from societal modernization to individual modernization, to theo-rize about the human aspects of social change and modernization. This was done in an attempt to understand why some societies were "modernizing" faster than others and why some were lagging behind. For about two decades from the late 1950s to the 1970s a great deal of research and theory undertook to reveal the psychological precursors for or factors in societal modernization. These ranged from "psychologi-cal reductionistic" propositions putting forth monistic key psychological explana-tions for modernization, such as the "emphatic personality" (Lerner, 1958), or the "innovative personality" (Hagen, 1962), or the "achieving personality" (McClelland, 1961) to more complex conceptualizations of "individual modernity."

The "individual modernity" conceptualizations typically pointed to a number of key psychological characteristics that seemed to characterize those individuals or groups who were more "modern" or open to change. Some of the commonly found characteristics forming the individual modernity syndrome were openness to change, a sense of efficacy, independence or self reliance, a present and future orientation (rather than a past orientation), low integration with relatives and kin, achievement motivation, and individualism, among others. These attributes, forming the theoreti-cal construct of individual modernity, were found in empirical research to distin-guish populations differing in exposure to western influences, urban/industrial life-styles and education.

Best known among the studies utilizing the individual modernity framework are the ones carried out by Inkeles in Argentina, Chile, India, Pakistan, Israel, and Nige-ria (Inkeles, 1969; Inkeles & Smith, 1974), Kahl in Brazil, Mexico, and the United States (1968), and Doob (1967) and Dawson (1967) in Africa. Several common "modern" characteristics emerged from these studies. For example Inkeles studies pointed to openness to new experiences, innovation and change; interest in national or other issues going beyond the immediate environment; present or future orienta-tion (rather than past orientation); planning; activism and faith in science and tech-nology; belief in merit-based distributive justice; valuing education and educational aspirations; and independence from traditional sources of influence, such as family and kinship. Kahl also emphasized low integration with relatives, individualism, activism, and risk taking, preference for an urban lifestyle, trust in people, and mass media participation.

Some others were conducted in a single country or society and related psycho-logical attitudes to social structural factors. For example, Guthrie (1970, 1977) stud-ied four different Filipino communities with his Tradition-Modern Interview Sched-ule and found more modern individuals to have greater individualism, independence from family and self-efficacy than traditional ones. Schnaiberg (1970) studying family and fertility behavior interviewed a large number of women in Ankara and four rural villages in Turkey. Kagitçibasi (1970) studied youth from urban and rural origins and family relations in different urban socioeconomic strata in Izmir, Turkey. Both studies found that individuals from urban and higher SES levels had more "modern" orientations, and Kâgitçibâsi found that the modern groups' child-rearing patterns included more affection than control. The lower control in child rearing reflected less compliance-oriented parenting, thus allowing for the development of autonomy in children.

Similarly Yang and associates (1981, 1988) conducted a series of studies in Taiwan pointing to various characteristics of the "modern" Chinese in the rapidly industrializing Chinese society. They developed three indigenous scales of individual modernity specifically applicable to the Chinese in Taiwan. They found that the more modernized Chinese had higher needs for or orientation toward exhibition and extraversion, dominance, autonomy, flexibility, tolerance, intraception, sexuality, individual-oriented achievement, preference for activity, self-indulgence, individualistic relationships, egalitarianism, internal control, and gender equality (Yang, 1988).

Thus, both the theory and research on individual modernity proposed "modernity" to be a *syndrome* of organized psychological characteristics, such that they all go together. This was the second most important assumption of modernization, particularly of psychological modernization, beyond the "convergence" hypothesis. Clearly, the "individual modernity syndrome" was construed in the image of the ideal-typical western individualistic human pattern, as that which is best fit to function in the modern society. Given the strong face validity of individual modernity, the research and theorizing continuing well into the 1970s helped establish this concept as common sense in the social sciences and in everyday parlance. This was the case even though serious criticism was raised within sociology (e.g., Bendix, 1967; Gusfield, 1967) having to do with the simplistic dichotomizing (traditional-modern) and "psychologizing" of complex social phenomena (see also Klages, this volume). Nevertheless, possibly because individual modernity was thus taken for granted, the research and writing on it subsided, only to be replaced, starting in the 1980s, with a new construct.

This new construct, functioning in exactly the same way as "individual modernity," is "individualism" of the individualism/collectivism paradigm. This was noted by some cross-cultural psychologists (Kagitçibasi, 1994, 1998; Yang, 1988) as a resurgence of the modernization paradigm in current thinking regarding the psychological underpinnings of global changes in human phenomena. Yang (1988) has in fact pointed to "individualism as the most important constituent of individual modernity" (p. 78) by showing that of some 20 "individual modernity" traits about two thirds reflected "individualism."

The popularity of individualism (/collectivism), just like the former psychological modernity, resides in its potential to explain the non-economic aspects of societal development. In this sense the construal of individualism is akin to that of individual modernity and more specifically to the achievement motive (McClelland, 1961), mentioned before. Indeed McClelland and Winters (1969) had endeavored to instill the achievement motive in managers in India to facilitate economic development, with meager results. Later on Hofstede (1980), using 1970s statistics showed a correlation of .82 between individualism and economic affluence (see also Klages, in this volume). Though Hofstede, himself, did not attribute a specific causal significance to individualism, many readers did. However, later Schwartz (1994) found this correlation to be in the order of .50. Beyond conceptual and measurement differences, the difference between the two correlations was probably due to the remarkable economic growth of the collectivistic Pacific Rim (Japan, Taiwan, Korea, Hong Kong, Singapore), in turn decreasing the overall association between individualism and economic wealth.

Where do we stand now?

Experience of the last few decades has provided evidence both supporting and opposing the modernization paradigm, thus necessitating fine-tuned distinctions to be drawn among the four different types of modernization (economic, political, sociocultural, and individual). They have also called for a reconsideration of the "convergence" hypothesis, thus unraveling modernization from westernization.

Considering supportive evidence, it may be said that several aspects of societal level modernization processes, particularly in the economic but also to some extent in the political and sociocultural spheres are occurring with wide scale prevalence. In this sense, global modernization has started and may even be considered to have materialized to a large extent, though there are regional and national variations in the degree and the extent of this process. Common patterns of change exist. Some of the most notable examples of these transformations are seen in economic modernization (industrialization; opening up to large scale financial markets; greater specialization of labor; greater use of scientific technology and energy resources), and in sociocultural modernization (urbanization; national and international mobility/migration; expansion of public education, telecommunications, and transportation), with political modernization (the establishment of political parties; universal suffrage and representational government) following suit, though with greater diversity and heterogeneity. "Globalization" is the current term to refer to these profound changes in world cultures.

Thus, in terms of societal patterns and structures, similarities in modernized/modernizing societies' lifestyles are notable. However, even at this level of societal transformations, the claim of a coherent "convergence" on the western model or the identification of modernization with westernization is not fully valid. This is because these modifications are manifested in more complex ways that make them somewhat different from the prototypical western patterns. For example, in the fast growing metropolitan cities in the "majority world," along with a highly specialized organized labor force, there is also an unspecialized, undifferentiated "informal" economy, as in the case of street vendors; or urban structures existing side by side with semi-urban settlements that manifest many rural/traditional patterns of living.

These complexities or variations from the western model constitute instances of evidence opposing the "convergence" hypothesis of the modernization paradigm. They are not to be easily brushed off as transitional "on their way toward" the western model. First of all, these more complex and diverse patterns appear to have a great deal of stability and resistance to change. Secondly, they tend to be more adaptive or functional solutions to problems faced by people undergoing rapid social change and development, as well as being more in line with their cultural outlooks and preferences.

The diversifications and complexities, thus, necessitate that "modernization" be distinguished from "westernization" and that it should be recognized that there might be multiple pathways to modernization or more generally to social change and development. Furthermore, in addition to different routes, there may also be different end points (other than the western endpoint). Indeed, there may be different modernizations, despite the commonalities noted above. This has also been recognized in sociological critiques of the modernization paradigm, who for example question the assumed antithesis between tradition and modernity and talk about the emergence of new "traditions" in the modern or the post modern era (e.g., Abraham, 1980). Thus "modernism" is now being contrasted with "postmodernism," not with tradition, and no progression from a less to a more "developed" societal state is assumed.

From a cross-cultural perspective, particularly focusing on the modernization experience of the East and South-East Asian countries in the last decades, Marsella and Choi (1993) make the point that the process is not "westernization" but rather "easternization." They note that "the doctrine of convergence" (toward the West) is ethnocentric and that "each society [...] modernize[s] by capitalizing on its own cultural heritage and traditions" (p. 206). Thus, it is claimed that the great economic "modernization" of the East has been accomplished not by acquiring western ideologies but rather by the consolidation and optimization of eastern worldviews for societal progress. The "Five Tigers" (Japan, Korea, Hong Kong, Taiwan, Singapore) adopted western technology but did not change their "psychologies" (Morishima, 1982); thus "they borrowed from the West, but they did not become Western"; instead, "they created a unique pattern and process of modernization that was specific to their cultural history and traditions" (Marsella & Choi, 1993, p. 203). In this process, many of the "individualistic" characteristics of modernization, such as individuality, materialism, self-sufficiency, independence from family, etc., were conspicuously absent; rather, "collectivistic" characteristics such as self-sacrifice, family ties, loyalty, endurance, respect for authority, etc., were optimally utilized for economic growth.

Individualization as Psychological Modernization

This last point brings us to the crux of the matter – the current status of psychological modernization or the individual modernity paradigm. The complexities and diversifications noted in economic, political, and sociocultural modernization, despite commonalities in changing lifestyles, are even more the case in psychological modernization. For example, Trommsdorff (1983) showed that strong traditional values such as group solidarity, interpersonal harmony, familism, etc., coexisted with "modern" values such as achievement and competition, and that along with democratic values there were beliefs in hierarchical relationships, obedience, and gender inequality among the Japanese. Similar complex findings defying the assumed coherence of modernization are reported in much research.

As shown by Yang (1988) and discussed above, most of the psychological characteristics constituting individual modernity in the research and thinking of the 1950s to 1970s can be subsumed under "individualism" as understood today in cross-cultural psychology (for reviews see Kagitçibasi, 1994, 1997; Kim, Triandis, Kagitçibasi, Choi, & Yoon, 1994; Triandis, 1995). The general assumption of much current research is that as societies and groups modernize, they become more individualistic (Georgas, 1989; Hofstede, 1980; Klages, this volume; Triandis, 1984, 1988, 1995). As Hofstede (1991) claims, "Modernization corresponds to individualization" (p. 74). In turn, as individualism is a prototypical human characteristic of the West, clearly, the modernization/westernization paradigm is still strong.

However, there is also a growing questioning of this perspective as being rather simplistic and not doing justice to the complexities in human patterns (e.g., Abraham, 1980; Jacobs, 1985; Kagitçibasi, 1996a, 1998; Marsella & Choi, 1993; Nash, 1984). It may be that just as in the case of societal patterns some of which undergo similar changes accompanying urbanization and social structural change while others present diversity, changing lifestyles may also differentially influence human patterns. In other words, while some human patterns change to become more similar in response to changing environmental demands, others may be oblivious to such demands. Which ones will change to become more similar across societies, and which ones will manifest diversity is an empirical question. Contextual/ functional conceptualizations can help in understanding the "what's" and the "why's" involved. The human patterns that have been under special scrutiny involve self-other relations, family relations, and child-rearing orientations.

Refinement in Conceptualization

Kagitçibasi (1990, 1996a, 1996b, 1997) has proposed a conceptual framework in an attempt to understand the nature of individualism/collectivism, the self, and the family in sociocultural context. Some of this conceptualization is of relevance to the issues discussed above.

To start out with, a distinction between "normative" and "relational" individual-ism/collectivism (Kagitçibasi, 1997, pp. 34-39) may provide clues with respect to the assumed "progression" toward individualism with modernization and economic development. Normative individualism/collectivism is more relevant at the cultural than at the individual level because it has more to do with societal values and con-ventions regarding what is right or wrong rather than individual tendencies. Basi-cally, normative collectivism is based on the premise that individual interests are to be subordinated to (in)group interests. Normative individualism, on the other hand, upholds individual interests against group domination. Most cross-cultural research and theory on individualism/collectivism have dealt with normative individual-ism/collectivism, particularly values (e.g., Georgas, 1989; Hofstede, 1980; Hui & Triandis, 1986; Triandis, 1988, 1995). Relational individualism/collectivism, on the other hand, has to do with the boundaries of the self and with self-other relations, particularly interpersonal distance. This refers to the degree of separateness or con-nectedness of individuals, ranging from the separated self (-other relations) to the related self (-other relations).

Given the above conceptualization, normative individualism/collectivism would be expected to be more responsive to modernization and societal change. Relational individualism/collectivism, however, would not be so much affected by societal changes because it is more of a psychological level variable and not necessitated or challenged to the same extent by social structural changes. Indeed, it is normative individualism/collectivism that gets confused with modernization vs. tradition. Since normative customs, values, and practices change in response to socioeconomic de-velopment, normative collectivism tends to weaken with changing lifestyles to be replaced by normative individualism, as predicted by modernization theory.

Common patterns of change in families in collectivistic societies undergoing so-cial structural changes, particularly urbanization, provide fertile ground for under-standing which human patterns change and which ones persist in the face of social structural change and why (Kagitçibasi, 1990, 1996a). For example, with increased urbanization, education, and affluence, the elderly become financially more self-sufficient, thus "material interdependencies" between generations decrease. In peas-ant society, children are the main source of "old-age security" for the elderly par-ents. In such a context, obedience oriented child rearing is seen, and the child's autonomy is not tolerated. This is because an autonomous child may grow up to be an independent adult who might attend to his own individual needs rather than be loyal to the family. Such an outlook is a threat to family integrity over the family life cycle. With urbanization and increased affluence, however, other sources of old-age security emerge, such as pensions, social security benefits, etc., which decrease reliance of the elderly parents on the grown-up offspring for financial support. When the growing child's autonomy is no longer a threat to family integrity, it is tolerated more, and full obedience to parents is not any longer aspired for. Thus, hierarchical intergenerational relations would also be expected to weaken (see also Nauck, this volume). This is an instance of normative collectivism decreasing with changing lifestyles.

However, the close "psychological" bonds between generations may continue, even though material interdependencies weaken (Kagitçibasi, 1990, 1996a). This latter has to do with relational collectivism at the interpersonal psychological level rather than at the normative level. Indeed, recent research shows that the changes in family interaction patterns often do not follow the linear route from collectivism to individualism, as predicted by modernization theory (for reviews see Kagitçibasi, 1996a, 2004). In "cultures of relatedness" where interpersonal distances are small between connected selves, individuals and families do not shift toward individualistic separateness with urbanization and socioeconomic development. As mentioned above, connectedness continues, though mainly in the realm of psychological interdependencies, while material interdependencies weaken with changing lifestyles. Thus, it may be claimed that psychological bonds may be untouched by normative changes; indeed how normative individualism/collectivism is realized at the individual level is not independent from relational individualism/collectivism. These transformations lead to a "family model of psychological interdependence" (Kagitçibasi, 1990, 1996a) that is different from both the traditional (rural) family, characterized by "total interdependence," and also the individualistic urban western middle class family, characterized by "independence." However, it is also similar to each in some ways. The functional underpinnings of the distinction between material and psychological interdependencies and why they are differentially affected by social structural changes are discussed below.

Autonomous-Related Self

The emerging pattern in the family model of psychological interdependence is complex, as it involves both autonomy and connectedness in child rearing, with the resultant "autonomous-related self" (Kagitçibasi, 1996b). Child rearing still involves control, rather than permissiveness, since the goal is not individualistic separation. However, autonomy also emerges in child rearing mainly for two reasons. First, autonomy of the child is no longer seen as a danger, since elderly parents are no longer dependent on their grown up offspring for their material livelihood. In the traditional interdependent family autonomy of the child is not desired because an autonomous child may grow up to be an independent (separate) adult who may look after his/her own self interest rather than supporting the elderly parents. This is a threat to the livelihood of the interdependent family through its life cycle. However, with increased affluence, material dependence on the grown up offspring decreases, with the corresponding tolerance of autonomy in child rearing.

Second, autonomy of the growing person is functional in urban lifestyles where, for example, decision making, rather than obedience, is required in school and in more specialized jobs. In the traditional context, age-old traditions may endure as worthwhile guidelines, as for example in subsistence agriculture. This makes obedi-ence to parents adaptive for rather stable lifestyles. However, with changing life-styles and particularly with urbanization, mere obedience does not get very far for advancing in education and specialized work contexts; autonomy becomes adaptive. Thus, with economic and sociocultural modernization parents come to tolerate, even possibly value, autonomy in child rearing. Nevertheless, this does not mean separa-tion. While autonomy is implicated for adaptation to urban technological society, there is no parallel implication for separateness. Socialization patterns and psycho-logical orientations that are not incompatible with the demands of changing life-styles continue to be maintained. Interpersonal connectedness appears to be such an orientation.

The coexistence of autonomy with connectedness is important, as the two are of-ten seen to be antithetical. Under the influence of psychoanalytic thinking, particu-larly object relations theory and the "separation-individuation hypothesis" (Mahler, 1972), separation is considered to be a requisite of autonomy in human develop-ment. Therefore, the implication is that connected selves cannot be adequately autonomous. This is an abiding view that has influenced both, psychological theory and application, particularly regarding adolescence, which is considered to entail the second separation-individuation process (Blos, 1979). Therefore, distancing (de-tachment) from parents is seen to be necessary for the development of autonomy (Kroger, 1998; Steinberg & Silverberg, 1986). It reflects the individualistic world-view stressing the value of independence, self-reliance, and self-sufficiency. It also greatly influences popular psychology, as in "self-help" books; a prime example is the title, "How to be Your Own Best Friend"!

An individualistic conceptualization of autonomy, construing it as separateness, in fact confounds two independent underlying dimensions. One of these has to do with interpersonal distance, ranging from separateness to relatedness. The other has to do with agency, ranging from autonomy to heteronomy (dependency) (Kagitçi-basi, 1996a). Given the logical and psychological independence of these two dimen-sions, it is possible to have different poles of each to coexist. Thus a combination of autonomy with relatedness is possible, though the understanding that one can be both autonomous and connected is not readily recognized in traditional developmen-tal, personality, and clinical psychology. However, more recently there is an increas-ing acceptance that both autonomy and relatedness are basic needs and are compati-ble (e.g., Blatt & Blass, 1996; Guisinger & Blatt, 1994; Raeff, 1997; Ryan & Solky, 1996).

Research and theory in adolescent adjustment, in particular, shows that a close, positive relationship with parents, rather than detachment from them, promotes the development of healthy autonomy (Grotevant & Cooper, 1986; Ryan, Deci, & Grol-nick, 1995; Ryan & Lynch, 1989). Attachment research also points to the positive association between "autonomous" (i.e. secure) attachment and positive relation-ships with parents (Grossmann, Grossmann, & Zimmermann, 1999; Zimmermann & Grossmann, 1997). This seems to be the case even in western individualistic society.

This is not to say that there are no differences between the western and non-western patterns, but apparently the differences are more a matter of degree than of kind. Thus the "autonomous-related self" and the "family model of psychological interdependence" that nourishes the development of this type of self appear to be more psychologically healthy models than the individualistic models upholding separateness.

Recent Research Evidence

Recent research evidence provides support for the complex synthetic patterns which differ from both the traditional collectivistic and the traditional (western) individualistic patterns.

The following are some studies that have supported or would imply "the family model of psychological interdependence" and/or "the autonomous-related self" (Kagitçibasi, 1996a, 1996b).

Kim, Butzel, and Ryan (1998) showed a more positive relation between autonomy and relatedness than between autonomy and separateness in both, Korean and American samples, providing support to the construct of the autonomous-related self. Chou (2000) found the two components of "emotional autonomy" (Steinberg & Silverberg, 1986), individuation, and de-idealization of parents, to be associated with depression in adolescents from Hong Kong, and Aydin and Oztutuncu (2001) found depression and negative schema to be associated with separateness in adolescents but not with high parental control. Finally, Ryan, and Lynch (1989) and Ryan, Stiller, and Lynch (1994) in the U.S. found positive rather than negative links between relatedness to parents and autonomy in adolescents.

A number of studies on parenting show the apparently conflicting tendencies of control and autonomy, often assumed to be incompatible, to coexist in child rearing, as proposed in the family model of psychological interdependence. For example, Lin and Fu (1990) found a combined autonomy and control orientation in Chinese parents, and Cha (1994) found both control and encouragement of autonomy in Korean parents' child rearing. Also in line with this family model, Imamoglu (1987) found low SES Turkish parents to stress material interdependence with their grown-up offspring, but modernized middle/upper SES Turkish parents to value autonomy and closeness. Similarly, Phalet and Schönpflug (2001) found that among Turkish immigrants in Germany parental autonomy goals for children do not imply separateness, and that achievement values are associated with parental collectivism, not individualism. Stewart, Bond, Deeds, and Chung (1999) in Hong Kong found persistence of family interdependencies together with some individualistic values. Family relatedness and parental control were seen in highly educated and affluent families, showing these family characteristics to be compatible with urban modern living. Similarly, Jose, Huntsinger, Huntsinger, and Liaw (2000) found Chinese and Chinese

American parents to endorse both relatedness and autonomy, together with high control of and closeness with their children.

The developmental roots may be located in mother-infant interactions. Keller and colleagues (Keller, et al., 2001) found German and Greek mothers to be similar in interactional orientations which lead to the development of agency in the young child but different in terms of promoting separateness, the German mothers stressing separateness more. Similarly, work with mother-child interactions in France (Suizzo, 2002) and in the Netherlands (Harkness, Super, & Tijen, 2000) has also noted an emphasis on agency but not on separateness. This is different from Anglo-American parents' insistence on separateness and disapproval of their children's displays of dependence (Suizzo, 2002, p.304).

Thus, research across cultures questions the assumed coherence (syndrome) of psychological modernization as individualization and the assumed convergence toward the western pattern, as westernization. Even the research conducted in the USA points to patterns other than the prototypical individualistic one, such as the coexistence of autonomy and relatedness, hitherto not adequately recognized in psychology. Indeed, it seems that accompanying multifaceted societal modernization, psychological modernization also manifests multiple outlooks. In this context, the autonomous-related self, entailing agency without separateness, appears to be a healthy model, since it addresses both of the two basic human needs, for autonomy and relatedness. As evidenced by recent research, this is more enriching than the prototypical individualistic and the collectivistic models that stress only autonomy or relatedness, respectively. Therefore, if there is a convergence of different human-family patterns, it is more likely to be toward the synthetic models of the autonomous-related self and the psychologically interdependent family.

Nevertheless, there is a caveat here. The above discussion is based on a functional analysis of individual- and family-society interface, pointing to the modifications in human-family patterns in adapting to changing lifestyles that accompany societal transformations. It does not address extraneous influences, particularly "cultural diffusion" through the mass media. With the increasing globalization of the mass media that is dominated by western, especially American sources, western individualistic patterns are being exported to the rest of the world as the "most advanced" human models to be emulated. Thus, even though not necessarily the most healthy or adaptive, the western individualistic model may indeed spread with globalization. However, if this happens, it would be because of cultural diffusion or acculturation, not because the individualistic pattern is the most adaptive to modern lifestyles, as assumed by the evolutionist "convergence" hypothesis of the modernization theory. If an awareness of the value of both autonomy and relatedness could be created at a global level, then such a trend could be thwarted. Culturally informed psychology could have a role to play in building such awareness.

Summary and Conclusion

Understanding and explaining change at various levels – societal, group, and individual – has been a challenge for the social and behavioral sciences. The modernization paradigm was put forth in facing this challenge. Modernization paradigm is an outgrowth of a social evolutionist worldview that considers whatever is different from the western pattern as deficient and bound to change with socioeconomic development. This change is thus seen to entail a necessary convergence on the western human model and is equated with westernization. In this way it provided a rather coherent portrait of global change as a convergence on the western pattern. Though some aspects of predicted changes have materialized to form common patterns, others have not, weakening the assumed coherence of westernization.

Though out of favor in sociology, modernization theory is nevertheless ubiquitous in everyday parlance, as well as in social science discourse, and appears to have acquired a new visage in "Individualism-Collectivism." The modernization prediction of a shift toward westernization is now being replaced with a prediction of a shift toward individualism. The basic issue is whether "Individualism-Collectivism" serves as a new "Modernization Paradigm" in explaining changes in societies.

To a large extent, psychology accepted the assumptions of unidirectional change. At the psychological level the concept of individual modernity, and its successor, individualism, were offered to explain the human aspects of the convergence toward the western model. However, more recent cultural and cross-cultural research has pointed to complex individual, interpersonal, and familial patterns that defy the assumption of a simple shift toward individualism and that require functional/contextual analysis. The observed diversities and complexities call for innovative approaches providing "integrative syntheses" of change and continuity, of the common and the different in human patterns.

This research challenges the "convergence" hypothesis underlying both modernization theory and individualism-collectivism. Indeed, as societies modernize (with increased urbanization, education, affluence, etc.), they do not necessarily demonstrate a shift toward western individualism. A more complex transformation is seen in family patterns of modernizing societies with cultures of relatedness. The emerging pattern shares important characteristics with both individualism and collectivism while as the synthesis of the two, it is significantly different from each. The implications for changes in families, parenting and the resultant development of the self are far reaching and need to be better understood.

References

Abraham, M. (1980). *Perspectives on modernization: Toward a general theory of third world development.* Washington, DC: University Press of America.

Aydin, B., & Oztutuncu, F. (2001). Examination of adolescents' negative thoughts, depressive mood, and family environment. *Adolescence, 36*, 77-83.

Bendix, R. (1967). Tradition and modernity reconsidered. *Comparative Studies in Society and History, 9*, 292-346.

Blatt, S., & Blass, R. B. (1996). Relatedness and self-definition: A dialectic model of personality development. In G. G. Noam & K. W. Fischer (Eds.), *Development and vulnerability in close relationships* (pp. 309-338). Mahwah, NJ: Erlbaum.

Blos, P. (1979). *The adolescent passage*. New York: International Universities Press.

Caldwell, J. C. (1977). Towards a restatement of demographic transition theory. In J. C. Caldwell (Ed.), *The persistence of high fertility* (pp. 25-122). Canberra, Australia: Australian National University.

Cha, J. H. (1994). Changes in value belief, attitude, and behavior of the Koreans over the past 100 years. *Korean Journal of Psychology: Social, 8*, 40-58.

Chou, K.-L. (2000). Emotional autonomy and depression among Chinese adolescents. *Journal of Genetic Psychology, 161*, 161-169.

Dawson, J. L. M. (1967). Tradition versus Western attitudes in West Africa: The construction, validation and application of a measuring device. *British Journal of Social and Clinical Psychology, 6*, 81-96.

Doob, L. W. (1967). Scales for assaying psychological modernization in Africa. *Public Opinion Quaterly, 31*, 414-421.

Eisenstadt, S. N. (1987). Historical traditions, modernization, and development. In S. N. Eisenstadt (Ed.), *Patterns of modernity* (pp. 1-11). London: Frances Pinter.

Georgas, J. (1989). Changing family values in Greece: From collectivist to individualist. *Journal of Cross-Cultural Psychology, 20*, 80-91.

Grotevant, H. D., & Cooper, C. R. (1986). Individuation in family relationships. *Human Development, 29*, 82-100.

Guisinger, S., & Blatt, S. J. (1994). Individuality and relatedness: Evolution of a fundamental dialectic. *American Psychologist, 49*, 104-111.

Gusfield, J. R. (1967). Tradition and modernity: Misplaced polarities in the study of social change. *American Journal of Sociology, 73*, 351-362.

Guthrie, G. M. (1970). *The psychology of modernization in rural Philippines*. Manila, Philippines: Ateneo de Manila University Press.

Guthrie, G. M. (1977). A socio-psychological analysis of modernization in the Philippines. *Journal of Cross-Cultural Psychology, 8*, 177-206.

Grossmann, K. E., Grossmann, K., & Zimmermann, P. (1999). A wider view of attachment and exploration. In J. Cassidy & P. R. Shaver (Eds.), *Handbook of attachment: Theory, research, and clinical applications*. (pp. 760-786). New York: The Guilford Press.

Grotevant, H. D., & Cooper, C. R. (1986). Individuation in family relationships: A perspective on individual differences in the development of identity and role-taking skill in adolescence. *Human Development, 29*, 82-100.

Hagen, E. E. (1962). *On the theory of social change.* Homewood, IL: Dorsey Press.

Harkness, S., Super, C. M., & van Tijen, N. (2000). Individualism and the "Western mind" reconsidered: American and Dutch parents' ethnotheories of the child. In W. Damon (Series Ed.), S. Harkness, C. Raeff, & C. M. Super (Vol. Eds.), *New directions for child and adolescent development, 87. Variability in the social construction of the child* (pp. 23-39). San Francisco, CA: Jossey Bass.

Hofstede, G. (1980). *Culture's consequences: International differences in work-related values.* Beverly Hills, CA: Sage.

Hofstede, G. (1991). *Cultures and Organizations: Software of the mind.* London: McGraw-Hill.

Hui, C. H., & Triandis, H. C. (1986). Individualism-Collectivism: A study of cross-cultural researchers. *Journal of Cross-Cultural Psychology, 17,* 225-248.

Huntington, S. P. (1966). Political modernization: America vs. Europe. *World Politics, 18,* 378-414.

Imamoglu, E. O. (1987). An interdependence model of human development. In Ç. Kagitçibasi (Ed.), *Growth and progress* (pp. 138-145). Lisse, The Netherlands: Swets & Zeitlinger.

Inkeles, A. (1969). Making men modern. On the causes and consequences of individual change in six developing countries. *American Journal of Sociology, 75,* 208-225.

Inkeles, A., & Smith, D. H. (1974). *Becoming modern: Individual changes in six developing countries.* Cambridge, MA: Harvard University Press.

Jacobs, N. (1985). *The Korean road to modernization and development.* Chicago: University of Illinois Press.

Jose, P. E., Huntsinger, C. S., Huntsinger, P. R., & Liaw, F.-R. (2000). Parental values and practices relevant to young children's social development in Taiwan and the United States. *Journal of Cross-Cultural Psychology, 31,* 677-702.

Kagitçibasi, Ç. (1970). Social norms and authoritarianism: A Turkish-American comparison. *Journal of Personality and Social Psychology, 16,* 444-451.

Kagitçibasi, Ç. (1990) Family and socialization in cross-cultural perspective: A model of change. In J. Berman (Ed.), *Cross-cultural perspectives: Nebraska symposium on motivation, 1989* (Vol. 37, pp. 135-200). Lincoln, NE: University of Nebraska Press.

Kagitçibasi, Ç. (1994). A critical appraisal of individualism and collectivism: Toward a new formulation. In U. Kim, H. C. Triandis, Ç. Kagitçibasi, S.-C. Choi, & G. Yoon (Eds.), *Individualism and Collectivism: Theory, method, and applications* (pp. 52-65). Thousand Oaks, CA: Sage.

Kagitçibasi, Ç. (1996a) *Family and human development across cultures: A view from the other side.* Hillsdale, NJ: Erlbaum.

Kagitçibasi, Ç. (1996b) The autonomous-relational self: A new synthesis. *European Psychologist, 1,* 180-186.

Kagitçibasi, Ç. (1997). Individualism and collectivism. In J. W. Berry, M. H. Segall, & Ç. Kagitçibasi (Eds.), *Handbook of cross-cultural psychology: Vol. 3. Social psychology* (2nd ed., pp. 1-50). Boston: Allyn and Bacon.

Kagitçibasi, Ç. (1998). Whatever happened to modernization: Individual modernity with a new name. *Cross-Cultural Psychological Bulletin, December, 8-11.*

Kagitçibasi, Ç. (2004). *Autonomy and relatedness in cultural context: Implications for family, parenting and human development.* Manuscript submitted for publication.

Kahl, J. A. (1968). *The measurement of modernism: A study of values in Brazil and Mexico.* Austin, TX: University of Texas Press.

Keller, H., Papaligoura, Z., Künsemüller, P., Völker, S., Papaliou, C., Lohaus, A., Lamm, B., Kokkinaki, N., Chrysikou, L., & Mousouli, V. (2001, August). *Concepts of Mother-Infant Interaction in Greece and Germany.* Paper presented at the X. European Conference on Developmental Psychology, Uppsala, Sweden.

Kim, U., Triandis, H. C., Kagitçibasi, Ç., Choi, S.-C., & Yoon, G. (Eds.). (1994). *Individualism and Collectivism: Theory, method and applications.* Thousand Oaks, CA: Sage.

Kim, Y., Butzel, J. S., & Ryan, R. M. (1998, June). *Interdependence and well-being: A function of culture and relatedness needs,* Paper presented at the International Society for the Study of Personal Relationships, Saratoga Spring, NY.

Kroger, J. (1998). Adolescence as a second separation-individuation process: Critical review of an object relations approach. In E. E. A. Skoe & A. L. von der Lippe (Eds.), *Personality development in adolescence: A cross-national and life span perspective. Adolescence and society.* (pp. 172-192). New York: Routledge.

Lerner, D. (1958). *The passing of traditional society: Modernizing Middle East.* New York: Free Press.

Lin, C.-Y., & Fu, V. R. (1990). A comparison of child-rearing practices among Chinese, immigrant Chinese, and Caucasian-American parents. *Child Development, 61,* 429-433.

Mahler, M. (1972). On the first three phases of the separation-individuation process. *International Journal of Psychoanalysis, 53,* 333-338.

Marsella, A., & Choi, S.-C. (1993). Psychological aspects of modernization and economic development in East Asian Nations. *Psychologia, 36,* 201-219.

Mazrui, A. (1968). From social Darwinism to current theories of modernization. *World Politics, 21,* 69-83.

McClelland, D. C. (1961). *The achieving society.* Princeton, NJ: Van Nostrand.

McClelland, D. C., & Winters, D. G. (1969). *Motivating economic achievement.* New York: Free Press.

Morgan, L. H. (1877). *Ancient society.* New York: Henry Holt.

Morishima, M. (1982). *Why has Japan "succeeded?" Western technology and Japanese ethos.* Cambridge, UK: Cambridge University Press.

Muschinske, D. (1977). The non-white as a child: G. Stanley Hall on the education of non-white peoples. *Journal of the History of the Behavioral Sciences, 13*, 328-336.

Nash, M. (1984). *Unfinished agenda: The dynamics of modernization in developing nations.* Boulder, CO: Westview Press.

Ozdalga, E. (2002). Contrasting modernities. In R. Liljeström & E. Ozdalga (Eds.), *Autonomy and dependence in the family* (pp. 3-16). Istanbul, Turkey: Swedish Research Center.

Phalet, K., & Schönpflug, U. (2001). Intergenerational transmission of collectivism and achievement values in two acculturation contexts. The case of Turkish families in Germany and Turkish and Moroccan families in The Netherlands. *Journal of Cross-Cultural Psychology, 32*, 186-201.

Raeff, C. (1997). Individuals and relationships: Cultural values, children's social interactions, and the development of an American individualistic self. *Developmental Review, 17*, 205-238.

Ryan, R. M., Deci, E. L., & Grolnick, W. S. (1995). Autonomy, relatedness, and the self: Their relation to development and psychopathology. In D. Cicchetti & D. J. Cohen (Eds.), *Developmental Psychopathology* (Vol. 1, pp. 618-655). New York: Wiley.

Ryan, R. M., & Lynch, J. H. (1989). Emotional autonomy versus detachment: Revisiting the vicissitudes of adolescence and young adulthood. *Child Development, 60*, 340-356.

Ryan, R. M., & Solky, J. (1996). What is supportive about social support? On the psychological needs for autonomy and relatedness. In G. R. Pierce, B. K. Sarason, & I. G. Sarason (Eds.), *Handbook of social support and the family* (pp. 249-267). New York: Plenum.

Ryan, R. M., Stiller, J., & Lynch, J. H. (1994). Representations of relationships to teachers, parents, and friends as predictors of academic motivation and self-esteem. *Journal of Early Adolescence, 14*, 226-249.

Schnaiberg, A. (1970). Rural-urban residence and modernism: A study of Ankara Province, Turkey. *Demography, 7*, 71-85.

Schwartz, S. H. (1994). Beyond individualism/collectivism: New cultural dimensions of values. In U. Kim, H. C. Triandis, Ç. Kagitçibasi, S.-C. Choi, & G. Yoon (Eds.), *Individualism and collectivism: Theory, method, and applications* (pp. 85-122). Thousand Oaks, CA: Sage.

Segall, M. H., Dasen, P. R., Berry, J. W., & Poortinga, Y. H. (1990). *Human behavior in global perspective.* New York: Pergamon.

Spencer, H. (1876). *Principles of sociology.* New York: D. Appleton.

Steinberg, L., & Silverberg, S. B. (1986). The vicissitudes of autonomy in early adolescence. *Child Development, 57*, 841-851.

Stewart, S. M., Bond, M. H., Deeds, O., & Chung, S. F. (1999). Intergenerational patterns of values and autonomy expectations in cultures of relatedness and separateness. *Journal of Cross-Cultural Psychology, 30*, 575-593.

Suizzo, M. A. (2002). French parents' cultural models and childrearing beliefs. *International Journal of Behavioral Development, 26, 297-307.*

Triandis, H. C. (1984). Toward a psychological theory of economic growth. *International Journal of Psychology, 19,* 79-95.

Triandis, H. C. (1988). Collectivism and individualism: A reconceptualization of a basic concept in cross-cultural psychology. In G. K. Verma & C. Bagley (Eds.), *Personality attitudes and cognitions* (pp. 60-95). London: MacMillan.

Triandis, H. C. (1995). *Individualism and Collectivism.* Boulder, CO: Westview.

Trommsdorff, G. (1983). Value change in Japan. *International Journal of Intercultural Relations, 7,* 337-360.

Tylor, E. B. (1865). *Researches into the early history of mankind and development of civilization.* London: John Murray.

Ward, R. E., & Rustow, D. A. (1964). *Political modernization in Japan and Turkey.* Princeton, NJ: Princeton University Press.

Werner, H. (1948). *Comparative psychology of mental development.* New York: Science Editions. (Rev. ed. 1957. New York: International Universities Press)

Yang, K. S. (1981). The formation of change of Chinese personality: A cultural-ecological perspective. *Acta Psychologica Taiwanica, 23,* 39-56. [Original in Chinese]

Yang, K. S. (1988). Will societal Modernization eventually eliminate cross-cultural psychological differences? In M. H. Bond (Ed.), *The cross-cultural challenge to social psychology* (pp. 67-85). London: Sage.

Zimmermann, P., & Grossmann, K. E. (1997). Attachment and adaptation in adolescence. In W. Koops, J. B. Hoeksma, & D. C. van den Boom (Eds.), *Development of interaction and attachment: Traditional and non-traditional approaches* (pp. 281-282). Amsterdam: North Holland.

12

Modernization and Value Change

Helmut Klages

Introduction

The relationship between modernization and value change is too complex as to be treated comprehensively in a paper such as the following one. Therefore, this chapter will proceed in a selective manner and explore *three aspects* of this theme. *First,* the dramatic nature of value change that the developed world has been experiencing since the sixties will be demonstrated. Data from Germany will serve as the main source in this context. *Second,* I wish to deal critically with a variety of outstanding attempts at conceptualizing the relationships between modernization and value change. Let it be stated beforehand that these attempts only fail because their explanative powers are too low in view of the available data. *Third,* a more successful approach of dealing with the obviously existing problem will be presented.

The Evidence of Rapid Value Change

To start off, time-series data from Germany is presented covering the period between 1951 and 2001, and demonstrating the remarkable scope of the ongoing value change:

The three lines in the chart depict the development of the scoring of three groups of educative values in the (West) German population (from top to bottom the labels of the groups read: "orientation to self-reliance and autonomy," "orientation to orderliness and diligence," and "orientation to obedience and subordination"). If one

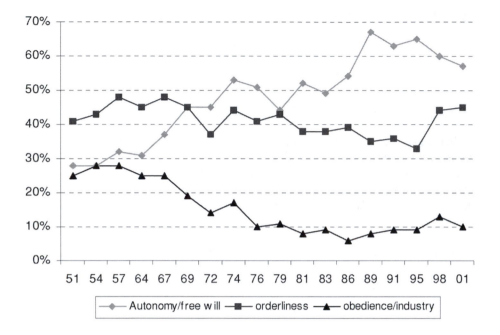

Figure 1. Preferential Educational Values in Germany from 1951 to 2001 (only former states of FRG). (Source: EMNID, 2001).

follows the top and bottom lines from left to right, one discovers a scissor-like movement of dramatic character. Self-reliance and autonomy rise during this period from an agreement-quota of 25% to more than 60%, whereas obedience and subordination descend from 28% to about 10% or less.

The available data from other countries quite clearly demonstrate that in all highly developed nations a rapid and deep-reaching value change has been taking place over the past decades. Furthermore the basic trend of this value change, indicated by the changing positions of the top and bottom lines in the chart, appears to proceed in the same direction in all these countries. If one exercises generosity with respect to differences in sampling-methods and labels, one may utilize the whole bulk of data from many nations presented, for instance, by Ronald Inglehart in his comparative work on "Culture Shift" (1990) for propping up this thesis with ample empirical evidence. Furthermore one might turn to the multi-national study "Culture's Consequences" by Geert Hofstede (2001) to find additional confirmation. In this volume Cigdem Kagitçibasi makes it clear that there is ample reason to not simply speak of "westernization" in this context, and to be cautious with respect to the categorization of the direction of the change. Nevertheless, one cannot fail to notice that there is near to unanimous agreement among researchers exploring value change as an international phenomenon, that the general course of this change (its "trajectory") can be labeled "individualistic," although Kagitçibasi is certainly right when she warns against a simplistic understanding of this term. When Hofstede computed the correlation of his Individualism Index with wealth in terms of GNP/capita, the correlation coefficient,was a striking r = .84*** (Hofstede, 2001, p. 251). If one takes GNP/capita as a measure of a country's level of socio-economic modernization, one will be able to infer that Hofstede's findings point towards a surprisingly strong individualistic direction in changing values, related to this process of societal change.

The *impact* of this value change on social attitudes and social behavior is enormous. Our research group analyzed this impact over several years in different areas. The result was that in nearly every case the value change was able to explain a larger portion of the respective variance in terms of R^2. So, for instance, it was found that the political attitudes of the (West) German population could be explained to a greater extent by value variables than by socio-demographic variables normally utilized in social sciences for explaining attitudinal characteristics. Again and again the hypothesis that value change is a variable with outstanding explanative and predictive power was confirmed for highly developed societies.

I must admit that over a long time I did not deal intensively with the reverse question of the *explanation* of value change. Exploiting the explanative and predictive power of value change required most of my time and energy (Klages, 1985). Even today my empirical research still concentrates in this direction. In the course of time it has become apparent to me, however, that the explanation of value change itself cannot be left out of consideration indefinitely, although it seemed clear from the very start that this was tricky territory (Klages, 2002).

According to a still lingering tradition of sociological thinking, rapid value change, as it is demonstrated by the chart, is strictly speaking impossible. According to this tradition of thinking, with its roots in basic premises of the American branch of cultural anthropology, individual value orientations are regarded as deeply embedded elements of the basic personality structure. They are seen as being internalized and fixed during the socialization process, preferentially in its first stages. If we look at the situation from this perspective, a rapid value change, comprising the majority of various age groups in the population, can hardly be expected. Inglehart, acting as one of the decisive pioneers in the discovery of the rapid value changing process, tried to move out of the firing-line by stressing those facts that pointed to intergenerational alterations as a source of value change, and by obliterating other facts that point at intragenerational changes (Inglehart, 1990). Nevertheless there are still several sociologists who regard the topic of rapid value change as suspect. Some have tried to avoid the problem by claiming that empirical value research has not actually been measuring genuine *value* orientations but *social attitudes*. Nobody, however, has been able to offer empirical methods measuring these assumed genuine value orientations behind the measured ones, or provide evidence of their deviating character. As a consequence the objections raised to the reality of rapid value change have been losing ground in sociology. But the basic question is still acute. How can rapid value change be explained without slaying one of the "holy cows" (challenging one of the basic fundamentals) of sociological thinking?

Actually a solution for the problem lies close at hand, and is possible merely by connecting some normally distinct pieces of sociological thinking. The very fact that rapid value change seems to be linked to the development of *modern* societies, or, stated more clearly, to the process of *societal modernization,* may serve as a bridge to the solution of the problem. It is generally accepted today that the process of modernization is substantially connected with a previously incomprehensible mutability and definitive alteration of structural patterns. When taking into account the ideas of Talcott Parsons (e.g., Parsons, 1978; Parsons & Shils, 1951) for instance, who is seen as one of the main representatives of structural-functional theory-building in sociology, one may understand rapid value change as the "subjective," i.e. attitudinal, aspect of rapid structural change occurring on an individual level. From there it may also become perceivable for traditionally minded sociologists that value orientations can possibly change in rapidly changing societies over the course of successive generations, or even within the life course of individual human beings.

It is clear, beyond a doubt, that the insight into a functional relationship between modernization and value change leads us a giant step forward. On the other hand, it is evident, that the modernization process as a whole cannot be used in an empirical meaningful way as an "explanans" of value change. Obviously this process has to be broken down into the variables that constitute it, if one wants to proceed to an empirically controllable explanation of its consequences on the attitudinal level.

Some Recent Attempts at Conceptualizing the Relationship between Modernization and Value Change

At this point the second aspect of the theme, mentioned previously, is considered. The following section of this paper intends to critically deal with some outstanding attempts at conceptualizing the relationship between modernization and value change, with the aim of setting up empirically controllable hypotheses. Here we propose to concentrate on *Geert Hofstede* and *Ronald Inglehart*; both prominent in the field of value research, and both border-crossers well known on an international level to sociologists and psychologists alike. Therefore it is plausible that both personalities are granted exclusive attention in an article whose limited scope imposes certain abbreviations in any case.

Geert Hofstede

Surprisingly enough *Hofstede* makes no attempt at utilizing structural-functional challenges or pressures in the process of societal modernization as a means of understanding rapid value change. Stated more directly, he does not deal with rapid value change at all. On the contrary, in the first sections of the Second Edition of his work "Culture's Consequences" he deals instead with the stability of national cultures. He makes it definitely clear that he regards the discovery and explanation of aspects of the stability of values as his decisive topic. In his words, the book is about "differences in national culture, and its primary objective is to provide evidence of differences and similarities among culture patterns of countries, these evincing in part very old historical roots (some, for instance, going back as far as the Roman Empire)" (Hofstede, 2001, p. 11).

In full accordance with the definition of his primary research interest, he develops a model of cultural dynamics that concentrates on "mechanisms in societies that permit the maintenance of stability in culture patterns across many generations." (Hofstede, 2001, p. 11) (see Figure 1).

In fact, scientific discovery, economy and technology show up in this model as forces that influence value systems. Hofstede, however, makes it clear that he is not in search of forces that trigger rapid cultural dynamics, but rather on mechanisms that enable culture to act as a "mental programming" making the "crystallization of history in the minds, hearts, and hands of the present generation" possible. (2001, p. 12) Consequently he is dealing in this context with national characters and national stereotypes and their origins in earlier stages of history (2001, p. 13 ff.).

One might be tempted to try to understand and categorize this theoretical position by tracing it back to a historically oriented research focus, in which aspects such as modernization and rapid change play no decisive role. In the following sections of his book Hofstede makes it quite clear, however, that he claims more than such a niche for individual predilections. In his words "cultures, especially national cultures, are extremely stable over time" (Hofstede, 2001, p. 34). He argues in this context against some authors, who hold the position that the contemporary world is under a growing influence of modern technology, and that based on this tendency a trend towards a cultural convergence among developed nations might be deduced.

Interestingly enough Hofstede – being an empirically minded researcher – states afterwards that "technological modernization is an important force toward cultural change that leads to somewhat similar developments in different societies, but does not wipe out variety" (2001, p. 34). There is no reason, in my opinion, to speak up against Hofstede when he formulates such statements. Here, as well as in other parts of his books, the reality of rapid change becomes visible through the wide gaps in the theoretical fence he has established around culture. One of these gaps occurs when Hofstede discovers the previously quoted striking correlation between GNP per capita and his Individualism Index. This index can be viewed as a suitable instrument for measuring dominant aspects of modern value structures and value changes. As was indicated before, the utilization of this instrument provides most convincing empirical evidence for the existence of a contra-intuitively strong relationship between socio-economic and technological modernization, and value change. It has to be regarded as another contra-intuitive fact, however, that Hofstede himself is not inclined to draw any substantial theoretical deference pointing in this direction from his own empirical data.

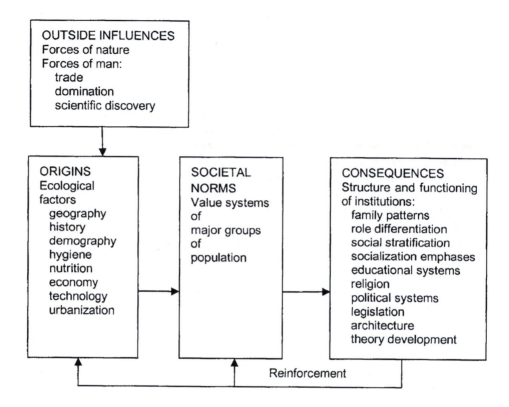

Figure 2. The Stabilizing of Culture Patterns According to G. Hofstede (2001, p. 12)

Ronald Inglehart

Differing sharply from Hofstede, Inglehart has persisted in bringing value change and modernization together by analyzing empirical data from several countries with hypotheses that clearly aim in this direction (Inglehart, 1990, 1997; Inglehart, Basanez & Moreno, 1998). In fact, he has been tremendously successful as an empirical researcher. He has considerably expanded existing knowledge on the character of contemporary value change in several parts of the world, and he is to be praised for this. Nevertheless, he also displays, though once again quite unwillingly, the enormous difficulties to be overcome, when wishing to snatch at the explanation of value change.

Inglehart deals with value change in modern societies by conferring prominence to the rise of so-called post-materialistic values, and develops an apparatus of hypotheses exactly suited to the explanation of this phenomenon. According to his scheme of explanation, value change can be traced back to the socio-economic components of the modernization process, specifically to the process of economic growth. According to Inglehart, a growing number of members of the younger generations, whose values have not yet been fixed, feel relieved by this progress away from former scarcity-pressures. They are set free to develop more idealistic values. Since older people stick to older materialistic values, which were at stake in former levels of economic growth, i.e., in the time of their formative years, a conflict of values arises in modern societies, in which established social and political institutions also participate. Since these are largely dominated by older individuals, they tend to take the position of the older values and to act as barriers against value-change. This value conflict becomes politicized and is eventually transformed into a conflict between political parties with conflicting value orientations.

According to Inglehart the decisive variable explaining value change is economic change. However, in his view economic change does by no means determinate the qualitative nature of emerging values. Value change is endogenously based in the structure of the personal system. This personal system does not directly react to external challenges and pressures, which would allow an interpretation in accordance with a sociological structural-functional paradigm. Economic change only serves as a trigger activating the potentialities of the personal system, and not as a cause. Inglehart's position is quite definitely marked by the postulation of a prefixed potential of value developments inside man. These are triggered by internal psychological mechanisms as soon as external conditions allow for this. Quite consequently post-materialist values are not functional with respect to the prerequisites of economic growth. On the contrary, Inglehart, who developed his explanative scheme in light of the Flower Power movement of the sixties, the New Social Movements and a New Left at the beginning of the seventies, derives from his view of value change the hypothesis that an inevitable slowing down of economic growth will be observed in the future. This is based on the fact that a growing number of post-materialists are quite definitively not interested in investing personal attachment in economic affairs.

Inglehart believes that eventually post-materialist values are of an obstructive nature, and only interpretable on the basis of a non-sociological theory of personal system. This rests on the assumption of meta-functional sources of self-development, which aim at independently pre-defined goals. Quite obviously this is a rather speculative assumption, whose source Inglehart only incidentally reveals when he refers to Abraham Maslow's (1954) theory of human personality.

At this point, however, Inglehart creates a theoretical shield with which he blocks and stifles his own empirical orientation. For several years now, many critics have been nagging at the fundamentals of Inglehart's scheme by pointing out the possibility of deriving quite divergent results from his own empirical data. The decisive point has always been that the available value change data, if taken as a whole, does not just indicate a shift from materialists to post-materialists, but rather the emergence of qualitatively distinct value structures, that is to say, a process of pluralization of values.

Unfortunately Inglehart, who has devoted many years to committed empirical research, has always turned a blind eye to the very fact that in his data a numerical
majority of cases fall into a no-man's land besides materialists and post-materialists,
and that this majority lying outside his conceptual scheme shows a tendency to grow
even more over time. Inglehart regards this expanding majority as irrelevant, because it does not possess the criteria that he regards as significant. By doing this, he
becomes prey to a pitfall similar to the one responsible for Hofstede's theoretical
wreck. His explanative scheme intervenes at this point into the process of handling
empirical data, which are quite obviously forced with some violence into concordance with its theoretical premises. The weakness here is by no means merely a
technical one. Rather the crux of it can be discovered when Inglehart first set up his
explanative scheme, stating that the main consequences of the process of modernization is modern man's relief from the pressures of scarcity, and the resulting emancipation of an inborn self-development potential. Since it is only the emergence of the
post-materialists that corroborates his central thesis, he concentrates exclusively on
the data providing the expected empirical evidence, attributing irrelevance to the rest
of data. Of course, this indicates once again a strategic departure, from the principles
of theory-building, characterized by a binding linkage to empirical research as its
controlling force. The reciprocal functions of both agents are reversed. Thus, the
explanative scheme serves as the normative controlling force instead of the data,
thereby avoiding the true enemy, all that data endangering its recognition.

"Subjective Modernization" in Perspective: Individualization of Values

Turning to the *third section,* a conceptualization of the relationship between modernization and value change will be described that appears to concur to a more satisfying degree with presently available empirical data.

For the moment I proceed alongside Inglehart by stating shortly that the available
data points to the uniform impact of the modernization process on the attitudes of
those affected by it, wherever it has been gaining momentum. Furthermore, I can go
along with Inglehart by stating equally shortly that the phenomenon of modern
value-change can for the most part be explained by analyzing this impact, and by
studying the reactions of the individual personal system to the impact. However, this
impact cannot be described sufficiently in characterizing it as a relief from former
scarcity pressures. By conceiving the relationship between modernization and value
change in such a way, the real situation is distorted twofold: First, the impact of
modernization is envisioned exclusively from the perspective of expanding "outputs" of modern economies, whereas the perspective of changing and expanding
"inputs" demanded by human beings is left out of consideration. Second, the reaction of the personal system is conceptualized in terms of the emancipation of a prefixed set of hierarchically ordered, basic instinctual desires, which substantially have
nothing to do with external influencing forces. Rather, societal modernization acts in

this process as a trigger that frees an agent from alien spheres from being caged up in the socio-economic and socio-cultural bottle.

It seems that the available data is better understood, when one builds on the assumption that human beings under the impact of the ongoing modernization process (i.e. so-called "globalization") are increasingly challenged to develop abilities that secure a satisfying balance in the relationship between their personal system and the societal system. This situation is often described under the heading of the "flexible man" (Sennett, 1998), who has to make his living beyond the physical securities of the former welfare-state, as well as beyond the metaphysical securities of institutionalized religion. Speaking more concretely, human beings are increasingly dependent of their ability to develop new capabilities of self-reliance, personal initiative and mobility, autonomous rational decision-making, and individual responsibility taking. If one combines these categories into a single expression, one might say that by developing new values, human beings are increasingly dependent of bringing about some kind of "subjective modernization" (Hradil, 1992).

As stated before, it seems possible to hypothesize that under the pressure of the ongoing process of modernization human beings tend to develop individualistic values and the available data confirms this throughout. The term "individualization" of values has to be clearly defined, however, if it is to allow for the development of hypotheses that adequately comprise the relations between ongoing modernization and value change in an adequate way. Stated more concretely, it has to be understood in a twofold way, which is to be discussed in the following section.

From integration of the societal, to integration of the personal system

First, the individualization of values concerns a shift of their functional focus away from the integration of the societal system, and towards the integration of the personal system. Such a shift seems to be necessary for the process of value-setting as soon as the logic of the societal system demands from human beings that they take care of themselves in an existentially relevant way. When human beings become existentially dependent on their personal ability to develop self-reliance, initiative and mobility, autonomous rational decision-making, and individual responsibility taking, it seems to be quite functional that their values channel the attention in this direction. In other words, human value systems have to develop, a primary focus on those values that sensitize and enable individuals to invest personal energy in meeting challenges, and making use of opportunities so that they can attain a satisfying balance between the two system-levels.

Things are quite different wherever the logic of the societal system demands human beings that they feel, think and behave according to social norms and common belief systems, in order to bring about collective performances. In such a case human beings are existentially dependent on their personal ability to develop a spirit of community, and it seems to be quite functional that their values channel their attention and energy invested in this direction. Their value systems, therefore, needs to be centered on values (and ideals) that affect the integration of the societal system.

Of course, in neither case those values that lie outside of the functional center are totally eliminated. Their presence is of indispensable importance for the well being of both the societal as well as personal system. Therefore, securing their coexistence and synergy with the more central values (Trommsdorff, 1983) is of vital functional importance. The decisive systemic variable is the relative weight of traditional and modern values. The differentiation between traditional and modern value systems is only justified, if it implies the concept of a functionally productive coexistence between the opposite values, whose prevalence constitutes the particular character of the respective system.

If one envisions on the basis of this clarification the structure of traditional and modern value systems in terms of concentric circles, one will in the second case find the individualistic values within an inner ring, whereas the collective values are situated within an outer ring (see Figure 3). In the first case the constellation of the two value categories will be the other way round. The collective values will be in the inner ring, whereas the individualistic values will be in the outer ring (see Figure 3). Of course the position of values in the inner or outer ring will determine the degree of importance and obligation they have for human beings. In the context of traditional value systems people will be ready to sacrifice personal interests quite willingly in order to serve the system, whereas in modern value systems collective values will have a minor importance and obligation for human beings. It goes without saying, however, that the quite frequent denouncement of modern values as egoistic or egocentric, and the communitarian lamentum over lost communal values that should be restored, points to a widespread misunderstanding of value-dynamics, and in particular to a misunderstanding of the logic of the societal life system under the conditions of an ongoing process of modernization.

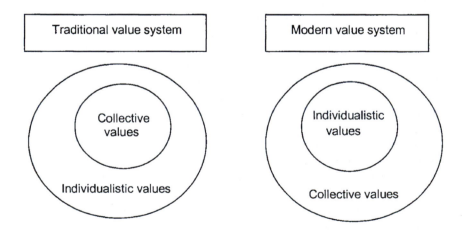

Figure 3. Alternative Constellations of Value Categories

It has to be acknowledged that under such conditions the shift of the focus of individual value systems from the integration of the societal system to the integration of the personal system, i.e., the first meaning of the individualization of values, is not only a functional prerequisite of the persistence of personalities. Rather it is also a functional prerequisite of the persistence of the societal system itself. The active involvement of people in the dynamics of the modernization process is not only necessary for the sake of their personal well being, but also for the sake of the development of the system. Modern organizations are deeply dependent on their ability to involve people and to motivate them to invest personal energy, intelligence and adaptive skills on the background of individualistic concepts of achievement. The book "Thriving on chaos" of the management-guru Tom Peters (1988) for instance provides a storehouse filled with evidence for the truth of this statement. Of course one may dream of a utopian society in which personality-centered and social system-centered values have equal weights. The structure of present reality is different, however, and it may remain different for a long time.

Individualization of decision-making

When we turn now to the *second meaning* of the individualization of values in the process of modernization, we have to qualify and, to a certain degree, reduce the statement that the available data point to a uniform impact of the modernization process on man. This impact is not uniform in the sense that it forces people into a standardized way of feeling, thinking, valuing, and acting. Such a standardizing impact is rather typical for pre-modern societies with a strong societal system-centeredness of values. Where individualistic value orientations in the sense defined above prevail, the uniformity of pressures acquires necessarily a different quality. Quite contrary to standardization it is intrinsically connected with a demand on individuals to expose themselves to opportunity structures that contain broad varieties of options. According to the logic of the system the individuals are expected to develop an ability to perform intelligent choices. It is a component of this systemic logic that the possession of a personality is being presupposed, that makes human beings capable of performing choices pro-actively in accordance to personal preferences, and in connection with deep-seated identifications. In other words, the logic of the system promotes the development of personal value orientations that concern the ability and propensity of practicing a subjective freedom of choice in view of opportunity-structures.

The objective fact behind this second dimension of the individualization of values has to be sought in that kind of social differentiation that has been one of the primary focuses of attention for modern sociology from Emile Durkheim (e.g., Durkheim, 1893/1984, 1895/1982) to Niklas Luhmann (e.g., Luhmann, 1982, 1995). Empirical evidence for the deep reaching importance of social differentiation can be found at nearly any angle of modern life systems. A quite instructive everyday-example is the differentiation of modern occupational structures, which force upon those individuals, who want to enter the labor-market, decisions between a nearly incalculable numbers of alternatives. Quite typically the individuals are expected to accomplish the necessary choice by relying on personal dispositions and desires.

There are even tests in use that assist people in finding their way to these dispositions and desires, which supposedly may be hidden to them on a conscious level. Occupational role-taking is left to individual decision-making on the basis of individualized values and preferences that act inside the personal system as agents of personality-based choices. By listening to these internal agents people are being enabled to conform to pressures that have their source quite clearly in functional prerequisites of the socio-economic modernization process.

One can grasp at a second dimension of a value-assisted individualization of decision-making that is functional with respect to the requirements of the modernization process by looking at the vertical (or hierarchical) aspect of modern role systems. Roughly speaking modern role systems offer a choice between different levels of personal involvement and investment of energy. Normally these different levels are being combined with different amounts of rewards, so that individuals can make a choice between a variety of options concerning their balance of inputs and outputs.

The logic of the system enables them, for instance, to opt for a "minimax"-strategy that gives them a chance to receive as much output as possible from the system by simultaneously minimizing their personal inputs. On the spur of the historical moment it was one of the big surprises of the seventies when the so-called "affluent workers" were discovered by Goldthorpe, Lockwood & Bechhofer (1969). This group of individuals displayed an instrumental orientation towards work by minimizing their effort and involvement, and yet nevertheless securing a satisfying level of earnings. Possibly it was still an even greater surprise, however, when some years later the Yuppies were discovered. These individuals adopted a sharply differing "maximax-strategy" of investing a large amount of effort and intrinsic involvement, and taking out large immaterial and material rewards in terms of social esteem, comfortable life and money.

Of course such contrasting strategies are intensely connected with contrasting values, which centre on differing self-images and life goals, being quite definitely individualistic. People, who adhere to such differing sets of values, do not have the feeling of acting according to prerequisites of the social system thereby. Rather they practice their options with strong feelings of self-assertion and self-development.

Aberrations from the Logic of the System - Areas of Conflict in the Relationship between Modernization and Value Change

Empirical research teaches us that the desire to experience such feelings is based on very strong values of self-assertion and self-development that can be found in growing parts of the populations of modernizing societies. These values seem to be located at the very center of the inner ring of individualistic values (see Figure 3). Empirical research teaches furthermore that the particular variant of these values found with the Yuppies (or presently with the Bobos) is expanding within the populations of modernizing societies, though it is still heavily competed by contrasting value sets. The functionality of such a development is obvious. The more this particular variant of values of self-development prevails, the more correspondence between the conditions of modernization and the direction of value change can be achieved. The reason is that self-development values that motivate people to maximize personal inputs and thereby to maximize outputs gained from the system, have the effect of supporting the logic of the dynamics of the socio-economic system on two essential sides. They add equally to maximizing the productive powers of the system as well as to maximizing the marketability and sale ability of their outputs that is to say to stabilize the basic conditions of its dynamics.

Quite ironically the functionality of this correspondence, which is overwhelmingly evident from the standpoint of an external observer, seems to be not yet fully realized by those strategic agents of the system that have the power and legitimacy to make system-influencing decisions. The reason for this astonishing aberration from the logic of the system seems to be that the full utilization of the maximax-values presupposes some kind of equalization of organizationally bundled social roles as a structural innovation. Roughly speaking, only such roles are sufficiently attractive for people with maximax-values and -desires that enable them to practice a considerable degree of self-responsibility.

Empirical evidence shows, however, that the hitherto prevailing organizational models are connected with more traditional concepts of hierarchy that favor a preferential allocation of chances for self-responsibility on higher organizational levels. Of course such status-oriented concepts find support with those stakeholders who profit from them, so that the existing structural barriers are being stabilized by vested interests. They are furthermore stabilized by the previously mentioned widespread misconceptions of the individualistically oriented value change as egoistic and egocentric.

These misconceptions which quite often are connected with utopian ideas of a reconciliation of individualistic values and community-oriented values, or of a restoration of the dominance of the latter category (see above), tend to form coalitions with structural neophobia and respective vested interests. As a result powerful resistances against a full utilization of system-conducive individualistic value orientations come into existence, whose detrimental influence on the modernization process is being hedged ideologically. In this way – and not via the continued value change itself, as Inglehart assumes – the process of modernization looses energy and is being slowed down.

If one evaluates this disturbance of the relationship between modernization and value change in a detached way from the point of view of an external observer, one may arrive at a more general conclusion. One is led to perceive this disturbance as a prominent aspect of system problems that are characteristic for advanced levels of the modernization process. As sociologists like Anthony Giddens and Ulrich Beck (Beck, Giddens & Lash, 1997; Giddens, 1991) have stressed during the past years that on such advanced levels the formerly spontaneous, unconscious, and self-propelling modernization process tends to change into a reflexive process, that is open for critical interpretations and interventions based upon them.

The sociologists mentioned above tend to assume that the transition of the modernization process into its reflexive stage adds to improving (i.e. optimizing and humanizing) the quality of modernization. The existence of chances of that kind is by no means to be denounced, though they cannot be taken for granted. Rather it might be argued that reflection on the conditions of influencing and possibly improving the relationship between social and individual development is presently in an early learning stage, in which the implicit logic of the modern life system is still expecting its discovery and analysis as a guiding principle of future-oriented thinking.

References

Beck, U., Giddens, A., & Lash, S. (1997). *Reflexive modernization: Politics, tradition and aesthetics in the modern social order*. Cambridge, UK: Polity Press.

Durkheim, E. (1982). *The rules of sociological method and selected texts on sociology and its method*. London: Macmillan. (Original work published 1895)

Durkheim, E. (1984). *The division of labour in society*. London: Macmillan. (Original work published 1893)

Gensicke, T. (2000). *Deutschland im Übergang: Lebensgefühl, Wertorientierungen, Bürgerengagement* [Germany in transition: Attitude towards life, value orientations, civic commitment] (Speyerer Forschungsberichte Nr. 204). Speyer, Verwaltungshochschule Speyer.

Giddens, A. (1991). *Modernity and self-identity: Self and society in the late modern age*. Cambridge, UK: Polity Press.

Goldthorpe, J. H., Lockwood, D., & Bechhofer, F. (1969). *The affluent worker in the class structure* (Cambridge studies in sociology, 3). Cambridge, UK: Cambridge University Press.

Hofstede, G. (2001). *Culture's consequences: Comparing values, behaviors, institutions and organizations across nations*. Thousand Oaks, CA: Sage.

Hradil, S. (1992). Die "objektive" und die "subjektive" Modernisierung ["Objective" and "subjective" modernization]. *Aus Politik und Zeitgeschichte, 29/30*, 3-10.

Inglehart, R. (1990). *Culture shift in advanced industrial society*. Princeton, NJ: Princeton University Press.

Inglehart, R. (1997). *Modernization and postmodernization: Cultural, economic, and political change in 43 societies*. Princeton, NJ: Princeton University Press.

Inglehart, R., Basanez, M., & Moreno, A. (1998). *Human values and beliefs: A cross-cultural sourcebook: Political, religious, sexual, and economic norms in 43 societies*. Ann Arbor, MI: University of Michigan Press.

Klages, H. (1985). *Wertorientierungen im Wandel: Rückblick, Gegenwartsanalyse, Prognosen* [*Value orientations in transition: Review, present situation, and forecast*] (2nd ed.). Frankfurt am Main, Germany: Campus.

Klages, H. (2002). *Der blockierte Mensch: Zukunftsaufgaben gesellschaftlicher und organisatorischer Gestaltung* [*The blocked man: Future tasks of societal and organizational formation*]. Frankfurt am Main, Germany: Campus.

Luhmann, N. (1982). *The differentiation of society*. New York: Columbia University Press.

Luhmann, N. (1995). *Social systems*. Stanford, CA: Stanford University Press.

Maslow, A. H. (1954). *Motivation and personality*. New York: Harper.

Parsons, T. (1978). *Action theory and the human condition*. New York: Free Press.

Parsons, T. & Shils, E. A. (1951). Values, motives, and systems of action. In T. Parsons & E. A. Shils (Eds.), *Towards a general theory of action* (pp. 45-243). Cambridge, MA: Harvard University Press.

Peters, T. (1988). *Thriving on chaos: Handbook for a management revolution*. New York: Knopf.

Sennett, R. (1998). *The corrosion of character: The personal consequences of work in the new capitalism*. New York: Norton.

Trommsdorff, G. (1983). Value change in Japan. *International Journal of Intercultural Relations*, 7, 337-360.

Part V

Acculturation

13

Acculturation

John W. Berry

Introduction

Acculturation is the process of cultural and psychological change that takes place as a result of contact between cultural groups and their individual members. Such contact and change occur for a variety of reasons, including colonization, military invasion, migration, and sojourning (such as tourism, international study, and overseas posting). Following these initial contacts, acculturation continues in most societies, particularly in those that are culturally plural, where many ethno-cultural communities maintain features of their heritage cultures. Adaptation to living in these culture-contact settings takes place over time; occasionally it is stressful, but often it results in some form of accommodation, in which both groups in contact experience change. Acculturation and adaptation are now reasonably well understood, permitting the development of policies and programs to promote successful outcomes for all parties.

Acculturation Concept

The initial interest in acculturation grew out of a concern for the effects of European domination of colonized and indigenous peoples (e.g., Herskovits, 1938). Research on acculturation thus became associated with the colonial enterprise, carried out mainly by anthropologists. Later, it focused on how immigrants (both voluntary and involuntary) changed following their entry and settlement into receiving societies. Much of this work was carried out by sociologists and psychiatrists, who often emphasized the negative consequences of acculturation (e.g., Stonequist, 1937). More recently, much of the work has been involved with how ethno-cultural groups relate to each other, and change, as a result of their attempts to live together in culturally plural societies (e.g., Chun, Balls-Organista, & Marin, 2002). During this phase, psychologists and psychological anthropologists became more involved in the study of acculturation, focusing primarily upon how individuals experience, and respond to, the acculturation that is taking place in their group. This phenomenon has become known as "psychological acculturation" (Graves, 1967). Nowadays, all three foci are important, as globalization results in ever-larger trading and political relations: indigenous national populations experience neo-colonization, new waves of immigrants, sojourners, and refugees flow from these economic and political changes, and large ethno-cultural populations become established in most countries (e.g., Berry, 1997; Portes, 1997).

Although much of this initial concerns and research was carried out in the traditional immigrant-receiving countries (Australia, Canada, New Zealand, USA), these issues have become increasingly important in Europe (e.g., Dacyl & Westin, 2000; Liebkind, 1989). As a cross-cultural psychologist, I take seriously the view that findings from research in one society cannot be generalized to others. Thus, the European experiences, ideologies, and sensitivities may alter the conceptions and empirical findings that are portrayed in this chapter. Nevertheless, some evidence exists to show that the very concept of acculturation, the various strategies adopted by immigrants and members of the national society, and the nature of the problems that may occur are rather similar to those identified in the research in other countries (e.g., Berry & Sam, 1997). It is, of course, up to European societies, their citizens, and the newcomers to assess the relevance and validity of this earlier work for their societies.

Early views about the nature of acculturation are a useful foundation for contemporary discussion. Two formulations in particular, have been widely quoted. The first is:

> Acculturation comprehends those phenomena which result when groups of individuals having different cultures come into continuous first-hand contact, with subsequent changes in the original culture patterns of either or both groups [...] under this definition, acculturation is to be distinguished from culture change, of which it is but one aspect, and assimilation, which is at times a phase of acculturation. (Redfield, Linton, & Herskovits, 1936, pp. 149-152)

In another formulation, acculturation was defined as

> culture change that is initiated by the conjunction of two or more autonomous cultural systems. Acculturative change may be the consequence of direct cultural transmission; it may be derived from non-cultural causes, such as ecological or demographic modification induced by an impinging culture; it may be delayed, as with internal adjustments following upon the acceptance of alien traits or pat-

terns; or it may be a reactive adaptation of traditional modes of life (Social Science Research Council, 1954, p. 974)

In the first formulation, acculturation is seen as one aspect of the broader concept of culture change (which results from intercultural contact), is considered to generate change in "either or both groups," and is distinguished from assimilation (which may be "at times a phase"). These are important distinctions for psychological work, and will be pursued later. In the second definition, a few extra features are added, including change that is indirect (not cultural but "ecological"), delayed (internal adjustments, presumably of both a cultural and psychological character take time), and can be "reactive" (that is, rejecting the cultural influence and changing towards a more "traditional" way of life, rather than inevitably towards greater similarity with the dominant culture).

Graves (1967) introduced the concept of *psychological acculturation*, which refers to changes in an individual who is a participant in a culture contact situation, being influenced both directly by the external culture, and by the changing culture of which the individual is a member. There are two reasons for keeping these two levels distinct. The first is that in cross-cultural psychology, individual human behavior is viewed as interacting with the cultural context within which it occurs; hence, separate conceptions and measurements are required at the two levels. Not everyone does accept this conception of culture and the individual as distinct entities.

However, in my view culture is both an "organismic" variable (i.e., is taken into individuals through the process of enculturation), and an "independent" variable (Berry, 2000). In this latter case, culture is seen as a set of contexts that pre-exists the arrival of any particular individual (whether by birth or migration), and maintains a collective status (i.e., is a characteristic of the whole group, rather than being embedded in any one individual). The second reason for considering culture and the individual as separate is that not every individual enters into, and participates in, or changes in the same way; there are vast individual differences in psychological acculturation, even among individuals who live in the same acculturative arena.

A framework that outlines and links cultural and psychological acculturation, and identifies the two (or more) groups in contact is presented in Figure 1. This Framework serves as a map of those phenomena which I believe need to be conceptualized and measured during acculturation research. At the cultural level (on the left) key features of the two original cultural groups (A and B) need to be understood prior to their major contact, the nature of their contact relationships, and the resulting dynamic cultural changes in both groups and in the emergent ethnocultural groups, during the process of acculturation. The gathering of this information requires extensive ethnographic, community-level work. These changes can be minor or substantial, and range from being easily accomplished through to being a source of major cultural disruption. For much of this group-level work, collaboration with anthropologists and sociologists is extremely valuable.

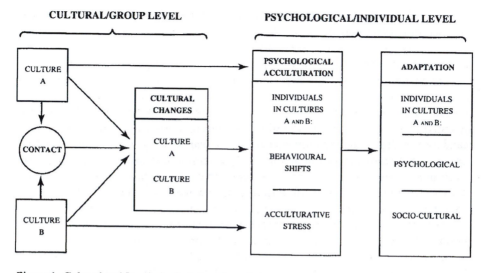

Figure 1. Cultural and Psychological Acculturation

At the individual level (on the right), the psychological changes that individuals in all groups undergo need to be considered, and their eventual adaptation to their new situations. Identifying these changes requires sampling a population and studying individuals who are variably involved in the process of acculturation. These changes can be a set of rather easily accomplished behavioral shifts (e.g., in ways of speaking, dressing, eating, and in one's cultural identity), often seen as acquiring a new set of social competencies (Ward, Bochner, & Furnham, 2001).

Sometimes they can be more problematic, producing acculturative stress as manifested by uncertainty, anxiety, and depression (Berry, 1976). Adaptations can be primarily internal or psychological (e.g., sense of well being, or self-esteem) or sociocultural, linking the individual to others in the new society as manifested for example in competence in the activities of daily intercultural living (Ward, 1996).

Acculturation Contexts

As for all cross-cultural psychology (Berry, Poortinga, Segall, & Dasen, 2002), it is imperative that we base our work on acculturation by examining its cultural contexts. We need to understand, in ethnographic terms, both cultures that are in contact if we are to understand the individuals that are in contact.

In Figure 1, we saw that there are five aspects of cultural contexts: the two original cultures (A and B), the two changing ethno-cultural groups (A and B), and the nature of their contact and interactions.

Taking the immigration process as an example, we may refer to the society of origin (A) and society of settlement (B), and their respective changing cultural features following contact (A^1 and B^1). A complete understanding of acculturation would need to start with a fairly comprehensive examination of the societal contexts: In the society of origin, the cultural characteristics that accompany individuals into the acculturation process need description, in part to understand (literally) where the person is coming from and in part to establish cultural features for comparison with the society of settlement as a basis for estimating how dissimilar the two cultures are, or their *cultural distance*.

The combination of political, economic, and demographic conditions being faced by individuals in their society of origin also needs to be studied as a basis for under-standing the degree of *voluntariness* in the *migration motivation* of acculturating individuals. Arguments by Richmond (1993) suggest that migrants can be ranged on a continuum between reactive and proactive, with the former being motivated by factors that are constraining or exclusionary, and generally negative in character, while the latter are motivated by factors that are facilitating or enabling, and gener-ally positive in character; these contrasting factors have also been referred to as push/pull factors in the earlier literature on migration motivation.

In the society of settlement, a number of factors have importance. First, there are the general orientations that a society and its citizens have towards immigration and pluralism. Some have been built by immigration over the centuries, and this process may be a continuing one, guided by a deliberate immigration policy. The important issue to understand for the process of acculturation is both the historical and attitu-dinal situation faced by migrants in the society of settlement. Some societies are accepting of cultural pluralism resulting from immigration, taking steps to support the continuation of cultural diversity as a shared communal resource; this position represents a positive *multicultural ideology* (Berry & Kalin, 1995) and corresponds to the integration strategy (see below).

Others seek to eliminate diversity through policies and programmes of assimila-tion, while others attempt to segregate or marginalize diverse populations in their societies. Murphy (1965) has argued that societies that are supportive of cultural pluralism (that is, with a positive multicultural ideology) provide a more positive settlement context for two reasons: they are less likely to enforce cultural change (assimilation) or exclusion (segregation and marginalization) on immigrants; and they are more likely to provide social support both from the institutions of the larger society (e.g., culturally sensitive health care, and multicultural curricula in schools), and from the continuing and evolving ethno-cultural communities that usually make up pluralistic societies. However, even where pluralism is accepted, there are well-known variations in the relative acceptance of specific cultural, "racial," and reli-gious groups (e.g., Berry & Kalin, 1995). Those groups that are less well-accepted experience hostility, rejection, and discrimination, one factor that is predictive of poor long-term adaptation.

Acculturation Strategies

Not all groups and individuals undergo acculturation in the same way; there are large variations in how people seek to engage the process. These variations have been termed *acculturation strategies*. Which strategies are used depends on a variety of antecedent factors (both cultural and psychological); and there are variable consequences (again both cultural and psychological) of these different strategies. These strategies consist of two (usually related) components: *attitudes and behaviors* (that is, the preferences and actual outcomes) that are exhibited in day-to-day intercultural encounters.

The centrality of the concept of acculturation strategies can be illustrated by reference to each of the components included in Figure 1. At the cultural level, the two groups in contact (whether dominant or non-dominant) usually have some notion about what they are attempting to do (e.g., colonial policies, or motivations for migration), or what is being done to them, during the contact. Similarly, the dings of changes that are likely to occur will be influenced by their strategies. At the individual level, both the behavior changes and acculturative stress phenomena are now known to be a function, at least to some extent, of what people try to do during their acculturation; and the longer term outcomes (both psychological and sociocultural adaptations) often correspond to the strategic goals set by the groups of which they are members.

Four acculturation strategies have been derived from two basic issues facing all acculturating peoples. These issues are based on the distinction between orientations towards one's own group, and those towards other groups (Berry, 1980). This distinction is rendered as a relative preference for maintaining one's heritage, culture, and identity and a relative preference for having contact with and participating in the larger society along with other ethno-cultural groups. This formulation is presented in Figure 2.

These two issues can be responded to on attitudinal dimensions, represented by bipolar arrows. For purposes of presentation, generally positive or negative orientations to these issues intersect to define four acculturation strategies. These strategies carry different names, depending on which ethno-cultural group (the dominant or non-dominant) is being considered. From the point of view of non-dominant groups (on the left of Figure 2), when individuals do not wish to maintain their cultural identity and seek daily interaction with other cultures, the *Assimilation* strategy is defined. In contrast, when individuals place a value on holding on to their original culture, and at the same time whish to avoid interaction with others, then the *Separation* alternative is defined. When there is an interest in both maintaining one's original culture, while in daily interactions with other groups, *Integration* is the option. In this case, there is some degree of cultural integrity maintained, while at the same time seeking, as a member of an ethno-cultural group, to participate as an integral part of the larger social network. Finally, when there is little possibility or interest in

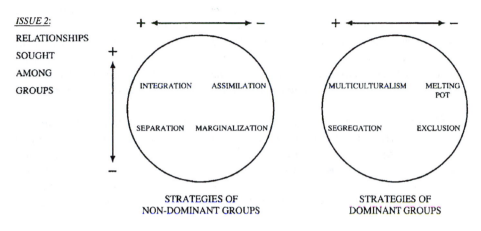

Figure 2. Varieties of Intercultural Strategies in Dominant and Non-Dominant Groups

cultural maintenance (often for reasons of enforced cultural loss), and little interest in having relations with others (often for reasons of exclusion or discrimination) then *Marginalization* is defined.

This presentation was based on the assumption that non-dominant groups and their individual members have the freedom to choose how they want to acculturate. This, of course, is not always the case. When the dominant group enforces certain forms of acculturation, or constrains the choices of non-dominant groups or individuals, then other terms need to be used (see below).

Integration can only be "freely" chosen and successfully pursued by non-dominant groups when the dominant society is open and inclusive in its orientation towards cultural diversity. Thus a mutual accommodation is required for *Integration* to be attained, involving the acceptance by both groups of the right of all groups to live as culturally different peoples. This strategy requires non-dominant groups to adopt the basic values of the larger society, while at the same time the dominant group must be prepared to adapt national institutions (e.g., education, health, labor) to better meet the needs of all groups now living together in the plural society.

These two basic issues were initially approached from the point of view of the non-dominant ethno-cultural groups. However, the original anthropological definition clearly established that *both* groups in contact would become acculturated. Hence, a third dimension was added: that of the powerful role-played by the dominant group in influencing the way in which mutual acculturation would take place (Berry, 1974). The addition of this third dimension produces the right side of Figure 2, and permits a comparison of the strategies being adopted by the ethno-cultural groups, and the larger society. *Assimilation* when sought by the non-dominant acculturating group is termed the "Melting Pot," but when demanded by the dominant group, it is called the "Pressure cooker."

When the dominant group forces *Separation*, it is "Segregation." *Marginalization*, when imposed by the dominant group, it is "Exclusion." Finally, *Integration*, when diversity is a feature of the society as a whole, including by all the various ethno-cultural groups, is called "Multiculturalism." With the use of this framework, comparisons can be made between individuals and their groups, and between non-dominant peoples and the larger society within which they are acculturating. The ideologies and policies of the dominant group constitute an important element of ethnic relations research (see Berry, Kalin, & Taylor, 1977; Bourhis, Moise, Perreault, & Senecal, 1997), while the preferences of non-dominant people are a core feature in acculturation research. (Berry, Kim, Power, Young, & Bujaki, 1989). Inconsistencies and conflicts between these various acculturation preferences are sources of difficulty for acculturating individuals. Generally, when acculturation experiences cause problems for acculturating individuals, the phenomenon of *acculturative stress* is observed.

Acculturation Stress

Three ways to conceptualize outcomes of acculturation have been proposed in the literature. In the first (behavioral shifts), we observe those changes in an individual's behavioral repertoire that take place rather easily, and are usually non-problematic. This process encompasses three sub-processes: *cultural shedding*; *culture learning*; and *culture conflict*. The first two involve the selective, accidental or deliberate loss of behaviors, and their replacement by behaviors that allow the individual a better "fit" with the society of settlement. Most often, this process has been termed adjustment, since virtually all the adaptive changes take place in the acculturating individual, with few changes occurring among members of the larger society (Ward et al., 2001). These adjustments are typically made with minimal difficulty, in keeping with the appraisal of the acculturation experiences as non-problematic. However, some degree of conflict may occur, which is usually resolved by the acculturating person yielding to the behavioral norms of the dominant group. In this case, *Assimilation* is the most likely outcome.

When greater levels of conflict are experienced, and the experiences are judged problematic but controllable and surmountable, then the second approach (acculturative stress) is the appropriate conceptualization (Berry, Kim, Minde, & Mok, 1987). In this case, individuals understand that they are facing problems resulting from intercultural contact that cannot be dealt with easily or quickly by simply adjusting or assimilating to them. Drawing on the broader stress and adaptation paradigms, this approach of advocates the study of the process of how individuals deal with acculturative problems on first encountering them, and over time. In this sense, acculturative stress is a stress reaction in response to life events that are rooted in the experience of acculturation.

A third approach (psychopathology) has had long use in clinical psychology and psychiatry. In this view, acculturation is usually seen as problematic; individuals usually require assistance to deal with virtually insurmountable stressors in their lives. However, contemporary evidence (e.g., Beiser, 1999) shows that most people deal with stressors and re-establish their lives rather well, with health, psychological and social outcomes that approximate those of individuals in the larger society.

Instead of using the terms *culture shock* (see Ward et al., 2001) to encompass these three approaches, we prefer to use the term *acculturative stress* for two reasons. First, the notion of *shock* carries only negative connotations, while *stress* can vary from positive (eu-stress) to negative (dis-stress) in valence. Since acculturation has both positive (e.g., new opportunities) and negative (e.g., discrimination) aspects, the stress conceptualization better matches the range of affect experienced during acculturation. Moreover, shock has no cultural or psychological theory, or research context associated with it, while stress (as noted above) has a place in a well-developed theoretical matrix (i.e., stress-coping-adaptation; Lazarus & Folkman, 1984). Second, the phenomena of interest have their life in the intersection of two cultures; they are intercultural, rather than cultural in their origin. The term "culture" implies that only one culture is involved, while the term "acculturation" draws our attention to the fact that two cultures are interacting, and producing the phenomena. Hence, for both reasons, I prefer the notion of acculturative stress to that of culture shock.

Relating these three approaches to acculturation strategies, some consistent empirical findings allow the following generalizations (Berry, 1997). For behavioral shifts, fewest behavioral changes result from the *Separation* strategy, while most result from the *Assimilation* strategy; *Integration* involves the selective adoption of new behaviors from the larger society, and retention of valued features of one's heritage culture; and *Marginalization* is often associated with major heritage culture loss, and the appearance of a number of dysfunctional and deviant behaviors (such as delinquency, and substance, and familial abuse). For acculturative stress, there is a clear picture that the pursuit of *Integration* is least stressful (at least where it is accommodated by the larger society) while *Marginalization* is the most stressful; in between are the *Assimilation* and *Separation* strategies, sometimes one, sometimes the other being the less stressful. This pattern of findings holds for various indicators of mental health (Berry, 1997; Berry & Kim, 1988).

Adaptation

As a result of attempts to cope with these acculturation changes, some long-term adaptations may be achieved. As mentioned earlier, adaptation refers to the relatively stable changes that take place in an individual or group in response to external demands. Moreover, adaptation may or may not improve the "fit" between individuals and their environments. It is thus not a term that necessarily implies that individuals or groups change to become more like their environments (i.e., adjustment by way of *Assimilation*), but may involve resistance and attempts to change their environments, or to move away from them altogether (i.e., by *Separation*) . In this usage, adaptation is an outcome that may or may not be positive in valence (i.e., meaning only well-adapted). This bi-polar sense of the concept of adaptation is used in the framework in Figure 1 where long-term adaptation to acculturation is highly variable ranging from well- to poorly-adapted, varying from a situation where individuals can manage their new lives very well, to one where they are unable to carry on in the new society.

Adaptation is also multifaceted. The initial distinction between psychological and sociocultural adaptation was proposed and validated by Ward (1996). Psychological adaptation largely involves one's psychological and physical well being, while sociocultural adaptation refers to how well an acculturating individual is able to mange daily life in the new cultural context. While conceptually distinct, they are empirically related to some extent (correlations between the two measures are in the +.4 to +.5 range; Ward, 1996).

However, they are also empirically distinct in the sense that they usually have different time courses and different experiential predictors. Psychological problems often increase soon after contact, followed by a general (but variable) decrease over time; sociocultural adaptation, however, typically has a linear improvement with time. Analyses of the factors affecting adaptation reveal a generally consistent pattern. Good psychological adaptation is predicted by personality variables, life change events, and social support while good sociocultural adaptation is predicted by cultural knowledge, degree of contact, and positive intergroup attitudes (Berry & Sam, 1997; Ward, 1996).

Research relating adaptation to acculturation strategies allows for some further generalizations (Berry, 1997; Ward, 1996). For all three forms of adaptation, those who pursue and accomplish *Integration* appear to be better adapted, while those who are *marginalized* are least well-adapted. Again, the *Assimilation* and *Separation* strategies are associated with intermediate adaptation outcomes. While there are occasional variations on this pattern, it is remarkably consistent, and parallels the generalization regarding acculturative stress.

Applications

There is now widespread evidence that most people who have experienced acculturation actually do survive! They are not destroyed or substantially diminished by it; rather they find opportunities, and achieve their goals sometimes beyond their initial imaginings. The tendency to "pathologize" the acculturation process and outcomes may be partly due to the history of its study in psychiatry and in clinical psychology. Second, researchers often presume to know what acculturating individuals want, and impose their own ideologies or their personal views, rather than informing themselves about culturally rooted individual preferences and differences. One key concept (but certainly not the only one) to understand this variability has been emphasized in this article (acculturation strategies).

The generalizations that have been made in this article based on a wide range of empirical findings allow us to propose that public policies and programs that seek to reduce acculturative stress and to improve intercultural relationships should emphasize the *Integration* approach to acculturation. This is equally true of national policies, institutional arrangements, and the goals of ethno-cultural groups; and it is also true of individuals in the larger society as well as members of non-dominant acculturating groups.

In some countries, the integrationist perspective has become legislated in as policies of *Multiculturalism*, which encourage and support the maintenance of valued features of all cultures, and at the same time support full participation of all ethno-cultural groups in the evolving institutions of the larger society. What seems certain is that immigration, acculturation, and the resultant cultural diversity are here to stay in all countries. Finding a way to accommodate each other poses a challenge and an opportunity to social and cross-cultural psychologists everywhere. Diversity is a fact of contemporary life; whether it is the "spice of life," or the main "irritant," is probably the central question that confronts us all, citizens and social scientists alike.

References

Beiser, M. (1999). *Strangers at the gate.* Toronto, Canada: University of Toronto Press.

Berry, J. W. (1974). Psychological aspects of cultural pluralism: Unity and identity reconsidered. *Topics in Culture Learning, 2,* 17-22.

Berry, J. W. (1976). *Human ecology and cognitive style: Comparative studies in cultural and psychological adaptation.* New York: Sage/Halsted.

Berry, J. W. (1980). Acculturation as varieties of adaptation. In A. Padilla (Ed.), *Acculturation: Theory, models, and findings* (pp. 9-25). Boulder, CO: Westview.

Berry, J. W. (1997). Immigration, acculturation, and adaptation. *Applied Psychology, 46,* 5-68.

Berry, J. W. (2000). Cross-cultural psychology: A symbiosis of cultural and comparative approaches. *Asian Journal of Social Psychology, 3,* 197-205.

Berry, J. W., Kalin, R., & Taylor, D. (1977). *Multiculturalism and ethnic attitudes in Canada.* Ottawa, Canada: Supply & Services.

Berry, J. W., & Kalin, R. (1995). Multicultural and ethnic attitudes in Canada: An overview of the 1991 National Survey. *Canadian Journal of Behavioural Science, 27,* 301-320.

Berry, J. W., Kim, U., Minde, T., & Mok, D. (1987). Comparative studies of acculturative stress. *International Migration Review, 21*, 491-511.

Berry, J. W., & Kim, U. (1988). Acculturation and mental health. In P. Dasen, J. W.
Berry, & N. Sartorius (Eds.), *Health and cross-cultural psychology* (pp. 207-
236). Newbury Park, CA: Sage.

Berry, J. W., Kim, U., Power, S., Young, M., & Bujaki, M. (1989). Acculturation
attitudes in plural societies. *Applied Psychology, 38*, 185-206.

Berry, J. W., Poortinga, Y. H., Segall, M. H., & Dasen, P. R. (2002). *Cross-cultural
psychology: Research and applications* (2nd ed.). New York: Cambridge University Press.

Berry, J. W., & Sam, D. L. (1997). Acculturation and adaptation. In J. W. Berry, M.
H. Segall, & Ç Kagitçibasi (Eds.), *Handbook of cross-cultural psychology: Vol.
3. Social behavior and applications* (pp. 291-326). Boston: Allyn and Bacon.

Bourhis, R., Moise, C., Perreault, S., & Senecal, S. (1997). Towards an interactive
acculturation model: A social psychological approach. *International Journal of
Psychology, 32*, 369-386.

Chun, K., Balls-Organista, P., & Marin, G. (Eds.). (2002). *Acculturation*. Washington, DC: APA Books.

Dacyl, J., & Westin, C. (Eds.). (2000). *Governance of cultural diversity in Europe*.
Stockholm: CEIFO/Unesco.

Graves, T. (1967). Psychological acculturation in a tri-ethnic community. *South-
Western Journal of Anthropology, 23*, 337-350.

Herskovits, M. J. (1938). *Acculturation: The study of culture contact*. New York:
Augustin.

Lazarus, R. S., & Folkman, S. (1984). *Stress, appraisal, and coping*. New York:
Springer.

Liebkind, K. (Ed.). (1989). *New identities in Europe*. Brookfield, VT: Gower.

Murphy, H. B. M. (1965). Migration and the major mental disorders. In M. Kantor
(Ed.), *Mobility and mental health* (pp. 221-249). Springfield, IL: Thomas.

Portes, A. (1997). Immigration theory for a new century. *International Migration
Review, 31*, 799-825.

Redfield, R., Linton, R, & Herskovits, M. (1936). Memorandum on the study of
acculturation. *American Anthropologist, 38*, 149-152.

Social Science Research Council (1954). Acculturation: An exploratory formulation.
American Anthropologist, 56, 973-1002.

Stonequist, E. V. (1937). *The marginal man*. New York: Charles Scribner.

Ward, C. (1996). Acculturation. In D. Landis & R. Bhagat (Eds.), *Handbook of
intercultural training* (2nd ed., pp. 124-147). Newbury Park, CA: Sage.

Ward, C., Bochner, S., & Furnham, A. (2001). *The psychology of culture shock*.
London: Routledge.

14

Long-Term Effects of International Student Exchange Programs

Alexander Thomas

Introduction

Many schools and youth organizations offer international exchange programs for children and adolescents. The aim of such programs is all in all quite clear: to provide students from different countries with the opportunity to become personally acquainted, to fully immerse in a foreign exchange partner's living environment, and to familiarize oneself with another country, its people, customs and culture. Through familiarization with a partner, one hopes that shared sympathies arise, encouraging students to develop an interest in their exchange partner and his or her culture, and so foster an intensified exchange. A more profound understanding of one's exchange partner, their living environment and culture, is cultivated, national and cultural differences are recognized and tolerated, and prejudices as well as stereotypes fade. This greater understanding then enables the path to be paved towards a relationship of trust and affection. If this occurs at an early age and is intensified in the following generation, it may contribute to a rapprochement across national borders, a strengthening of tolerance, friendship between people and a peaceful world. A systematic survey of students in regard to their experiences and the lasting effects of the exchange are to be presented here.

Until now, very few investigations into the long-term effects of intercultural experiences have been made during international student exchange programs. As exciting, fascinating and eventful the participation in a student exchange program may be it is only a relatively short-term event in the stream of experiences and activities that are part of the developmental processes of an individual. Compared to an important examination a student has prepared for over a lengthy period of time, and the results which are of key importance for his further education, the experiences gained from an international exchange are possibly of so little consequence that they may be lost in the tide of events or at the most leave only a small trace, of which the person is no longer conscious or can be made conscious of.

An eventful international student exchange is most probably useful for the personal development of an individual (see also Kobayashi, this volume). However, what effects exactly result from such an exchange, and how and when they come about, may even be difficult for individuals to identify for themselves. One reason may be that at the end of a successful student exchange, having taken place without any hitches and enjoyed by all participants, no one thinks to investigate its long-term effects. For the students themselves, as well as for others closely concerned such as parents and teachers, this project has been completed from a psychological point of view, with little left to ask about or discuss (Thomas, 1988).

Many who gain international experience, regardless of the circumstances – be it as a student, a student assistant enjoying a year's study abroad, or a foreign staff member profiting from a three-year overseas tenure – often complain that on returning to their familiar settings no one appears to be truly interested in their experiences abroad. They find that their wish to recount their experiences often meets with dismissal rather than interest. Seen psychologically, all these are signs of a so-called "completed action," or – gestalt psychologically expressed – the course of action is seen and assessed by all those concerned as being "of a good gestalt" and therefore completed. Consequently, students and parents do not consider it necessary to concern them with this subject any further. Moreover, the organizations that run the programs are intent on organizing the next program. What concerns them is that everything went smoothly, that the students enjoyed themselves, that the program received a positive endorsement, and that their "clients" (students, parents, teachers, etc.) were satisfied. At most, interested academics might wish to find out whether the experiences gained during the international student exchange had any long-term effects on those who participated, how they would describe their experiences, and what aspects of their personality and fields of activity were affected.

A publication analysis reveals that not only in Germany, but internationally as well, very little research has been undertaken into the long-term effects of such exchange programs. The state of research on this topic can only be defined as particularly insufficient. At present, no scientifically based findings exist on the subject. Consequently, the following is a report on the course and outcome of a relevant study that should best be seen not as a final but rather as a pilot study.

Theoretical Background

The concept of acculturation provides the theoretical framework for this study in conjunction with Seymour Epstein's self-theory (1979) and its extension, the cognitive experiential self-theory (Epstein, 1990, 1991, 1993a). In the following, both components and their consequences for the actual study are presented.

The concept of "acculturation"

Acculturation – understood as a condition – is defined by Gudykunst and Hammer (1988) as follows: "Intercultural adaptation refers to the fit between individuals and their environment. Individuals, who have adapted to "foreign" environments, have worked out a good "fit" between themselves and their environment" (p. 111). But – seen as a process – acculturation can only be effective, if both the guest and the guest-culture work together. Berry (1994) defines psychological adaptation as a process, through which an individual changes his psychological characteristics, the surrounding context, or the extent of contacts in order to achieve a better "fit" with other aspects of the system in which he lives (see also Berry, this volume). The goal of this study is to describe and strive to explain long-lasting effects of such acculturation processes.

The actual study also refers to Brislin (1994), who states that acculturation can be operationalized in three aspects of cross-cultural experience: emotional, cognitive, and behavioral. Many studies point out three decisive dimensions for acculturation: the subjective satisfaction or respectively the absence of stress-relevant symptoms, the quality of social relations to natives, and the degree of task-fulfillment. In summary, the concept of acculturation is based on three theoretical branches.

First, acculturation can be seen as a learning-process. Kühlmann (1995) postulated that an individual has to learn "which behavior leads to which consequences in which social situations" (p. 15).

Second, acculturation is understood as adaptation. The basic idea is that the behavior of a person aims at achieving a "fit" between the person and the environment. According to Shaffer and Shoben (1956; in Anderson, 1994), the process of acculturation is activated when a person is confronted with obstacles. In this sense, the process of acculturation never ends – a central idea of the following study.

Third, coping strategies form the theoretical background that will be described in the following.

Self-theory of Epstein

In his self-theory, Epstein succeeds in resolving obvious contradictories by integrating four different theoretical positions (Epstein, 1993a). The first is a phenomenological orientation, meaning that the internal living-world of the subject is demonstrated. Second, he refers to Kelly's concept of personal constructs (Kelly, 1955). In both concepts, a hierarchical structured system of constructs and schemes organizes perception, reasoning and acting. The third position is based on integration theory that contains depth-psychological aspects and terms. The fourth theoretical position taken is based on a learning-theoretical approach (Maturana & Varela, 1987).

The central aspect of the third theory mentioned above, the integration theory, is the correlative and functional relation between the self and environment theory: For example, the way a person views, recognizes, and values their environment expresses to a high degree their self-cognitions and vice versa (Epstein, 1979, p. 16). As a consequence, a person constructs specific "hypotheses" as to their attitude towards the environment, how to deal with it and how to evaluate it. This individual self-theory is a tool used to satisfy one's own needs. Epstein (1993b) postulates four basic needs that need to be met in order to maximize pleasure and minimize pain: need for pleasure and avoidance of lack of enthusiasm, need for coherence, need for affiliation, and need for increase of self-esteem (p. 404). Well-adjusted people fulfill their basic needs in a harmonious, even synergistic manner, with the fulfillment of one need contributing rather than competing with the fulfillment of other needs (Epstein, 1993b). An intraindividual change of personality happens whenever a person modifies their individual theory of reality.

Conclusions for the actual study

A central assumption of this study refers to the fact that long-term changes in the adolescent personality, i.e., development, maturation or growth, can be observed in three different fields of personality-organization: self theory, reality theory, and integration theory (interactions between the two theories mentioned above) (Reed, 1996).

In this study, the integration theory as described above plays an important role. It is relevant for the construction and the functioning of a relative stable, resilient motivation of curiosity and exploration. A balanced relation between the self theory and the environment theory results in situation-adequate responses that support on the one hand the assimilation, i.e. finding adequate solutions for problems. At the same time, acculturation occurs within this process, i.e., the integration of foreign and new elements change the individual's theory of reality. Epstein's theory will be more pertinent for this study than the concept of acculturation.

The Study

With this background in mind, it seems quite risky to interview participants some ten years after the exchange, as to how they believed their experiences during the program influenced their personality and the further course of their lives. Also, it could not be guaranteed that they would be capable of stating exactly what effects the exchange program had on them. Moreover, it was not at all clear whether it would be possible to contact these students or whether they would be prepared to participate in an interview about something which had happened such a long time ago.

With considerable logistical and financial support from the "Bayerischer Jugendring" (Bavarian Youth Ring), a study was carried out in 1997/98 into the long-term effects of intercultural experiences resulting from an exchange program, entitled "Schüleraustauschprogramm auf Gegenseitigkeit" ("Mutual Student Exchange Program"). Organized by the "Bayerischer Jugendring," its purpose was to study the development of the participants' personality and the further course of their lives.[1] From records kept at the "Bayerischer Jugendring" in Munich, the current addresses of 30 Australian and 30 German former exchange students were found and these students were subsequently contacted by mail. 11 Australians and 12 Germans (18 women and 7 men), between the ages of 26 and 30 at the time of the interview, were asked about their experiences during the exchange some 10 to 13 years back.

The student exchange program, in which the interviewees had participated, is a program that the "Bayerischer Jugendring" has been offering for several decades and one that is both very popular and highly esteemed. In this program, students from Bavaria stay with students abroad, e.g., Australia, for three months. The student lives with the host family, goes to school with the exchange student, and spends his or her free time with them, as well. Shortly afterwards, the foreign student, e.g., an Australian, lives with the German counterpart in a similar situation. Each participant gains intercultural experiences in the target country as well as with their counterpart, with whom they became familiar, in their own home country. Whether the student visits the target country first and then receives their partner, or whether they first receive their partner and then travel to the target country is not fixed but a matter of coordination and timing.

The former participants were visited at their present addresses, and, with the help of a semi-structured interview, asked about their intercultural experiences at the time, and whether they had observed any noteworthy consequences resulting from this exchange. The interviews were tape recorded and fully transcribed. The contents of the text material were analyzed based on Epstein's personality theory (1993b). Each interview lasted about one and a half hours and their transcription covered 600 pages.

Results

All interviewees were capable of reflecting on the experiences they had made during the exchange and its perceived effects in a coherent, clearly structured and differentiated manner. The experiences acquired such a long time ago had not simply been lost or forgotten, but instead were easily recalled. They had left distinct impressions and were linked to vital incidents in the person's life. Sometimes causal relationships of the following type were made:

---

[1] Diana Hetzenecker carried out the interviews and the data analysis (Hetzenecker, 1999). The thesis can be obtained from the Institut für Auslandsbeziehungen, Stuttgart.

"I am convinced that I would not have done this (X), or that I would not have thought in that way (Y), if I had not had that experience (Z) in Australia/Germany."

This seemingly self-evident relationship seen between exchange experiences that were made in a specific and relatively short period of time in life, and the lengthy process of personal development or the development of specific interests and careers, is surprising and in fact not at all self-evident. It would not have been revealed in the analysis of answers to questionnaires had they been completed shortly after the exchange, in respect to the circumstances surrounding the exchange and how it progressed.

Generally, such investigations occur when thoughts and emotions connected with the exchange are still very salient (for short-term effects see Kobayashi, this volume), whereas ten years down the line completely different influences are at work. In the interviews there is no glorification of former experiences rather a detailed account is offered of the problems involved in coping with emotionally stressful foreign experiences, and the initially useless attempts to extract personal gain from these exchange experiences. Evidently, exchange experiences have a lasting effect on the development of an individual's personality. Thereby, the long-term duration of the effect is certainly an important factor explaining the ability to supply details of its effect.

The interview material that has been analyzed reveals the experiences participants made in regard to the foreign culture, and their own culture, as well as the specific intercultural situation. Findings indicate that three aspects were affected in particular: (a) an increase of self-efficacy, (b) growth of self-decentralization, and (c) individual variations of the effects.

Increase in self-efficacy

Self-efficacy consists of the conviction of being able to combine already existing cognitive, social and action-related abilities with new strategies for action in order to master new and unknown situations. A high assessment of one's self-efficacy leads to a person actively seeking out new challenges. In this sense, the exchange experiences had long-term effects on the following individual processes[2].

General confidence in one's own abilities
Such a general confidence can be seen in the following statements:
"Since then I believe that nothing can go wrong in my life, that everything will work out somehow."
"The many new experiences made me more mature. One gains a wider perspective and one's own understanding of things is broader and sounder. One

---

[2] In the following text, excerpts from the original German interview transcripts that have been translated into English are cited in quotation marks.

has a trove of experiences that one can delve into when necessary, and which gives one a sense of security."

"The exchange gave me the confidence 'to do something quite different and something by myself'. That confidence made it easier for me to join the army and do further traveling which were very influential experiences as well."

"The biggest thing that I got out of it was that it actually taught me that I can control my own destiny and my own survival."

"The one thing I got out of the three months was a certain level of independence which I didn't have before that."

Increased willingness to take risks

Such willingness is illustrated by the fact that the persons who have decided to undertake something preferred the risk of failure to that of not daring to carry out the undertaking in the first place:

"An important effect from the exchange was the willingness to take risks and to go out and do something. Like I found after that trip I just went off to Paris by myself and didn't have any problem with going by myself for more than a year."

"So (when I came back) I began to question what other people thought my life and my future should be about and learnt that I can make my own decisions and I live by them. And if they work out they work out and if they don't they don't. [...]. I would rather do something and have it not work out than not do it at all."

Staying power

This power manifests itself in the belief that, despite smaller setbacks, the consequential setting and following of goals lead to success:

"It [the exchange] has taught me that I can do something on my own. It is not always going to be easy and there is always going to be little hurdles along the way and there is always going to be times when you look at it and say 'Why on earth did I do this?' but the end result is that I obtained something. I came back and [...] I felt that I had achieved something as an individual, as a person in terms of my own personal growth."

"I achieved what I set out to achieve – that's one hurdle so where's the next hurdle sort of approach."

"I am really surprised how many things I actually complete, that I carry on through to the end, that I accomplish through thick or thin, and I do believe that it comes from the fact that I simply learned to do so."

Steadfastness

Steadfastness shows itself in that the persons had learned to a greater extent than before to believe in the correctness of their own opinions and decisions even when their beliefs were contrary to those of the majority:

"A strength of character developed out of it which I hadn't previously had."

"I became a bit stronger in personality as well and I did start to think different from the norm [...] and I wasn't quite as afraid to voice my opinion on things."
"Since then I have taken all that into other things that I have done and instead of being the sort of person that is quite easily swayed by what the main stream is going to do, I have got fairly set ideas on what I want to achieve and what I want to do. And I stick to that even if everybody else is going off in that direction."

The ability to handle crises
The ability to handle crises is evident in the better mastery of current psychologically difficult situations. Persons who, at the time of the exchange experience, felt themselves to be rather nervous and insecure reported this:
"Before I went to Germany I was quite an anxious person because I seemed to have a lot of things to worry about at the time."
"That was one of the reasons why my parents wanted to send me because they were worried about me as well – being highly strung – I think that is what you would call me at the time."
"At that age I was always worried about myself. I was quite shy and uncomfortable with myself as a teenager growing up before."
"A couple of months before I went to Germany a very close friend had killed herself. So I was still in mourning about all this when I went to Germany."

Improvement of psychological well being
A long-term improvement in psychological well being, through the ability to cope more productively with crisis situations can be seen in the following statements:
"I tapped into who I really am and I did find that it was a releasing experience for me."
"When I came back I brought most of the real me back – I had a totally different approach to my studies when I came back as well. I was much more relaxed and I just took it as I took it and whatever happened, happened – my psychological health was incredibly improved."
"My life has only got better since, that's what I am saying so it made a real change in my life."
"I lost some of that self-consciousness and became more comfortable in myself."
"I was still quite unhappy after I got back because I didn't like school and I was missing my friend but I was a bit stronger anyway and I knew that I could do some things."

Increase in self-decentralization
The term "self-decentralization" denotes the willingness and ability to accept different and foreign aspects, to alter one's own perspectives, to overcome ethnocentricity, to favor ethnically relativistic attitudes, and to come to terms with that which is unfamiliar and different. It has to be noted that the process of decentralization is activated and accelerated through (1) concern about unsatisfactory social contacts in

a foreign cultural setting (pressure to assimilate) and (2) insufficient gratification of the need for coherency as the result of increased cognitive dissonance. An increase in self-decentralization can be seen on three central levels of personality, that is, on cognitive, emotional and behavioral levels.

Effects on the cognitive level

Acceptance of unfamiliar/foreign viewpoints, opinions and behavior patterns
"You learn to confront a situation and not to back away from it when you don't get along so well with somebody." "You can understand better when people are different, [...] because you have got to know so many different people, that you say, O.K., there are cultures where people are totally different, and that one is not scared about it but accepts it and sees the positive side of it."
"My stays abroad are experiences that have perhaps made it easier for me to accept completely different ways of living or to take completely different people as they come."
"In Australia, I learned to be more open minded, and since then I try harder to accept other people as they are and not to categorize and judge people too quickly – unfortunately I still sometimes do that, but I do try to talk to them first."

Understanding of other points of view
"I learnt not to jump to conclusions, to try and understand where somebody has come from and what influence that has had on them and why they might be doing what they are doing."
"I am probably a lot less judgmental – that was the beginning of learning how to be less judgmental and trying to be more analytical and get to the bottom of somebody or something."
"The exchange made me more receptive to other people and other cultures and probably more tolerant of other people."
"I am willing to see other people's points of view more."

Increased readiness to learn new things; to acquaint one with that, which is foreign or unfamiliar so as to become more knowledgeable
"Another thing that I began to learn was that I didn't know very much and there was a lot to learn in the world."

Interest in other worldviews, in other perspectives of the world and of humanity
"The exchange influenced my interests – I'm interested in speaking to people and finding out what other people do with their lives – even if what they are doing is working in a shop and going home and then going to the pub – I mean it might be a completely different experience to what I am doing."

"So it changed a lot of my opinions on people. Just on meeting people – every single person you meet has something – they are interesting – there is something interesting about their life or what they do or their background."

Several participants reported, in particular, that their relationship to their parents improved considerably after their return home since they had more understanding for their parents' point of view and could constructively evaluate their standpoint:

"I felt a bit more understanding when I got home. [...] It made it easier in the family because less stress and hassle."

"When I came home even though it didn't all work out beautifully with my mother it certainly made me start to think more clearly about doing things for myself – that everything didn't just happen automatically and that I needed to be more cooperative."

Increased intercultural sensitivity

This sensitivity is manifest on the part of the participants in an increased attentiveness and receptiveness towards culturally related differences:

"That made me a lot more sensitive to the cultural differences of people and that those differences influence everything."

"I have an understanding of where people are coming from in Germany."

The reported development of intercultural sensitivity often referred initially to the culture of the guest country, but in the course of time also included other cultures:

"I have broadened my interest to other cultures too and not just the German culture. [...] I have opened up to other cultures now and perhaps had a bit of a closed mind to some of those other countries before."

Effects on the emotional level

Lessening of the fear of that which is foreign

"And not being frightened of new cultures – having like a real fear of new cultures being beaten out of me at an early age.

Seeing that which is foreign as a positive challenge

"I am very interested in gaining overseas experience in my career as soon as possible. To go to another country, to start something new, to come to grips with a new situation, that's the best thing that could happen to me."

Effects on the behavioral level

Interest in travel abroad

"I wonder whether I would have traveled at all or whether I would have had this big passion for travel."

"I just love meeting new people, new cultures and I don't think necessarily that would have happened if I hadn't had the opportunity to go over."

"I find my life is constantly gearing around saving for the next trip to go back."

International career orientation
"It has influenced it [my career goal] in the certain sense that travel and meeting people and working with people from other countries has then become an important part of what I want in a career."
"So there is a preparedness to go somewhere else – to move and to assimilate to that culture.

Interest in international friendships
Such interest also includes persons of other cultures living in one's own country:
"I got back from Germany and the first big difference was that I made so many new friends because I began to see that what my group of friends were – it was a fairly confined little group that stuck together for stupid reasons and there are a hell of a lot of different people out there and just because somebody doesn't fit in your little group that you have set doesn't mean that you can't get along with that person."
"I found that over time I was developing my friendships where there were parts of things that we had in common but we didn't have everything in common."

A less critical attitude towards people in their own environment
"It definitely has influenced my perception of people and also – I mean everybody has their quirks – there is always going to be something about somebody that is not going to agree with you and there is always going to be things about them that do."
"One of the things you learn when you are over there is that you just have to lump whatever you've got."

Social compatibility
Social compatibility refers to the ability to adapt to different types of persons in different cultural contexts:
"The exchange has made me today a very adaptable person."
"Later on in life I haven't found it too much of a problem to actually get on with different people."
"From the social aspect, it's helped me a lot, [...], that is to communicate with people you don't know, to cope with other people, to have to get along with them."

Individual variations in the chronology of influential effects
As has previously been explained, through the exchange, a process of self-decentralization is activated that continues after the end of the program. An active search for new experiences is pursued, whereby new and unknown fields of learning

are opened up. The process of self-decentralization is a long-term process and not just limited to the exchange itself or to a short period thereafter:

"I am probably a lot less judgmental – that was the beginning of learning how to be less judgmental and trying to be more analytical and get to the bottom of somebody or something."

"I did find that I started to broaden my horizons and enjoyed different commonalities with different people. [...] And there were different things that I enjoyed doing with other people that I couldn't have been able to do with the same group of people."

The results of the research show that the process of self-decentralization does not begin immediately after the exchange experiences for all people. To the contrary, the effects were delayed for the majority of interview partners:

"At the time I did not have the feeling at all that I was learning anything new. Except the language, of course [...] But apart from that, I never had the feeling that, what do you say, that I had learned any social competence or the like."

"Looking back on it, when I went over the exchange again in my mind, I found I had learned a lot about myself."

"It took me a long time to realize what it had really meant. [...] But slowly I realized over the next year or probably more what has happened in that exchange."

Altogether, three different courses of development can be recognized: initial, delayed and carried-over development.

Initial development

The process of self-decentralization is in many cases activated by the very acute anxiety that the participant will not be sufficiently able to satisfy his or her need for social contacts in his or her guest country. This impending lack of contacts leads to the necessity for the exchange student to actively try to react to the foreign partners in a sensitive manner. "These endeavors can either consist of a general 'friendliness,' or of an attempt to adopt the schemata of the interacting partner that are relevant for interaction; that is to undergo a change in perspectives. In the terminology of Epstein's Theory of Personality this means that the automatic strategies of behavior no longer hold up" (Hetzenecker, 1999, p. 58). Patterns of action, constructed from one's own experiences of life, are reconsidered when compared to other patterns of action and then modified according to the norms and rules of behavior of the target culture. "In Australia I behaved differently and I realized later on that this behavior was better." Figure 1 shows a graphic representation of the initial development:

A complete consciousness of this process of learning, and consequently the possibility of consciously putting these new strategies to use at home as well, even though the need for contacts was no longer so acute, often first occurred a long time after returning home. The interviewees said that the reason for this was that initially,

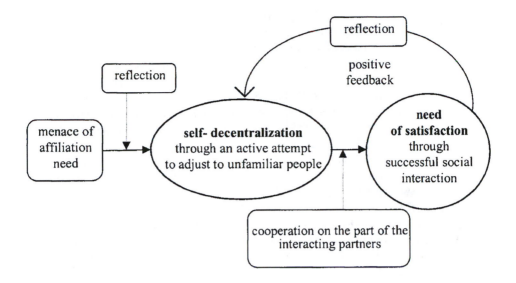

Figure 1. Initial Development

during the reintegration phase, they were incapable of reflecting on what they had experienced.

Delayed Development
With quite a few people, the self-decentralization process begins only after a certain delay in time. These persons initially interpret their experiences abroad based on their experiences in their own culture, that is, they activate the orientation system of their own country. Consequently, the people in the guest country sometimes experience their partners' actions as being very strange, and regard them as wrong, incomprehensible, and useless. Confrontation with an unfamiliar reality leads to an increase in cognitive dissonance and threatens the need for coherence. Thus, cognitive processes increasingly start focusing on experiences made, in which the discrepancy between one's own and the foreign system of orientation becomes obvious, and the possibility for a reduction in the dissonance is critically examined. A possible result of this process of reflection is that the participant goes through a change in perspective, changing his perspective in such a way that the incorrectly interpreted experiences are interpreted in a culturally adequate manner. Like this, a gradual and belated self-decentralization begins. Figure 2 represents this delayed development of the effect.

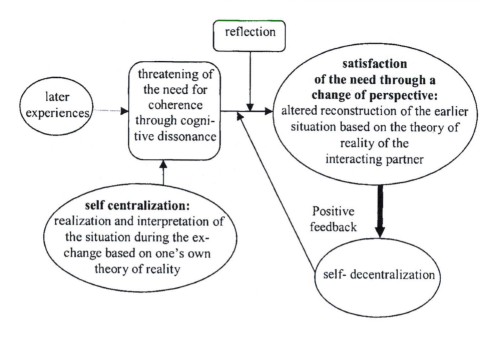

Figure 2. Delayed Development of the Effect

Carried-over development
In the interview material, there are cases where the process of decentralization is set in motion during a further trip abroad. The interviewees, however, see the origin for it being set in motion in their intercultural experiences during the student exchange. A basic willingness to learn is established during the student exchange, that allows for the easier start up and development of the self-decentralization process during a next stay abroad. Figure 3 shows the process of a carried-over development:

According to Epstein's theory of personality a satisfaction of needs through increased self-efficacy leads to an expansion of the theory of reality, coupled with an increased willingness to learn. It can therefore be presumed that the foreign exchange experience creates a certain basis that can be built upon in a following international exchange and at a higher level of learning. During the first international exchange, the willingness to learn was probably noticeably reduced because a strong threat to an adequate satisfaction of the need for control was experienced. This resulted in a noticeable restriction of the theory of reality. An increased willingness to acquire intercultural experiences leads, when combined with increased self-decentralization, to an increasingly satisfied need for control during a further intercultural exchange. The result is also an improvement in feelings of self-efficacy.

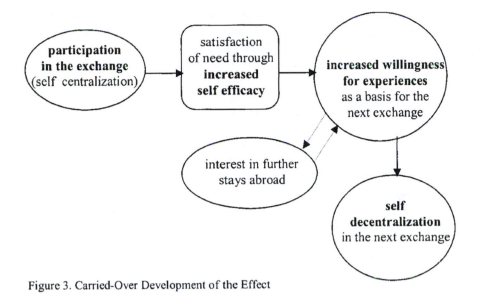

Figure 3. Carried-Over Development of the Effect

Conclusions

The results strengthen the hypothesis that experiences abroad cause, in one form or another, a change in the theory of reality: As far as the further course of life is concerned, such a change in the theory of reality starts up a 'chain reaction', that can be easily reconstructed using the data provided. The opening up of the theory of reality, brought about by the exchange, permits the individual to encounter new experiences, thereby offering the chance for increasing perceived self-efficacy. An increase in self-efficacy, in turn, offers the possibility of opening up the theory of reality even further. Due to this continuously self-strengthening feedback process, the possibility is increased that, during the course of life, critical incidents can be handled productively. It can thus be said that the biographical significance of the changes in personality caused by the exchange lies in the fact that psychological "protective factors" for avoiding or coping with critical events in life are built up (Filipp, 1983). "People who believe in their own competence, effectiveness, and control cope better and achieve more" (Myers, 1993, p. 109).

This pilot study showed that intercultural exchange experiences, occurring within the framework of an international youth exchange program, have a lasting effect on young people's personality development and the course of their lives. Also, it was shown that persons concerned are actually able to report on these effects. At least, they are able to report at the time of the interview the memories they have of the exchange as well as its effects, although, these accounts must possibly be considered as rather subjective constructions of reality. Of course, the actual perceptions, thoughts, appraisals, and actions of the time cannot be reconstructed from an external, objective point of view. The account will inevitably be from an inner perspective, influenced by construction and interpretation processes.

A generalization of the long-term effects of international student and youth exchanges based on the results described should be ruled out, since the interviewees participated in a very specific program that not only permitted a three-month stay in a guest culture but also involved a three month cohabitation with a guest student in one's home country.

Further investigations should examine what types of programs generate which long-term effects. The general validity of the results is greatly restricted by the fact that, of the 60 former exchange students who were contacted by mail, only 25 subjects participated in the inquiry. As far as those who were not willing to participate in the inquiry are concerned, nothing is known about their experiences with the exchange program and its effects. It is very possible that only those persons who took part in the inquiry positively assessed their participation in the exchange program.

It is generally recognized, and this recognition can also be generalized, that it is often useful for organizers of student and youth exchange programs of this type to participate in scientific research that inquires into the long-term effects of their programs. In this manner alone, these organizations can receive scientifically based findings, as well as a differentiated understanding of the processes of learning that were initiated during the student exchange and their long-term effects. In addition, through this exploratory investigation, using partly structured, focused or narrative interviews, important cognitive processes that occurred during the course of the program and the years thereafter, can, at least from the point of view of the participants, be reconstructed in a differentiated manner. The resulting text material can, with the help of scientific concepts and theories, be analyzed, allowing valuable knowledge for the organizers of international youth exchanges to be won, as well as an improved theoretical understanding of – in view of globalization and internationalization – the increasingly important field of "International Student and Youth Exchanges."

References

Anderson, L. E. (1994). A new look at an old construct: Cross-cultural adaptation. *International Journal of Intercultural Relations, 18*, 293-328.

Berry, J. W. (1994). Acculturation and psychological adaptation: An overview. In A.-M. Bouvy & F. J. R. van de Vijver (Eds.), *Journeys into cross-cultural psychology* (pp. 129-14). Bristol, PA: Swets & Zeitlinger.

Brislin, R. W. (1994). *Intercultural communication training*. Thousand Oaks, CA: Sage.

Epstein, S. (1979). Entwurf einer integrativen Persönlichkeitstheorie [Scheme of an integrative theory of personality]. In S.-H. Filipp (Ed.), *Selbstkonzept-Forschung* (pp. 15-45). Stuttgart, Germany: Klett-Cotta.

Epstein, S. (1990). Cognitive-experiential self-theory. In L. A. Pervin (Ed.), *Handbook of personality: Theory and research* (pp. 165-192). New York: The Guilford Press.

Epstein, S. (1991). Cognitive-experiential self-theory: An integrative theory of personality. In R. C. Curtis (Ed.), *The relational self: Theoretical convergences in psychoanalysis and social psychology* (pp. 111-137). New York: The Guilford Press.

Epstein, S. (1993a). Entwurf einer integrativen Persönlichkeitstheorie [Scheme of an integrative theory of personality]. In S. H. Filipp (Ed.), *Selbstkonzept-Forschung: Probleme, Befunde, Perspektiven* (3rd ed., pp. 15-45). Stuttgart, germany: Klett-Cotta.

Epstein, S. (1993b). Implications of cognitive-experiential self-theory for personality and developmental psychology. In D. C. Funder, R. D. Parke, C. Tomlinson-Keasey, & K. Widaman (Eds.), *Studying lives through time: Personality and development* (pp. 399-438). Washington, DC: American Psychological Association.

Filipp, S. H. (1983). Die Rolle von Selbstkonzepten im Prozess der Auseinandersetzung mit und Bewältigung von kritischen Lebensereignissen [The role of self-concepts for dealing and coping with critical life events]. *Zeitschrift für Personenzentrierte Psychologie und Psychotherapie, 2,* 39-47.

Gudykunst, W. B., & Hammer, M. R. (1988). Strangers and hosts. In Y. Y. Kim & W. B. Gudykunst (Eds.), *Cross-cultural adaptation* (pp. 106-139). Newbury Park, CA: Sage.

Hetzenecker, D. (1999). *Analyse der langfristigen Auswirkungen eines internationalen Schüleraustauschprogramms auf die Persönlichkeit und den weiteren Lebenslauf der Teilnehmer [Analysis of the long-term effects of an international student exchange program on the personality of the participants and the further course of their lives].* Unpublished Diploma thesis, University of Regensburg, Germany.

Kelly, G. A. (1955). *The psychology of personal constructs* (Vol. 1). New York: Norton.

Kühlmann, T. M. (1995). Die Auslandsentsendung von Fach- und Führungskräften: Eine Einführung in die Schwerpunkte und Ergebnisse der Forschung [The dispatch of skilled employeees and senior staff to foreign countries: An introduction of main issues and results of research]. In T. M. Kühlmann (Ed.), *Mitarbeiterentsendung ins Ausland: Auswahl, Vorbereitung, Betreuung und Wiedereingliederung* (pp. 1-30). Göttingen, Germany: Verlag für Angewandte Psychologie.

Maturana, H. R., & Varela, F. J. (1987). *Der Baum der Erkenntnis [The tree of knowledge]*. Bern, Switzerland: Scherz.

Myers, D. G. (1993). *Social Psychology*. New York: McGraw-Hill.

Reed, E. S. (1996). *Encountering the world*. New York: Oxford University Press.

Thomas, A. (Ed.). (1988). *Interkulturelles Lernen im Schüleraustausch [Intercultural learning in exchange of students]*. (SSIP-Bulletin No. 58). Saarbrücken, Germany: Breitenbach.

15

Collective Self-Esteem and Acculturation: A Case Study of European and Japanese Internship Students

Makoto Kobayashi

Introduction

This study deals with the role of the collective self-esteem for acculturation processes in a foreign cultural context and provides the example of European students visiting Japan in comparison to Japanese students visiting Europe. The study of acculturation is an important topic in international education today and is in step with the increased mobility of people beyond national boundaries. Intercultural tolerance is a generally required skill today enabling people to live together peacefully and contributing to the prevention of intercultural conflict. From a psychological viewpoint, the function of the self-concept, especially self-esteem – the evaluative aspect of the self-concept –, is important as it represents a fundament of social cognition and behavior in collective interaction between members of various cultural groups. This study attempts to explore culturally variant and universal aspects of collective self-esteem and its function with regard to the promotion of intercultural tolerance in a Euro-Japanese comparison. Thereby, the acquisition of a theoretical and methodological basis for the development of educational programs promoting intercultural tolerance is pursued.

One important factor in the research of acculturation is the length of stay. As previous studies have shown, a short-term stay in a foreign culture is connected in part with certain problems and tasks with respect to psychological adaptation (Thomas, 2000; see also Thomas in this volume). In today's global age, people are increasingly paying attention to the effects of the experience acquired by staying abroad. The short-term stay has become an especially popular topic; it is often integrated in company training programs and studied in academic institutions. Thus, it will be of great interest to explore from a psychological viewpoint the characteristic processes of acculturation typically observed during short-term stays in a different cultural context.

Intercultural Tolerance

In accordance with progressing globalization, people have come to recognize education as an international issue transcending the autonomous system within national boundaries. In this contemporary context, the promotion of "understanding, tolerance and friendship among all nations, racial or religious groups" has become a significant objective of education (United Nations, 1948: Universal Declaration of Human Rights, Article 16). The question is what constitutes the psychological foundation of a tolerant attitude towards cultural diversity, particularly in international relations. Obviously, it is an important task of intercultural education to find and analyze the psychological conditions for the promotion of intercultural tolerance, which is the main objective in the educational UNESCO program "Culture of Peace" (Kobayashi, 1998; Reardon, 1997; Yoshitani, 2001).

In this respect, cross-cultural psychology is expected to provide a theoretical and empirical contribution towards the development of educational program aimed at the promotion of tolerance and its related psychological features, even though it is not the central issue of cultural psychology. Intercultural tolerance can be defined as the psychological readiness to accept people with different racial, ethnic, religious and ideological background for living together with mutual respect in peaceful relations. This intercultural tolerance is supposed to be a significant factor predicting the quality of the acculturation of immigrants in an unfamiliar cultural context.

One important aspect of acculturation is that it contains not only interindividual interactions, but is also closely related to collective perceptions. It corresponds to the phenomenon, for example, that a foreign resident is normally regarded not as an idiosyncratic individual, but rather as a foreign national (i.e., one sample of the concerned ethnic or national group), at least in the first phase of human interactions with citizens of the host country. Berry's model of acculturation (Berry & Sam, 1997) is basically concerned with the individual strategy to adapt oneself to the foreign cultural context. The image held of the cultural or ethnic groups, which the interacting individuals respectively belong to, influences the quality of the interactive communication. The stereotyping of the communication partner on account of his or her nationality or socio-cultural background tends to happen with higher intensity at the beginning of an intercultural encounter (Gudykunst, Yoon & Nishida, 1987). Therefore, the socio-cultural attributes of the individual who enters into a different cultural environment must be a significant factor deciding the type of acculturation that will result. Taking this collective aspect of acculturation into consideration, it is necessary to pay attention to the collective components, which affect intercultural tolerance (see Berry, this volume).

The factors influencing intercultural tolerance can vary according to different sets of personal and situational conditions. The combination of the cultural backgrounds of two interaction partners is important, of course. However, the quality of the interaction between these two partners also depends on the question who is dealing with foreign guests in his own country and who is staying abroad as a foreigner and interacting with people of the host country (Furnham & Bochner, 1986). This makes a substantial difference because the motivational baseline for cultural adaptation is expected to be different: people who enter a foreign culture based upon their own free decision are supposed to possess a generally higher level of interest in the host country and also a higher level of motivation to learn about and experience the foreign culture.

The contact made with foreign nationals in one's own country or community, however, is often a forced situation, which does not necessarily enhance motivational readiness to learn more about the foreign culture. It is expected, therefore, that travelers to a foreign culture are more open (at least in the initial phase of their sojourn) towards acculturation processes including perception and value change. As for this openness, it should also be taken into account that the contextual background of an intercultural encounter plays a significant role here as well; for example, the position of a visitor (a tourist, a student, a business person, a military officer in a belligerent situation, an immigrant or a refugee etc.) is a decisive factor influencing the quality of personal interaction. Furthermore, the life domain concerned with regard to tolerance, i.e. whether it concerns customs in daily life, occupational life, private life including marriage, political or religious ideology, is another factor that can affect the quality of acculturation.

In addition, the quality of acculturation depends on the duration of the sojourn in the foreign culture. This means not only the time-related stages of acculturation processes (Adler, 1975), but it is also related to the goals set and therefore the expectations of the visitor and of the host persons with regard to the stay. The present study focuses on internship students' short-term stay abroad, and data analysis will also be confined to this particular kind of experience of intercultural encounter. It is expected that from the beginning this kind of short-term internship is connected with very different acculturation problems and tasks, than those that business people confront during their long-term stays in a foreign country, or the problems immigrants and refugees encounter who have no definite schedule to return to their own country. Thus, the specification of the concrete setting of the transcultural experience is essential for the psychological study of acculturation.

Collective Self-Esteem as a Predictor of Intercultural Tolerance

Considering the significance of the collective aspects of acculturation, it seems to be necessary to examine the role of cultural identity, particularly the *collective self-esteem* as the evaluative aspect of cultural identity.

The concept of collective self-esteem (Crocker & Luthanen, 1990) is derived from the general self-esteem. According to the classic definition by Rosenberg, self-esteem is understood as the feeling of self-acceptance based on one's own recognized superiority (Rosenberg, 1965). In most cases, the role of self-esteem has only been taken into consideration at the individual level. However, intercultural understanding contains a group interaction aspect. The consciousness of the cultural backgrounds always influences the quality of interaction between individuals with different cultural affiliations on account of their mutual image reflections. James has already indicated that the social self is a fundamental aspect of the self, along with the physical and spiritual self (James, 1890/1950).

It is assumed that in intercultural communication this socio-cultural aspect of the self is activated to a higher level than in communication within the domestic context. Collective self-esteem is defined as an *evaluative feeling or attitude towards the socio-cultural group* (culture, nation, country, region, social or occupational group etc.) *to which a person belongs* (Crocker & Luhtanen, 1990). Due to the activation of the socio-cultural aspect of self in the intercultural context, this collective self-esteem is supposed to play an important role in the formation of intercultural tolerance, regardless of whether the person interacts with foreign guests in their own country or the person goes abroad into a foreign cultural context.

A variety of psychological studies on acculturation have shown that ethnic and cultural identities play a crucial role influencing the psychological well being of immigrants (e.g. Silbereisen, Lantermann & Schmitt-Rodermund, 1999; Sam, 2000; Weinrich, Luk & Bond, 1996). In these studies, collective self-esteem has been dealt with mostly as an indicator for the success or failure of the acculturation process. It seems to be necessary, however, to consider self-esteem not only as an indicator for the acculturation, but also as a precondition for the facilitation of the acculturation process. Nozaki (1999) pays close attention to the important function of collective self-esteem in the promotion of international education; assuming that the feeling of one's superiority or at least equality could provide the readiness to accept others with different backgrounds. This research seems to suggest that positive collective self-esteem constitutes the fundament of a positive attitude towards interaction with people from different cultural backgrounds.

Collective self-esteem has increasingly attracted the attention of researchers in the study of acculturation and cultural adaptation (Trimble, Helms, & Root, 2002). In the guidelines for international education issued by UNESCO (Japanese National Commission for UNESCO, 1982), the self-consciousness of one's own culture and the respect for other cultures are both listed as compatible educational objectives to be pursued. Self-consciousness of one's own culture can be interpreted as a positive collective self-esteem, while the respect for other cultures is regarded as a basic aspect of intercultural tolerance. It shall provide a basic orientation for the curriculum development in education for intercultural understanding.

The question is, whether (positive) collective self-esteem even may constitute a psychological prerequisite for intercultural tolerance. Such relations are indirectly confirmed by studies that have shown that the confidence in one's own group identity, i.e. positive collective self-esteem, tends to promote an open-minded attitude towards other groups, enhancing the willingness to share ideas and assumptions with other groups (Berry & Kalin, 1995; Derman-Sparks, 1989); and this may foster intercultural tolerance. To the contrary, the perceived threat to one's own group identity would easily lead to the aggressive and exclusive attitude towards outsiders (Berry & Sam, 1997) and block the fostering of intercultural tolerance. Collective self-esteem comprises at least two different aspects, which have to be differentiated: the degree of identification with the group and the degree of evaluation. These two aspects will be described in the following.

Object and degree of identification of collective self-esteem

Normally a person belongs to various social groups at the same time. For example, an individual can be an Asian, a Japanese national, a citizen of a city, a member of a university, a psychologist, a member of an association, of a family etc. If the so-called collective self-esteem is object-specific, it means that a person represents several collective self-esteems at the same time. From the perspective of personality integrity, however, these plural collective self-esteems must be integrated into one single evaluative system attributed to the individual personality. In this respect, it appears to be necessary that the subjective importance of each socio-cultural group to which the individual belongs be assessed, in order to make clear which social attribute is more or less important for evaluative self-awareness of the concerned individual. For the purpose of cultural comparisons of collective self-esteem, this cannot be ignored. In terms of cross-cultural equivalency, it must be checked whether the same identity object, such as the national identity, has the equivalent subjective importance for the self-esteem of the different samples concerned. The functional equivalency of the same concept in various cultural contexts is a crucial point, which should always be taken into consideration in such cross-cultural studies (Trommsdorff, 2003; van de Vijver & Leung, 1997).

This subjective importance of a social category relates to the degree to which a person identifies himself with the social group. If the person feels strongly attached to his own culture or ethnic group, the degree of identification shall bear a high value. The *identification* is defined as the *degree of how strong the person perceives the social group as one part of his self*. A high level of identification does not necessarily mean, though, that the person evaluates the concerned social group positively or highly. In the conceptualization by Crocker and Luthanen (1993), this relative weight of various group objects according to the degree of identification is not taken into account. To understand the structural complexity of collective self-esteem, however, this is an indispensable aspect to be reflected in the theory formation.

Degree of evaluation as part of collective self-esteem

The degree of identification should be differentiated from the *degree of evaluation*, namely *how positively the person estimates his own socio-cultural background*. This differentiation has not been taken enough into consideration in the previous studies on self-esteem (e.g., Rosenberg, 1986), but it is an important point for the clarification of the self-esteem structure. On account of this differentiation, it becomes understandable that a person strongly identifies with his own culture but suffers from an inferiority complex in regard to this same cultural belongingness. The survey by NHK on the consciousness structure of the Japanese people provides us with an example of this point: 97% of the inquired 5000 Japanese citizens answered that they are happy to be born as Japanese, while, at the same time, most of them answered that Japan is inferior or backwards in many aspects when compared to western countries (NHK Broadcasting Culture Research Institute, 2000).

This consideration leads to the question: What actually makes a person feel attached to his own culture even if it cannot correspond with the highest evaluation? In his theory of the multidimensional self-concept validation, Bracken assumes that the self-concept always implies some validation (Bracken, 1996; Enomoto, 1998). This point is also relevant for the differentiation between "knowledge of one's own culture" and "recognition of one's own culture by the other." As generally discussed, self-esteem contains cognitive elements. In so far, whether the person thinks that he has good knowledge (cognitive fundament) of his own culture shall be a significant precondition, which provides the person's collective self-esteem with some solid stability.

The problem is that this cognition is connected with evaluation of collective self-esteem. When it is concerned with evaluation, the other's reflective evaluation about one's own culture (the perception of how far the own culture is acknowledged and evaluated by foreign people in the international society) significantly contributes to the formation of one's collective self-esteem. Due to the reflective nature of self-esteem, whether it is on the personal or collective level, the perceived evaluation of one's own culture by the other, and also the desire for better acknowledgement by the international community, in connection with this perceived evaluation, needs to be estimated independently from the perceived knowledge of one's own culture, which does not contain the evaluative perspective of the others.

The image of the host country also contains evaluative elements. This is related to the direct evaluation of another culture, in difference to the perceived or presumed evaluation by the other. But as previous studies have indicated (Phinney, 1995; Yamazaki, Kuramoto, Nakamura, & Yokoyama, 2000), the image of the host country is influenced by the reflected self-image in the eyes of the other. This image of the host country then again has some degree of influence on the quality of interaction with the people of the host country. On account of this process model, the image of the host country will be assessed as an indicator for the acculturation, particularly with regard to the readiness for interpersonal relationships in the foreign context.

Characteristics of European and Japanese Culture

For effective implementation of a cross-cultural study, the assurance of intercultural equivalence of core concepts is a key issue. In this concern, it is a crucial question to determine whether national identity has the same psychological substance for European and Japanese people. First, as Triandis (1989) pointed out, the assumption is plausible that for members of a collectivist culture, collective identity has more significance in self-construction as compared to members of an individualistic culture, to which most European countries are assumed to belong.

Whether Japan is to be regarded as a collectivist culture is subject to various disputes, and the intra-continental variety within European countries with regard to the individualism-collectivism scale should not be ignored either (see also Kagitcibasi, this volume; Klages, this volume). It can be assumed at least, however, that the different construal of the self in relation to others, as revealed in the cross-cultural study of Markus and Kitayama (1991), makes a considerable difference as to the perceived meaning of the collective identity for Japanese (possessing interdependent view of the self) and Europeans (possessing independent view of the self). Second, the supra-national identity that characterizes the identity formation of European people at the EU-level in the current geo-political situation is far from any psychological reality for the most Japanese people, whose collective identity appears to be fixed to the national boundaries.

As mentioned earlier, acculturation is not an abstract concept, but always a concrete process of change that is taking place within a specific cultural encounter context. So far it is necessary to take into consideration the specific cultural backgrounds of the visitor and the host. There are many cross-cultural studies in psychology comparing America and Japan, or Europe and America, but only few have focused on comparing Europe and Japan. Due to the expected structural difference of collective identity, the Euro-Japanese comparison in psychological terms will provide us with valuable information about behavioral tendencies, particularly in the intercultural encounter.

With regard to acculturation tasks, it is assumed that European students staying in Japan and Japanese students staying in Europe are confronted with different quality of challenges. Generally speaking, some training of self-assertion and behavioral management of the individual's initiative will be necessary for Japanese students visiting Europe to study, work or take part in an internship. European students, on the other hand, who go to Japan will be more concerned with the acculturation task of adapting themselves to a more group-oriented way of behavior or attitude, which is often more functionally adaptive than direct self-assertion based on the consciousness of one's individual originality.

Reciprocal expectations and perceptions of Europe and Japan
As for the difficulty level of the acculturation task, there are striking perspectives due to the unique features of the Euro-Japanese relationship. Since the Meiji Restoration in 1868, Japan has maintained positive relations to European countries with few political or economic conflicts. This is mainly owing to Europe's role as a model of modernization for Japanese society. This socio-historical condition has resulted in the fact that there have been many more Japanese students visiting Europe, the model of modernization, than European students going to Japan. For a long time, Japan has been merely the object of exotic interest for many Europeans. This historically conditioned one-sidedness in the cultural exchange between Europe and Japan, reflected in the asymmetrical number of exchange students, implies that Japanese students generally have more knowledge of European society and culture than Europeans know about Japan. In this respect, it can be supposed that Japanese students have a better starting point for acculturation in Europe than European students coming to Japan. It should also be pointed out that the image of Europe possessed by Japanese people is generally much more positive than Europeans' general image of Japan (e.g. Wilkinson, 1980).

Aspects of collective self-esteem in Europe and Japan
How is this property of the Euro-Japanese relationship reflected in the collective self-esteem of Japanese and European students? The traditional one-sidedness of the Euro-Japanese relationship leads to the assumption that the collective self-esteem of European students will be higher than that of Japanese students. In addition, as Heine, Kitayama and Lehman (2001) point out, Japanese people have the tendency to accept negative self-relevant information, whereas Americans are strongly influenced by self-enhancing motivation in their self-assessment. In comparing the general level of collective self-esteem cross-culturally, however, it needs to be also examined whether and how far the motivational and behavioral function of collective self-esteem is culturally equivalent. In the present study, a critical question will be to see whether there is a culture-specific function of the collective self-esteem for the acculturation process in the case of European and Japanese students.

Research Questions

The questions and hypothesis investigated in this study primarily relate to European students since no Japanese data could be collected at the end of the internship for administrative reasons.

Do the European students' collective self-esteem and their image of Japan change over the duration of the short-term stay?

Do European and Japanese students differ in regard to the collective self-esteem and the main object of group identity in the beginning of the internship?

The main goal was to examine the function of the collective self-esteem of the European students for their acculturation process in Japan. The hypothesis is that positive collective self-esteem concerning one's own cultural background will foster the acculturation process in a foreign cultural context through the enhancement of intercultural tolerance.

Study about Collective Self-Esteem and Acculturation

Methods

Sample

50 European students, who stayed in Japan in the summer of 1999 for a two-month internship at Japanese companies as participants of the EU internship program "Euro-Asia Business Internship Program (EABIP)," participated in this study. The EABIP was founded and financed by the European Commission and is managed by the DAAD (German Academic Exchange Service).

The 35 male and 15 female students came from 13 EU countries: Great Britain (10), Germany (7), Sweden (6), Austria (5), Belgium (4), France (3), Spain (3), Netherlands (3), Greece (3), Italy (2), Portugal (2), Denmark (1) and Finland (1). Their age ranged from 20 to 29 years, with an average age of 22.5 years. As for their academic specialty, 34 of the European students were students of economics or business management, and 16 were majoring in engineering and technology.

This sample was divided into two subgroups: students from Mediterranean countries and those from Transalpine countries. However, no significant differences were found between the two subgroups concerning the variables. Thus, the division along geographic regions was not included in the following data analysis.

49 Japanese students, who took up a two-month business internship in Europe for the same program EABIP as their European counterparts, participated. This group consisted of 25 male and 24 female students and came from 13 Japanese universities (6 State and 7 private universities). Their age ranged from 21 to 29 years, with an average of 22.2 years. Thus the age of the Japanese students was almost equivalent with that of the European students. As for the academic specialty, 20 Japanese students were studying economics or business management, 8 law, 8 engineering and technology, and 7 politics. In addition, 4 Japanese students were majoring in international relations, one student in German literature and one student in European studies. As mentioned above, the Japanese data were only collected during the initial phase of their departure to Europe, so that the cross-cultural comparison between European and Japanese students was only partly possible.

Instruments

A questionnaire was developed by the author for the assessment of the collective self-esteem of the participating students, their image of the host country as an indicator for their intercultural tolerance towards acculturation, and the national or supra-national level of identification. The questionnaire consisted of 22 questions on the collective self-esteem* of the students, 23 questions on their image of the host country. All items were answered on a 5-point scale from 1 – totally false to 5 – very true. One question concerning the level of identification asked whether they identify themselves more with their country (national identity) or more with the supra-national identity (Europe/Asia).

The Japanese supervisor of each European student evaluated the internship student by answering a general assessment sheet. Each host company submitted this assessment to the European Commission in respect to the EABIP and the trainees they hosted. This sheet consisted of three evaluations. (a) Evaluation of the student's Working Attitude: 1 – reluctant to work, lacks enthusiasm; 2 – does what is required but without much enthusiasm; 3 – usually shows enthusiasm, has a steady approach to routine work; 4 – prepared to work hard as and when required; 5 – high level of enthusiasm throughout the internship and always works hard. (b) The intern's relationships with Japanese colleagues in the company: 1 – difficulty in communicating with others; prefers to work alone; 2 – cooperates readily but lacks confidence to work in teams; 3 – communicates well with most people; useful team member; 4 – communicates well with all levels of staff; a strong team member. 5 – excellent communicator; inspires and improves team performance. (c) A general assessment: 1 – unsatisfactory, 2 – below average, 3 – average, 4 – very good, 5 – outstanding.

Procedure
The European students were asked to fill in the researcher's questionnaire immediately after their arrival in Japan. The Japanese students answered the questionnaire shortly before their departure for Europe. This means that both European and Japanese data were collected in Japan. However, cultural bias expected from this location is supposed to be eliminated because in each case the research team consisted of Japanese *and* European members. After their two-month internship in Japan, the supervisors of the Japanese host companies were requested to evaluate their internship student. The European students were asked by the bi-cultural research team, consisting of Japanese and European members, to answer the second questionnaire immediately before returning to Europe, in order to measure their image of Japan during the internship (post-test).

Variables
Four aspects of *Collective Self-Esteem* were measured: (1) *Positive Feeling*, i.e., positive degree of evaluation: The degree of evaluation of collective self-esteem was measured by 8 items, e.g. "I believe that the culture of my country is superior to

---

* In a previous paper of the author, the first variable was called "cultural identity" (Kobayashi, 2002). However, as the items consisting this variable are concerned mainly with affective-evaluative aspects of the cultural identity, it shall better be called "collective self-esteem" in more specific sense.

other cultures." (2) *Belonging*, i.e. degree of identification with one's own culture: The degree of identification included 5 items, e.g. "I get angry if foreign people criticize my country." (3) *Knowledge* of one's own culture was measured by 3 items, e.g., "I have no difficulty explaining the culture of my country to foreign people." (4) *Recognition*, i.e., desire for international recognition: This scale contained 4 items, e.g., "I feel that the culture of my country is underestimated in the international community."

The *level of identification* was dichotomously coded, higher identification with the national identity or with the supra-national identity (Europe/Asia).

The *Image of the Host Country* actually referred to the image of Japan because these questions were only put to the European students. Five dimensions were assessed: (1) *Interest in Japan* consisted of 4 items, e.g., "I want to make Japanese friends." (2) *Evaluation of Japan* contained 6 items, e.g., "Japan is a highly developed society." (3) *Evaluation of the Openness of Japan* consisted of 4 items, e.g., "It is easy to make real friends among Japanese." (4) *Knowledge of Japan* was measured by 2 items, e.g., "I have a good knowledge of Japanese history," and (5) *Collectivist View of Japan* was assessed by the item: "Japanese people always behave collectively."

Supervisors' evaluation of the student: The supervisors of the Japanese host companies were requested to evaluate their internship student with regard to (1) their working attitude, (2) their interpersonal relationships with Japanese colleagues in the company and (3) a general assessment (see above).

The internal consistency of the scales reached intermediate levels for collective self-esteem: Positive Feeling: α = .68 (Europeans), α = .72 (Japanese); Belonging: α = .54 (Europeans), α = .54 (Japanese); Knowledge: α = .69 (Europeans), α = .72 (Japanese); Recognition: α = .61 (Europeans), α = .53 (Japanese).

For the Image of the Host Country only data of the European sample were available. The internal consistencies revealed a rather modest pattern: Interest: pretest: α = .53; posttest α= .75; Evaluation: pretest: α = .57; posttest: α = .42; Openness: pretest: α = .44; posttest α = .65; Knowledge: pretest: α = .71.

Results

Collective self-esteem and the image of Japan for European students
Differences in cultural self-esteem, image of Japan and changes in the image of Japan were tested for the European students by taking gender and academic specialty into account (see Table 1). There were no differences in cultural self-esteem. One significant effect appeared for the image of Japan. The students of business administration showed significantly higher level of knowledge of Japan than the students of engineering (see Table 1). Concerning the changes of image, the evaluations before and after the internship were compared and two significant effects appeared: The female students' evaluation of Japan changed more into a negative direction during their stay in Japan in comparison to the male students (see Table 1).

Table 1
Collective Self-Esteem and the Image of Japan in European Students

Variable	Total Sample	Gender		Faculty	
		Male	Female	Business	Engineering
	(N = 50)	(n = 35)	(n = 15)	(n = 34)	(n = 16)
	M (SD)	M (SD)	M (SD)	M (SD)	M (SD)
Collective Self-Esteem					
Positive Feeling	3.47 (.59)	3.50 (.60)	3.38 (.58)	3.55 (.56)	3.29 (.65)
Belonging	3.20 (.70)	3.16 (.68)	3.31 (.78)	3.13 (.76)	3.36 (.56)
Knowledge	3.68 (.73)	3.59 (.72)	3.89 (.74)	3.67 (.79)	3.71 (.63)
Desire for Recog-nition	3.37 (.65)	3.44 (.65)	3.22 (.63)	3.46 (.64)	3.17 (.64)
Image of Japan					
Interest	3.63 (.60)	3.67 (.62)	3.56 (.58)	3.68 (.59)	3.54 (.64)
Evaluation	4.30 (.47)	4.27 (.41)	4.39 (.63)	4.27 (.45)	4.38 (.55)
Openness	2.87 (.50)	2.89 (.53)	2.83 (.42)	2.88 (.42)	2.85 (.64)
Knowledge	2.14 (.83)	2.06 (.86)	2.33 (.75)	**2.32* (.83)**	**1.75*(.68)**
Collectivism	3.38 (.99)	3.29 (1.04)	3.60 (.83)	3.35 (1.04)	3.44 (.89)
Change of Image					
Interest	-.09 (.87)	-.16 (.87)	.07 (.87)	**-.24* (.91)**	**.23* (.68)**
Evaluation	-.20 (.54)	**-.09* (.46)**	**-.49*(.64)**	-.24 (.57)	-.12 (.50)
Openness	.23 (.70)	.29 (.68)	.10 (.76)	.15 (.75)	.42 (.55)
Collectivism	.17 (1.10)	.03 (1.19)	.50 (.76)	.15 (1.09)	.20 (1.15)

Note. * *p* < .05

With regard to the academic specialty, the students of engineering showed a positive change concerning their interest in Japan, while the interest of business students in Japan decreased during their stay (see Table 1).

Cross-cultural comparison in collective self-esteem
The cross-cultural comparison of the four dimensions of collective self-esteem yielded two significant effects (see Table 2). With regard to Knowledge of one's own culture, the European students scored significantly higher than their Japanese counterparts, $t(95) = 3.34$, $p < .001$ and Desire for Recognition proved to be significantly higher for the Japanese students than for the Europeans, $t(95) = 5.62$, $p < .001$. Japanese students feel their own culture is less acknowledged abroad and want it to be recognized higher as well as broader in the international circle, than is currently the case. It can be interpreted as a sign for an inferiority complex, which the Japanese students have towards their own cultural background.

As for Positive Feeling and Belonging there were no significant differences between the two samples. Japanese students showed a similar emotional attachment to

Table 2
Collective Self-Esteem in Euro-Japanese Comparison

Collective Self-Esteem	Europeans ($n = 50$) M (SD)	Japanese ($n = 49$) M (SD)	T-values
Positive Feeling	3.47 (.59)	3.51 (.60)	.37
Belonging	3.20 (.70)	3.22 (.78)	.11
Knowledge	3.68 (.73)	3.15 (.84)	3.34***
Recognition	3.37 (.65)	4.07 (.58)	5.62***

Note. ***$p < .001$.

their own culture like the European students. This means that an intensive feeling of belongingness or attachment to one's own culture does not necessarily contradict with the presence of inferiority feeling. This is an indirect evidence for the necessity to differentiate between the degree of identification and the degree of evaluation. As a Japanese interviewee stated, "I love my country and feel strongly attached to it even though I think my country is not superior to other countries in many respects."

Cross-cultural comparison of the identity object
As for the European students, about half of the sample preferred the supra-national European identity (48%, $n = 24$) to the national identity (52%, $n = 26$) while Japanese students showed apparent preference for the Japanese national identity (77.6%; $n = 38$) and only 22.4% ($n = 11$) for the Asian identity. The difference of the distribution between both samples concerning both answers reached a statistically significant level, $\chi^2(1) = 9.23, p < .01$). The concept of the supra-national identity "Europe" seems to have some psychological substance for many of the European students, while Japanese students have little sense of solidarity with Asian people in the framework of their collective identity.

Relations between collective self-esteem and the evaluation by the host side
Correlations were calculated between the average values of the subcategories that constitute the collective self-esteem of the European students, and the students' assessments by the Japanese supervisor of the host company (see Table 3). The results showed significant positive correlations between the positive degree of identification and the general assessment by the supervisor, $r(48) = .30; p < .05$, as well as between the intensity of belonging and the assessment of the intern's human relations in the Japanese host company, $r(48) = .33; p < .05$.

This means that the European students who have strong feeling of belongingness to their home culture tended to develop better human relations with their Japanese colleagues in the Japanese host company. And they also enjoyed a better evaluation by their supervisor in general. This result supports the hypothesis that positive col-

Table 3
Correlations between the Collective Self-Esteem of European Students and the Assessment by the Supervisor

Assessment	Collective Self-Esteem			
	Positive Feeling	Belonging	Knowledge	Recognition
General Assessment	-.04	.30*	.04	-.09
Working Performance	-.14	.02	.09	.01
Human Relations	.08	.33*	.11	.07

Note. * $p < .05$.

lective self-esteem fosters acculturation processes, and thereby enables better adaptation to the foreign cultural context. However, there was no significant correlation between the positive degree of evaluation and the assessment of the supervisor. Neither the knowledge of one's own culture nor the desire for international recognition showed any significant correlation with the supervisor's assessment. This result suggests that the degree of identification with one's own culture serves as a more important factor for the facilitation of acculturation process, than the degree of evaluation or the knowledge of one's own culture.

Discussion

The present cross-cultural study has aimed at exploring the function of collective self-esteem for the acculturation process as one aspect of intercultural tolerance, thereby focusing on the psychological features characteristic for a short-term stay in a foreign culture. The main hypothesis was that a positive collective self-esteem promotes or facilitates the acculturation processes. The study has several limitations: small sample size and lack of post-test for Japanese students. On account of these limitations, the present study should be seen as a pilot study, which may be developed into a large-scale, multidimensional study (with a more complete research design) for the cross-cultural comparison of acculturation. Nevertheless, several findings relevant to the examination of the hypothesis could be acquired. They relate particularly to the cultural comparison of collective self-esteem, the object of the collective identity (national vs. supra-national identity), and the validity of the differentiation between two components of the collective self-esteem: the degree of evaluation and the degree of identification.

First, the short-term stay did not effect any changes of the European students' collective self-esteem. Furthermore, the changes of Japan's image were also small and specific. The fact that students in business lost interest whereas students in engineering gained interest can be interpreted as follows: The work in business administration is subject more strongly to cultural variance than the work in engineering. For instance, the demand for Japanese proficiency was obviously higher for the business students than for the engineering students who could mostly get through with English in their working tasks. It implies that the business students were generally loaded with heavier psychosocial burdens in the process of cultural adaptation in comparison to the engineering students who could start with rather universalistic positions in their working ethos. Taking the short term of the stay into consideration, this higher demand for business students through more direct exposure to cultural difference seems to have played a significant role for decreasing their positive interest in the host country because they did not have enough time to meet this higher psychosocial demand. In addition, it should also be noticed that the engineering students in general could be integrated more easily into the working processes of the host company thanks to the wider universality of engineering and natural sciences, which provided them with greater chance to learn efficiently about the ongoing novelties in the Japanese host companies. The latter might also contribute to the increased interest of engineering students in Japan. The result that female students evaluated Japan less positively after the stay compared to the male students who did not change their evaluation might point to the fact that the Japanese society still does not meet enough the requirement of gender equity in working settings as well as in general, at least from the perspectives of European women. In this concern, the comparison of these European students' data with the gender difference of Japanese students in the changing process of their evaluation towards the European host societies would be an interesting question for future research.

Second, this study revealed cultural differences in several aspects of the collective self-esteem of European and Japanese students. Japanese students attributed a lower level of knowledge of their own culture and showed a stronger desire for broader recognition of their own culture by the international community in comparison to their European counterparts. These differences can be interpreted that Japanese students' collective self-esteem is characterized by inferiority feelings. At the same time, they show a similar intensive attachment to the collective identity like the European students. These results clearly point to the multidimensionality of the concept of collective self-esteem. In line with this argumentation, the different relations between the aspects of collective self-esteem with acculturation process also speak in favor for a differentiation of the structure of collective self-esteem at least between the degree of identification and the degree of evaluation.

In the present study we found an apparent difference in the preferred accent between European and Japanese subjects concerning the framework of their collective identity. European students seem to possess a double-leveled structure of collective identity and realize some kind of balancing between national and supra-national identity. On the contrary, the collective identity of the Japanese students obviously converges on the national level. The supra-national identity seems to have no psychological reality for Japanese subjects. There are surely various socio-cultural and historical factors, which contribute to this cultural difference. In this concern, we should also consider the significant socio-historical difference between both cultural constructs, "Europe" and "Asia": Whereas Europe has a common historical and cultural background in spite of its diversity, such as the Christian tradition and its Greek-Roman heritage, Asia should be understood rather as a fictive construct which has almost no common cultural factor among its member states other than its geographical location. Therefore, the two groups are not equivalent and one has to use different units, for example an East Asian identity might be less fictive. And another question is to differentiate between Western Europe and Eastern Europe identities.

When we investigate the functions of collective self-esteem further from a cross-cultural perspective, this difference in the structure of the collective identity, must be taken into consideration. The crucial point for our interest is the implications of these different frameworks for the development of collective self-esteem. It also puts the validity of the comparable measurement of collective identity into question because the national level of collective identity could have quite a different meaning and different weight for European and Japanese students. The question as to how to guarantee cross-cultural equivalency in the measurement of collective self-esteem shall be pursued further, taking into account the ipsative characteristics of collective identity, valid in each cultural context. In this respect, the dichotomy of European individualism and Japanese collectivism is not sufficient; it requires a qualitative analysis of the culture-specific model ("naïve theory") about the relation of the individual and the cultural attribute of the society, including its variability due to the ongoing process of social change (Kornadt & Eisler, 1998; Teichler, 1998).

Our hypothesis that positive collective self-esteem fosters the acculturation process in a foreign cultural context was partially supported, namely with regard to Belonging. The European students that reported strong feelings of belonging to their own cultural background tended to be evaluated more positively by their supervisors in respect to their relationship with their Japanese colleagues and their adaptation to the Japanese society in general. This result is in line with the finding that European students who had positive feelings about and strong attachment to their own culture tended to regard Japan as an open society (Kobayashi, 2002).

General conclusions and outlook

The short duration of the sojourn by the internship students in the host country must be pointed out as an important aspect of the present study. According to the acculturation model of Adler, the two-month stay is regarded as just the outset of the crisis period (Adler, 1975). The further process of recovery and integration beyond that initial period would be crucial for our interest in acculturation. For a more exact assessment of the acculturation process, a longitudinal research of these students would be necessary, including the analysis of the long-term adjustment processes after their return to the home country (see Thomas, this volume).

In order to obtain more general findings, it is necessary to realize cross-cultural comparison to test the consequences of the collective self-esteem for the acculturation processes. It is also necessary to assess the internship experience by the students themselves. Finally, the assessment of long-term effects of such short-term stays abroad on the collective self-esteem and on the development of intercultural tolerance would be a further interesting research question from the perspective of developmental psychology (see Thomas, this volume).

The present study revealed cultural variability of collective self-esteem and the significance of this collective self-esteem for the adaptation process in a foreign cultural context. The necessity to differentiate the two aspects of collective self-esteem, namely the degree of evaluation and the sense of belonging or identification is also a significant finding which shall be taken into consideration for further study on this topic. The systematic analysis of the multidimensional structure of the collective self-esteem on the one hand and the specification of the valid indicators for the intercultural tolerance on the other hand will be the next research tasks which we shall be confronted with towards the establishment of a systematic model for intercultural understanding. However, this result is too restricted to allow one to derive a general conclusion about the function of collective self-esteem. In order to obtain more general findings, it would have been desirable to compare the results with those of the Japanese students who implemented a two-month internship in Europe as well. Unfortunately this was not possible due to an insufficient data set at the time. This would have allowed us to analyze the consequences of the identity object for the acculturation processes in cross-cultural comparison. At the same time, it will be necessary to compare the assessment by the host company also with the subjective assessment of the internship experience by the students themselves. A long-term effect of the collective self-esteem upon the development of intercultural tolerance after the return to their home country would be an especially interesting research question from the perspective of developmental psychology.

References

Adler, P. S. (1975). The transitional experience: An alternative view of culture shock. *Journal of Humanistic Psychology, 15(4)*, 13-23.

Berry, J. W., & Kalin, R. (1995). Multicultural and ethnic attitudes in Canada: An overview of the 1991 National Survey. *Canadian Journal of Behavioural Science, 27*, 301-320.

Berry, J. W., & Sam, D. L. (1997). Acculturation and adaptation. In J. W. Berry, M. H. Segall, & C. Kagitcibasi (Eds.), *Handbook of cross-cultural psychology: Vol. 3. Social behavior and applications* (2nd ed., pp. 291-326). Boston: Allyn & Bacon.

Bracken, B. A. (1996). Clinical applications of a context-dependent, multidimensional model of self-concept. In B. A. Bracken (Ed.), *Handbook of self-concept* (pp. 463-503). New York: Wiley.

Crocker, J., & Luhtanen, R. (1990). Collective self-esteem and ingroup bias. *Journal of Personality and Social Psychology, 58*, 60-67.

Derman-Sparks, L. (1989). *Anti-bias curriculum: Tools for empowering young children*. Washington, DC: National Association for the Education of Young Children (NAEYC).

Enomoto, T. (1998). *Jiko-no Shinrigaku. Jibun-sagashi eno Sasoi* [Psychology of the Self: An introduction into self-exploration]. Tokyo: Saiensu-sha.

Furnham, A. & Bochner, S. (1986). *Culture shock: Psychological reactions to unfamiliar environments*. London: Methuen.

Gudykunst, W. B., Yoon, Y. C., & Nishida, T. (1987). The influence of individualism-collectivism on perceptions of communication in ingroup and outgroup relationships. *Communication Monographs, 54*, 295-306.

Heine, S. J., Kitayama, S., & Lehman, D. R. (2001). Cultural differences in self-evaluation: Japanese readily accept negative self-relevant information. *Journal of Cross-Cultural Psychology, 32*, 434-443.

James, W. (1890/1950). *The principles of psychology*. New York: Dover.

Japanese National Commission for UNESCO (1982). *Guidelines for international education*. Tokyo: Ministry of Education, Culture, Sports, Science and Technology.

Kobayashi, M. (1998). "The Culture of Peace" and education: A new transdisciplinary concept from UNESCO. *International Education, 4*, 64-74.

Kobayashi, M. (2002). Cultural identity and adaptation of European students in Japan. In U. Teichler & G. Trommsdorff (Eds.), *Challenges of the 21st century in Japan and Germany* (pp. 65-78). Lengerich, Germany: Pabst.

Kornadt, H.-J. & Eisler, A.-C. (1998). Psychological indicators of social change in Japan and Germany. In G. Trommsdorff, W. Friedlmeier & H.-J. Kornadt (Eds.), *Japan in transition. Sociological and psychological aspects* (pp. 243-258). Lengerich, Germany: Pabst.

NHK Broadcasting Culture Research Institute (2000). *The consciousness structure attitudes and awareness of Japanese today (5th Edition)*. Tokyo: Japan Broadcasting Publishing.

Markus, H. R., & Kitayama, S. (1991). Culture and the self: Implications for cognition, emotion, and motivation. *Psychological Review, 98*, 224-253.

Nozaki, S. (1999). Theoretical implications of the concept of self-esteem from psychological studies. *International Education, 5*, 40-53.

Phinney, J. (1995). Ethnic identity and self-esteem: A review and integration. In A. Padilla (Ed.), *Hispanic psychology: Critical issues in theory and research* (pp. 57-70). Thousand Oaks, CA: Sage.

Reardon, B. A. (1997). *Tolerance – the threshold of peace*. Paris: UNESCO Publishing.

Rosenberg, M. (1965). *Society and the adolescent self-image*. Princeton, NJ: Princeton University Press.

Rosenberg, M. (1986). Self-concept from middle childhood through adolescence. In J. Suls & A. G. Greenwald (Eds.), *Psychological perspectives on the self* (Vol. 3, pp. 107-136). Hillsdale, NJ: Erlbaum.

Sam, D. L. (2000). Psychological adaptation of adolescents with immigrant back-grounds. *Journal of Social Psychology, 140*, 5-25.

Silbereisen, R. K., Lantermann, E.-D., & Schmitt-Rodermund, E. (1999), Akkultura-tion von Aussiedlern: Viel gelernt – noch mehr zu tun [Acculturation of ethnic German repatriates: Learned a lot – still more to do]. In R. K. Silbereisen, E.-D. Lantermann, & E. Schmitt-Rodermund (Eds.), *Aussiedler in Deutschland: Akkulturation von Persönlichkeit und Verhalten* (pp. 367-381). Opladen, Germany: Leske+Budrich.

Teichler, U. (1998). Bildung und Beschäftigung in Japan und in Deutschland. Kon-traste und Gemeinsamkeiten [Education and work in Japan and Germany: Con-trasts and similarities]. In A. Takahashi & U. Teichler (Eds.), *Berufliche Kompetenzentwicklung im Bildungs- und Beschäftigungssystem in Japan und Deutschland* (pp. 183-190). Baden-Baden, Germany: Nomos.

Thomas, A. (2000). Globalisierung und interkulturelle Managementkompetenz [Globalization and intercultural management competence]. In B. Fahrenhorst & S. A. Musto (Eds.), *Grenzenlos. Kommunikation, Kooperation, Entwicklung (pp. 162-174).* Berlin, Germany: Society for International Development.

Trimble, J., Helms, J., & Root, M. (2002). Social and psychological perspectives on ethnic and racial identity. In G. Bernal, J. Trimble, K. Burlew, & F. Leong (Eds.), *Handbook on Racial and Ethnic Psychology.* Thousands Oaks, CA: Sage.

Triandis, H. C. (1989). The self and social behavior in differing cultural contexts. *Psychological Review, 96*, 506-520.

Trommsdorff, G. (2003). Kulturvergleichende Entwicklungspsychologie [Cross-cultural developmental psychology]. In A. Thomas (Ed.), *Kulturvergleichende Psychologie. Eine Einführung* (2nd ed., pp 139-179). Göttingen, Germany: Hogrefe.

United Nations (1948). *Universal Declaration of Human Rights.* Proclaimed in the General Assembly of the United Nations on 10 December 1948.

van de Vijver, F. J. R., & Leung, K. (1997). *Methods and data analysis for cross-cultural research.* Newbury Park, CA: Sage.

Weinrich, P., Luk, C. L., & Bond, M. H. (1996). Ethnic stereotyping and identifica-tion in a multicultural context: "Acculturation," self-esteem and identity diffu-sion in Hong Kong Chinese university students. *Psychology & Developing So-cieties, 8*, 107-169.

Wilkinson, E. (1980). *Misunderstanding - Europe vs. Japan.* Tokyo: Chuokoron-sha.

Yamazaki, M., Kuramoto, N. T., Nakamura, S., & Yokoyama, T. (2000). Formation of attitude of Asian students toward the Japanese and other cultures: Understand-ing in terms of ethnicity. *Japanese Journal of Educational Psychology, 48 (3)*, 305-314.

Yoshitani, T. (2001). Intercultural tolerance in European society: To cope with mul-ticultural setting of society. *Intercultural/Transcultural Education (Bulletin of Intercultural Education Society of Japan), 15*, 14-30.

Author Index

Aberle, D. F. 13
Abraham, M. 262-263, 281
Achenbaum, W. A. 44
Ackerman, B. P. 127
Acredolo, L. 172
Adamopoulos, J. 10
Adelson, J. 233, 239
Adler, P. S. 325, 338
Aiken, L. S. 217
Ainsworth, M. D. S. 77-83, 86, 88-90, 101-103, 106, 109-110, 112, 115, 117-119
Albas, C. A. 126
Albas, D. C. 126
Albert, I. 207, 225
Allen, J. P. 105, 241-242
Allport, G. W. 234
Alzate, G. 83, 109
Ames, E. W. 92
Anderson, L. E. 307
Angelillo, C. 100
Arenas, A. 83, 109
Armstrong, E. 78
Arnold, F. 209, 211
Aviezer, O. 82-83
Aydin, B. 267
Azuma, H. 99, 104, 116-118

Badinter, E. 77
Balls-Organista, P. 294
Bandura, A. 234-236
Barnes, R. H. 155

Basanez, M. 34, 209, 280
Baumrind, D. 241
Bechhofer, F. 286
Beck, U. 287
Beiser, M. 301
Bell, K. L. 241
Bell, S. M. 77-78, 82-83, 90
Bell-Krannhals, I. 85
Belsky, J. 105
Bem, D. J. 247
Bendix, R. 260
Bengtson, V. L. 44
Berry, J. W. 4-5, 11, 13, 15-18, 20, 32-33, 54, 153, 155, 157, 159, 258, 294-302, 307, 324, 327
Bharati, A. 47
Bickel, B. 158
Bilsky, W. 212, 214
Bischof-Köhler, D. 5, 78
Blass, R. B. 266
Blatt, S. J. 266
Blehar, M. C. 80
Block, W. 208
Blos, P. 266
Bochner, S. 296, 325
Boesch, E. E. xvii, 12, 19, 54
Bond, M. H. 267, 326
Bornholt, L. 206, 223
Bornstein, M. H. 83, 104
Boski, P. 19
Bourhis, R. 300

Bowlby, J. 77-79, 101, 113, 118-119
Bracken, B. A. 328
Bradshaw, D. L. 135
Bretherton, I. 84
Brislin, R. W. 18, 20, 307
Bronfenbrenner, U. 13
Bronstein, P. 9
Brown, P. 156-157
Bruner, J. S. 78, 100, 113
Bruschi, C. J. 136, 139, 146
Bujaki, M. 300
Burger, C. 236
Buss, D. M. 76, 78
Bustamante, M. R. 83, 109
Butzel, J. S. 267

Caldwell, J. C. 257
Campbell, D. T. 13, 18-19
Campos, J. J. 104, 135
Camras, L. A. 135
Cantril, H. 234
Carbonell, O. A. 83, 109
Carlson, D. S. 208
Carlson, E. 84
Carlson, V. 104, 116
Carter, M. C. 92
Carver, C. S. 237
Caspi, A. 247
Caudill, W. 135
Cha, J.-H. 209, 267

Chakkarath, P. 2, 32-34, 46, 99, 208
Chan, D. K.-S. 208, 212, 214
Chao, R. K. 79, 135, 206, 210, 224, 241-242
Charnov, E. L. 109
Chen, C. 223
Chen, S. Y. 84
Chen, S.-J. 104
Chen, X. 242
Chen, X. P. 208
Chisholm, K. M. 92
Cho, E. 84
Chodynicka, A. M. 19
Choi, I. 33
Choi, S.-C. 258, 262-263
Choi, S.-H. 208-209
Chou, K.-L. 267
Choy, G. 136
Chun, K. 294
Chung, S. F. 267
Clark, F. L. 214
Clark, H. 157
Claussen, H. A. 114-115
Cohen, A. K. 13
Cohen, J. 217
Cohen, P. 217
Cohen, R. 18
Cole, M. 2, 15, 18, 54, 56, 61, 64, 68
Cole, P. M. 104, 106, 136, 139, 146
Coleman, J. S. 185
Collins, W. A. 204, 207
Coon, H. M. 33, 129, 205

Cooney, G. H. 234-235, 238
Cooper, C. R. 241, 246, 266
Coopersmith, S. 236
Cosmides, L. 78
Cottereau-Reiss, P. 163, 169, 172-173
Cournoyer, D. E. 213
Crittenden, P.M. 114-115
Crnic, K. 105
Crocker, J. 326-327
Crockett, L. J. 239
Cronbach, L. J. C. 12, 212-213
Cross, S. 235
Cumming, E. 44
Cummings, E. M. 99, 115, 119

Dacyl, J. 294
Damasio, A. R. 133-134
Danziger, E. 158, 161, 165, 173
Darling, N. 210, 241
Darroch, R. K. 199
Darwin, C. 78, 126, 258
Dasen, P. 3, 18, 45, 153, 155-157, 159, 161, 163-165, 168-174, 258, 296
Davidson, D. 117
Davies, P. T. 115
Davis, A. 13
Dawson, J. L. M. 12, 20, 259
De Wolff, M. S. 82, 114-115
Deci, E. L. 266
Deeds, O. 267

deMause, L. 191
Dennis, T. A. 106
Derman-Sparks, L. 327
Dinnel, D. L. 19
Doi, T. 135
Donald, M. 76
Dong, Q. 242
Donnell, F. 82-83
Donovan, B. R. 213
Doob, L. W. 259
Dornbusch, S. M. 206, 210, 224
Douvan, E. 233, 239
Drenth, P. J. D. 12
Durkheim, E. 285

Eccles, J. S. 237
Egeland, B. 92
Eisenstadt, S. N. 258
Eisler, A.-C. 338
Ekman, P. 126-127, 130, 133
Elder, G. H. 247
Ellsworth, P. 126-127
Engel, C. 190
Enomoto, T. 328
Enriquez, V. G. 34
Entin, E. E. 236-237
Epstein, S. 4, 307-309, 316, 318
Erickson, M. 92
Erikson, E. H. 233
Essau, C. A. 134, 248

Fawcett, J. T. 185
Felton, W. 56
Fernandez, D. R. 208
Field, T. 135
Filipp, S. H. 319
Fine, G. A. 56, 58

Fiske, A. P. 103
Fiske, D. W. 13
Folkman, S. 301
Forgays, D. K. 19
Fraleigh, M. J. 206
Frank, L. K. 234
Fremmer-Bombik, E. 80
Friedlmeier, W. 3, 31, 79, 84, 99-100, 104-106, 131, 133-136, 139, 145, 192, 203-204, 206-208, 223-225
Friedman, D. 185
Friesen, W. V. 126-127, 130, 133
Frijda, N. H. 127-128
Fu, V. R. 267
Fuchsle, T. 236
Furnham, A. 296, 325

Ganapathy, H. 34, 39, 43
Gannon, M. 22
Gardiner, H. 13
Gardner, W. 109
Gauvain, M. 163
Gay, J. 18
Geertz, C. 132
Gelberg, Y. 236
Georgas, J. 21, 263-264
Gergely, G. 133, 135
Gergen, K. J. 11, 33-34
Gerris, J. R. M. 246
Giddens, A. 287
Gillespie, J. M. 234
Gjerde, P. 79
Gladwin, T. 155
Gleitman, L. 173

Glick, J. 18
Goeke-Morey, M. C. 115
Golby, B. 84
Gold, R. 206
Goldthorpe, J. H. 286
Goncu, A. 113
Goodnow, J. J. 204, 207
Graves, T. 294-295
Gray, M. R. 241
Greenfield, P. M. 34, 69, 205
Greenholtz, J. 130
Grolnick, W. S. 266
Grossmann, K. 2, 80, 82-86, 88-92, 101, 112-113, 140, 266
Grossmann, K. E. 2, 77, 80, 82-86, 88-92, 101, 112-113, 140, 266
Grotevant, H. D. 235, 241, 266
Gudykunst, W. B. 307, 325
Guisinger, S. 266
Gulerce, A. 11, 33
Gumperz, J. J. 157
Gur-Lev, S. 236
Gusfield, J. R. 260
Guthrie, G. M. 259
Gwartney, J. 208, 222

Hagen, E. E. 259
Halabi-Kheir, H. 234-235, 238
Hammer, M. R. 307
Harkness, S. 13, 33, 114, 135, 204, 206, 225, 246, 268

Harold, G. T. 115
Harris, M. 13, 15
Harter, S. 215
Harwood, R. L. 104-107, 109, 116, 118, 206, 212
Hatwell, Y. 172
Haun, D. 173
Hauser, S. T. 241
Hayes, S. A. 19
Hechter, M. 185
Heckhausen, H. 237, 239, 242
Heelas, P. 33
Heider, K. 126
Heine, S. J. 130, 330
Helms, J. 326
Henry, W. 44
Herbart, J. F. xvii
Hermans, H. J. M. 16
Heron, A. 155
Herskovits, M. J. 18, 293-294
Hetzenecker, D. 309, 316
Hinde, R. A. 77
Hiruma, N. 104
Hitchcock, J. T. 43
Ho, D. F. Y. 32-33
Hoffman, L. W. 183-184, 209, 212
Hoffman, M. L. 183-184
Hofstede, G. H. 4, 15, 22, 47, 128, 205, 208, 261, 263-264, 276, 278-280, 282
Hogan, J. D. 10
Holenstein, E. 157
Holodynski, M. 131, 133-135

Hoppe-Graff, S. 209
Hradil, S. 283
Hrdy, S. B. 80
Hui, C. H. 264
Huinink, J. 187
Huntington, S. P. 257
Huntsinger, C. S. 267
Huntsinger, P. R. 267
Hutchins, E. 54, 155
Hyun, K. J. 209

Imamoglu, E. O. 267
Imhof, A. E. 77
Inglehart, R. 4, 34,
    209, 276-278, 280-
    282, 287
Inhelder, B. 154,
    156, 163-164
Inkeles, A. 258-259
Irizarry, N. L. 106
Israeli, N. 82-83,
    234-235, 238-239,
    242, 244-245, 247
Izard, C. E. 126-127

Jacobs, A. 79, 83,
    109
Jacobs, N. 263
Jahoda, G. xvii, 5,
    10-12, 54
James, W. 326
Johnson-Laird, P.
    157
Jöreskog, K. G. 242
Jose, P. E. 267

Kagan, J. 135
Kagitçibasi, Ç. 4,
    129, 154, 185, 189,
    209, 223, 246, 257-
    258, 260, 263-267,
    276
Kahl, J. A. 259

Kakar, S. 39
Kalin, R. 297, 300,
    327
Kanazawa, S. 185
Keller, H. 43, 105-
    106, 113, 268
Kelly, G. A. 307
Kemmelmeier, M.
    33, 129, 205
Kempen, H. J. G. 16
Keppler, A. 2, 86, 91,
    101, 112, 140
Khaleque, A. 210
Killen, M. 205
Kim, H.-O. 209
Kim, J.-O. 209
Kim, K. W. 209
Kim, U. 32-33, 203,
    208-209, 263, 300-
    301
Kim, Y. 267
Kindler, H. 80
Kita, S. 158, 173
Kitayama, S. 20, 33,
    103, 128, 329-330
Klages, H. 4, 129,
    257, 260-261, 263,
    277, 329
Klineberg, O. 10
Kluckhohn, C. 23, 54
Kobayashi, M. 5,
    306, 310, 324, 332,
    338
Kondo-Ikemura, K.
    79, 108, 113
Kornadt, H.-J. 5, 20,
    46, 140, 191, 203-
    205, 224, 338
Krell, R. 76
Krewer, B. 10
Kroeber, A. L. 54
Kroger, J. 266
Kudoh, T. 126-127

Kühlmann, T. M.
    307
Kuhn, M. H. 214
Kupperbusch, C. 130
Kuramoto, N. T. 328

Lamb, M. E. 109
Lamborn, S. D. 210
Lamm, H. 236, 238-
    239
Land, D. 105
Landers, C. 43
Lantermann, E.-D.
    326
Lanz, M. 246
Lash, S. 287
Latzko, B. 209
Laurendeau, M. 163-
    164
Lawson, R. 208
Lazarus, R. S. 127,
    134, 301
Lebra, T. S. 135
Lee, S. J. 209
Lee, S.-I. 209
Lehman, D. R. 330
Leibenstein, H. 188
Leiderman, H. 206
Lens, W. 234, 236
León, L. de 158
Lerner, D. 259
Lerner, R. M. 247
Leung, K. 17-18,
    126, 213-214, 327
Levenson, R. W. 126
Leventhal, H. 127
LeVine, R. A. 105,
    107, 109, 111, 203
Levinson, S. C. 154,
    156-158, 161, 163,
    173
Levi-Strauss, C. 196
Levy, M. 13

Lewin, K. 233-234
Lewis, S. 155
Li, P. 173
Liaw, F.-R. 267
Liebkind, K. 294
Liegel, M. 86, 91
Lilach, E. 236
Lin, C.-Y. 267
Lindenberg, S. 186
Linton, R. 294
Lock, A. 11, 33
Lockwood, D. 286
Lonner, W. J. 2, 5, 10, 12, 18, 20, 23-24, 32, 126
Lucy, J. 157
Luhmann, N. 285
Luhtanen, R. 326
Luk, C. L. 326
Lynch, J. H. 266-267

Maccoby, E. E. 206, 213
Mahajna, S. 238, 244-245, 248
Mahler, M. 266
Malinowski, B. 85
Marcia, J. E. 237
Marin, G. 294
Markam, S. 128
Markus, H. R. 20, 33, 103, 128, 235, 329
Marsella, A. 258, 262-263
Martin, J. A. 206, 213
Martinot, C. 169, 173
Mascolo, M. F. 34, 47
Maslow, A. H. 281
Masutani, M. 126

Matsumoto, D. 19, 126-127, 129-130, 133, 136, 146
Maturana, H. R. 308
Mayer, B. 207, 225
Mayseless, O. 82-83
Mazrui, A. 257
McClelland, D. C. 15, 259, 261
McCluskey, K. W. 126
McCrae, R. R. 21-22
McGillicuddy-DeLisi, A. V. 244
McPartland, T. S. 214
Meins, E. 78
Meltzoff, A. N. 135
Merritt, A. 208
Mesquita, B. 127-128, 145
Meyer, P. A. 199
Miller, G. 157
Miller, J. G. 45, 106
Miller, P. M. 109
Minde, T. 300
Minturn, L. 43
Mishra, R. C. 3, 155, 157, 159, 161, 170, 174
Misra, G. 11, 33-34
Mistry, J. 113
Miyake, K. 79, 84, 89, 101, 103-104, 108, 135
Mizuta, I. 104, 106
Mohanty, A. K. 157
Mohay, H. 136
Moise, C. 300
Mok, D. 300
Monks, F. 234
Moore, M. K. 135

Morelli, G. 3, 79, 101, 108, 135
Moreno, A. 34, 209, 280
Morgan, L. H. 258
Morishima, M. 262
Morrison, S. J. 92
Mosier, C. 113
Mounts, N. S. 210
Murphy, H. B. M. 297
Murray, H. A. 23
Muschinske, D. 259
Myers, D. G. 319

Nagy, L. K. 163
Nakamura, S. 328
Naroll, R. 18
Nash, M. 263
Nauck, B. 3, 183, 189, 199, 203, 264
Nicholson, J. D. 208
Nicolopoulou, A. 61, 64, 67
Niraula, S. 159, 161, 170, 172, 174
Nisbett, R. E. 33, 45, 103
Nishida, T. 325
Norenzanan, A. 33
Noyman, M. S. 236, 238
Nozaki, S. 326
Nurmi, J. E. 234-236, 238-239, 241, 245
Nussbaum, M. C. 135
Nuttin, J. 234, 236

O'Connor, T. G. 241
Ogino, M. 104
Oumar, F. 83, 109

Oyserman, D. 33, 205
Ozanne-Rivierre, F. 155
Ozdalga, E. 257
Oztutuncu, F. 267

Pandey, J. 13, 54
Paranjpe, A. C. 34
Park, Y. Y. 209
Parsons, T. 278
Paul, S. 21
Pederson, E. 158, 165
Peng, K. 33, 130
Perreault, S. 300
Perregaux, C. 157
Peters, T. 285
Pettengill, S. M. 206, 210
Phalet, K. 267
Phinney, J. 328
Piaget, J. 13, 45, 154-156, 163-164
Pike, K. L. 13, 15
Pike, R. 215
Pinard, A. 163-164
Pisani, L. 83, 109
Poole, M. E. 234-236, 238
Poortinga, Y. H. 13, 19-20, 54, 155, 157, 258, 296
Portes, A. 294
Portmann, A. 77
Posada, G. 79, 83, 108-110, 112, 117-118
Pott, M. 79, 101, 103, 108
Power, S. 129, 184, 205, 281, 300
Przeworski, A. 18

Pulkkinen, H. 235, 239, 241, 245
Pulkkinen, L. 239, 241, 245

Quina, K. 9

Raeff, C. 266
Rapisardi, C. 34
Rasch, B. 173
Raymond, C. 54, 239
Raynor, J. O. 236-237
Reardon, B. A. 324
Redfield, R. 294
Reed, E. S. 308
Richmond, M. K. 297
Riksen-Walraven, J. M. 83, 108
Ritter, P. L. 206
Rivers, W. H. xvii
Roberts, D. F. 206
Rogoff, B. 100, 113, 163
Rohner, E. C. 213
Rohner, R. P. 206, 210, 213, 223
Roll, S. 213
Root, M. 326
Rose, E. 56
Roseman, I. J. 128
Rosenberg, M. 236, 242, 326, 328
Rosenberger, K. 105
Rosenthal, D. A. 206, 223, 236
Rothbaum, F. 3, 79, 101, 103, 105, 107-108, 110-113, 134-135, 223
Ruiter, J. P. de 158

Russell, J. A. 127, 236
Rustow, D. A. 257
Ryan, R. M. 266-267

Sagi, A. 79-80, 82-84, 86, 101, 108, 111, 113, 117
Sam, D. L. 294, 302, 324, 326-327
Sander, L. 77
Saraswathi, T. S. 34, 39, 43, 153
Sato, K. 128
Sattler, D. N. 19
Scabini, E. 246
Schäfermeier, E. 3, 5, 204, 207
Schaie, K. W. 45
Scheier, M. F. 237
Scherer, K. R. 127
Scheuerer-Englisch, H. 80
Schieche, M. 89
Schiefenhövel, W. 75-76, 85-86
Schiffauer, W. 194
Schimmack, U. 129
Schlesinger, R. 234, 244
Schmidt, R. W. 238-239
Schmidt-Atzert, L. 126
Schmitt-Rodermund, E. 326
Schnaiberg, A. 260
Schölmerich, A. 206
Schönpflug, U. 267
Schulze, P. A. 206

Schwartz, S. H. 15, 22, 212, 214, 225, 261

Schwarz, B. 3, 46, 208-209

Scribner, S. 18

Sebald, H. 247

Segall, M. H. 18, 32, 155, 157, 258, 296

Seginer, R. 3, 134, 234-240, 244-245, 248

Senecal, S. 300

Senft, G. 155, 158, 172

Sennett, R. 283

Setiadi, B. N. 19

Sharp, D. 18

Sherman, B. R. 213

Shils, E. A. 278

Shweder, R. 32

Sigel, I. E. 208, 244

Sigman, M. 133

Silbereisen, R. K. 326

Silverberg, S. B. 266-267

Singarimbun, M. 199

Sinha, D. 32-34, 47, 159

Smith, A. 186

Smith, D. H. 258-259

Smith, P. B. 22

Snir, N. 236

Snyder, S. S. 134

Sogon, S. 126

Solky, J. 266

Sörbom, D. 242

Spangler, G. 82, 89

Spencer, H. 258

Spitz, R. A. 92

Sroufe, L. A. 84, 135

Stansbury, K. 133

Stayton, D. J. 77-78

Steinberg, L. 210, 224, 239, 241, 266-267

Sternberg, R. J. 79

Stevenson, H. W. 206, 223

Stewart, S. M. 267

Stiller, J. 267

Stonequist, E. V. 294

Suess, G. 82

Suizzo, M. A. 268

Suleiman, M. A. 246-247

Summerfield, A. B. 127

Suomi, S. J. 110-112

Super, C. M. 13, 33, 114, 135, 204, 206, 225, 246, 268

Supratiknya, A. 19

Sutton, F. X. 13

Takahashi, K. 84, 104

Tamang, B. L. 136-137, 139, 146

Tamis-LeMonda, C. S. 104, 206

Tartaglini, A. 10

Taylor, D. 300

Taylor, H. A. 154

Teichler, U. 338

Teune, H. 18

Thomas, A. 4-5, 306, 324, 338-339

Thomas, R. M. 34, 39

Thompson, R. A. 82, 84, 109, 133

Thorndike, R. M. 18, 20

Thurnwald, R. xvii

Tobin, J. 117

Tomasello, M. 78

Tooby, J. 78

Triandis, H. C. 11, 18, 33, 129, 205, 208, 214, 263-264, 329

Trimble, J. 326

Tripathi, R. C. 47

Troadec, B. 169, 173

Trommsdorff, G. xvii, 1, 3, 5, 21, 31, 45-46, 79, 84, 104-106, 116, 133-134, 139-140, 145, 153, 175, 183, 190-192, 203-208, 213, 223-225, 234-236, 238-239, 241, 245, 248, 263, 284, 327

True, M. M. 83, 109, 110, 112-113, 117-118

Tversky, B. 154

Tyler, F. L. 11

Tylor, E. B. 258

Uher, J. 76

Unzner, L. 82

Valenzuela, M. 82, 83, 109-110, 118

Valsiner, J. 100, 114, 132, 135

van de Vijver, F. J. R. 17-18, 20, 126, 213, 327

van IJzendoorn, M. H. 79-80, 82-84, 86, 101, 108, 111, 113-115, 117, 246

van Leeuwe, J. F. J. 246
van Lieshout, C. F. M. 83
van Tijen, N. 268
Varela, F. J. 308
Vasconcellos, V. 204, 207
Vasquez, O. 56, 65-67
Ventura-Cook, E. 206
Vereijken, C. J. J. L. 108
Vermulst, A. A. 245-246
Villareal, M. V. 214
Voland, E. 190
Völker, S. 105
Vygotsky, L. S. 55, 58, 126, 131, 132

Wainryb, C. 205
Waitz, T. xvii
Walden, T. A. 135
Wall, S. 80
Wallace, M. 234
Wallbott, H. G. 127
Wang, S. 206

Ward, C. 20, 296, 300-302
Ward, R. E. 257
Wassmann, J. 154-158, 165, 168-169, 171-174
Waters, E. 80, 99, 110, 113, 118-119
Watson, J. S. 133, 135
Weiner, A. B. 85
Weinrich, P. 326
Weinstein, H. 135
Weisz, J. R. 79, 101, 103, 108, 134
Werner, H. 259
West, S. G. 217
Westin, C. 294
White, M. I. 107
Whiting, B. B. 191
Whiting, J. W. M. 191
Wiers, R. 128
Wigfield, A. 237
Wilkins, D. 158
Wilkinson, E. 330
Williams, R. 54-55

Willis, S. L. 45
Wilson, S. P. 78, 206
Winter, M. 92
Winters, D. G. 261
Wu, D. 117
Wundt, W. xvii

Yamaguchi, S. 105
Yamazaki, M. 328
Yang, K. S. 257-258, 260, 263
Yokoyama, T. 328
Yoon, G. 263
Yoon, Y. C. 325
Yoshitani, T. 324
Young, M. 236, 300
Yovsi, R. D. 105
Yowell, C. M. 233

Zahn-Waxler, C. 104, 106
Zelditch, M. 192
Zelizer, V. A. 191
Zevalkink, J. 83
Zimmermann, P. 80, 90, 92, 266
Zusho, A. 206

Subject Index

Absolutism 16, 22, 24

Acculturation 20, 157, 268, 293-296, 298-303, 307-308, 323-326, 329-332, 336-339
  strategies 298, 301-303

Acculturative stress 296, 298, 300-303

Achievement 69, 106, 184, 191, 206, 210-212, 215-223, 242, 244-245, 260, 263, 267, 285
  motivation 20, 259, 261

Action theory 185, 198-199

Activity system 55-56, 69-70

Adaptation 75, 80, 90, 108, 159, 266, 293, 295-297, 300-302, 307, 324-326, 336-339

Adolescence 42-43, 45, 59, 111, 209, 211, 224, 233-235, 238-242, 244-248, 266-267, 305, 308

Allocentrism 129, 173, 205, 214-216, 219, 222-223

Anthropology
  cultural 20, 33, 78, 277
  psychological 9

Approach
  culture-sensitive 126, 128-129, 131, 135, 146
  thematic 233-235
  three-component 234, 236-237, 248

Arabs 235, 239-240, 244-247

Assimilation 294-295, 297-298, 300-302, 308, 313, 315

Attachment 46, 75-83, 85-87, 90-93, 99, 100-104, 107-108, 110, 112-114, 116-119, 135, 191-192, 266, 327-328, 334-335, 337-338
  antecedents of 79, 82, 102-104, 108
  consequences of 79, 102-104, 106-108, 111
  -exploration balance 80-81, 86, 88, 90-91, 107, 112
  nature of 102-104, 107-108, 112
  non-attachment 38, 46-47
  organization 86, 91
  quality of 77-78, 81-82
  security 82-87, 90-92, 100, 103-105, 107-111, 113-116, 119, 191-192, 266

Attribution 45, 54, 132

Australia 136, 158, 205-206, 223, 235, 238, 294, 309-310, 313, 316

Autonomy 103-107, 115, 129, 190-192, 205, 223, 241-242, 247, 260, 264-268, 275-276, 283, 294, 324

Bali 155-159, 165, 168-169, 171-174

Beliefs 35, 37, 43, 56, 100, 104, 112-113, 116, 135, 160, 203-205, 207-208, 212, 225, 236, 244-246, 248, 259, 263, 283, 311

Cameroon (Nso) 105-106

Canada 205, 294

Caregiving 41, 46, 75-77, 79-80, 82-83, 87, 90, 100, 102-106, 109, 111, 113-119, 132-135, 140, 145, 204, 207, 214, 223

Caste 35-36, 40-41, 43, 46, 136

Change, structural 257, 263-265, 278

Child rearing 31, 80,
   82-83, 86, 92, 111,
   125, 135, 146, 190,
   206-207, 222, 224,
   239, 260, 263-267
   goals 203-212,
      214-225
Chile 83, 101, 109,
   259
China 21, 104, 106,
   136, 183, 206, 211,
   224, 260, 267
Cognition 36, 43-45,
   155, 157, 171, 323,
   328
Collectivism 33, 47,
   129, 145, 204-210,
   217-219, 222-223,
   260, 262-264, 267-
   269, 329, 338
Columbia 101, 108,
   110
Committed compli-
   ance 84, 92, 105
Computer games 56,
   58, 62, 69
Costa Rica 106
Cross-cultural com-
   parison 10, 53,
   67, 183-184, 188,
   205, 224, 327,
   331, 334-336, 338-
   339
Cross-cultural psy-
   chology 9-13, 15,
   18-20, 22-25, 32,
   53, 118, 125, 135,
   146-147, 260, 263,
   294-296, 303, 324
   contemporary
      trends in 11, 20-
      22
   definitions 13

Handbook of 18-
   19, 25
historical develop-
   ments in 10-11
International Asso-
   ciation for
   (IACCP) 9-12,
   19
Journal of (JCCP)
   9-10, 12, 18
maturing of 19,
   22
modern era of 10
Cultural context 13,
   17, 33-34, 43, 45-
   46, 48, 59, 64, 79,
   101, 109, 111, 114,
   118, 125, 171, 189,
   204, 208, 223, 225,
   238, 248, 263, 295-
   296, 302, 315,
   323-324, 326-327,
   331, 336, 338-339
Cultural dynamics
   69, 279
Cultural norms 35,
   83, 126, 133, 135,
   146-147, 184, 190,
   196, 203-204, 207,
   209, 223, 283, 300,
   316
Cultural patterns 16,
   24, 54, 58, 130,
   139, 211, 217, 222,
   225, 238, 245, 261,
   263, 267-268, 279-
   280, 294
Cultural psychology
   9, 15, 19-20, 24,
   32-33, 70, 135,
   324
Culture
   definitions 54, 58

immediacy of 135,
   147
of collaborative
   learning 58, 61
shock 301
Curiosity 80, 84, 86,
   90-91, 115, 308

Decision making
   183, 191-192, 247,
   265, 283, 285-286
Development
   carried-over 316,
      318-319
   cognitive 13, 45,
      68, 133, 153-
      155, 161, 163,
      168, 170-171,
      174
   delayed 316-318
   emotional 93, 125,
      132, 135, 140,
      146
   initial 316-317
   language 76, 78,
      157-159, 171
   life-span 31, 35,
      38-39, 42, 44-45,
      48
Developmental
   niche 13, 31, 33,
      204, 222, 225,
      246
   stages 11, 39-47,
      155, 277
Disengagement
   theory 44
Druze 235, 238-239

Ecology 55, 75,
   118, 153, 159-160,
   167, 171, 175, 294-
   295

Educational activities, afterschool 53, 56
Emic/Etic 15, 102, 104, 110, 116-117, 155
Emotion(s) 23, 38, 41, 44, 76-78, 90, 125-137, 139-140, 143, 145-147, 310
basic 126-127
experience of 37, 87, 104, 113, 127-130, 132-133, 136-138, 140, 145-146
expression of 76-77, 126-127, 130, 132-137, 139-142, 145-146
negative 83, 90, 135, 137, 140-146, 236
regulation 44, 90, 110, 128, 131-137, 139-141, 143-147
socialization 136, 140
Ethnotheories 32, 43, 48, 146, 204, 207, 224-225
Europe 77, 79, 82-83, 155-158, 169, 205-206, 257-258, 293-294, 323, 329-339
Evolutionary perspective 75-76, 257
Exploration 17-18, 48, 80, 86, 88-92, 100, 103, 105-107, 111-113, 115, 206,

237, 239, 244, 308

Family
exclusivity of 189, 196-198
settings 233, 239
size 189
Feeling of
belongingness 24, 328, 335
inferiority 328, 334-335, 337
Fertility 183-186, 188, 190, 199, 260
Fifth Dimension 56-62, 64-69
France 169, 173, 258, 268, 331
Future orientation 233-239, 241-248, 259

Gender
differences 46, 161, 194, 238-239
relationships 189, 194
Germany 21, 79, 82-84, 89, 105-106, 139-145, 183, 203-224, 239, 241, 267-268, 275-277, 306, 309-310, 312, 314-315, 331
Globalization 261, 268, 283, 294, 320, 324

Hindu Psychology 35, 41-42, 44-46, 48

Human
condition 36-38, 43
relationships 335
Hypothesis
competence 83-84, 90-91
convergence 258, 260-262, 268-269
normativity 81, 86
sensitivity 82, 109
universality 80, 126

Identity, supra-national 329, 332-333, 335-337
Idiocentrism 129, 205
Idioculture 55-56, 58-62, 64-65, 67-70
Immigrants 66, 105, 267, 293-294, 297, 324-326
India 32, 34-36, 38, 40, 43-47, 106, 113, 153, 157-159, 161, 167-168, 171-175, 259, 261
Indigenous
peoples 293-294
psychology 9, 15, 31-35, 38, 45, 47-48, 101, 107, 109, 116, 186, 260
Individualism 33, 47, 77, 105, 107, 129-130, 145, 154, 204-208, 210, 218, 222-

223, 259-260, 262-
263, 265-269, 277,
285-286, 329, 338
Individualism/collec-
tivism
normative 264-265
relational 264-265
Individualization
of decision making
285-286
of values 282-286
Indonesia 19, 83,
156, 183, 205, 211,
224
In-group 47, 130,
136
Integration 187, 205,
of the personal
system 283, 285
of the societal
system 283, 285
Intercultural
experiences 306,
309, 318
Intercultural tolerance
323-324
Interdependence
material 264-265,
267
psychological/emo-
tional 103, 106,
112, 205, 225,
265, 267
Intergenerational
relationships 46-
47, 187, 189,
190, 192, 198-
199, 264
transmission 111,
186, 233-234,
245-248
Internship 323, 325,
329-333, 338-339

Intertwining tactics
233-234, 247-248
Israel 83-84, 183,
211, 235, 238-239,
244-245, 247, 259
Israeli Jews 235,
238-240, 242, 244-
247

Japan 21, 79, 84, 89,
102-103, 105-107,
128, 130, 135, 139-
145, 158, 206, 261-
263, 323, 326-339

Kenya (Gusii) 105
Kinship systems 193,
196, 198
affinal 192-198
descent 192-199
Korea 104, 183, 203-
205, 207-224, 261-
262, 267

Language 16-17, 54,
78, 84, 108, 132,
147, 153-162, 165-
175, 316
Levels of analysis
69
Life cycle 39, 41-44,
46, 264-265
Life goals 38-39, 44,
286

Mali (Dogon) 83-84,
101, 109-110, 113
Marginalization 297,
299, 300-302
Materialism 262,
281-282
Maternal support 83,
86, 91-92, 215

Mexico 65, 69, 156,
158, 259
Modernism 20, 262
Modernity, individual
259-261, 263, 269
Modernization 222,
224, 257-266, 268-
269, 275, 277-288,
330
psychological 258-
260, 263, 268
subjective 282-283
Mother-child inter-
action 69, 79, 268
Motivation 10, 36-
37, 44-45, 47-48,
76, 79, 90, 185,
207, 233, 236-239,
241-244, 247, 285,
287, 297-298, 308,
325, 330
Multicultural ideol-
ogy 297

Naïve theory 190,
338
NEO-PI-R 20, 22
Netherlands 156,
158, 207, 268, 331
New Zealand 294

Old-age security
264
Ontogenetic perspec-
tive 69, 75
Out-group 46, 136

Papua New Guinea
75, 85, 87-88, 155
Parenting
acceptance 209-
211, 213, 215-
216, 220, 223,

241-243, 247, 266

autonomous-accepting 241-244, 247-248

control 104, 116, 190-193, 206, 208, 210-211, 215, 221-222, 224, 267

egalitarian 215-216, 221

strictness 104, 211, 217

Parents as models 245-246

Phylogenetic perspective 23, 76, 126

Plural societies 281, 293-294, 297, 299

Postmaterialism 280-282

Postmodernism 262

Primates (non-human) 77, 111, 113

Protection 76, 79-80, 84, 88, 90, 115

Psychology
cross-cultural See Cross-cultural psychology
cultural See Cultural psychology
Hindu See Hindu psychology
indigenous See Indigenous psychology
Western See Western psychology

Puerto Rico 104-107, 118

Refugees 294, 325

Relativism 16, 24, 32, 99, 312
linguistic 154, 157, 159, 168, 172-174

Religion 32-36, 38-39, 42, 118, 135, 160, 167, 184, 212, 224, 283, 297, 324-325

Responsiveness 77-78, 80, 82-84, 87, 92, 100, 103-106, 108-111, 114-116, 140-145, 206, 314

Rituals 39-41, 191

Schooling 39, 43, 154, 156-157, 159, 161, 168-170, 174-175

Secure base 80-81, 90, 92, 100, 102-103, 107, 111-112

Segregation 195, 297, 300

Self
assertion 103, 136-137, 286, 329
autonomous-related 265, 267-268
concept 47, 207, 235, 323, 328
decentralization 310, 312-313, 315-318
efficacy 260, 310, 318-319

esteem 44, 46, 103, 115, 128, 235, 242-243, 296, 308, 323, 326-328, 330-339
fulfillment 47, 206, 214, 223
regulation 44, 48, 132, 145, 196
reliance 191-192, 206, 209, 212, 215, 218, 220-221, 223-224, 266, 275-276, 283
theory 307-308

Sensitivity See Responsiveness

Separation 42, 80, 86, 90, 192, 194, 265-266, 298, 300-302

Social
change 209, 222, 259, 262, 338
competence 84, 100, 103, 106-107, 110-111, 316
differentiation 285
production function 186-188, 193, 196, 198-199

Societal change 257-258, 264, 277

Sociocultural theory 100, 104, 114

Sociohistorical approach 126, 131

Sociology 10, 257, 260, 269, 277-278,

285, 287-288, 293,
295
Sojourners 293-294,
325, 338
Spatial frames of
reference 154,
158, 172-174
deictic 154, 166-
167, 169-170,
174
egocentric 154,
156-160, 162-
163, 165-166,
170-172, 174
Euclidian 154-155,
159, 164, 166,
175
extrinsic 154
intrinsic 154, 158,
166, 169-170,
173
projective 154-
155, 157, 164-
166, 170, 172,
174
topological 154,
164
Student exchange
305-306, 308-311,
313, 315-316,
318-320, 330-
331
Subjective theories
See Ethnotheories
Sustainability as
method 68-69

Tahiti 173
Taiwan 106, 260-
262
Transmission of cul-
tural knowledge
125, 131-132

Trobriand Islands 75-
76, 84-91, 101, 172
Turkey 12, 183, 211,
258, 260, 267

Uganda 79, 82, 101-
103, 109-110, 112,
115, 117-119
UNESCO 11, 324,
326
Universalism 15-17,
21-24, 32-33, 35,
75-80, 85, 90-93,
99-103, 105-113,
125-128, 132, 140,
147, 157, 186, 210,
222-225, 323,
337
Urban/rural compari-
son 106, 114,
153, 158-161,
171, 174, 209,
259-260, 262, 265-
267
USA 9, 18, 21, 56,
82-83, 88-89,
102-108, 110,
117, 127, 130,
135-137, 139,
173, 205-207,
210, 242, 258,
267-268, 277,
294, 330

Value change 275-
283, 287, 325
Value of children
(VOC) 20, 183-
186, 188, 191, 198-
199, 203, 211-220,
222, 224
children as inter-
mediate goods

186, 192- 193,
195-196, 198-
199
costs of children
184-185, 189-
190, 196-197
emotional utility of
children 185,
188-189, 190,
192, 196-199
income utility of
children 184-
185, 187, 189,
190-191, 194-
196, 198
insurance utility of
children 185,
187-191, 193,
195-197
labor utility of
children 188,
194, 196
status attainment
utility of chil-
dren 188, 190-
191, 195-196,
198
Value orientations
129, 146, 205,
207-208, 210,
212, 215, 217-
219, 222-223,
277-278, 281, 285,
287
Value systems 38,
46-47, 185, 279,
283, 285
modern 284
traditional 209,
222, 263, 284
Values
collectivistic 205,
207, 210, 212,

215, 217-218, 222, 285, 287, *See also* Collectivism

individualistic 205, 207, 210, 212, 215, 217-218, 222, 267, 277, 283-287,

See also Individualism

Western psychology 19, 33-35, 42-45, 47-48, 100-101, 103, 105-106, 108-109, 112, 114, 117-118, 154, 168

Westernization 257-258, 261-263, 268-269, 276

Worldview 32-34, 234, 262, 266, 313

Hindu 35-36, 38, 43

social evolutionist 258, 269